D1473816

BIOGRAPHICAL SKETCHES
OF
AMERICAN ARTISTS

COMPILED BY

HELEN L. EARLE

FIFTH EDITION, REVISED AND ENLARGED

GARNIER & COMPANY

Booksellers   Publishers

Charleston, South Carolina

This limited edition, published in 1972, is an unabridged
republication of the edition originally published by
the Michigan State Library in 1924.

GARNIER & COMPANY

192 King St.

Charleston, South Carolina

FOR
PATTY & BETSY

TABLE OF CONTENTS

PAINTERS.

Abbey, Edwin Austin
Adams, Wayman
Aid, George C.
Alexander, John White
Allston, Washington
Alten, Mathias J.
Anderson, Karl
Anschutz, Thomas Pollock
Armstrong, D. Maitland
Baker, Elizabeth Gowdy
Baker, Ellen Kendall
Barlow, Myron
Barse, George R., Jr.
Beal, Gifford
Beaux, Cecilia
Beckwith, James Carroll
Belcher, Hilda
Bellows, George Wesley
Benson, Frank Weston
Betts, Louis
Bierstadt, Albert
Bisbing, H. Singleton
Blakelock, Ralph Albert
Blashfield, Edwin Howland
Blum, Robert Frederick
Blumenschein, Ernest Leonard
Blumenschein, Mary Shepard Green
Bogert, George
Borglum, J. Gutzon M.
Bouguereau, Elizabeth Gardner
Bowen, Benjamin James
Breckenridge, Hugh Henry
Breuer, Henry Joseph
Bridges, Fidelia
Bridgman, Frederick Arthur
Brown, George Loring
Brown, John George
Browne, George Elmer
Brush, George DeForest
Cadwalader-Guild, Emma Marie
Carlsen, Emil
Carlson, John F.
Carpenter, Francis Bickwell
Cassatt, Mary
Champney, James Wells
Chanler, Robert W.

Chapman, John Gadsby
Chase, William Merritt
Christy, Howard Chandler
Church, Frederick Edwin
Church, Frederick Stuart
Clarke, Thomas Shields
Coe, Ethel L.
Cole, Thomas
Coman, Charlotte Buell
Cooper, Colin Campbell
Cooper, Emma Lampert
Copley, John Singleton
Couse, Eanger Irving
Cowles, Genevieve Almeda
Cox, Kenyon
Cox, Louise
Craig, Charles
Crane, Bruce
Crowninshield, Frederic
Curran, Charles Courtney
Cushing, Howard G.
Dabo, Leon
Dabo, Theodore Scott
Daingerfield, Elliott
Dannat, William T.
Davies, Arthur B.
Davis, Charles Harold
Deakin, Edwin
Dearth, Henry Golden
De Camp, Joseph Rodefer
DeHaven, Frank
Deming, Edward Willard
Dessar, Louis Paul
Dewey, Charles Melville
Dewing, Maria Oakey
Dewing, Thomas Wilmer
Dillaye, Blanche
Dixon, Maynard
Dodson, Sarah Paxton Ball
Dolph, John H
Donoho, Gaines Ruger
Dougherty, Paul
Dufner, Edward
Dunlap, Mary Stewart
Duveneck, Frank
Eakins, Thomas

Eaton, Charles Harry
Eaton, Wyatt
Elliott, Charles Loring
Elliott, John
Enneking, John Joseph
Farny, Henry
Fenn, Harry
Fisher, William Mark
Flagg, James Montgomery
Foote, Will Howe
Forbes, Edwin
Foster, Ben
Fournier, Alexis Jean
Fowler, Frank
Frieseke, Frederic Carl
Fromuth, Charles Henry
Fry, John Henning
Fuller, George
Garber, Daniel
Gaul, William Gilbert
Gay, Walter
Genth, Lillian Matilde
Gibson, Charles Dana
Gies, Joseph W.
Gifford, Robert Swain
Glackens, William J.
Grayson, Clifford Provost
Groll, Albert Lorey
Grover, Oliver Dennett
Gruppe, Charles Paul
Guerin, Jules
Gutherz, Carl
Haggin, Ben Ali
Harding, Chester
Harding, George
Harper, William A.
Harrison, Lovell Birge
Harrison, Thomas Alexander
Hassam, Childe
Hawthorne, Charles Webster
Healy, George Peter Alexander
Henri, Robert
Higgins, Eugene
Higgins, Victor
Hitchcock, George
Hoffman, Malvina
Homer, Winslow
Hopkin, Robert
Hopkins, Edna Boies
Horton, William Samuel
Houston, Frances C. Lyons

Hovenden, Thomas
Howe, William Henry
Hubbell, Henry Salem
Hunt, William Morris
Hutchens, Frank Townsend
Hutty, Alfred H.
Hyde, Helen
Inman, Henry
Inness, George
Inness, George, Jr.
Isham, Samuel
Ives, Halsey Cooley
Ives, Percy
Johansen, John Christen
Johnson, Eastman
Johnson, Marshall
Johnston, John Humphreys
Jones, Hugh Bolton
Keith, William
Kendall, William Sergeant
Kent, Rockwell
Kirk, Maria Louise
Knight, Daniel Ridgway
Knox, Susan Ricker
Koopman, Augustus
Kost, Frederick W.
Lachman, Harry B.
LaFarge, John
Lauber, Joseph
Lawson, Ernest
Leigh, William R.
Leroy, Anita
Leutze, Emanuel
Lie, Jonas
Linde, Ossip L.
Little, J. Wesley
Loeb, Louis
Longpre, Paul de
Low, Will H.
Lucas, Albert Pike
Luks, George Benjamin
MacCameron, Robert Lee
MacEwen, Walter
MacKay, E. Murray
McLane, M. Jean
MacMonnies, Frederick W.
Macomber, Mary L.
Marin, John
Martin, Homer Dodge
Maynard, George W.
Melchers, J. Gari

Metcalf, Willard Leroy
Miller, Richard
Millet, Francis Davis
Minor, Robert Crannell
Mitchell, John James
Monks, John Austin Sands
Mora, F. Luis
Moran, Edward
Moran, Mary Nimmo
Moran, Peter
Moran, Thomas
Mosler, Henry
Murphy, John Francis
Myers, Jerome
Nast, Thomas
Newcomb, Maria Guise
Newell, George Glenn
Nicholls, Rhoda Holmes
Noble, John
Nordfeldt, Bror J. Olsson
Nourse, Elizabeth
Ochtman, Leonard
Osthaus, Edmund Henry
Page, Walter Gilman
Palmer, Walter Launt
Pape, Eric
Parker, Edgar
Parker, Lawton S.
Parrish, Stephen
Parton, Arthur
Paulus, Francis Petrus
Paxton, William McGregor
Peale, Charles Wilson
Pearce, Charles Sprague
Peixotto, Ernest Clifford
Penfold, Frank C.
Perrault, I. Marie
Picknell, William Lamb
Platt, Alethea Hill
Pope, Alexander
Potthast, Edward Henry
Powell, William Henry
Prellwitz, Edith Mitchell
Prellwitz, Henry
Proctor, Alexander P.
Pyle, Howard
Quinn, Edmond T.
Ranger, Henry Ward
Read, Thomas Buchanan
Redfield, Edward Willis
Reid, Robert

Remington, Frederic
Reuterdahl, Henry
Richards, William Trost
Robinson, Theodore
Rolshoven, Julius
Rungius, Carl
Ryder, Albert Pinkham
Sargent, John Singer
Sartain, William
Schille, Alice
Schneider, Otto J.
Schofield, W. Elmer
Scott, Emily Maria Spaford
Shannon, James Jebusa
Sharp, Joseph Henry
Shinn, Everett
Shirlaw, Walter
Shulz, Adolph Robert
Simmons, Edward Emerson
Singer, William H., Jr.
Slade, C. Arnold
Sloan, John
Smedley, William Thomas
Smillie, James D.
Smith, Francis Hopkinson
Smith, Jessie Willcox
Smith, Letta Crapo
Sonntag, William Louis
Speicher, Eugene
Stanley, James M.
Steele, Helen McKay
Sterne, Maurice
Sterner, Albert E.
Stewart, Julius L.
Stuart, Gilbert
Sully, Thomas
Sylvester, Frederick Oakes
Symons, George Gardner
Tanner, Henry Ossawa
Tarbell, Edmund C.
Taylor, William Ladd
Thayer, Abbott Henderson
Tiffany, Louis Comfort
Tillinghast, Mary Elizabeth
Trumbull, John
Tryon, Dwight William
Tucker, Allen
Turner, Charles Yardley
Turner, Helen M.
Turner, Ross Sterling
Twachtman, John Henry

Ufer, Walter
Ulrich, Charles Frederick
Vail, Eugene
Van Elten, Kruseman
Vedder, Elihu
Vinton, Frederic Porter
Volk, Douglas
Vonnoh, Robert William
Walden, Lionel
Walker, Henry Oliver
Walker, Horatio
Walter, Martha
Watkins, Susan
Waugh, Frederick J.
Webster, Herman A.
Weeks, Edwin Lord
Weir, Julian Alden

Wendt, Julia M. Bracken
Wendt, William
Wentworth, Cecile de
Whistler, James Abbott McNeill
White, Thomas Gilbert
Whittredge, Worthington
Wiggins, Carleton
Wiles, Irving Ramsey
Williams, Frederick Ballard
Winter, Ezra A.
Woodbury, Charles Herbert
Woodwell, Joseph R.
Wyant, Alexander Helwig
Wyeth, N. C.
Yates, Cullen
Young, Mahonri

SCULPTORS.

Adams, Herbert
Aitken, Robert I.
Ball, Thomas
Barnard, George Grey
Bartlett, Paul Wayland
Baxter, Martha Wheeler
Beach, Chester
Bitter, Karl Theodore
Blumenschein, Mary Shepard Green
Borglum, John Gutzon M.
Borglum, Solon Hannibal
Boyle, John J.
Brenner, Victor David
Burroughs, Edith Woodman
Cadwalader-Guild, Emma Marie
Calder, A. Stirling
Clarke, Thomas Shields
Couper, William
Crunelle, Leonard
Dallin, Cyrus Edwin
Davidson, Jo
Deming, Edward Willard
Donoghue, John
Donoho, Gaines Ruger
Duveneck, Frank
Eberle, Abastenia St. Leger
Elwell, Frank Edwin
Evans, Rudulph
Ezekiel, Moses Jacob
Fairbanks, Avard

Farnham, Sally J.
Fraser, James Earle
French, Daniel Chester
Frishmuth, Harriet W.
Fry, Sherry Edmundson
Fuller, Meta V. Warrick
Grafly, Charles
Hammer, Trygve
Hoffman, Malvina
Hosmer, Harriet
Hyatt, Anna Vaughn (Huntington)
Kelly, James Edward
Kemeys, Edward
Konti, Isidore
Ladd, Anna Coleman
Lamb, Ella Condie
Lauber, Joseph
Lewis, Edmonia
Linder, Henry
Longman, Evelyn Beatrice (Batchelder)
Lopez, Charles Albert
Lucas, Albert Pike
Lukeman, H. Augustus
Macdonald, James Alexander Wilson
McKenzie, R. Tait
MacMonnies, Frederick W.
MacNeil, Carol Brooks
MacNeil, Hermon Atkins
Manship, Paul
Mears, Helen Farnsworth

Nadelman, Eli
Neandross, Sigurd
Ney, Elizabeth
Niehaus, Charles Henry
O'Connor, Andrew, Jr.
Paeff, Bashka
Partridge, William Ordway
Piccirilli, Attilio
Piccirilli, Furio
Polasek, Albin
Pope, Alexander
Potter, Edward Clark
Potter, Louis
Pratt, Bela L.
Proctor, Alexander P.
Quinn, Edmond T.
Reed, Earl H.
Remington, Frederic
Rhind, J. Massey

Rogers, John
Roth, Frederick G. R.
Ruckstuhl, Frederick Wellington
Saint-Gaudens, Augustus
Schuler, Hans
Scudder, Janet
Shrady, Henry Merwin
Taft, Lorado
Tilden, Douglas
Vedder, Elihu
Vonnoh, Bessie Potter
Walker, Nellie Verne
Ward, John Q. A.
Warner, Olin L.
Weinman, Adolph Alexander
Wendt, Julia M. Bracken
Whitney, Gertrude Vanderbilt
Yandell, Enid
Young, Mahonri

ILLUSTRATORS.

Abbey, Edwin Austin
Ahrens, Ellen W.
Alexander, John W.
Anderson, Karl
Bellows, George W.
Birch, Reginald Bathurst
Blashfield, Edwin H.
Blum, Robert F.
Blumenschein, Ernest Leonard
Borglum, J. Gutzon M.
Breuer, Henry Joseph
Chandler, George W.
Christy, Howard Chandler
Church, Frederick S.
Clark, Walter Appleton
Cory, Fanny Y.
Cox, Kenyon
Cox, Louise
Crowninshield, Frederic
Daingerfield, Elliott
Deming, Edward Willard
Dewing, Maria Oakey
Dielman, Frederick
Dillaye, Blanche
Eaton, Charles Harry
Elliott, John
Emmet, Lydia Field
Fenn, Harry

Fisher, Harrison
Flagg, James Montgomery
Fournier, Alexis J.
Fowler, Frank
Frost, Arthur Burdett
Gaul, William Gilbert
Gibson, Charles Dana
Glackens, William J.
Green, Elizabeth Shippen
Guerin, Jules
Harding, George
Harrison, L. Birge
Hitchcock, George
Hitchcock, Lucius Wolcott
Hutt, Henry
Keith, William
Keller, Arthur I.
Kelley, James Edward
Kemble, Edward Windsor
Kent, Rockwell
Kinney, Margaret West
Kinney, Troy
Kirk, Maria Louise
Lamb, Ella Condie
Leigh, William R.
Leroy, Anita
Loeb, Louis
Low, Will H.

McCarter, Henry
McLane, M. Jean
Maynard, George W.
Millet, Francis Davis
Mora, F. Luis
Moran, Thomas
Nast, Thomas
Newell, Peter
Nicholls, Rhoda Holmes
Oakley, Violet
Pape, Eric
Parrish, Maxfield
Peixotto, Ernest Clifford
Pennell, Joseph
Plowman, George Taylor
Potthast, Edward Henry
Preston, Mary Wilson
Pyle, Howard
Reinhart, Charles Stanley
Remington, Frederic
Reuterdahl, Henry
Robinson, Boardman

Robinson, Theodore
Rungius, Carl
Seton, Ernest Thompson
Sherwood, Rosina Emmet
Shinn, Everett
Shinn, Florence Scovel
Sloan, John
Smedley, William Thomas
Smith, F. Hopkinson
Smith, Jessie Willcox
Steele, Helen McKay
Stephens, Alice Barber
Sterner, Albert Edward
Stillwell, Sarah S.
Taylor, William Ladd
Turner, Ross Sterling
Vedder, Elihu
Wenzell, Albert Beck
Wright, M. Louise Wood
Wyeth, N. C.
Yohn, Frederick Coffay

MURAL PAINTERS AND STAINED GLASS DESIGNERS.

Abbey, Edwin Austin
Alexander, John W.
Armstrong, D. Maitland
Ballin, Hugo
Barlow, Myron
Benson, Frank W.
Blashfield, Edwin H.
Blum, Robert F.
Burd, Clara Miller
Chanler, Robert W.
Cowles, Genevieve Almeda and Maud
   Alice
Cox, Kenyon
Crowninshield, Frederic
Daingerfield, Elliott
De Camp, Joseph Rodefer
Deming, Edwin Willard
Dewing, Thomas Wilmer
Dielman, Frederick
Dixon, Maynard
Dodge, W. DeLeftwich
Duveneck, Frank
Elliott, John
Frieseke, Frederic Carl
Guerin, Jules

Gutherz, Carl
Heinigke, Otto
Herter, Albert
Hunt, William Morris
LaFarge, John
Lamb, Charles Rollison
Lamb, Ella Condie
Lamb, Frederick Stymatz
Lathrop, Francis
Lauber, Joseph
Low, Will H.
MacEwen, Walter
Marsh, Fred Dana
Maynard, George W.
Melchers, J. Gari
Metcalf, Willard LeRoy
Millet, Francis Davis
Mora, F. Luis
Mowbray, Henry Siddons
Oakley, Violet
Parrish, Maxfield
Pearce, Charles Sprague
Peixotto, Ernest Clifford
Potthast, Edward H.
Pyle, Howard

Reid, Robert
Sargent, John Singer
Sears, Taber
Sewell, Robert V. V.
Shinn, Everett
Shirlaw, Walter
Simmons, Edward E.
Sperry, Edward Peck
Steele, Helen McKay
Thayer, Abbott H.
Tiffany, Louis Comfort

Tillinghast, Mary E.
Turner, Charles Yardley
Van Ingen, William B.
Vedder, Elihu
Walker, Henry O.
Weir, J. Alden
Whistler, James McNeill
Wiles, Irving Ramsey
Willet, William
Winter, Ezra A.

ETCHERS.

Aid, George C.
Bacher, Otto
Beatty, John W.
Benson, Frank W.
Blum, Robert F.
Brown, George Loring
Cassatt, Mary
Chandler, George W.
Chapman, John Gadsby
Church, Frederick S.
Dielman, Frederick
Dillaye, Blanche
Duveneck, Frank
Farrer, Henry
Fenn, Harry
Forbes, Edwin
Gifford, Robert Swain
Greatorex, Eliza
Hassam, Childe
Higgins, Eugene
Hopkins, Edna Boies
Hornby, Lester G.
Hutty, Alfred H.
Hyde, Helen
Lauber, Joseph
Loeb, Louis
MacLaughlin, Donald Shaw
Marin, John
Merritt, Anna Lea

Mielatz, Charles Frederick William
Mitchell, John James
Monks, John Austin Sands
Moran, Mary Nimmo
Moran, Peter
Moran, Thomas
Myers, Jerome
Nordfeldt, Bror J. Olsson
Parrish, Stephen
Paulus, Francis Petrus
Pennell, Joseph
Pitts, Lendall
Plowman, George Taylor
Potter, Louis
Reed, Earl H.
Roth, Ernest David
Schneider, Otto J.
Sloan, John
Smillie, James D.
Sterne, Maurice
Stevens, Helen B.
Van Elten, Kruseman
Washburn, Cadwallader
Webster, Herman A.
Weir, Julian Alden
Whistler, James McNeill
Woodbury, Charles Herbert
Young, Mahonri

MINIATURE PAINTERS.

Ahrens, Ellen Wetherald
Baer, William J.
Baker, Elizabeth Gowdy
Baker, Martha Susan
Baxter, Martha Wheeler
Bayliss, Lillian
Beckington, Alice
Coudert, Amalia Kussner
Dix, Eulabee
Edgerly, Mira
Emmet, Lydia Field
Fuller, Lucia Fairchild
Hallowell, George H.
Hawley, Margaret F.
Hills, Laura Coombs
Humphreys, Marie Champney
Inman, Henry

Josephi, Isaac E.
Kendall, Margaret Stickney
Malbone, Edward Greene
Marsh, Alice Randall
Otis, Amy
Peixotto, Ernest Clifford
Redfield, Heloise Guillou
Schille, Alice
Sherwood, Rosina Emmet
Southwick, Elsie Whitmore
Stanton, Lucy May
Thayer, Theodora W.
Turner, Helen M.
Welch, Mabel R.
Whittemore, William John
Wright, M. Louise Wood

AMERICAN ARTISTS

OF THE

LEGION OF HONOR.

The Legion of Honor of France is the most vital and democratic order in the world. It is an order of merit and has a genuinely international significance.

In the Paris salon the insignia of the order—the "red ribbon"—is the highest award given to exhibitors.

The following American painters and sculptors have received this coveted prize.

Abbey, Edwin Austin
Alexander, John White
Armstrong, D. Maitland
Bartlett, Paul Wayland
Bierstadt, Albert
Bisbing, H. Singlewood
Bridgman, Frederic Arthur
Cassatt, Mary
Dannat, William T.
Frieseke, Frederic Carl
Gay, Walter
Gibson, Charles Dana
Harrison, T. Alexander
Hitchcock, George
Howe, William Henry
Hyatt, Anna Vaughn
Johnston, John Humphreys
Knight, Daniel Ridgway

LaFarge, John
MacCameron, Robert Lee
MacEwen, Walter
MacMonnies, Frederick William
Melchers, J. Gari
Miller, Robert E.
Millet, Francis Davis
Mosler, Henry
Pearce, Charles Sprague
Saint-Gaudens, Augustus
Sargent, John Singer
Stewart, Julius L.
Tanner, Henry O.
Tiffany, Louis Comfort
Vail, Eugene
Wentworth, Cecile de
Whistler, James McNeill

(It is regretted that it has been impossible to complete the above list.)

AMERICAN ART IN THE LUXEMBOURG.

In 1916 M. Benedité, curator of the Luxembourg Museum, Paris, was quoted by the correspondent to the New York Sun as stating that the foreign schools of art in the Luxembourg are represented as follow:

American	35
Belgian	29
British	30
Dutch	8
German and Austrian	11
Italian	30
Russian	4
Scandinavian	17
Spanish and Portuguese	10
Swiss	6
Turkish	2

It will be noted that the American works purchased by the French Government outnumber those of any other country.

MICHIGAN ARTISTS.

Barlow, Myron ....Ionia, 1873
Barse, George R., Jr..Detroit, 1861
Church, Frederick Stuart....................................Grand Rapids, 1842
Couse, E. Irving...Saginaw, 1866
Dabo, Leon ....Detroit, 1868
Dabo, T. Scott...Detroit, 1870
Foote, William Howe.......................................Grand Rapids, 1874
Frieseke, Frederic Carl...Owosso, 1874
Gies, Joseph W...Detroit, ...
Hopkins, Edna Boies..Hudson, ...
Horton, William Samuel...................................Grand Rapids, 1865
Houston, Frances C. Lyons................................Hudson, 1867-1906
Hutty, Alfred H..Grand Haven, 1877
Ives, Percy ....Detroit, 1864
MacKay, Edwin Murray.......................................Sebewaing, ...
Marsh, Alice Randall..Coldwater, ...
Melchers, J. Gari...Detroit, 1860
Newell, George Glen.......................................Berrien County, 1870
Parker, Lawton S...Fairfield, 1868
Paulus, Francis P...Detroit, 1862
Perrault, I. Marie...Detroit, ...
Pitts, Lendall ....Detroit, 1875
Rolshoven, Julius ....Detroit, 1858
Smith, Letta Crapo..Flint, 1862
Wenzell, Albert B...Detroit, 1864
White, Thomas Gilbert ....Grand Rapids, ...
Winter, Ezra A...Traverse City, 1886

ABBREVIATIONS.

Am Art News—American Art News
Am M—American Magazine
Am M of Art—American Magazine of Art (continuation of Art and Progress)
Arch Rec—Architectural Record
Art & Archaeol—Art and Archaeology
Art & P—Art and Progress
Art in Am—Art in America
Art W—Art World
Artist—The Artist
Arts—The Arts
Arts & D—Arts and Decoration
Atlan—Atlantic
Bay View M—Bay View Magazine
Bkbuyer—Bookbuyer
Bk-Lovers M—Book-Lovers Magazine
Bookm—Bookman
Bk News M—Book News Monthly
Brush & P—Brush and Pencil
Bul Pan Am U—Bulletin of Pan American Union
Burlington M—Burlington Magazine
Canad M—Canadian Magazine
Catholic W—Catholic World
Cent—Century
Chaut—Chautauquan
Craftsm—Craftsman
Cosmopol—Cosmopolitan
Country L—Country Life
Cur Lit—Current Literature
Cur Opin—Current Opinion
Delin—Delineator
Ecl M—Eclectic Magazine
Good H—Good Housekeeping
Harper—Harper's Monthly Magazine
Harper B—Harper's Bazar
House & G—House and Garden
House B—House Beautiful
Illus W—Illustrated World
Ind—Independent
Int Studio—International Studio
Jour of Am Hist—Journal of American History
Lit Digest—Literary Digest
Liv Age—Living Age
McCl—McClure's Magazine
Mag of Art—Magazine of Art
Mo Illus—Monthly Illustrator
Nat Cyc Am Biog—National Cyclopedia of American Biography

Nat M—National Magazine
New Eng M—New England Magazine
New Repub—New Republic
19th Cent—Nineteenth Century
No Am—North American Review
Outl—Outlook
Overl—Overland Monthly
Print Coll Q—Print Collector's Quarterly
Pub Opin—Public Opinion
Quart Illus—Quarterly Illustrator
R of Rs—Review of Reviews
St N—St. Nicholas
Scrib M—Scribner's Magazine
South Lit Mess—Southern Literary Messenger
Sunset M—Sunset Magazine
Studio—Studio (London)
Tech W—Technical World
Touchst—Touchstone
Woman's H C—Woman's Home Companion
W To-day—World To-day
W Work—World's Work

BIOGRAPHICAL SKETCHES

BIOGRAPHICAL SKETCHES.

ABBEY, EDWIN AUSTIN, (P., I., Mural P.) b. Philadelphia, Pa., April
1, 1852; d. London, England, August 1, 1911. At the age of four he
produced pen sketches worthy of more than passing attention and when
not more than fourteen, Harper accepted some of his pen illustrations.
He studied a year in the Pennsylvania Academy of the Fine Arts and
in 1871, went to New York, where he joined Harper's art staff. In 1878
he was sent by that publishing house to England to gather material to
illustrate Herrick's poems. His first painting in oil, "May day morn,"
was exhibited at the Royal Academy, London, in 1890 and "Fiametta's
song" in 1894. He was unexcelled by any living artist in rendering
mediaeval subjects. His notable paintings in this line are "Richard III
and Lady Anne," "Hamlet," "Trial of Queen Katherine," "The penance
of Eleanor," "Daughters of King Lear," "Crusaders sighting Jerusalem,"
"Columbus in the new world."

His series of decorations in the Boston Public Library embodying
the story of the "Holy Grail" is the most popular wall-painting in
America.

In 1909 he was commissioned to paint the coronation scene of King
Edward VII. This painting now hangs in Windsor Castle. He declined
the invitation to paint the official picture of King George's coronation.

Mr. Abbey was honored by membership in the leading art societies of
Europe and America and received decorations from several European
governments in recognition of his artistic ability. He had a marvelous
technique, was an illustrator of the greatest power and originality and
has been mentioned as one of the four greatest draughtsmen of the 19th
century.

Of his brushwork, Henry Strachey says: "He knows how to wield the
magic of the brush so that his painting apart from its color or form is
eloquent."

At the time of his death he was engaged upon the commission from
the state of Pennsylvania for decorative panels in the state capitol at
Harrisburg; less than half of the work had been accomplished.

Royal Cortissoz, the art critic, says: "He was very gay and likeable,
you felt in him honesty and force and you could see just how his sterling
nature poured itself into his work. In it he sought the truth, he wanted
to make it live; with all his strength and with all his conscience he
strove for a reality that would touch men, make them think and feel.
He achieved this aim and made his best monument in the decorations
at Harrisburg."

In the Craftsman, Louis A. Holman, closes an article on the late Mr. Abbey and his work as follows: "I feel confident Abbey will hold his place as one of America's foremost colorists, as one of her rarest draughtsmen, as the most poetic painter of mediaeval subjects in his time and as the greatest illustrator that America has yet produced."

Abbey's paintings are very rare in the United States but the Butler Art Institute, Youngstown, Ohio, has recently purchased and imported from England his "Lady Anne." The color is rich and the figure has grace and refinement. His pen and ink drawing called "Corinna's going a Maying" has also been added to the institute's collection.

ADAMS, HERBERT, (S.) b. West Concord, Vermont, January 28, 1858. He studied sculpture five years under Mercié in Paris. On his return to the United States in 1890, he engaged as art instructor in the Pratt Institute, Brooklyn, N. Y., where for eight years he criticised the modeling. Mr. Adams is a member of the Society of American Artists; he was elected associate member of the National Academy of Design in 1898; full member in 1899; and president in 1917-18.

While a descendant of New England ancestors, Mr. Adams' sculpture has nothing of the puritanical character. "The extreme refinement of his art and the beauty of finish of all his work are much more akin to the productions of the southlands, of those master-craftsmen of the cinque-cento—Donatello, Mino da Fiesole, or the Pollaiuoli—who forgot that sculpture meant cold classic marble and expressed themselves in delicate poems of marble or bronze." (Am M of Art 12:151)

His group which surmounts the fountain in McMillan Park, Washington, D. C., erected by citizens of Michigan in honor of the late James McMillan, U. S. Senator from Michigan, attracts particular attention. The three maidens on the pedestal represent three water nymphs; they have not only technical excellence but grace and charm.

The "Nymph" modelled for the Cooper estate of Cooperstown, N. Y., is another charming figure.

Mr. Adams' nudes are beautiful, chaste, and modest.

His portrait busts have rare refinement and beauty. Hartmann says: "The best bust ever made in America is, in my opinion, Herbert Adams' bust of his wife."

Taft in his "History of American sculpture," says: "In Mr. Herbert Adams, the whole fraternity recognizes a master almost unequaled in a certain form of sculpture as rare as it is exquisite—the creation of beautiful busts of women . . . . . There is nothing so distinctive in his figures of men."

Mr. Adams' experiments in coloring his busts are exceedingly interesting. He has shown a beautiful color bust of "St. Agnes," a "Portrait
of a young lady" in tinted marble in bronze decorations, and the "Rabbi's
daughter" in pink marble, with dress and ample wide spread sleeves in
wood with gold decorations. "It is in his choice and treatment of these
heads that Mr. Adams reveals his true personality." (Lorado Taft)

In his love of details he is closely akin to M. Dampt and M. Rivière-
Théodore, the French sculptors.

His work in reliefs deserves special mention, those best known being
the Welch, Hoyt, and Choate memorials. He also designed the relief
for the tomb of Ellen Louise Axson Wilson (Mrs. Woodrow Wilson).

His portrait statues are imposing figures: William Cullen Bryant
in Bryant Park, New York City; William Ellery Channing, Public Gardens, Boston, Mass.; Justices John Marshall and Rufus Ranney on Court
House grounds, Cleveland, Ohio.

One of his finest statues is the symbolic statue of Michigan on the
Vicksburg National Military Park.

The work of early Italian sculptors is recalled in his bronze doors
for the Library of Congress, Washington, D. C. and for St. Bartholomew's church, New York City.

ADAMS, WAYMAN, (P.) b. Muncie, Ind., September 23, 1883. Studied
with Chase in Florence and Henri in Spain.

His sketches of Spain, Chinatown, San Francisco, and New Orleans
were done, it is said, for his own amusement; but they are very interesting. His serious work, however, is portrait painting.

The portraits of Booth Tarkington and Alexander Ernestinoff were
the first to win recognition. "The art jury" and "The conspiracy" are
portraits of well-known artists cleverly painted in groups. "Irvin S.
Cobb and his daughter," shown at the National Academy of Design
this spring, was a favorite with the critics. "Old New Orleans mammy"
is a very characteristic canvas.

Mr. Adams is a "lightning" artist, painting his portraits at one sitting.

AHRENS, ELLEN WETHERALD, (Min. P., I.) b. Baltimore, Md., June 6,
1859. Pupil Boston Museum of Fine Arts under Grundemann, Pennsylvania Academy of the Fine Arts under Eakins, Drexel Institute under
Pyle.

Received second Toppan prize, School of Pennsylvania Academy of
the Fine Arts, 1884, and other prizes for oil painting and miniatures.

AID, GEORGE CHARLES (E., P.) b. Quincy, Ill. A pupil of Laurens and Benjamin-Constant in Paris.

Mr. Aid won quite an enviable reputation for painting while in Paris, being a follower of Richard Miller, and like Frieseke revived Fragonard's subjects—women in interiors.

Taking up etching and choosing architectural subjects, he was first attracted to Holland, then to the cathedral towns of France; later fell under the spell of Italy.

He etches "with a grace and spirit that Whistler would have enjoyed .... He is an excellent observer and does not disdain accuracy." (Arts & D 4:446)

AITKEN, ROBERT I., (S.) b. San Francisco, California, May 8, 1878. Pupil of Mark Hopkins Institute, San Francisco. Won the Barnett prize of the National Academy of Design, 1908. He is a member of the National Sculpture Society and recently has been elected a member of the National Academy.

Mr. Aitken began his art work by painting. After studying sculpture for six months under a French master, he decided to work alone. Later he went to Paris. His monuments to the navy and to President McKinley are among the finest works of art in San Francisco. He has completed a statue of the late Frederic Remington placed at the new station of the Boston, Westchester, & N. Y. R. R., which runs through the Remington property at New Rochelle, N. Y.

His busts are said to possess evidence of perception of character and of subtle discernment. Those most characteristic are:
George Bellows
Willard Metcalf
Prof. Nathaniel Shaler
Henry Arthur Jones, playwright
John W. Gates, financier
"That he possesses those subtle qualities distinguishing the genuine portraitist becomes more and more apparent from close study of his busts." (Overl 60:108)
At the Panama-Pacific Exposition at San Francisco, 1915, Mr. Aitken was represented in the Court of the Universe by four heroic figures typifying the elements—fire, air, water, earth; and his Fountain of Life in the Court of Abundance tells the story of human life in its many phases. "Destiny," symbolized by two enormous arms and hands, gives life with one and takes it with the other. His groups at the exposition were of elaborate and complicated symbolism.

"He has injected much personal charm, shown the grandeur of life, along with the physical perfection of man and womanhood in their alluring quality of youth, and the figures pulsate with life." (Int Studio 54: sup xv)

"Comrades in arms," an Alpha Delta Phi memorial, is among his recent works, and bronze replicas are to be placed in twenty-five chapter houses in the United States and Canada.

ALEXANDER, JOHN WHITE, (P., I., Mural P.) b. Allegheny, Pa., October 7, 1856, d. New York, May 31, 1915. A pupil of Prof. Benczur of the Royal Academy, Munich, and of Frank Duveneck in Munich, Venice, and Florence. He was awarded many medals and won much distinction at home and abroad; was elected chevalier of the Legion of Honor, 1901; a member of Société Nationale des Beaux Arts, Paris; Munich Secessionists; International Society of Artists, London; and Vienna Society of Painters; president of the National Society of Mural Painters; associate member of National Academy of Design, 1901; full member, 1902; and later president.

Mr. Alexander was a painter of portraits, of mural decorations, and of many figure pictures with a distinct decorative purpose. His "Woman in gray" hangs in the Luxembourg; "The green bow" and "The picnic" have also been purchased by the French government. His "Pot of basil" reveals his talent for ideal figure subjects. Of his "Sunlight" which was awarded first-class medal at the 1911 spring exhibition of the Carnegie Institute, it was said: "For grace of lines, relative beauty of color and tone, and illusion of light—sheer necromancy of the painter—this work is without a peer in the exhibition."

Other characteristic pictures are:

"The Mirror"	"A butterfly"
"Woman in pink"	"A rose"
"Flowers"	"Pandora"
"The piano"	"Quiet hour"
"A summer day"	"In the cafe"
"A ray of sunlight"	"A little mother"
"Peonies"	"Study in black and white"
"The blue bowl"	"The ring"
"Memories"	"Autumn"
"Tenth muse"	"A meadow flower"
"A toiler"	"The gossip"

His artistic instinct was decorative, but his portraits of Mrs. Alexander, Auguste Rodin, Walt Whitman, Prof. Chandler of Columbia, Mrs. Wheaton, and others, show he could also master character.

Armand Dayòt, the French critic, says: "From simply caressing the canvas, his brush has become penetrating and the pictures he now shows us possess—and this we consider the highest praise that can be bestowed upon his talent—not only the charm of life but also an intensity of thought."

"He sees, as did Constable, only the beautiful, and the beautiful life is normal."

His mural paintings, "Apotheosis of Pittsburg" in the Carnegie Institute, and "The evolution of the book" in the Library of Congress (both represent the glorification of labor) are among the noteworthy achievements of this branch of art in America.

His combination of piquancy of form and piquancy of color is known as the "Alexander liquid style." "This 'liquidity' is simply music expressed in terms of painting." (Outl 95:171) With Mr. Alexander the real subject is a pictorial harmony based on the human form.

The "John W. Alexander Memorial Studio" at Peterborough, N. H., which is a part of the MacDowell Colony, was completed last summer. The studio suggests a Swiss votive chapel and includes an exhibition gallery.

ALLSTON, WASHINGTON, (P.) b. Waccamaw, S. C., November 5, 1779; d. Cambridge, Mass., July 9, 1843. At six years of age his favorite amusement was making little landscapes about the roots of an old tree near his home. In 1800 he graduated from Harvard and in company with Edward Green Malbone soon after went to London where through the assistance of Benjamin West, who was then president of the Royal Academy, he studied at that school. In 1804 he visited Paris and spent four years in Rome where he obtained the name of the "American Titian."

His first work of importance, "The dead man revived," gained a prize of two hundred guineas from the British Institute and was purchased by the Pennsylvania Academy of the Fine Arts. This was followed by "St. Peter liberated by the angel," "Uriel and the sun," "Jacob's dream," and several smaller pictures which are in private galleries in England.

In 1818 he opened a studio in Boston and spent the remainder of his life in his native country. The most choice of his works were done after he returned to the United States, and are now in Boston. His wonderful wealth of color was his great distinction.

Allston's reputation as a poet and novelist was second only to that he enjoyed as a painter.

ALTEN, MATHIAS J., (P.) b. Gusenburg, Germany, February 13, 1871. A pupil of Constant, Laurens, Prinet, Girrardo, and Whistler in Paris. Mr. Alten's home has been in Grand Rapids, Michigan, for many years. His specialty is portrait painting. His latest, and by many considered his finest, work is a portrait of the late Justice Stone of the Michigan Supreme Court.

ANDERSON, KARL (P., I.) b. Oxford, Ohio, January 13, 1874. Studied in Paris, Holland, Italy, and Madrid as well as in the United States.

When a boy he was apprenticed to the harness making trade but decorated the walls of the shop with his drawings. Going to the city and searching for work he found work in a photographer's studio retouching photographs. Then he advanced to illustration; and later he worked at engraving, attending art school evenings. He studied drawing in Paris and was a member of George Hitchcock's sketching class in Holland. Here he met the late J. J. Shannon, the expatriate, who encouraged him. In 1910 he spent the winter at Madrid copying Velasquez and the next summer worked with Frieseke, at Giverny, France. The canvas painted there, "The idlers," won the silver medal at the Carnegie Exhibition and was bought by the Chicago Art Institute.

A few of his admired canvases are:

"Apple gatherers"   "Pegasus"
"The stubborn goat"   "Wistaria"
"Children of the well"   "The princess"
"The Venetian candelabra"   "Youth in autumn"
"The infant St. John, the Baptist"

"Not alone the fragrance of some hidden beauty is found in Anderson's pictures, but also delicious color and entrancing motion of design, not violent or agitating, but rather subtle, liquid, with the freshness of the morning dew, pearl-like and pure. . . . There is that about his color which seems fused and molten into unity." (Int Studio 76:138)

ANSCHUTZ, THOMAS POLLOCK, (P.) b. Newport, Ky., October 5, 1851; d. Fort Washington, Pa., June 16, 1912. He studied art at the National Academy of Design, New York, and at the Pennsylvania Academy of the Fine Arts, Philadelphia; also with Doucet and Bouguereau in Paris; was a member of the faculty of the Pennsylvania Academy of the Fine Arts, and had served the institution for an uninterrupted period of thirty-two years. He received medals and prizes for his canvases shown in competitive exhibitions and was the painter of the popular Sketch Club portraits which form the artistic frieze of the club rooms in Philadelphia.

Mr. Anschutz painted in pastels, water color, and oils but devoted his time mainly to teaching. As a teacher his popularity was almost without precedent. The Pennsylvania Academy of the Fine Arts owns two of his finest works: "The Tanagra" and "Becky Sharp."

ARMSTRONG, D. MAITLAND, (P., Stained glass designer,) b. Newburg, N. Y., June 12, 1836; d. May 26, 1918. He graduated at Trinity College, Hartford, Conn., 1858; practiced law a few years; studied art in Paris and Rome; was United States consul to Italy; director American Art Department, Paris Exposition, 1878; member of the Society of American Artists, 1879; also of the Architectural League. Associate member National Academy of Design, 1907; also a chevalier of the Legion of Honor of France.

Mr. Armstrong was a professional decorative artist, specializing in stained glass work. The round dome of opal and amber glass, also the side windows of the court room in the New York appellate court building, are his work and rank with the best in this line of art produced in America.

BACHER, OTTO, (E.) b. Cleveland, O., March 31, 1856; d. Lawrence Park, Bronxville, N. Y., August 16, 1909. Began his career as an art student in 1874. In September, 1874, he went abroad and spent some time at Munich, from there he went to Venice with Mr. Duveneck and his band of pupils. His first experiments in etching were made in 1876, and were not successful. He established himself in Europe and again took up the work in 1879, this time with success.

Member of Society of Painter-Etchers, London; associate member of National Academy of Design, 1906.

His first etchings were mostly of picturesque German villages and bits; but later works portray the beauties of Venice. He has produced a large plate of Milan cathedral; one of the interior of Saint Mark's and another of the Grand canal, Venice.

Mr. Bacher was one of our ablest etchers. Sir Seymour Haden said that his series of Venetian etchings evinced a strong artistic feeling and was characterized by "bold and painter-like treatment." The London Times speaks of him as "a most formidable rival of Whistler."

Knaufft says "Celebrated as an etcher, he draws landscape in pen and ink that nearly equals his etching, and he is unsurpassed in pen renderings of still life."

"Unlike Mr. Duveneck, he dwells more upon human than upon the architectural elements in the Venetian panorama. His most characteristic plates show work people of the sea-city at their labors, show lace-makers and bead stringers and washerwomen, either in some dim interior or in some sunny courtyard, or under some shadowy archway by the water."

BAER, WILLIAM J., (Min. P.) b. Cincinnati, O., January 29, 1860. A pupil of the McMicken School of Design, Cincinnati, and of Loefftz at the Munich Royal Academy.

Mr. Baer was first an illustrator of magazines and a teacher of drawing. His portrait of Alfred Corning Clark in 1892 was a success and he afterwards produced it in miniature.

The history of miniature-painting of the present generation in this country began with the work done in this field by Miss Laura C. Hills and Mr. William J. Baer, both of whom were inspired by a love of small things, and admiration for the paintings of the old masters which is more or less reflected in their work. There was a revival of a demand for portraits on ivory and in 1899 the American Society of Miniature Painters, was founded.

In Mr. Baer's "Primavera" he combines many of the best qualities of a good oil painting with a luminosity and brilliancy of texture only to be achieved on ivory. This and such productions as his "Golden hours" will no doubt in time rank with the best work of Malbone, while his only rivals in portraiture today are Josephi, Miss Beckington and the late Theodora W. Thayer. (Int Studio 33 :sup C)

"In his ideal pictures, such as "A girl with a rabbit," he accomplishes much of his best work." (Critic 47 :522)

His flesh tints are exquisite.

He has chosen to erect a very high standard in miniature painting.

At a recent exhibition of the American Society of Miniature Painters, "Mr. Baer showed one large ivory—a full-length female figure, entitled "Egeria," painted in richer, heavier colors than is his custom; also four small portraits done in his usual masterly style. The likeness of Mrs. William Arrindell Shearson in lavender and white lace revealed his skill in exquisite finish and delicacy of touch." (Int Studio 43 :sup xxi)

BAKER, ELIZABETH GOWDY, (P., Min. P.) b. Xenia, O., 1860. A pupil of the Cooper Union, Art Student's League of New York, New York School of Art, Pennsylvania Academy of the Fine Arts, Cowles Art School, Boston; under Frederick Freer, William M. Chase and H. Siddons Mowbray.

Received medal at Cooper Union; is a member of the Boston Art Students' Association and Art Workers' Club for Women, New York.

Mrs. Baker's specialty is portraits in water-color. She is especially successful with pictures of children.

In her work she uses a heavy imported paper and claims that her method enables her to get the strength of oil with the daintiness of water-colors.

Mrs. Baker rarely exhibits and her portraits are in private homes.

BAKER, ELLEN KENDALL, (Mrs. Harry Thompson), (P.) b. Fairfield, N. Y., d. December 4, 1913 at her home, The Croft, Chalfant, St. Giles, England, at the age of 74 years. Studied in Paris under Charles Müller, Paul Soyer, and Harry Thompson, an English artist, whom she married in 1896.

Mrs. Thompson has exhibited in the Paris salons since 1879, also at Munich, St. Petersburg, New York, Philadelphia, Chicago, and Detroit, and is represented in Buffalo, Detroit, and Minneapolis.

A characteristic painting "The young artist," was exhibited in the Paris salon of 1885, and is now owned by the Detroit Museum of Art.

BAKER, MARTHA SUSAN, (Min. P.) b. Evansville, Ind., December 25, 1871; d. Chicago, Ill., December 21, 1911. A pupil of the Chicago Art Institute, she won the Municipal Art League Purchase prize, 1895; first prize for miniature in the Arché salon Chicago, 1897; bronze medal for miniature painting at St. Louis Exposition, 1904; silver medal Art Institute, Chicago, 1905, and received honorable mention for oil painting at the Carnegie Institute, Pittsburgh, 1904. A well-known writer in a review of her work, says: "Her subsequent progress has been as steady and brilliant as it has been well-deserved." She was instructor both in the Art Institute and at the Academy of Fine Arts and one of the four Chicago artists represented at the Paris Exposition in 1900.

At the twelfth annual exhibition of the American Society of Miniature Painters, she exhibited a large composition entitled "Springtime"—a nude child playing with chrysanthemums on the floor. Two small heads were also exhibited—"Master Gifford Ewing" and "Miss Marion Tooker" —painted against a pure ivory background. Although less ambitious, these miniatures were more representative of Miss Baker's gift for strong penetration of character and showed her individual technique.

She has also done some mural work—decorations in the hall of the Fine Arts Building, Chicago.

A gem in water-colors is her "Lake front—Chicago."

"Her style is characterized by an almost masculine force and directness, a naïve obedience to truth and a delightful simplicity. Her knowledge of form is ably expressed in her unerring draughtsmanship." (Int Studio 21:85)

BALL, THOMAS, (S.) b. Charleston, Mass., June 3, 1819; d. December 11, 1911. His first studies were devoted to portrait painting and his most celebrated painting is a full length portrait of Daniel Webster. He also painted several scripture subjects which were highly praised for fine coloring.

Among his first works in sculpture was a small bust of Jenny Lind. After studying in Europe he returned to America and made busts of Rufus Choate, statuettes of Webster and Clay and the equestrian statue of Washington for Boston. Mr. Ball returned to Florence, Italy, in 1865 where he resided until 1897. His works considered his best are the colossal Webster in Central Park, New York; Edwin Forrest as "Coriolanus" in Philadelphia; Governor John A. Andrews of Massachussetts in Boston; and the group "Emancipation" in Washington, D. C.

As a musician, Mr. Ball ranked high and for years was known as a famous baritone singer. During his early struggles in art he supported himself entirely by his musical talents.

BALLIN, HUGO, (Mural P.) b. New York City, 1879. His father was a manufacturer but his grandfather had been a court artist and very early he was encouraged to take up painting. After studying at the Art Students' League of New York, he went abroad to continue his art studies in Italy. While there he was privileged to travel with Robert Blum and to study with him the mural decorations in Lombardy and Umbria. Since his return to the United States he has won many medals and prizes. He is a member of the Society of American Artists and an associate member of the National Academy of Design, 1906. His works have been reproduced in the Critic, Century, and International Studio.

In writing of his art, Homer St. Gaudens, (Critic 47:497) says: "Though in theory Ballin lays greater stress on color and composition than on drawing in decorative work, yet for the most part in practice he applies his skill as a draftsman to aid in conveying his museful conceptions......His drawing discloses in place of assertion an elusiveness and insinuation of contour. The fluency of his lines and the masses of his broad and simple drapery never become angular or extravagant or pale."

BARLOW, MYRON, (P., Mural P.) b. Ionia, Michigan, 1873. A pupil of the Art Institute, Chicago; Gérome and Ecole des Beaux Arts in Paris. He received his first medal in 1894 when he exhibited at the Academie Colarossi; and when elected a member of the Société Nationale des Beaux Arts in 1907 he was the only American to receive the honor at that time. He is a member of the Paris American Artists' Association.

One of his salon pictures, "The fisherman's pride" has brought Mr. Barlow much favorable comment.

Lena M. McCauley in writing of the twenty-third exhibition of the Chicago Art Institute (Art and Progress 2:49), says: "The blue-toned interiors with figures—"Fatigue," "A chat," and "Embarrassing question"—by Myron Barlow, have been displayed with discriminating tact which permitted none of their delicacy to be lost. They are novelties in color but so harmonious and individual that they are a pleasure to look upon."

E. A. Taylor in writing of American artists in Paris says of Mr. Barlow's art: "To simplify an understanding of his art, I might say he paints the luxury of the poor........ Mr. Barlow designs his work; he is not a slave to nature ready-made; his work is always decorative, not decorated, and his color, broad and simple; though bright at times, it is never disturbing by a lack of harmony."

"He claims to be one of the first in the art world to paint blue pictures. These are high in key, and his figures are generally placed against a very light or white background. Vermeer is the old master whose work he constantly studies." (Int Studio 54:sup xxviii)

One of the latest and strongest pieces of work that Mr. Barlow has done is "The prophet," the first of a series of four murals to be painted for the new Temple Beth El, Detroit, Michigan, and which he painted while in Picardy, France. The remaining three—"The patriarch," "The student," and "The immigrant,"—for which color sketches already exist, will be finished during 1923, probably in Etaples, France, where the artist lives most of the time.

"Mother love" is in the Pennsylvania Academy of the Fine Arts; "Liseuse" in the Palais des Beaux Arts, Douai, France; and "Pecheuse" in the Detroit Museum of Art.

BARNARD, GEORGE GREY, (S.) b. Bellefonte, Pa., May 24, 1863. As a youth he developed a taste for natural history; became familiar with birds and their habits and, self-taught, attained skill as a taxidermist. Apprenticed to a local jeweler, he became a skilled letterer and engraver. At the age of sixteen he went to Chicago and entered the Art Institute. With $350 which he was paid for a portrait bust, he went to Paris and studied in the Atelier Cavelier. After three years he took up a studio at Vaugirard, near the port of Versailles, where in 1885 he finished the "Boy" in marble and in 1887 began the "Brotherly love" for a Norwegian monument. He began the group called "Two natures" (suggested by a line from one of Victor Hugo's poems) in 1890, and put it into marble in 1894. That year his work was exhibited in the salon of the Champs de Mars, and he was immediately elected an associate of the Société Nationale des Beaux Arts.

The Figaro said: "Mr. Barnard is possessed of very great qualities, the first of which is the freshness of eternal youth."

M. Thiebault-Sisson, art critic of the Temps, said: "We have a new-comer, George Grey Barnard, who possesses all the qualities of a great master."

Mr. Barnard returned to the United States in 1896 and made a public display of his works in the Logerot Gardens, New York. His "Pan" surmounts the fountain at Columbia University, New York, and has been pronounced "one of the strongest and most original things yet done in sculpture." "The hewer" shows not only sculptural "bigness" but "reveals an unusual emphasis in the matter of straight lines and planes, which gives it remarkable carrying power." The "Rose maiden," a memorial figure, is a work in which a new and tender element has entered. "The figure is a poem of sweetness and mystery, and grows fragrant with dew of spring."

William A. Coffin says: "He is an analyst in thought, and a synthesist in execution. His work shows decided psychological bent. He apparently cares more for force and vitality than for so-called beauty . . . . The splendid vigor and pure artistic power of his work entitled it to be received with enthusiasm."

A late triumph is his work—two groups composed of more than thirty heroic figures—for the façade of the Pennsylvania capitol.

On Fort Washington Heights—One hundred and eighty-ninth street, New York, is located "The Cloisters," the first Gothic museum in the United States.

The story of the assembling of this collection is an interesting one. Mr. Barnard says that he has long been ambitious to reconstruct the outlines of a great epoch in art and gain for himself, and others, a new inspiration from the labors of the sculptors who lived and wrought in mediaeval times. While studying in France he took long tramps through the peasant districts and there discovered and personally excavated these relics of the 12th and 13th centuries. During the French Revolution abbeys, chapels, churches, and cathedrals were stripped of their treasures and practical use made of them; columns, statues, and memorials were used to support and strengthen walls, wine vats, and farm outhouses of the peasantry. Mr. Barnard's account of how he gained possession of some of these rare relics is most interesting.

In writing of the interior of "The Cloisters," Elbert F. Baldwin says: "Within is one of the most remarkable collections of sculpture ever exhibited in this country. Indeed, outside of the Louvre and Cluny museums, it may be the finest of any collection of French Gothic statues, bas-reliefs, capitals, and altar carvings." (Outl 109:199)

But it looks now as though this fine collection of French Gothic is to be lost to New York. A heavy assessment put upon the property decided Mr. Barnard to sell, and, as no person offered to purchase the Cloisters and present it intact to the public of New York City, negotiations were entered into with Los Angeles. This city is planning to spend $35,000,000 in beautifying Palos Verdes, a coast suburb, and the Cloisters will probably be one of the many features of this proposed "Athens of America."

Barnard's fine works grace John D. Rockefeller's estate at Pocantico Hills, N. Y. One is the graceful figure, "Woman," in marble; another is "Adam and Eve."

His Lincoln statue which excited a great controversy was finally erected in Manchester, England, instead of in London as originally planned.

BARSE, GEORGE R., JR., (P.) b. Detroit, July 31, 1861. He received first Hallgarten prize in 1895, and in 1898 at the exhibition of the Society of American Artists his pictures formed part of the Shaw purchase in accordance with the finding of the jury of artists. In 1898 he was elected associate member of the National Academy of Design and full member in 1899.

His pictures have a note of ideality about them, varied in subject from landscapes to allegories. "His Italian landscapes have in them the intense light and luminous shadows of the Mediterranean climate and a good deal of poetry. . . . His New England scenes true to the locality, 'possess no less the keynote of the idealist.' " (Detroit Bulletin, Oct. 1907)

BARTLETT, PAUL WAYLAND, (S.) b. New Haven, Conn., 1865. As a boy modeling in the garden of his home at Marly, France, he attracted the attention of the famous sculptor Frèmiet who gave him instructions in his class in animal sculpture and drawing in the Jardin des Plantes in Paris. At the age of fourteen he exhibited in the salon a bust of his grandmother, and a year later he entered the Ecole des Beaux Arts; at twenty-two his group, "The Bohemian bear tamer," was shown in the salon. He did some remarkable things in bronze casting, and a collection of his bronzes was exhibited in the salon of 1895 and won for him honors. Later achievements occupy places of honor in the United States. In the reading room of the Library of Congress are three well-known statues by him—"Law," "Columbus," and "Michelangelo." Of the last mentioned, the editor of "The artist," says: "One of the noblest modern statues in America is undoubtedly that of Michelangelo .... by Paul Wayland Bartlett, in the Library of Congress."

His "Dying lion" is a work of appealing strength and beauty. His statue of General Warren, the early martyr of the revolution, is at Roxbury. The "Death of Warren" in low relief on the pedestal, has been called "a funeral march in bronze." His equestrian statue of Lafayette, which the school children of the United States presented to France, stands in the court of the Tuileries, "the most coveted site in Paris."

Carriès, the French potter sculptor, says of him: "He reminds me of those artisans of the renaissance who had nothing but art in view and mind." (New Eng M 33:369)

"Mr. Bartlett is primarily a sculptor of the specific. What he most delights in is the presentation of actual characters of history or of definite emotions." (Craftsm 16:437)

The French have showered upon this American sculptor nearly every honor in their gift; he was elected chevalier of the Legion of Honor at the age of thirty, since which time his works have been hors concours in the Paris salons. Elected an associate member National Academy of Design, 1916; full member, 1917.

Mr. Bartlett was selected from a list of sculptors submitted by the National Sculpture Society to design the group of figures to be placed in the pediment of the House wing of the Capitol at Washington, D. C. The work, now completed, consumed seven years of time. The subject is the "Apotheosis of Democracy." "Peace" is the central figure protecting "Genius." Figures in one half of the pediment represent agricultural and pastoral occupations; in the other, various forms of industry—printing, ironworking, textile manufacturing. The ends symbolize the Atlantic and Pacific oceans.

"The entire composition is remarkable for its variety and interest. The figures are grouped in masses of light and shadow, avoiding the monotony of the usual pediment groups .... Mr. Bartlett has shown in his work how sculpture can become modern without ceasing to be monumental." (Arch Rec 39:265)

His decorative group for the New York Public Library, six symbolic figures on the attic above the colonnade of the main entrance on Fifth Avenue, is a great achievement. Mr. Cass Gilbert, the architect, says that Mr. Bartlett has happily solved an interesting problem, the most difficult ever presented to a sculptor in this country. These figures represent the principal things a library contains—History, Philosophy, Romance, Religion, Poetry, Drama.

His colossal statue of Benjamin Franklin, recognizing him as the founder of American public libraries, has been placed in Library Park, Waterbury, Connecticut. It journeyed by team in a flower-decked float, guarded by boy scouts from Baltimore, Maryland, to its permanent location. This unique caravan was received at the New York City Hall by Mr. Bartlett and had a triumphant passage through the streets of Boston.

Mr. Bartlett's "Pilgrim mother and child," designed to commemorate the tercentenary of the landing of the Pilgrims in 1620, is in Provincetown, and this group is one of the two in the United States in memory of the brave women of the Mayflower.

The statue of Robert Morris, the financier of the American Revolution, stands near Independence Hall, Philadelphia.

The design for the Oklahoma Soldiers' State Memorial was modeled by Mr. Bartlett. The monument, one hundred and fifty feet wide and ninety feet high and equipped with elevators, is to be chiseled in granite.

A late design of interest is that for a statue of Agassiz to be erected at the Calumet and Hecla group of mines in Michigan.

BATCHELDER, EVELYN B. LONGMAN (Mrs. Nathaniel Horton Batchelder) (S.) b. Winchester, O., November 31, 1874.

A member of the National Sculpture Society, the American Numismatic Society, and the American Federation of Arts; associate member of the National Academy of Design, 1909; full member, 1919.

To lighten her father's burden of caring for a large family she found employment—at the age of fourteen—in a large wholesale house in Chicago and at the same time attended night school at the Art Institute. Six years later, with her savings, she went to Olivet College, Michigan, then returned to Chicago after a year and a half to become a pupil of Lorado Taft. Miss Longman became a teacher and took charge of the summer school of modeling. Going to New York she worked with Hermon A. MacNeil and Isidor Konti, and later became a valued assistant in the studio of Daniel Chester French.

Her first piece of importance was a "Victory" which she was chosen to execute for the St. Louis Exposition. Contrary to tradition she designed "Victory" as a male figure, and it proved her victory in actual fact; it won for her a silver medal.

The bust of Kate Parsenow, a German actress (called by the sculptor "Aenigma"), has generally been accepted as one of Miss Longman's masterpieces of character study.

She has made two remarkable pairs of bronze doors; one for the entrance chapel of the U. S. Naval Academy at Annapolis; the other for the library building at Wellesley College.

Jonathan A. Rawson, Jr., says (Int Studio 45:sup ciii) : "Mr. French with just pride in the renown that has come to his former pupil is fond of saying that Miss Longman is the last word in ornament."

"Miss Longman's art is noticeable for its refinement and strength, characteristics infrequently found together."

In writing of the winter exhibition of the National Academy of Design, a well known art critic says: "Evelyn Beatrice Longman's contributions were many and dignified; they showed an individual appreciation of classicism which drove them above servility, the classicist's danger."

Miss Longman won in competition the $50,000 commission for the design for the monument to the late Senator Allison of Iowa.

In her "Genius of telegraphy" and "Consecration" the masculine figures are delineated with truth and power. "Consecration," better known as "L'Amour," is a beautiful two-figure group. It was exhibited at the Panama-Pacific Exposition at San Francisco, 1915, as was also her figure representing "Ceres" which surmounted the fountain in the Court of the Four Seasons.

Miss Longman was married to Mr. Nathaniel Horton Batchelder, June 28, 1920.

BAXTER, MARTHA WHEELER, (Min. P., S.) b. Vermont, 1869. A pupil of the Pennsylvania Academy of the Fine Arts and the Art Students' League of New York under Mowbray, Cox, Beckwith, and F. V. DuMond. Studied miniature painting under Mme. de Billemont-Chardon and Mlle. Schmitt in Paris and Mme. Behenna in London.

Received honorable mention at the Paris Exhibition of 1900. Is a teacher.

BAYLISS, LILLIAN, (Min. P.) Has received recognition as a miniature painter. Her ivory work of Madame Gabrielli displays a distinct power of characterization .... As a whole she produces results peculiar for a refinement, a simplicity of tone and surface, and a dignity of the use of color. (Critic 47:527)

BEACH, CHESTER, (S) b. San Francisco, Cal., 1881. Pupil of Verlet and Roland in Paris. Received Barnett prize, National Academy of Design, 1909. Associate member National Academy of Design, 1908; also member of Paris American Artists' Association and National Sculpture Society.

Of his small bronzes, a critic writes: "His expression is symbolic to a considerable degree and is the outcome of a serious and thoughtful mind. His statuettes suggest beautiful pictures that direct themselves princi-

pally to the imagination and by their gentle and graceful motion remind one of passages of music beautifully phrased and perfect in
rhythm. (Arts & D 2:106) "Of the more purely imaginative sculpture, the largest and in some respects the most ambitious work in this
exhibition (110th Pennsylvania Academy of Fine Arts) was Chester
Beach's "Unfolding of life"—figures in white marble of about half life-
size." (Scrib M 55:666)

BEAL, GIFFORD, (P.) b. New York City. A pupil of Chase, DuMond,
and Ranger, his student days were spent entirely in this country. His
subjects are American and one might say his art is completely American.
He became associate member of the National Academy of Design in 1908;
full member in 1914. His paintings have won many prizes and medals
and he is represented in several of our art museums.

His subjects cover garden parties, circuses, landscapes, and marines,
so there is no typical or characteristic style to his work.

"On the whole he is inclined toward color that is rich and strong. The
garden scenes have masses of deep and gleaming foliage over the gay
scenes below. The circus pictures are resplendent in hue. He takes the
rich green that crowns the cliffs at Montauk and with it gives depth and
richness to their tawny sides. The ocean in "Sword fisherman" is an
intense blue, neither light nor dark, and full of almost imperceptible
shadings.

"There is something about his recent painting that suggests he has
made some illuminating discovery or gained a sudden increase of power."
(Int Studio 77:242)

BEATTY, JOHN W., (E) b. Pittsburgh, Pa., July 8, 1851. Director of
Fine Arts, Carnegie Institute, Pittsburgh, since 1896. Student at
Munich Academy of Fine Arts. He was a member of the jury on painting
for Pennsylvania and New York at Columbian Exposition, 1893; member
National advisory board Paris Exposition, 1900; fine arts committee
Pan-American Exposition, Buffalo, 1901; and National advisory commit
tee St. Louis Exposition, 1904.

Executed the etching "Return to labor." His two well-known landscapes are "Plymouth hills" and "Chiltonville." Author of "An appreciation of Augustus Saint-Gaudens."

BEAUX, CECILIA, (P.) b. Philadelphia, Pa., 1863, and is a French descent. Mrs. Thomas A. Janvier gave her her first lessons in drawing;
she was also a pupil of William Sartain and won general recognition as
an able portrait painter. The first of her works to bring her fame was

"Last days of infancy," which was exhibited at the Philadelphia Academy in 1885, and won the prize for the best painting by a resident woman artist; she also won the same prize in 1887, 1891, 1892. Miss Beaux spent the winter of 1889-90 in Paris studying in the life classes of the Académie Julien under Bouguereau, Robert-Fleury, and Benjamin-Constant; also at Colarossi's where her drawings were criticised by Courtois and Dagnan-Bouveret. Spending the summer at Concarneau, she was aided by suggestions from Alexander Harrison and Charles Lasar. After a visit to Italy and England she returned to Philadelphia. In 1893 she won the gold medal of the Philadelphia Art Club for the portrait of Dr. Grier; also the Dodge prize of the National Academy of Design for her portrait of Mrs. Stetson. Miss Beaux was the seventh woman to whom the honor of an election to membership in the Society of American Artists was awarded. In 1894 she was elected associate of the National Academy of Design, being the third woman to gain admission; elected full member in 1902. She is recognized here and abroad as the most distinguished of living woman painters.

To the salon of the Champs de Mars, Paris, 1896, she sent six paintings. These were hung in a group, an unusual distinction and brought to her an election as an associate of the Société Nationale des Beaux Arts. (Nat Cy Am Biog)

Her figures are usually represented in repose or at least in arrested action, but "Dorothea and Francesca" shows her power in rendering motion with equal success. Her portrait of Mrs. Roosevelt is one of her happiest creations. "The dreamer," "New England woman," "Sita and Sarita," "The Cynthia," "Ernesta and her little brother," are all portraits. Miss Beaux's portraits are never composite; they are not in any sense types. Her individuality is developed in two characteristics: brilliancy and refinement. (Int Studio 41:337)

Her "Banner bearer" is referred to as "a work of compelling strength and convincing simplicity—a work utterly without mannerism."

Giles Edgerton says: "It is not once in a generation that a woman so subverts her essentially characteristic outlook on life to her work that her art impulse becomes universal as that of the greatest men often is. One feels that Cecilia Beaux has done this in her portrait work, as George Eliot did in her stories."

Since the honor conferred upon Miss Beaux by the National Art Committee to paint the portraits of Premier Clemenceau of France, Cardinal Mercier of Belgium, and Admiral Beatty of England, she has been known as the "painter of heroes."

The late Gutzon Borglum in writing of Miss Beaux and her art, said: "She boasts no abnormality of genius, she did not run away from opposing parents or starve for a quarter of a century 'just to paint.' She just sanely labored with color and oil and brush, and so found the minds and moods and motives of human existence and painted them."

BECKINGTON, ALICE, (Min. P.) b. St. Charles, Mo., July 30, 1868. A pupil of Art Students' League, New York; Lefebvre, Benjamin-Constant, and Lazar, Paris.

She received honorable mention at the Pan-American Exposition, Buffalo, 1901; bronze medal at the St. Louis Exposition, 1904; is a member of the New York Woman's Art Club and also of the American Society of Miniature Painters. Instructor at Art Students' League, New York.

Miss Beckington's work reveals a feeling for the impressionistic and a charming application of it. The portrait of Mrs. Buford is the best example of her work.

"She treats her sitters with a clear directness and absence of nonsense, selecting and refining her essentials with sanity and taste ......
Her portraits increase steadily in naturalness and an unwavering yet delicate definition of facial character." (Critic 47:525)

"Mrs. Beckington," a portrait of the artist's mother, was accepted by the Paris salon in 1894, and is now the property of the Metropolitan Museum of New York City.

"This picture is essentially characteristic of Miss Beckington, representing her straightforward and sincere simplicity combined with an appreciation of subdued color harmonies."

Her miniatures have a pleasing warmth of color. "It is, in fact, as values of exquisite subtlety that Miss Beckington sees color. Her kinship is with Dewey, with Whistler, and with Thayer." (Scrib 67:384)

BECKWITH, JAMES CARROLL, (P.) b. Hannibal, Mo., September 23, 1852; d. New York City, October 24, 1917. Studied painting in Chicago where his father was a merchant. Began his art studies in 1868 under Walter Shirlaw and in 1873 entered the studio of Carolus-Duran, subsequently studying at the Ecole des Beaux Arts. Returned to the United States in 1878, opened a studio in New York and began his profession as a portrait painter. He was at once elected an instructor in the Art Students' League. Became an associate member of the National Academy of Design, 1886; full member, 1894.

Mr. Beckwith received honorable mention in the Paris salon of 1887, and painted portraits of many distinguished residents of New York.

At the Paris Exhibition in 1878, he exhibited "The falconer" painted when he was only twenty-five years old. His portrait of Mrs. R. H.

McCurdy, shown at the Academy Exhibition of 1879, gave him a definite position among the painters of New York; that of Captain Joseph Lentilhon, exhibited in the Paris salon in 1887 and at the Universal Exposition of 1889, received awards in both cases. His picture, "The authoress," has been called a modern Mona Lisa. In "A baptism at Onteora" all the figures are portraits, and the artist and his wife are viewing the procession from the shadow of the chimney to the right.

Mr. Beckwith's skill in figure drawing is shown in the following:

"La Cigale"   "Under the lilacs"
"The nautilus"   "The Christian martyr"
"Danse antique"   "Mother and child"
"The awakening   "The blacksmith"
"The falconer"   "Judith"
"Azalia"

"Mr. Beckwith's work is distinguished by a breadth of style and an unerring grace which is rarely met with outside of continental schools." (American Artists)

Mr. Beckwith wrote and lectured on art and conducted a summer school in painting at Onteora-in-the-Catskills.

One of Mr. Beckwith's most notable achievements was as president of the Free Art League, which succeeded, in September 1894, in having removed the duty on paintings imported into this country. A duty of ten percent was imposed in Civil War days which was later raised to thirty percent. The Free Art League had the duty removed.

During a period covering forty years, Mr. Beckwith made a series of copies of paintings by the old masters in the galleries of Paris, Vienna, Madrid, Haarlem, Florence, and Dresden. These copies were circulated by the American Federation of Arts. Mr. Blashfield says: "The intrinsic value of the collection of copies made by Carroll Beckwith is great; its relative interest is perhaps even greater; relative, that is to say, as to art education and to the situation which governs our acquaintance with the masterpieces of the artists of the past."

He was best known as a painter of portraits. The portrait of Mrs. Beckwith, shown at the Paris Exposition of 1900, is one of his most notable achievements. "Mark Twain", an intimate-portrait of the great humorist, painted at Onteora Park, in the Catskills, the summer home of these comrades, both born in Hannibal, Mo., is now in the possession of Mrs. Ossip Gabrilowitsch, the daughter of Mr. Clemens.

BELCHER, HILDA, (P.) b. Pittsford, Vermont. Studied at the New York School of Art.

The International Studio (46:237) writes of her "Little Boston girl": "It is one of those delightful portrayals of the ingenuous child character that are always acceptable as subjects of the painter's analytical study."

A few of her best paintings are:

"Sibyl"
"The checkered dress"
"Portrait of Miss P"
"The mother"
"Red mitts"
"Speculation"
"Auburn and white"

"Unrepentant"
"Young girl in white"
"The old ladies"
"Fellow traveler"
"Listening"
"The fairy book"

BELLOWS, GEORGE WESLEY, A. B., (P., I.) b. Columbus, O., August 12, 1882. Studied in New York School of Art under Robert Henri. Exhibited at International Exposition, Venice; Royal Academy, Berlin; Royal Society, Munich; Kensington Museum, London; and in principal cities of the United States. Elected as associate member of the National Academy of Design in 1908; full member in 1913.

Mr. Bellows is one of the modern impressionists. In his out-of-doors scenes—landscapes and marines—he shows a liking for sharp contrasts. An example of his snow pictures is "The Palisades."

Among his best known pictures are:

"Up Hudson" (one of his finest works), Metropolitan Museum, New York.
"North River," Pennsylvania Academy of the Fine Arts, Philadelphia.
"Blackwell's bridge," Toledo, Ohio.
"Love of winter," Art Institute, Chicago.
"A day in June," Detroit Institute of Art.

At college Mr. Bellows was a great foot ball player, and athletic subjects portrayed by him in paint are full of strength and power as well as action.

Bellows' greatest achievement is in his figure composition—his handling of a type or a character study. His art has been described as having "breeziness," "snap," "plenty of go," "red blood," gumption," etc.

"As a painter of the propitious, strenuous, or dramatic moment he indeed lives up to his intention." (Int Studio 56:242)

"Should any one look for a literary parallel to Bellows, he would, I think, stop at Kipling, as the one who most nearly approaches it. Both deal with the great realities of life, its pathos, and both treat these in a big, general way." (Art and P 3:679)

"The execution of Edith Cavell" is a fine example of lithography as well as an eloquent document of history. Royal Cortissoz says: "It is quite the finest thing Mr. Bellows has ever done, really rich in that deep, tenderly-felt beauty which as a rule he would appear to disdain. The scale of color used in this canvas is not very broad. But the play of light and shade exploited within it is so subtile as actually to enrich the artist's tones."

His war pictures are his individual interpretations of the press notices and the personal anecdotes of returned soldiers. Of these war pictures Mr. Bellows says: "In presenting these pictures of the tragedies of war, I wish to disclaim any intention of attacking a race or a people—guilt is personal, not racial."

Charles L. Buchanan in discussing his prize fights, games, and circus says: "Bellows has too often suggested the sporting edition of an evening paper, a statistician's accounting, the report of a charitable organization. In company with the large majority of his generation he is engaged in pushing art over its boundary lines, in utilizing it as a medium for the expression of things which are actively and permanently antagonistic to it."

At the International Exhibition at the Carnegie Institute in 1922, Mr. Bellows was given the medal of the first class for his portrait group, "Eleanor, Jean, and Anna," a painting recognized as his greatest work and as one of the finest achievements in American portraiture.

BENSON, FRANK WESTON, (P., E., Mural P.) b. Salem, Mass., March 24, 1862. Studied art at the Boston Museum of Fine Arts, also under Boulanger and Lefebvre in Paris. He has been the recipient of a remarkable number of artistic distinctions, the chief significance of which is that they have been awarded by the artistic profession. Since 1892 he has been instructor in drawing in the Boston Museum of Fine Arts. In 1905 he was elected to full membership in the National Academy of Design and his list of honors and prizes received is a long one. He has also won distinction by his sympathetic and understanding interpretation of child life.

"Open-air work is the most familiar side of Benson's art, and figure subjects in the open air have made him a student of the sea as well as of landscape, and especially of both viewed under the effect of sunlight."

"Against the sky," which Mr. Benson considers one of the best things that he has ever done, like "Eleanor," has the quality of freedom for which the "Ten" seceded. His " Moonlight at sea" has all the beauty of romance and technique. "Summer" is one of his most successful decorative paintings.

A few of his representative canvases are:

"Orpheus"	"My little girl"
"Winter storm"	"Lamplight"
"Girl with veil"	"Girl with black hat"
"Portrait of three sisters"	"Calm morning"
"In an old garden"	"Girl playing solitaire"
"Woman reading"	"In the spruce trees"
"The hill top"	"Portrait in white" (his wife.)
"Summer afternoon"	

"He set before us visions of the free life in the open air, with figures of gracious women and lovely children, in a landscape drenched in sweet sunlight and cooled by refreshing sea breezes. The purity and charm of the sentiment match the purity and charm of the color." (Arts & D 1:195)

His wife and children have been his models for his popular figure canvases.

"Mr. Benson's paintings (apart from his portraits) have much shimmering color and radiance of light, a subtle effect of seeking the decorative in nature herself." (Int Studio 35:sup xcix)

A fine group of water colors exhibited last year resulted from a winter spent in the West Indies.

"The play of sunlight on the water and sunlight in the eyes, the ripple of the sea and the roll of surf, scudding sail boats and dories and black-skinned figures in the sun are all motives for the pattern of his art. He has great knowledge of the limitations of aquarelle."

Mr. Benson's drawings and etchings of wild fowls have marked an epoch in American art. He is an ardent huntsman and his etchings of flying water fowls have been called his playtime specialty. It has been said that no other artist has approached him in his ability to accurately reproduce the rapidity of motion of wild birds in flight.

"The majority of his etchings and dry-points have reference to the life of wild birds, various kinds of ducks and geese, which he often represents in flight. His compositions, showing flocks of wild geese and wild ducks flying, are very remarkable."

Adam E. M. Paff in referring to his etchings says: "His work so far marks him as one who uses etching, not as a means for the making of pictures, but as an intimate and personal medium of expression."

"His etchings and wash drawings are magnificent proofs of his genius, showing how a true artist can express in a few strokes both life and character."

Forty-eight etchings by Mr. Benson were displayed at a New York gallery in 1915. This was his first appearance as an etcher and shows that "he has a bold and strong line and, as in his paintings, a fine composition, sense of the picturesque, and love of nature."

Mr. Benson has also done mural painting. "The Graces" and "The Seasons" in the Library of Congress are his work.

BETTS, LOUIS, (P.) b. Little Rock, Arkansas, October 5, 1873. His father was a landscape painter and his mother was also an artist. At an early age his father encouraged him in his love of pictorial art and was his first instructor. He became a pupil at the Pennsylvania Academy School and won a traveling scholarship which gave him his first trip to Europe.

Mr. Betts was elected an associate member of the National Academy of Design in 1912; a full member in 1915.

When fourteen years of age he painted his first portrait, for which he received instruction on the violin, his favorite instrument. Painting and music have been his vocation and avocation since this youthful age.

Mr. Betts has been successful as a portrait painter not only in Chicago and New York but in London, Paris, Amsterdam, and Madrid. His portrait of Scott Libbey, Jr., a handsome lad, is regarded as a perfect representation of American childhood and also as one of his finest achievements. His "Apple blossoms" is in the Art Institute, Chicago.

"His grasp of character and essentials is revealed in a broad and dashing manner .... He is a painter's painter in the truest meaning whose work will ever appeal to connoisseurs." (Int Studio 64: sup lxxi)

Among his best portraits of those who have attained national prominence are those of Michael Cudahy, Ella Flagg Young, and D. Thomas Wakefield Goodspeed of the Chicago University.

BIERSTADT, ALBERT, (P.) b. Düsseldorf, Germany, January 7, 1830; d. New York, February 18, 1902.

When one year old he was taken to New Bedford where his youth was spent. At twenty-four he returned to his native town in Germany and studied art under Lessing for four years, and in Rome for one year, making summer sketching tours to Switzerland. He returned to the United States in 1859 but made frequent trips to Europe. In 1857 he accompanied General F. W. Lander's expedition to the Rocky Mountains and collected material for his most important pictures.

"Settlement of California by the Spanish priest, Father Junipero Serra," and "The discovery of the Hudson river" in the Capitol at Washington; "View on the Kern river" and "Sunset among the Sierra Nevada mountains" in the Hermitage, St. Petersburg; "Great trees of California" in the Imperial palace, Berlin; "Estes Park" owned by the earl of Dunraven; "Laramie Peak" in the Academy of Fine Arts, Buffalo; and "A mountain peak" in the Corcoran gallery at Washington are among some of his best known works.

Tuckerman says: "No more genuine and grand American work has been produced than Bierstadt's "Rocky mountains."

Medals were awarded to him in Austria, Germany, Bavaria, and Belgium. He was made a chevalier of the Legion of Honor of France, received the order of St. Stanislaus of Russia and the Imperial order of the Madjidi from the sultan of Turkey. Mr. Bierstadt was elected member of the National Academy of Design, 1860.

BIRCH, REGINALD BATHURST, (I.) b. London, England, May 2, 1856; came to the United States at the age of sixteen; later studied art in Munich and Italy. He has drawn much with the pen, mostly for "St. Nicholas," and may, indeed be called the "Children's Gibson." Illustrated "Little Lord Fauntleroy," "Lady Jane," and "The story of Betty."

Mr. Birch is the illustrator par excellènce for children's stories and fairy tales. His line is graceful and his use of blacks exceedingly skilful.

BISBING, H. SINGLETON, (P.)—American cattle painter—b. Philadelphia, Pa., January 31, 1849. Began his artistic career by studying wood-engraving. In 1872 he was employed on Appleton's Art Journal. He entered upon a course of study under Profs. Barth and Loefftz at Munich in 1876 and three years later became a pupil of J. H. L. deHaas, the celebrated animal painter of Brussels. In 1884 he removed to Paris where he continued his studies under Felix du Vuillefroy, also a noted animal painter.

His pictures, mostly animal subjects, have been exhibited at the Paris salon.

He received third-class medal at Paris salon in 1891; Temple gold medal at the exhibition of Pennsylvania Academy of Fine Arts in 1892, and was made a chevalier of the Legion of Honor of France in 1902.

His works are in the Pennsylvania Academy of the Fine Arts, Philadelphia; Berlin National Gallery; and in the private collection of the royal family of Saxony. Mr. Bisbing is a member of the Paris Society of

American Painters and his paintings are hors concours at the Paris salon.

"Bisbing paints large landscapes, saturated by light and air, with cows somnolently resting in the sun." (Müther.)

BITTER, KARL THEODORE, (S.) b. Vienna, Austria, December 6, 1867; d. New York City, April 10, 1915, of injuries received when he was run down by an automobile. Studied art in the Vienna Academy of Fine Arts. From the age of sixteen he made efforts to come to America but did not receive the consent of his parents until 1889 when he sailed for New York. The first year in New York, unknown and practically friendless, he won in competition the order for one of the Astor Memorial gates of Trinity Church.

Mr. Bitter was connected with the Columbian Exposition as a decorator, with the Pan-American and St. Louis expositions as official director of sculpture, and with the Panama-Pacific as chief of the department of sculpture.

Of his "Standard bearers" in heroic size (a personal contribution to the Pan-American Exposition), Lorado Taft says: "They were among the finest things ever devised for any exposition." His "Villard memorial" and "Hubbard memorial" are beautifully modeled and have about them an atmosphere of poetic gravity quite unfamiliar in Mr. Bitter's sculpture. His bust of Dr. Pepper, provost of the University of Pennsylvania, is a gratifying success and shows beyond its admirable workmanship a subtle union of kindliness and reserve which makes it a convincing expression of individuality.

Among Mr. Bitter's works are many figures and figure reliefs for the residences of the Vanderbilts, C. P. Huntington, John Jacob Astor, and others. More numerous are his decorations for public buildings, libraries, churches, stores, etc. Notable are the enormous reliefs for the Broad street station of the Pennsylvania Railroad at Philadelphia. His groups of children are happy ideas for small fountains.

He was elected an associate member of the National Academy of Design, New York, in 1902; full member, 1903; and was a member of the National Sculpture Society, New York Architectural League and Society of American Artists.

Mr. Bitter's statue of Thomas Jefferson for the University of Virginia was unveiled a few days after his death. He was to have been the guest of honor at the ceremonies. His last work was the Hendrik Hudson statue to be placed on Spuyten Duyvil Hill.

BLAKELOCK, RALPH ALBERT, (P.) b. New York, October 15, 1847. d. in the Adirondacks, August 9, 1919. The son of a physician, he was educated with a view to adopting his father's profession, but he was naturally gifted in the line of music and painting and the science and practice of medicine did not attract him. Renouncing the career of a physician and resolving to take up the profession of painting, with no art training whatever, without guidance or assistance, he opened a studio in New York. The story of his life is a pitiful one—one of the saddest in the history of American art. The hardships and privations which he endured unsettled his mind and he was confined in an insane asylum for nearly seventeen years.

After fifteen years confinement, the National Academy of Design elected him to associate membership—a tardy recognition of his genius. He was freed from the asylum and permitted to visit the exhibition of his paintings held in April, 1916, at the Reinhardt Gallery to raise a fund for his benefit. After this exhibition he was advanced to full membership in the National Academy of Design.

Eleven paintings which brought Blakelock less than $2,000 were sold in the Lambert collection for $46,990. "Brook by moonlight" was bought by the Toledo Museum of Art for $20,000 (Blakelock sold it for $500). A few years ago another "Moonlight" which Blakelock sold for $50 was purchased by a well-known art collector for $14,000.

Characteristic examples of his work are:

"Moonrise"
"At nature's mirror"
"Solitude"
"Sunset, Nevarra Ridge"
"The mountain brook"
"Sunset off the coast"
"Sunset through the wood"
"Morning"
"Moonlight"
"Cool wooded shades"
"The oak tree"

"October sunshine"
"Redwoods, California"
"Indian girl, Uinta tribe"
"Navajo blanket makers"
"Indian fisherman"
"Bannoch wigwam in peaceful vale"
"The captive"
"The canoe builder"
"Abode of the stately deer"
"Story of the buffalo hunt"

"A characteristic Blakelock is a twilight thing conceived in mellow browns and russets, accented with deep yellows and a dash of scarlet, and relieved by a patch of blue .... Blakelock was keenly sensitive to music, and the elusive quality of the more modern harmonies is in his pictures." (Review 1:314)

"His preoccupation was with the romantic quality of the white moonlight, of the glowing sunset, against which he could arrange his dark masses of foliage into an agreeable composition."

"Praise of Blakelock has been excessive. Probably the truth is, that though he can never rank with the masters, ... still in the history of American landscape painting he will not be altogether forgotten." (Nation 109 :254)

BLASHFIELD, EDWIN HOWLAND, (P., Mural P., I.) b. New York, December 15, 1848. Was educated in Boston Latin School. Studied in Paris, 1867, under Leon Bonnat; also received advice from Gérome and Chapu. Exhibited at the Paris salon 1874-9, 1881, 1891, 1892; also several years at Royal Academy, London. Returned to the United States in 1881. Elected a member of the National Academy of Design, New York, in 1888; president since 1919. He is also President National Society of Mural Painters.

He has exhibited genre pictures, portraits, and decorations and lectured on art at Columbia, Harvard, and Yale and in prominent cities of the United States, his lecture on "Municipal art" being regarded one of the best lectures on art ever given in this country.

In collaboration with his wife he prepared numerous illustrated articles for Scribner, Century, and other leading magazines on subjects connected with mediaeval or renaissance art, or noted places of the old world. Among the most noteworthy and interesting of these may be mentioned: "With Romola in Florence," "The man at arms," "Castle life," "A day with a Florentine artist of the 15th century," "Ravenna and its mosaics," "The Paris of the musketeers," "Afloat on the Nile."

Most notable of his paintings are:

"Christmas bells"	"All souls day"
"The choir boys"	"Inspiration"
"The angel of the flaming sword"	"Young poet"
"Spring time"	"Toreador"

Mr. Blashfield's strength lies in decorative painting in which his drawing is as elegant as his color is fragile in tone. His best mural work is seen in the Library of Congress, Washington; court house, Baltimore; and the Minnesota and Iowa state houses. He painted the design for the dome piece for the new state capitol at Madison, Wis., said to be the largest canvas ever painted in America, and the figure which typifies the state of Wisconsin is thirteen feet sitting, the largest figure ever painted.

"In his art he demonstrates his understanding of drawing, elevated without losing strength, of refined felicitous light, of controlling unified tone, of the grace, sweetness and reticence in simple gesture and of the power in an organized whole." (Int Studio 35 :sup lxix)

A most notable mural work of Mr. Blashfield is in the new public library of Detroit, Michigan. The scheme is a combination of symbolism and portraiture placed on the walls of the grand central staircase. Two long panels represent Symphonic Music and the Graphic Arts. At the top of the Music panel St. Cecilia is enthroned between two maidens with violin and 'cello. In the middle is a figure seated at an organ representing Ecclesiastical Music. In the Arts panel Pegasus gallops across the top, figures representing various forms of architecture come in the center, and portraits of artists are at the bottom. The large lunette over the south window symbolizes "Poetry" and contains thirty-seven figures. The Muse is seated at the top, and portraits of musicians and writers of opera are on one side, poets on the other. The large lunette opposite—over the north window—symbolizes "Prose works" and grouped on either side and below the Muse are thirty-three portraits of famous persons in the world's literature.

Mr. Blashfield has recently been in Rome and Venice to arrange for the execution of a series of mosaics for St. Matthew's church, Washington, D. C. The design, sixty feet in diameter, represents the largest work of the kind in America and two years will be required for its completion.

Mr. Blashfield is the author of "Mural painting in America"—an authoritative and much valued work.

BLUM, ROBERT FREDERICK, (P., I., E., Mural P.) b. Cincinnati, O., July 9, 1857; d. New York, June 8, 1903. He was apprenticed in a lithographing shop in 1871 and attended night classes at McMicken Art School of Design, Cincinnati; studied nine months at the Pennsylvania Academy of the Fine Arts, Philadelphia; went to New York in 1879 and made trips to Europe during the years 1880-89. In 1890 he accompanied Sir Edwin Arnold to Japan in order to illustrate his "Japonica."

His "Lace makers" won a medal at the Paris Exposition in 1889; "Bead stringers" occasioned his election as an associate of the National Academy of Design, and the exhibition of his "Ameya" ("Itinerant candy vender") brought him into full membership of the academy in 1893. At his election he was the youngest member of the association.

Upon his return from Japan in 1892, after completing his Japanese drawings and paintings, he took up mural decoration and reached the highest perfection of art in the magnificent decorations in Mendelssohn Hall, New York, illustrating the "Moods of music."

The charm of Blum's pictures lies in the execution rather than in the subjects which are chosen from every land except America. His "Itinerant candy vender" in the Metropolitan Museum of New York is full

of color, with exactitude of line and a charming sense of foreign parts.
(Isham.)

His pen drawings of Venice, dated 1880, have in all the progress of
that special art, never been excelled.

"He paints Japanese street scenes full of sunlight and lustrous color."
(Müther.)

A few Japanese pictures are:

"Flower market, Tokio"	"Musse-night"
"The geisha"	"Siesta"
"Cherry blossoms"	"The terrace"
"The bath"	

While Mr. Blum's reputation as an illustrator and etcher was well
established, it is probable that he will be longest remembered by his
work as a colorist.

BLUMENSCHEIN, ERNEST LEONARD, (P., I.) b. Pittsburgh, Pa., May 26,
1874. Pupil of Cincinnati Art Academy; Art Students' League of New
York; Benjamin-Constant, Laurens, and Collin of Paris. Member of Society of Illustrators and Paris American Artists' Association. Elected
associate member of the National Academy of Design, 1910.

Illustrator for Century, Scribner's, McClure's, Harper's, American,
and other magazines and books; also portrait painter and teacher.

Blumenschein was one of the first American artists who found their
theme in the pictorial suggestion of the Taos region in New Mexico.

"Superstition" is the painting that was awarded the Altman prize
at the National Academy of Design in 1921 when it was withdrawn
from Carl Rungius, a foreign-born competitor, who was, because of this
fact, not eligible. It represents an old Indian holding on his lap a
pottery jar out of which arises a little wraith of an Indian. The background is composed of Taos motives with crude, dull reds and browns
predominating. The work is thoroughly typical of the Southwestern
school.

"The gift," one of his typical canvases, is very popular.

"The chief speaks" was awarded the Potter Palmer gold medal and
$1,000 at the exhibition at the Art Institute, Chicago, 1917.

"Blumenschein has passed beyond the anecdotal stage in dealing pictorially with the Indians of the great Southwest . . . . In his group
pictures especially he handles the pomp and ceremony of these latter-day
red men in much the same clear, concise way that the Venetians told
their tales of Venice when she was queen of the seas. The splendor of

costume, the warmth of complexion, the brilliant sunlight, the picturesque details of Indian life he co-ordinates in compactly designed canvases."

BLUMENSCHEIN, MARY SHEPARD GREEN, (P., S.) (Mrs. E. L. Blumenschein) b. New York. Pupil of Herbert Adams of New York, Collin of Paris. Received third-class medal in the Paris salon of 1900; second-class medal in salon of 1902; silver medal of St. Louis Exposition, 1904.

Mrs. Blumenschein was the first American woman to receive a medal of the second class from the Société des Artistes Francais.

BOGERT, GEORGE, (P.) b. New York, 1864. Pupil of National Academy, also of Puvis de Chavannes, Aime Morot, and E. Boudin, Paris. Received honorable mention at the Pennsylvania Academy of the Fine Arts, 1892; Webb prize, Society American Artists, 1898; first Hallgarten prize, National Academy, 1899. Associate member of National Academy of Design, 1899.

"October moonlight" is much admired, as is also "Approach of evening, Venice," ablaze with the vibrating colors of the sky at sunset.

"He has done a great amount of work, much varied, not only in subject—landscapes, marines, views of cities chosen from all over the world—but also in handling and in color scheme." (Isham.)

His work is largely reminiscent, the works of Constable, Diaz, Maris being reflected in his canvases; but his two most interesting canvases, "Approaching storm" and "Day after the storm" are strong works and derived evidently from independent study and a personal outlook. (Artist 24:sup lxi)

"His technique is strong, and if his ideals were simpler and more direct, his art could be enthusiastically admired. He has force, dramatic quality, and knows how to put a picture together." (Brush & P 4:125)

Other popular pictures are:

"Eventide"	"Rainbow at sea"
"The last rays"	"Summer morning, Manomet"
"Chateau Gaillard, moonrise"	

BORGLUM, JOHN GUTZON MOTHE, (S., P., I.) b. California, March 25, 1867. Pupil of San Francisco Art Association and Academie Julien in Paris; a member of the Royal Society of British Artists and Société Nationale des Beaux Arts, Paris.

As a lad in a western Jesuit college he carved crucifixes on his slate and copied in his books reproductions of pictures by the old masters.

After studying in Paris and spending a year in Spain he returned to the United States but in 1896 went to London and remained there until 1901; settled in New York in 1902.

His earlier works in sculpture were western in subject — "Indian scouts," "Death of a chief," "Apaches pursued by U. S. troops." Later works are "The seer," "The Boer," "Remorse," gargoyles for the dormitory building at Princeton, bronze statuette of John Ruskin, and portrait bust of Lincoln. Of this bust of Lincoln a writer on works of art says: "In profound insight into character and in subtleness of portrayal, Gutzon Borglum's "Head of Lincoln" must be accounted among the greatest achievements in portrait sculpture that have been made by any American artist." (Craftsm 14:26)

The masterly rendering of "The mares of Diomedes" places this group among the great works of art. Here he has given movement—the fury of high-strung steeds.

In 1898 he was commissioned to make the decorations for the Queen's Hotel at Leeds and chose for his subject the story of "Pan." Here his real personality showed itself and his special genius came into play.

In his New York studio he painted a series of mural decorations for the Midland Hotel Concert Hall at Manchester, England—subject: "The coming of Guinevere," also painted twelve panels illustrating "Midsummer night's dream" for a private residence in New York.

His statuette of John Ruskin evinces that broad thought with which he approaches his subject.

In writing of the art of the Metropolitan Museum of New York (where are his "Mares of Diomedes" and the bronze statuette of Ruskin) David C. Preyer says: "Nothing could be in more striking contrast— the mad stampede of the tumbling mass of horses and the quiet dignified repose of the writer and thinker."

A contributor to the International Studio says: "A certain impressionistic tendency shows itself in Mr. Borglum's recent work."

His works are so varied and his manner so versatile that classification and general exposition is almost out of the question.

"The reason for building any work of art," he says, "can only be for the purpose of fixing in some desirable form a great emotion, or a great idea, of the individual or the people."

Mr. Borglum is preparing to execute on Stone Mountain, Ga., (sixteen miles from Atlanta) the largest sculptural work in the history of the world—a memorial to the confederate armies, to be built by the south of today. On the granite mountain will be carved a frieze 2,000 feet long, 50 feet wide and five stories high at an expenditure of

$2,000,000. Twelve years will be the time required to complete the work. The New York Times, January 2, 1916, gave a detailed description of this unprecedented undertaking.

BORGLUM, SOLON HANNIBAL, (S.) b. Ogden, Utah, December 22, 1868, d. Stamford, Conn., January 30, 1922. Was reared among the frontiersmen in a typical prairie town and worked on a stock ranch while young. In 1893 he decided to give up ranch life and to study art; became a student in the Cincinnati Art School and studied under Louis Rebisso and Fremiet in Paris. Associate member of National Academy of Design, 1911; founder of the School of American sculpture in New York City.

When he went to Cincinnati he obtained admission to the U. S. stables and began to model his first group which, when exhibited in the annual school exhibit, won him a special prize of $50, and during his second year at the art school he won the prize of a scholarship. In Paris his groups were accepted by the salon and he received encouraging words of approval from Fremiet, the French sculptor.

His group called "Lassoeing wild horses" was his first exhibit in the Paris salon; "Stampede of wild horses" was next, and "The lame horse" brought him honorable mention. Returning to the United States in 1900, he made a special study of western life, living among cow-boys and Indians, and producing "One in a thousand," "The blizzard," and "The plainsman."

"In such works as "The last round-up," "Our slave," and "On the border of white man's land" Mr. Borglum has hit upon a very large and impressive treatment which is distinctly sculptural in its inspiration; while in the tiny "Burial on the plains" there is a mysterious emotional note which has been touched by few indeed of our sculptors, a sentiment that might easily have been dissipated by a more insistent technic." (Taft's "History of American sculpture")

"There is that in his work which challenges the shams and insincerities of our drawing rooms and which makes the money-getting occupation of our trammeled lives seem suddenly trite. His art is not the expression of his personality, but of that part of the universe by which he was environed and is therefore as untrammeled as nature."

"He stands pre-eminently as a sculptor of American life in one of its distinctive phases .... His groups embody in marble and bronze the free primitive life of the great west." (Craftsm 12:382)

His five colossal busts of Civil War generals which are in the Vicksburg National Park and his statue, "The pioneer," in the Court of Honor, Panama-Pacific Exposition, 1915, are among his best known works.

"Fighting bulls" (typifying the clash between untamed nature and civilization) is in the Metropolitan Museum, New York.

His "Napoleon" is more than the portrait bust of an historical figure. One sees latent in this marble the baffled spirit of man, "his ambition arrested by the voice of God whom in his vain might he has defied."

"Aspiration" and "Inspiration," symbolized by two figures, are works of a late period.

During the World War he served in France as a Y. M. C. A. secretary and was awarded the Croix de Guerre for courage under fire at Chateau-Thierry. He was the first American artist in the service of the allies to receive this distinguished honor.

In a tribute to his late, lamented brother, Gutzon Borglum says: "The poetic charm, the rhythm that harmonized action—that gives action its true psychology—he felt as no other American of our day, and as the life he drew has largely passed it is more than doubtful if any ability of his kind, should it appear, can parallel his contribution to the pioneer days of America's ascendance in fine art accomplishment."

BOUGUEREAU, ELIZABETH GARDNER (Madame W. A. Bouguereau), (P.) b. Exeter, N. H., 1851; d. Saint Cloud, France, January, 1922. Received honorable mention in Paris salon, 1879; gold medal, 1889; hors concour. Her professional life has been spent in Paris where she was a pupil of Hugues Merle, Lefebvre, and Bouguereau whom she married.

When Miss Gardner went to Paris to study art, women were not admitted to the Julien Academy, but, determined to have the benefit of the teaching there given, she donned boy's clothes. Bouguereau was her teacher and his interest and kindness won from her a confession of her secret. The great French artist's sense of justice was aroused and through his efforts the doors of the famous academy were opened to women, and the name of the first woman artist to be enrolled in the academy was that of Elizabeth Gardner of the United States. Twenty years later, after the death of Bouguereau's mother who opposed the marriage, he and Miss Gardner were married. (Cur Lit 39:391)

Elizabeth Gardner Bouguereau literally opened the Paris schools of art to the women of the world. As a pathfinder her place is assured in the history of the fine arts.

Her birth place, Exeter, New Hampshire, will receive many of her paintings if the French law forbidding the removal of works of art from that country does not prevent.

One of her best known paintings, "Impudence," won the gold medal of the Paris Salon.

Being criticized for not boldly asserting her individuality, she said: "I would rather be known as the best imitator of Bouguereau than be nobody."

BOWEN, BENJAMIN JAMES, (P.) b. Boston, Mass., February 1, 1859. After receiving his education he went into business for some time. Later he became the pupil of Lefebvre, Robert Fleury, and Carrière in Paris and after studying the works of the old masters in the various art galleries of Europe he took a studio at Concarneau, France, and there painted his .first successful picture. He has exhibited in the Salon des Artistes Francais and in America.

"The first thing that strikes us in Mr. Bowen's pictures is the skillful management of light—fine shadow masses illumined with bursts of light; this is admirably illustrated in his three salon pictures: "Le mousse blessé," "Mending the sail," and "Pardon de Notre Dame de la joie."

"His work is honest and strong, and in looking at his pictures one seems to share the simple homeliness of the life they reveal." (English Illustrated Magazine 47 n. s. :10)

BOYLE, JOHN J., (S.) b. New York, January 12, 1852; d. New York City, February 10, 1917. Pupil of Pennsylvania Academy of the Fine Arts, Philadelphia, under Thomas Eakins; Ecole des Beaux Arts under Dumont, Thomas, and E. Millet in Paris; received honorable mention Paris salon 1886, and has also won many medals.

Among his best known works are the Benjamin Franklin statue in front of the Philadelphia post office, the replica of which was erected in Paris by the French government in April, 1906, and the Bacon and Pluto statues in the Library of Congress.

Lorado Taft says: "His most valuable contribution to our national art is undoubtedly in his favorite field of aboriginal subjects.......... For the expression of power, for monumental simplicity,. and integrity of conception his groups "The alarm" in Lincoln Park, Chicago, and "The stone age," in Fairmount Park, Philadelphia, have not been surpassed."

BRECKENRIDGE, HUGH HENRY, (P.) b. Leesburg, Va., October 6, 1870. Pupil of the Pennsylvania Academy of the Fine Arts, Philadelphia, and Bouguereau, Doucet, and Ferrier in Paris. Received honorable mention at Paris Exposition in 1900 and several prizes and medals since that time. Member of the Philadelphia Water Color Club and instructor and secretary of the faculty of the Pennsylvania Academy of the Fine Arts since 1894.

Mr. Breckenridge's portrait of Dr. James Tyson was exhibited at the 107th annual exhibition of the Pennsylvania Academy of the Fine Arts and the International Studio says that it "was painted, with thoroughly masterful technique and was decidedly the most creditable example of the artist's work ever seen on the Academy walls and certainly added tremendously to his reputation."

Other representative paintings are:

"A thread of scarlet"	"The nautilus"
"Autumn"	Portrait of Dr. Edgar Fohs Smith
"Moonlight"	Portrait of Howard B. French

BRENNER, VICTOR DAVID, (S.) b. in Russia, 1871; came to America at the age of nineteen. Later in Paris he studied under the great Roty and soon reached a high stage of proficiency in the art of the medallist.

"In honor of motherhood" is characteristic of his work and excellent in itself.

"For the expression of a large idea, indeed, a medal is to sculpture what a sonnet is to poetry, and each calls for the greatest ability of the artist or the poet." (Warren Wilmer Brown, Arts & D 2:24)

"The Motherhood medal is the fourth of a series being struck under the auspices of this circle of connoisseurs and admirers of this expression of art."

BREUER, HENRY JOSEPH, (P., I.) b. Philadelphia, Pa., August 18, 1860. Began his art studies in Buffalo, N. Y. Was a Rookwood pottery decorator in Cincinnati, 1880-2; lithographic designer, 1882-4; mural decorator, New York, 1884-8; illustrator San Francisco Chronicle, 1890-2; art editor California magazine, 1892-3; landscape painter since 1893. Studied in Paris where he came under the influence of the Barbizon school and was especially impressed by Corot. Is a member of the Society of American Artists of Paris.

"As an aid to development along individual and original lines he has spent many years in California where the 'atmosphere' is individualistic in all activities, and he was there isolated to an extent from the 'schools' and of necessity studied nature more than art."

"Having a splendid eye for details, he applies it in a creative imagination evidenced in his synthetic method, which gives a balance and sense of completeness to his compositions." (Int Studio 39: sup. xlix)

He was commissioned to paint pictures of the Arroyo Seco of the San Gabriel Valley for the St. Louis Exposition in 1904.

Characteristic works are:

"Yosemite valley"   "Mt. Brewer in the Sierras"
"A California sunset"

BRIDGES, FIDELIA, (P.) b. Salem, Mass., May 19, 1834; d. May 14, 1923. One of the few pupils of the late William T. Richards. She was elected associate member of the National Academy of Design, 1874.

At the forty-fifth annual exhibition of the American Water Color Society she exhibited two paintings of characteristic charm and finesse; "Flowers in the beach grass" and "A wide beach."

"Miss Bridges is unique in her remarkable application of the principles of Japanese art in landscape painting and in the delineation of flowers and birds, the last, indeed, being as inseparable from her name as are cats from the name of Henriette Ronner."

BRIDGMAN, FREDERIC ARTHUR, (P.) b. Tuskegee, Ala., November 10, 1847. Was an apprentice in the engraving department of the American Bank Note Company, New York, 1864-5. Studied in Brooklyn Art School and National Academy, New York; and was a pupil of Gérome and at the Ecole des Beaux Arts, Paris, 1866-71. Since then he has had a studio in Paris, occasionally visiting New York. A member of the National Academy of Design since 1881.

Mr. Bridgman has a well-established reputation for his Oriental and archaeological pictures. He paints almost exclusively scenes from Algiers. The first picture by which he became widely known was "The burial of the mummy." This won for him the decoration of the Legion of Honor. Of this picture the severe critic of the Paris Figaro said: "Gérome himself might have signed it, so high is the merit." This painting with "The pastime of an Assyrian king" and "The procession of the sacred bull, Apis" are his chief pictures.

He has made special study of Algiers, Egypt, and Nubia and the Nile and is regarded as the authorized painter of the south shore of the Mediterranean. In 1881 he brought together in all 330 pictures of the East at an exhibition in New York. His favorite studies are curious mixtures of Arab camel drivers, French zouaves and cosmopolitan tourists. These pictures belong to what is called Mr. Bridgman's salon manner.

"White draperies, dark skin tints, shining marble, and keen blue atmosphere, ethnographical accuracy, and a taste for anecdote are the leading characteristics of his pictures." (Müther's "History of modern painting.")

Some of his Brittany studies, chiefly landscapes, are more interesting —they possess a different quality. The effects of light are subdued and very delicate. (Artist 29:138)

His works are now hors concours in the Paris salon.

Well-known paintings are:

"Up early"	"Girls in the way"
"Apollo bearing off Cyrene"	"Interior of the harem"
"Illusions of high life"	"Bringing in the corn"
"The American circus in Paris"	"A Moorish interior"
"In the Pyrenees"	"Tete-a-tete in Cairo"
"Chapel—noon"	"Bay of Dinard, moonlight"
"Greek girls on the seashore"	"Hour of reverie"
"The morning bath"	"In the silence of the evening"
"Lady of Cairo visiting"	"Gathering seaweed"

BROWN, GEORGE LORING, (P., E.) b. Boston, Mass., February 2, 1814; d. Malden, Mass., June 25, 1889. At the age of twelve he was apprenticed to Alonzo Hartwell, an artist, to learn the art of wood-engraving; when sixteen he went to Europe with money earned by painting and through the influence and assistance of John Cheney, an American engraver living in London, he was enabled to study in Paris, enduring many hardships, however. Two years later he returned to Boston, opened a studio, and worked with Washington Allston. In 1840 he went to Paris again and studied under Isabey, then took up his residence in Rome where his brilliant and poetical pictures found ready sale.

Among his famous paintings are:

"Doge's palace and Grand Canal"	"Bay of Naples"
"Doge's palace at sunrise"	"Fountain of Trevi"
"Palermo"	"Niagara by moonlight"
"Atranti"	

The Art Museum in Rome owns his "Moonlight scene" (a prize picture) and the late King Edward VII bought his "Crown of New England" when, as the Prince of Wales, he visited the United States.

"Brown's 'Sunset, Genoa,' is one of those gorgeous, idealized, hazy Italian scenes for which this artist is so much noted in the vein of Turner." (Art Journal, May, 1875)

His etchings executed in Rome are much freer in handling and more suggestive in color than are those of John Gadsby Chapman.

BROWN, JOHN GEORGE, (P.) b. Durham, England, November 11, 1831; d. New York City, February 8, 1913. As a boy he lived at Newcastle-on-Tyne and there served seven years' apprenticeship in learning the glass trade. He studied art in the Newcastle School of Design and at the Royal Academy and began to paint portraits before he came to the United States in 1853. In 1861 he was elected an associate member of the National Academy of Design, a full member in 1863, and vice president in 1899.

Mr. Brown was the most popular of American painters of genre. He belonged to the earlier school of painters; he was always "telling a story," and was widely known as the painter of newsboys and bootblacks.

"His first cigar" was his first work to attract attention. "Curling in Central Park," painted for Robert Gordon, elected him to membership in the National Academy of Design. "Allegro and Penseroso" and "The Longshoreman's noon" are in the Corcoran Gallery, Washington, D. C.; "Jack in the box," Detroit Museum of Art; "Meditation," Metropolitan Museum of Art, New York.

Well-known pictures are:

"Passing show"　　　　　　　　"Training the dog"
"Dress parade"　　　　　　　　"The gang"
"Three (scape) graces"　　　　"The thrilling moment"
"A merry air and a sad heart"

For more than fifty years Mr. Brown worked in the same studio in New York.

BROWNE, GEORGE ELMER, (P.) b. Gloucester, Mass., May 6, 1871. Studied at Museum of Fine Arts and at Cowles Art School, Boston, and Académie Julien, Paris; exhibited in Paris salon and has been represented at nearly all prominent American exhibitions. Received medal at the Charitable Mechanics Association, Boston, 1895, and the Inness Jr. prize, Salmagundi Club, New York, 1901.

His painting entitled "Selling bait at Cape Cod," exhibited in the Paris salon, 1904, was purchased by the French government.

Popular paintings are:

"Fishing boats at Boulogne-sur-　"On the beach at Scheveningen"
mer"　　　　　　　　　　　　　"The old gate at Moret"
"A peasant's cottage"　　　　　"The wain team"
"Storing the grain"

Many of his best subjects have been the depicting of city life and scenery along the water front and streets of New York, also life and scenery along the Seine, from the Parisian boulevards, the banks of the Thames, and the canals of Holland.

The eminent art critic, W. Lewis Fraser, in Brush and Pencil, 14:107, says: "The charm of his pictures is the tender elusiveness of their somewhat somber airtones."

Mr. Browne's painting entitled "Morning Sottomarina" has also been purchased by the French government and is now hanging in the permanent collection of the Luxembourg.

Correctness of line enables him to express unmistakably what he wants to say.

BRUSH, GEORGE DE FOREST, (P.) b. Shelbyville, Tenn., September 28, 1855. Pupil of Gérome. He received the first Hallgarten prize of the National Academy of Design, New York, 1888; Temple gold medal of the Pennsylvania Academy of the Fine Arts, 1897; gold medal at the Paris Exposition, 1900; Saltus medal of the National Academy of Design, New York, 1909. A member of the academy since 1901.

Began as a genre painter of Indians and in his story-telling pictures of Indians he represents the most poetical treatment of the subject that has yet been achieved. Best examples are "Silence broken," "Mourning her brave," "The Indian hunter," "The Indian and the lily." For a number of years he has confined himself to one subject—the modern madonna, his wife and children serving as his models. His "Madonna" in the Corcoran Gallery of Art, Washington, is one of his strongest works. "In the garden" and "The family" are more pictorial.

Technically Brush's work does not attract, but intellectually it is full of beauty.

"His drawing is strong and distingué and his figures are interpreted with truth of expression." (Hartmann.)

Another critic says: "He has not yet solved the mysterious affinity between certain colors and certain emotions."

Kenyon Cox says: "George de Forest Brush is one of the few painters outside the ranks of the mural decorators who concerns himself primarily with line and a severe conception of form. He has often fine color, also in a restrained key, and always a profound feeling for character and for the beauty of childhood. In its composition of long flowing lines, its firm clean drawing, its subtle modeling and above all in the beautifully expressive heads and the radiant charm of blond infancy, his "In the garden" is worthy of one of those fifteenth century Florentines with whom Mr. Brush has much more affinity than with the average painter."

"In his 'Madonna pictures' he shows the pathos of motherly love."

BURD, CLARA MILLER, (Stained glass designer) b. New York City. Studied art at the National Academy of Design, also with Wm. M. Chase. Later she studied with Courtois and Renarde in Paris.

Since returning to the United States, Miss Burd has been known as a stained glass artist and specializes in memorial windows for churches.

The Architectural Record 35:163 has a very interesting article on Miss Burd and her ideas on art.

BURROUGHS, EDITH WOODMAN (Mrs. Bryson Burroughs), (S.) b. Riverdale-on-Hudson, N. Y., October 20, 1871; d. Flushing, L. I., January 6, 1916. A pupil of the Art Students' League, New York, under Saint-Gaudens; also studied with Injalbert and Merson in Paris. Mrs. Burroughs was a member of the National Sculpture Society and was awarded the Shaw prize of the National Academy of Design in 1907.

At the exhibition of the National Sculpture Society held in Baltimore, April, 1908, her "Summer sea" was shown; and at the academy exhibition in New York, 1909, she presented a marble bust, "Scylla," and her portrait-bust of John LaFarge.

In Mrs. Burroughs' work—statuettes, portraits in low relief, busts, and decorative sculpture—"the fine quality of what we may call the lyric subjectivism is noticeable, because of its fineness, its delicacy." (Scrib. M 47:639)

"Her figures have dignity and refinement, reached through lessons of art, perhaps, but nevertheless captivatingly expressive of life." . . . .

"Her work has a charm and a strength that are purely womanly." (Arts & D 5:190)

An exhibition of Mrs. Burroughs' sculpture was recently held in New York and thirty-nine examples were in the collection. Four especially mentioned are "At the threshold," "Acquiescence," "Summer sea," "Fountain design." In these the sculptor is seen at her best. "Here she is severe without being cold, dignified without being pompous."

Her "Fountain of youth" at the Panama-Pacific Exposition balanced Mrs. Harry Payne Whitney's "Fountain of El Dorado" at the other end of the court.

CADWALADER-GUILD, EMMA MARIE, (S., P.) was born in New England but most of her work has been done in England and Germany, and is better known there than here.

Ambassador White after seeing her work in Germany urged her to return to the United States and make a bust of President McKinley.

Through correspondence, sittings were agreed upon; she came but they were not given; she then modeled the bust from prints. Mr. Hanna entered a bill in Congress for the purchase of the bust, so pleased was he with it, and it is now in the president's room of the Capitol at Washington.

Mrs. Guild has also made a striking bust of Lincoln. John Hay said of it: "The power of the head is remarkable. It is a great expression of the personality of the man."

Her two busts of Gladstone—one in bronze, one in marble, are the only ones for which Mr. Gladstone gave sittings.

When her bust of George Frederick Watts was completed he said: "When I look at that bust I can understand how that man could have painted that picture" (pointing to one of his own.)

Mrs. Guild numbers royalty among her distinguished patrons.

Her idealistic heads and statues are as remarkable as her portraits. Of her "Lotos," the German Times says: "This psychic masterpiece stamps Mrs. Guild unequivocally as an artist of the very first rank." A bronze statuette called "Freed" has been exhibited in the Paris salon; at the Royal Academy, London; and at Munich. Her "Head of St. Monica, the mother of St. Augustine," is a charming study. The German government purchased her "Electron" and placed it in the Post-museum at Berlin. The pose of her "Endymion" is not to be found in either modern or ancient sculpture.

"Mrs. Guild is careful in her anatomical study but works without model; and her results strengthen the suspicion that in poses involving a representation of movement, however slight, the appearance of a stationary model is false in detail to the exact appearance in motion."

Mrs. Guild is a painter as well as sculptor and known abroad as one of superior merit.

CALDER, ALEXANDER STIRLING, (S.) b. Philadelphia, Pa., 1870. He studied four years in the Academy of Pennsylvania and two years in Paris under Chapu and Falguiére and has been connected with the Philadelphia school ever since his return to America. He was appointed assistant chief of the Department of Sculpture of the Panama-Pacific Exposition, 1915. In 1906 he was elected an associate member of the National Academy of Design; full member in 1913.

Calder has been called an Aristotelian. "His work reveals a beauty beneath the exterior, not of soul merely, but of quality."

His various works range from the study of a child's head to monumental archways.

He made the statue of Dr. Samuel D. Gross for the army medical museum, Washington, D. C.; also six figures of heroic size for the exterior of the Witherspoon building, Philadelphia—six representative Presbyterians. "The rugged figures are admirably characterized." He also made the Washington group, Washington Arch, New York City; the statue of Philippe Francois Reneault, French explorer, for the St. Louis Exposition; the Celtic cross memorial to General William Joyce Sewell of New Jersey; statue of Marcus Whitman, (famous in the struggle for Oregon) called "Spirit of the Far West," for the Seattle Exposition; a series of monumental archways for the Throop Polytechnic Institute at Pasadena, California; a unique sun-dial in a sunken garden in Fairmount Park, Philadelphia; and the two great groups which surmounted the arches of the Rising and Setting Sun at the Panama-Pacific Exposition, San Francisco, 1915; also the Fountain of Energy.

Mr. Calder lived in the west several years studying the Indians. "The past, the present, and the future of the red people is beautifully delineated in Calder's subtly modeled figures." (Craftsm 28:154)

One of Mr. Calder's most attractive groups is the Depew Memorial fountain erected in Indianapolis to the memory of Dr. Richard J. Depew. A daughter of Pan with cymbals surmounts the fountain and suggests music, while below is a frieze of twenty-eight jumping fish encircled by eight dancing nude children. Although a memorial, the idea of the fountain is to express exuberance, youth, and joy.

Mr. Calder was awarded the contract to execute the 128 foot frieze across the front of the new capitol building for the State of Missouri. The subject will be the history of Missouri and it will be portrayed in a relief cut into the stone from six inches to a foot in depth.

CARLSEN, EMIL, (P.) b. Copenhagen, Denmark, October 19, 1853. Was educated in his native city and came to the United States in 1872. He has what the late Frank Fowler has described as a kind of specialized vision, very charming and very fine. Coming from Denmark he brought with him the old Vikings' love of the great waters. His poetic interpretation of their beauty has met with universal recognition. Medals and prizes have been awarded him in many exhibitions and he was elected a member of the National Academy of Design in 1906.

"He contents himself with quiet middle tones, never forcing his gamut to extremes of light or shades, but his surfaces are lovely, his paintings invariably mature." (Int Studio 39:10)

"His landscape work has the quality of his still-life studies of game or fish; broad unbroken masses of color strongly relieved against each other, whether sunlit trees against a deep blue sky or a white swan

against a dead wall, the contrast not being relied on alone for the effect,
—but the color being made as absolutely true as in his vigorous works."
(Isham)

Admired paintings are:

"The quiet sea"   "Wild swan"
"Meeting of the seas"   "May morning"
"The open sea"   "The panel"

Kenyon Cox says: "Beauty is his aim, and the facts and the force of
nature are both subordinated to decoration. In the "Open sea" it is
the exquisitely varied blues and grays of sky and water that have
charmed him, while in his "Surf" it is not crash and roar that we are
made to feel, but the bold pattern of black and white and blue."

At the one hundred and tenth annual exhibition of the Pennsylvania
Academy of the Fine Arts was shown Emil Carlsen's "O, ye of little
faith," a vision of Christ walking on the waters. The artist refuses to
sell this work and calls it his religion.

"In an infinite glory of sea and sky, in a burst of silvery light, un-
matched by anything in art since the days of Rembrandt, along the
luminous pathway trod the Son of Man .... It was almost too precious for public display, too far above the heads of those in the motley
throng who commented on the perfect framing or wondered why the
figure was drawn so small." (Bk News M 33:378)

CARLSON, JOHN F., (P.) b. in Sweden, 1875. Member of the New York
Watercolor Club, American Watercolor Society, Salmagundi Club, and
Washington Watercolor Club. Associate member of the National
Academy of Design, 1911. Instructor Art Students' League Land-
scape School, Woodstock, New York.

Mr. Carlson is a landscape painter who specializes in winter scenes.
His "Winter rigor" was awarded the Carnegie prize. "Sylvan laby-
rinths" is perhaps the very epitome of Carlson's work. "Here we have
a most important canvas in his most characteristic manner depicting
one of nature's scenes of perfect beauty in which he so delights ...... It
is curious that Carlson's snow pictures are the darkest and richest
of all such crystalline themes .... One cannot get away from the
musical feeling in his work, perhaps because of its all-pervading harmony." (Fine Arts Journal, March, 1917)

Royal Cortissoz says: "They call it 'Twilight in the woods.' The
brook is flecked with sunset, the snow is iced and blue. I wonder if

the artist thought of the Erl King's deeds, of dryads and of solemn fairy tales. They hailed me in chorus as a corner of the painting came in view. A well set stage it is for fantastic dreams."

"Summer night" is an unusually successful interpretation of moonlight. One of his most beautiful paintings is called "The brook in winter." It has been compared with the work of the late J. Francis Murphy. "Woods in winter" is in the Corcoran Gallery, Washington, D. C.; "Woodland repose" in the Toledo Museum. Other paintings noted for beauty of form, poetic color, and musical tone are: "November woods," "Passing winter," "Morning mists," "Autumn beeches," and "Winter dream days."

CARPENTER, FRANCIS BICKWELL, (P.) b. Homer, N. Y., August 6, 1830; d. New York, May 23, 1900. He was a pupil of Sanford Thayer at Syracuse, N. Y. He won much fame as a painter and also possessed much literary ability.

His painting "Arbitration," representing the signing of the treaty of Washington, was accepted by Queen Victoria and hung in her private collection. His portrait of President Fillmore was purchased by the city of New York and hangs in the City Hall. "First reading of the Emancipation proclamation before the cabinet" now hangs on the stairway of the House of Representatives, Washington.

Mr. Carpenter was elected associate member of the National Academy of Design in 1852.

CASSATT, MARY, (P., E.) b. Pittsburgh, Pa., 1855. Her first studies in art were at the Pennsylvania Academy of the Fine Arts, Philadelphia. After traveling extensively in Spain, Italy, and Holland she settled in Paris; and Degas, convinced of her ability and sincerity, consented to take her as a pupil and for fifteen years she studied and worked with him, achieving in time a position not far below his own.

At various intervals Miss Cassatt has devoted herself to painting in oils and pastels, to color-etching, dry point, and even lithography. While her range of expression is wide, her choice of motive is restricted. For the most part she transcribes the intimate relationship of mother and child. She always avoids a sentimental version of child life. "Beauty is there, but not a sugary, waxen beauty."

Among her most characteristic works are:

"The toilet"	Earlier works are:
"Women and child"	
"The caress"	"At the French theater"

"Baby arises"   "After the bullfight"
"The cup of tea"   "Music lesson'
"The reading lesson"   "On the balcony"
"Children playing. with a cat"
"Mother and child"
"Supper-time"

Miss Cassatt, a follower of Manet, sends her canvases to the Impressionists' exhibitions in Paris, but she refuses to exhibit in the salons, and in her indifference to their applause she stands alone. All other American artists in Paris have regularly displayed their works in the great competitive exhibitions. Miss Cassatt is a member of the Legion of Honor of France, and her work takes rank beside that of the foremost modern masters.

"Her work is resolute, thoughtful, and lucid. Much of her master's strength of line is there, and much also of his solemn, almost classic restraint. Miss Cassatt has never faltered in her allegiance to the tenets of Impressionists." (Int Studio 27: sup i)

"She has succeeded in creating a new style and lending to prose and realism a decorative quality best displayed in her colored etchings. In sheer force and breadth of view few men artists could rival her 'Mother and child' pictures." (Hartmann)

"Perception of and sympathy for the wonderfully intimate relation existing between mother and child are qualities which stand out prominently in the work of Miss Cassatt." (Elizabeth Anna Semple)

"Chief distinction of Miss Cassatt's art is closeness of interpretation united to the impressionist's care for the transitory aspect of things." (Elizabeth Luther Cary)

"The secret of compressed statement is hers, of condensed significance." (Frank Weitenkampf)

At the exhibition of the Pennsylvania Academy of the Fine Arts, held in 1914, Miss Cassatt was awarded the gold medal of the academy. She accepted it. It is the only honor which she has accepted in her long and distinguished life.

CHAMPNEY, JAMES WELLS, (P.) b. Boston, Mass., July 16, 1843; d. New York, May 1, 1903. Began his art education with a wood engraver in Boston. Studied in Europe under Edouard Frére, Paris, and at Antwerp under Van Lerius, 1868-9. In 1882 he was made associate member of the National Academy of Design. An exhibitor of oil paintings at the Centennial Exhibition, 1876, and of pastels at World's Columbian Exposition, 1893.

On account of the number of Boston artists bearing his surname, he signed his early pictures "Champ," but later gave his full name.

Early and popular pictures are:

"Not as ugly as he looks"	"The best scholar"
"Boy shelling peas"	"Which is umpire"
"Hearts and diamonds"	"Grandma's pet"
"The seer leaf"	"Don't touch"
"Your good health"	"Children roasting apples"
"Speak, sir"	

The most successful paintings are genre subjects, quiet and simple in their nature.

During the last few years of his life, Mr. Champney made a specialty of pastel pictures and achieved remarkable success in this branch of art.

A few of his later pictures are:

"The squire's daughter"	"The flower of New England"
"Ophelia"	"Sylvia"
"Indian summer"	"Mignon"
"A song without words"	"Little Mistress Dorothy"
"The best scholar"	

CHANDLER, GEORGE W., (E., I.) b. Milwaukee, Wis. He early evinced artistic tendencies and was employed as an illustrator on the New York daily papers. After some foreign travel, entered the Academie Julien, Paris, in the classes of Jean Paul Laurens. In 1908 received honorable mention at the salon.

India forms the setting for some of his finest plates:

"The minarets, Benares"
"The burning ghats, Benares"

Parisian scenes:

"Les travaux du Métro"	"Le dejeuner"
"Dans l'Avenue de Saxe"	"Aux bords de la Seine"

Evidence of his versatility, as well as his understanding of pastoral beauties, may be found in "Le Moulin Moret," "The old lock," "Cour de

Cerf," and "Cour à pont l'Arche"; "Le portail de St. Maclou, Rouen" is an expression of sombre beauty.

"He gives us not only the lacy fret work of the vaulted doorway, but we enter with him into the shadow of a dim interior, heavy with the incense of a by-gone age." (Marie Bruette)

CHANDLER, ROBERT WINTHROP, (P., Mural P.) b. New York City, 1872. He first studied art under private tutors, then traveled extensively, and while in Rome became interested in sculpture and studied under Mariano Benlliure. After a sojourn in Italy, he attended the art schools and academies of France and it was while in Paris that he renounced clay for crayon and color. He returned to Italy to study the decorations of Pinturicchio in the Vatican and the frescoes of Gozzoli in the Riccardi Palace, Florence. Later he explored Africa for art material.

Mr. Chanler's screens have become famous in Europe as well as in the United States. The originality of his massive, gorgeous, and bewilderingly fanciful work is most striking.

It was at the first exhibition of the International Society of Painters and Sculptors that his art gained recognition in this country. Eight or ten of his screens were displayed in the entrance chamber and attracted attention by reason of their originality and delightfully decorative aspect.

"The giraffes" is probably the best known of Mr. Chanler's screens. It received honorable mention at the Paris salon and has crossed the Atlantic six or seven times. It has been purchased by the French government and has found its home in the Luxembourg Gallery, Paris. "The swans," painted on mahogany in blue, silver, and gold, is noted for charming arrangement; "Wolves" is a dramatic composition; "White peacocks" is ornately beautiful; "Variations in metal," a panel in which butterflies and large flower petals appear on a seemingly metallic surface; "Marching Martians," a screen with humorous figures. "Wanderer" is a set of six panels with nude figures; "Leopard and the deer" resembles a Beardsley drawing in mastery of the grotesque; "Porcupine screen" is a harmony of dull blues, silver, and white. "Deep-sea fantasy" is a six-paneled screen in which aquatic monsters are used as symbols of nature's forces. "Flame," a symbolic picture, is an elaborate decorative panel in Mrs. Whitney's studio.

Entirely lacking the lyrical qualities of the above named screen work is the panel entitled "Death of the white hart." Here the fears of the mind are symbolized in a terrible black beast that leaps upon and devours "with the suddenness of implacable fate," his victim, an unprotected little white antelope.

Mr. Chanler's compositions are of infinite variety and delightful originality, and at times the influence of the arts of China and Japan is very
impressive.

"The one outstanding feature of Chanler's art is its primitive dynamic
symbolism which manifests itself now in the nature of designs, then
again in the rich color harmony or gorgeous combinations of gold and
silver backgrounds." Int Studio 75:470)

The mural decorations of the Colony Club, New York, are the most
important decorations of public buildings he has done, much of this class
of Mr. Chanler's work being in private palatial homes. His treatment of
the loggia is famous. We see "the vivid life of southern air and jungle
and the extravagant forms and colors in tropical waters."

"Mr. Chanler's great achievement is that just as the great Cretan
artists in 2000 B. C. took their hints from the wild life of the sea and
land and also used themselves as material for mural decorations, so he,
nearly 4000 years later, has gone to the fauna and flora of the sea and
the fauna and flora of the land to say nothing of the human form and
all natural aspects for his patterns." (Am M of Art 13:534)

"He is a Sinbad bringing tropical rarities to the feet of those who,
like himself, require them for diversion." (Arts and D 12:418)

CHAPMAN, JOHN GADSBY, (E., P.) b. Alexandria, Va., December 8,
1808; d. Brooklyn, N. Y., July 6, 1890. One of the most important of
the early etchers in the United States, he made his first attempt at etching in 1843; etched in Rome from 1852 to 1857, where he studied art. He
first became known as an etcher in New York City where he did much
good work for Harper & Bros.

His versatility was remarkable—portraits, landscapes, engraving, and
etching being alike within the compass of his ability. For fifty-three
years he was a member of the National Academy of Design.

His "Baptism of Pocahontas" in the rotunda of the Capitol at Washington is the painting by which he is best known.

Mr. Chapman was the first American to write on etching.

CHASE, WILLIAM MERRITT, (P.) b. Franklin, Ind., November 1, 1849;
d. New York City, October 25, 1916. At the age of nineteen began the
study of art in Indianapolis; he studied in New York, later in the Munich
Royal Academy, and afterwards had Alexander Wagner for a teacher;
also was a pupil of Karl von Piloty. He refused a professorship in the
Munich Royal Academy and returned to America. In 1885 he was elected
president of the Society of American Artists and re-elected every year
thereafter for ten years. After conducting winter classes at the Art

Students' League for eighteen years, in 1897 he organized a distinct
school of his own known as the "Chase School for Art." Aside from his
work in New York, he taught for a number of years at Pennsylvania
Academy of the Fine Arts and at the Hartford Art School. His summer
school at Shinnecock, L. I., was famous. His influence as an instructor
is the most far-reaching of any artist in America and probably of any
country, and his traveling classes abroad were a feature in the progress
of American art. He was one of the foremost landscapists and portrait-
ists, and the best "still-life" painter in America. A member of the
National Academy of Design since 1890.

In 1876 he exhibited his "Court jester" and established his reputation
as a painter; and five years later his "Smoker" (portrait of Frank
Duveneck) won prizes in Paris and Munich.

His most famous portraits are those of his mother, "My daughter
Helen," Mrs Tyler, Dr. Osler, and Thomas Dolan. Among his fanciful
pictures are "Alice," "Dorothy and her sister," "The red box," "Ring
toss," "Girl with dog," "Ready for the ride," "The gray kimona," "The
open Japanese book." These serve well to illustrate the distinctive
quality of Chase's color sense.

"One of Chase's most significant contributions to the history of American art, however, is his painting of the figure in relation to its environment—the figure in relation to the interior (not the figure against a background), the figure in the landscape." (Craftsm 18:38)

Mr. Chase was world-famous for painting of brass and other metals;
and he painted the gold frame of the picture within the picture with sufficient skill to stand comparison with the real frame.

Mr. Chase's portrait hangs in the Uffizi, Florence, Italy, in the famous
gallery devoted to the portraits of painters by themselves. This is an
emphatic recognition of his achievement and his standing in the profession of art.

In 1903 he was elected a member of "Ten American Painters" to fill
the vacancy caused by the death of John Henry Twachtman.

"In his portraits one may discover echoes of Franz Hals and Sargent
as well as Whistler, while his colorful, broadly-executed still-life paintings betray his unqualified admiration of Vollon and Chardin."
(J. Nilsen Laurvik)

On May 29, 1923, a bust of the late William M. Chase was unveiled
in the Gould Memorial Library at the New York University. Ninety-two
former pupils (American men and women) subscribed to the fund. The
bust of Chase was the seventh to take its place in the reading room.
Those already installed are of George Inness, Carroll Beckwith, Clinton

Ogilvie, Frank Duveneck, Walter Shirlaw, and J. Q. A. Ward. It was the work of Albin Polasek, the Chicago sculptor.

CHRISTY, HOWARD CHANDLER, (P., I.) b. Morgan county, Ohio, January 10, 1873. Was educated at Duncan Falls, Ohio. At the age of twenty he entered the National Academy of Design, New York, and in two months had won honorable mention and one bronze medal. He studied under William M. Chase and later became instructor in Cooper Union, the Chase School, New York School of Art, and the Art Students' League.

During the Spanish-American war he was with the Rough Riders before Santiago and established his reputation by his Cuban pictures and types of the navy and army men. He wrote war stories and illustrated them for Scribner's and Leslie's Weekly, and has made hundreds of illustrations for other publications.

Among his best known and most popular works were his pictures illustrating "Miles Standish" and "Evangeline." Mr. Christy is famous as the painter of the American girl.

His art is of a high romanticism in conception and academic in its execution.

Howard Chandler Christy has been commissioned by the United States Shipping Board to paint six portraits of as many presidents of the United States for vessels of the board's passenger fleet in the "President class." The following are the ones to be painted: John Adams, John Quincy Adams, James Monroe, Martin Van Buren, James K. Polk, and James A. Garfield. Each portrait will be hung in the main lounge of the ship named for the president. The late President Harding's portrait is hung in the passenger liner, Leviathan.

CHURCH, FREDERICK EDWIN, (P.) b. Hartford, Conn., May 4, 1826; d. New York, April 7, 1900. The pupil of Thomas Cole, he resided with him at Catskill, N. Y., thus gaining the first inspirations along the shores of the Hudson and amid the beautiful regions of the legendary Catskills. He established a studio in New York and was elected a member of the National Academy of Design in 1849. Made sketching tours in South America in 1853 and 1857; later, on the coast of Labrador and in Jamaica. In 1868 visited Europe and the Holy Land and Mexico in 1883.

Church's "Niagara" was immediately recognized as the first satisfactory delineation in art of one of the greatest natural wonders of the western world, and this is in itself extraordinary praise. It received a medal at the Paris Exposition of 1867. When Ruskin first saw this painting he pointed out an effect upon water which he declared he had often seen in nature among the Swiss waterfalls, but never before on canvas.

Among his works sketched on his extensive tours are:

"Icebergs"	"Rainy season in the tropics"
"A South American landscape"	"Heart of the Andes"
"The afterglow"	"El Khasmé Petrà"
"Andes of Ecuador"	"Cotopaxi"
"Chimborazo"	"Twilight in the wilderness"
"Morning in the Cordilleras"	"View of Quebec"
"Jerusalem"	"Aurora borealis"

Church's works are generally composite rather than a transcription of actual landscape.

CHURCH, FREDERICK STUART, (P., I., E.) b. Grand Rapids, Mich., December 1, 1842, died 1924. Studied in the Chicago Academy with Walter Shirlaw and later in the National Academy of Design and Art Students' League of New York, and for some years occupied a studio in that city. His first popularity was gained by his drawing in black and white; he furnished book and magazine illustrations for Scribner's and other publication houses; then his oil and water-color work attracted attention.

Mr. Church was a member of the National Academy of Design, New York; Society of Painter-Etchers, London; and the New York and Philadelphia etching clubs.

"Una and the lion," "The lion in love," "Beauty and the beast," "The black orchid," "The sorceress," and "Twilight" are familiar examples of his graceful realization of purely fanciful themes.

Of his works, Isham in his "History of American painting" says: "They are not profound, they are not subtle .... yet if they have the simplicity of a story told to children, they have also freshness and charm. If the drawing is loose, it is also graceful."

There are probably no more popular etchings than his, wherein a graceful and humorous fancy charms us all. His "Mermaid" is a well-known plate.

CLARK, WALTER APPLETON, (I.) b. Worcester, Mass., June 24, 1876; d. New York City, December 27, 1906. With purely local art training of some three years, he established himself as one of the leading illustrators of the day. Taught classes at the Art Students' League and Cooper Union, N. Y., and at the Pennsylvania Academy of the Fine Arts.

A picture of his on the wall of the Art Students' League, while a student, attracted the attention of the art editor of Scribner's magazine; this led to his being employed to illustrate one of Kipling's stories. Among his last works was the illustration of the modern version of "Canterbury Tales" by Percy Mackaye.

"Mr. Clark's strong point is his execution, he has a nice clean dexterity of touch, employed with nobility and ease."

"In finish he obtains the feeling noticeable in the color work of Vibert and his compositions are handled with the adroitness of Fortuny, with less dash, however, but with more delicate sympathy and refinement."

CLARKE, THOMAS SHIELDS, (S., P.) b. Pittsburgh, Pa., April 25, 1860. Graduated at Princeton University in 1882. While a student at the Art League in New York, he made illustrations for magazines. Going to Paris, he studied drawing under Boulanger and Lefebvre, modeling under Chapu and painting under Gérome in the Ecole des Beaux Arts; later was instructed by Dagnan-Bouveret; also studied art in Florence, Rome, and Venice. Associate member of National Academy of Design, 1902.

His paintings and sculpture have brought him honor at home and abroad, he having been represented at international expositions at Berlin, Madrid, London, and Paris.

His "Night market in Morocco" received official recognition at the Berlin Exposition in 1891; "A fool's fool" was shown at the Paris salon, and upon its merits he was admitted to membership in the Society of American Artists, New York. "A gondola girl," "Morning, noon and night" and other Venetian works are attractive.

His bronze group—fountain design—"The cider press," displayed at the Madrid Exposition, brought him a medal of honor, presented personally by the King of Spain.

Four caryatides—"The seasons"—on the New York Appellate Court building are dignified and graceful. His more important work in sculpture is "Alma Mater and her son, Alumnus" for Princeton University.

"These figures are splendidly modeled and thoughtfully conceived."

Mr. Clarke has also done some notable mural decoration.

COE, ETHEL L., (P.) b. Chicago, Illinois. Pupil of Hawthorne and Sorolla. Instructor in University of Chicago.

When Sorolla, the Spanish painter, was in Chicago in 1911, he became interested in the work of Miss Coe, and he influenced her to accompany him to Spain to continue her painting under his instruction. After two years in Spain, the Indians of Taos, N. M., attracted her as subjects; then a trip to Morocco and Tangiers resulted in a series of pictures of Moors and Arabs with local background.

Miss Coe is called "a disciple of light." She says that a shadow is nothing but the absence of light. "There is a certain blue in her pictures of Tangiers that impresses one as being a new color .... In her New Mexican picture "A horse to trade" and in the little nude study "The crystal ball" it is possible to see how well she learned Sorolla's lesson of attention to accurate portrayal." (Am M of Art 13 : 308)

COLE, THOMAS, (P.) b. Bolton-le-Moor, Lancashire, England, February 1, 1801; d. Catskill, N. Y., February 11, 1848. He was of American parentage, and in 1819 the family returned to America, taking up their residence at Steubenville, Ohio, where he began the study of painting under a portrait painter named Stein. Not successful in portrait work, he took up landscape painting. In 1825 he went to New York and subsequently became intimately acquainted with Durand and Trumbull. He was one of the founders of the National Academy of Design and had a picture at its first exhibition in 1826. A patron sent him to Europe in 1829 to complete his art education and he remained there about three years sketching and painting in England, France, and Italy. After his return he painted two allegorical series, "The course of empire" and "Voyage of life." These soon won him great contemporary popularity. (Noble's "Life and works of Thomas Cole.") These paintings were exhibited in the rooms of the New York Art Union in 1848 and were visited by half a million people. Other paintings depict scenes from an extreme range of landscape.

"All are remarkable for imagination, composition, and the most refined and picturesque truth to the details, as facts and influences of nature." (Tuckerman)

His most beautiful illustrations of Italian scenery are "l'Allegro" and "Il Penseroso," companion pieces. Of American views one of the most attractive is "The hunter's return." One of his most highly finished works is a picture illustrating Mrs. Hemans' poem "The cross in the wilderness." "The tone of the picture is quite Claude-like." (Tuckerman.) Caffin says: "Cole forms a link between the new enthusiasm for nature study and the older predilection for historical and 'grand style' subjects." According to this authority his more enduring claim, however, to be remembered consists in his having aroused an appreciation of the pictorial possibilities of the Catskill, and of American landscape in general. He makes nature the vehicle for moral allegories.

COMAN, CHARLOTTE BUELL, (P.) b. Waterville, New York, 1833. Studied in Paris with Harry Thompson and Emile Vernier; spent six years in France and Holland and exhibited at the Paris salons for two years. Mrs. Coman's specialty in painting is landscapes and she was thirty years of age before she commenced the study of art. She received the Shaw memorial prize of the Society of American Artists, and the second prize of the Washington Society of Artists, 1906. Was elected associate member National Academy of Design, 1910. Mrs. Coman is represented in the Evans collection, Washington, D. C., the Metropolitan Museum, New York; and in the permanent collections of several western clubs.

"Clearing off" is one of her strongest, and "A misty morning at the farm" one of her best.

Craftsman 21:491: "But to return to the academy walls one seeks again and again Charlotte Coman's beautiful painting of hills and clouds. What sunlight pours over the friendly little house nestling in the shadowy meadows, a delightful study, tenderly painted, a thing to remember and rejoice in."

Mrs. Coman was one of a hundred representative American artists chosen to exhibit at the Detroit Museum's exhibition of "best pictures from current shows." Her "Well-worn path" was selected by the committee.

Critics of high repute declare that Mrs. Coman has been doing her best work since she reached the age of eighty. At ninety she is still painting.

COOPER, COLIN CAMPBELL, (P.) b. Philadelphia, Pa. Studied in Pennsylvania Academy of the Fine Arts, Philadelphia; Académie Julien, and other art schools in Paris. Is a member of many leading art clubs in this country, and has been awarded many medals and prizes; is an associate member of the National Academy of Design. He has spent much time in Europe painting figure and architectural subjects, architecture and street scenes being his specialty. "Beauvais cathedral," one of the notable historical structures of France, is considered his finest work. Mr. Cooper's notable achievement is his long series of canvases depicting the picturesque charm of the modern sky-scraper; he began this work in 1902. He sees beauty, sublimity, and grandeur in the structures that the average person is wont to call monstrosities.

He handles water-colors on canvas so cleverly that his water-colors can scarcely be distinguished from oils.

"Broad street, New York," "Rush hour, Brooklyn bridge," "Broadway," "The chain gate," "The Flatiron building," "Walton hotel, Philadelphia," and a scene in Penn Square, are additional proof of his skill in clothing the commonplace brick and mortar of the business block with rich warm colors of their own.

"That Cooper has the natural gift of seeing the beauty of what to most people are prosaic structures, and the patience and persistence to perfect his delineation of street and building, is the secret of his success as an architectural painter." (Brush & P 18:72)

Mr. Cooper has recently returned from the Far East and has exhibited Indian paintings in New York. Among his architectural works which are said to possess "such charm as to make them dreams of beauty" are:

"Taj Mahal, Agra"
"White Mosque, Bombay"
"Maharajah's palace, Udaipor" (Venice of India)

He has also given his poetic version of the famous "Bathing Ghat, Benares" and "Akbar's Baths, Agra." "Bombay harbor at sunrise" is an impressive and splendidly painted view of the Himalayan peak of Kungchenjunga.

"Perhaps the most striking work in the display is the "Palace gate, Udaipor," which pictures the inner gate in the Maharajah's palace during a procession, a remarkable portrayal of the rich colored, moving, strange life of an ancient city under tropic skies."

COOPER, EMMA LAMPERT (Mrs. Colin Campbell Cooper), (P.) b. Nunda, New York. d. Pittsfield, N. Y., July 30, 1920. Began the study of art at the Cooper Union and Art Students' League in New York and later was the pupil of Harry Thompson in Paris, J. Kever in Holland, and William M. Chase in New York; has also studied in Italy.

Mrs. Cooper has had charge of the art department at Foster School, Clifton Springs; also of the painting classes at Mechanics' Institute, New York.

Interiors and street scenes from France, Holland, Belgium, Italy, and Switzerland, painted in oils and water colors, are her favorite subjects.

Representative pictures are:

"Morning near Riverdale"   "News of the day"
"High noon, Cape Ann"   "Weaving homespun"
"Mother Claudia's fireside"   "Swiss fireplace"
"The breadwinner"   "Canal at Lisieux"
"Breton bakery"   "Old dye house"

COPLEY, JOHN SINGLETON, (P.) b. Boston, Mass., July 3, 1737; d. London, England, September 9, 1815. At the age of seventeen he produced his first grouped picture—an allegorical study of Mars, Venus, and Vulcan. From that time he was recognized as a painter. Through the influence of Benjamin West his "Boy with the squirrel" was exhibited in London in 1766, and in 1772 he was elected a fellow of the Society of

Artists. In 1774 he settled in London and became a notable painter of historical scenes. In 1776 he was elected associate of the Royal Academy, and in 1779, academician; and presented, on admission, his "Tribute money." His "Death of the Earl of Chatham" established his fame in England.

He opposed the classical productions of the age by his vigorous representations of events of history and war. Among his numerous subjects in this line are: "Death of Major Pierson," "Siege of Gibraltar," "Surrender of Admiral de Windt to Lord Camperdown," "Charles I demanding the five impeached members," "Charles I signing Stafford's death warrant," "Offer of crown to Lady Jane Grey," "Assassination of Buckingham." He also painted religious subjects and large portrait groups of noted English families. But of his earlier work—that done before he left Boston, which consists of a long series of portraits of our colonial dignitaries, divines, judges, and merchants—Isham says: "These paintings are the most authentic records of our pre-revolutionary ancestors which have come down to us."

Copley's best known portraits in America are those of John Adams and John Hancock.

Caffin says: "Copley was the most distinguished in skill of craftsmanship of all the pre-revolutionary painters."

Copley was not poetical, but he produced splendid prose.

CORY, FANNY YOUNG (Mrs. F. W. Cooney), (I.) b. Waukegan, Ill., October 17, 1877. Studied art at the Metropolitan School and the Art Students' League of New York. Married to F. W. Cooney, 1904.

Mrs. Cooney has made illustrations for the Century Company and Harper Bros., and illustrated numerous books, including "Alice in Wonderland," "Through the looking glass," etc.

Favorite children pictures are:

"Do you make saucer pies?"
"On the dark stair"
"Shoo!"

COUDERT, AMALIA KUSSNER, (Min. P.) b. Terre Haute, Ind., March 26, 1876; began her artistic career in New York in 1892 and afterwards went to London and painted miniature portraits of King Edward and most of the highest aristocracy of England; later she was summoned to Russia to paint portraits of the Czar and Czarina and the Grand Duchesses Vladimir and Ellen and also went to Africa to paint the portrait of the late Cecil Rhodes.

COUPER, WILLIAM, (S.) b. Norfolk, Va., September 20, 1853. Pupil of Thomas Ball and Cooper Institute in New York; also studied in Munich and Paris.

Lorado Taft says: "His 'Moses' in the appellate court building is a magnificent conception and justly admired, its only weakness is over-elaboration .... Mr. Couper has made particular and sympathetic study of winged figures. They are not merely pretty but they are beautiful, radiant creations, gracefully conceived, carefully drawn and exquisitely carved."

Mr. Couper is a member of the National Sculpture Society.

COUSE, EANGER IRVING, (P.) b. Saginaw, Mich., 1866. Pupil of National Academy of Design, New York; Bouguereau; Robert-Fleury; and Ecole des Beaux Arts, Paris. Received the Shaw prize for black and white, at Salmagundi Club, 1899; second Hallgarten prize, National Academy, 1900; Proctor prize, Salmagundi Club, 1900; honorable mention, Paris Exposition, 1900; first Hallgarten prize, National Academy, 1902. Associate member National Academy of Design, 1902; full member, 1911.

Mr. Couse devotes himself to the Pueblo or town Indians of the southwest, painting them in their actuality or with ideal touch in their home in New Mexico. Part of the year he passes at Taos, for the portrayal of the Taos Indians is his particular art.

He had much difficulty in securing interesting and picturesque models, as it is a matter of belief with these Indians and in fact with others, that the soul of the sitter passes out into the portrait when the picture is completed, and naturally, until the prejudice is overcome, there is not much enthusiasm about posing.

"He paints the Indian not primarily as the actor in a wild savage drama, as Remington and Schreyvogel have, but as the peaceful dweller in primitive scenes, revealing them often as more poetical and philosophical than the more so-called civilized races." (Craftsm 18:619)

Admired works are:

"The mountain hunter"
"The magic forest"
"Trout ripples"
"An Indian shepherd"
"The voice of the falls"
"Elk-foot"
"San Juan pottery"
"Mending the war bonnet"

"The weary hunter"
"Bear cubs"
"Returning to camp"
"Medicine fires"
"The trout streams"
"The brook"
"The tom tom maker"

At the winter exhibition of the National Academy of New York the Carnegie prize of $500 for the most meritorious oil painting by an American artist went to Mr. Couse for his "Indian making pottery." An unusually fine Indian subject is his "Rain-god maker."

COWLES, GENEVIEVE ALMEDA AND MAUD ALICE (twin sisters), (Mural P. and stained-glass decorators) b. Farmington, Conn., February 23, 1871. These sisters always lived in an atmosphere favorable to the cultivation of their naturally artistic tastes. They took up drawing at the age of seven; a little later they were taken to Europe and in Florence, Giotto, Fra Angelico, and Botticelli impressed their imaginations deeply. Their first series of children were drawn for Scribner's. They have done much work for magazines, executed stained glass windows in various churches, also specialized in mural decoration.

Their mural decorations in Christ Church, New Haven, Conn., are especially noteworthy. They represent: "Prayer of the prisoner," "Prayer of the soul in darkness," and "Prayer of old age." These are paintings of states of the soul and of deep emotions. They are records of human lives and not mere imagination.

Other works are a memorial window and a decorative border for the chancel of Saint Michael's Church, Brooklyn; a window in memory of the deaconess, Miss Stillman, in Grace Church, New York. They have executed many windows and other decorative works for churches.

Miss Maud Alice died during the summer of 1905.

Miss Genevieve writes: "I desire especially to work for prisons, hospitals and asylums—for those whose great need of beauty seems often to be forgotten."

She contributed to the Craftsman (10:97) a most interesting article on "Building a stained glass window."

COX, KENYON, (P., I., Mural P.) b. Warren, O., October 27, 1856, d. New York City, March 17, 1919. Studied in Cincinnati and Philadelphia; also in Paris under Carolus-Duran and Gérome, 1877-82; returned to New York.

Received second Hallgarten prize at the Academy exhibition in 1888, and the same year received two prizes for works at the Paris Universal Exposition. His pictures are principally portraits and figures. He painted two decorations in the Library of Congress; one in Walker Art Gallery, Bowdoin college; one in Iowa state capitol; also frieze in court room of appellate court building, New York. Associate member of National Academy of Design, 1900, full member, 1903; also a member of American Academy Arts and Letters.

"A lady in black" was exhibited in the salon during his Paris student days and on the merits of this work he was elected to the Society of American Artists.

Best known paintings are:

"Jacob wrestling with the angel"   "Painting and poetry"
"Vision of moonrise"   "Flying shadows"

"Mr. Cox is regarded as a colorist of distinction, but especially excels as a draughtsman. He is also well known by his critical writings of art and by his work in black and white, including his illustrations to Rossetti's 'Blessed damozel.'" (Int. Studio 32:3)

Cox, Louise, (Mrs. Kenyon Cox), (P. and I.) b. San Francisco, Cal., June 23, 1865. Pupil of the National Academy of Design, Art Students' League under Kenyon Cox in New York. Received third Hallgarten prize, National Academy of Design, 1896; bronze medal, Paris Exposition, 1900.

"Mrs. Cox makes a specialty of children's portraits and some of her happiest results have been obtained when her own charming children have acted as the models." (Overl 40:111)

Craig, Charles, (P.) b. Morgan county, Ohio, November 1, 1846. He went west in 1865 and lived among the Indians for four years. In 1869 he came east for technical instructions and became a student at the Pennsylvania Academy of the Fine Arts, remaining there until 1873 when he entered the studio of Peter Moran. Eight years later he returned to Colorado, opened a studio at Colorado Springs, and became known as a painter of Indians and western scenes.

Mr. Craig has exhibited in eastern galleries and many of his pictures have gone to Europe. Count Orloff Davidorff of St. Petersburg and the Duchess of Buckingham and Chandos are among distinguished people who own his pictures. Representative pictures are:

"Trailing in"   "Medicine man"
"Scouting party"   "Hualipi"
"A Sioux lookout"

"Mr. Craig's knowledge is so accurate that the student of Indian costume may be sure that every detail is correct. If a Sioux warrior is depicted on the war path his streaks of paint are in the proper place and

of the proper color .... Each canvas is an historical record." (Int
Studio 52: sup xciv)

CRANE, BRUCE, (P.) b. New York, October 17, 1857. Studied art under
Alexander H. Wyant. At the age of seventeen while residing in Elizabeth, New Jersey, he entered the office of an architect and builder and
there had actual experience as a practical draughtsman. In 1878 he
went abroad, visiting the galleries of Liverpool, London, and Paris. His
first picture, "An old mill pond on Long Island," was exhibited at the
National Academy in 1879. The summer of 1882 he spent in the historic
old town of Grez, near the forest of Fontainebleau.

He received the Webb prize, Society American Artists, 1887; bronze
medal, Paris Exposition, 1900; the George Inness' memorial gold medal,
National Academy, 1901. He was elected an associate member of the
National Academy of Design in 1897; full member in 1901. He belongs
distinctly to the plein air school of landscape painters and chooses only
native subjects. As a teacher he has met with remarkable success.

Mr Crane has produced a long list of charming, poetic canvases, being one of America's most idyllic landscape painters.

His most notable canvases are:

."Winter"   "November woods"
"A haystack"   "Peace at night"
"Apple blossoms"   "A black cloud"
"Brown and sere"   "Waste land"
"Ripening grain"   "White fields"
"The gray hill"   "A New England meadow"
"Rainbow"   "Harvest field"
"Indian summer"   "After the rain"
"Awakening hills"

He writes: "A work of art is not a scientific statement. It is enough
if it be true to itself, that is to say, harmonious."

"It is by the simple selection of colors and the conscientious pains-
taking methods that Crane has achieved his notable successes." (Brush
& P 11:1)

"Fond as he is of the russets and tans and mauves of the autumnal
season shown in the tender combination called "Old clearing," he occasionally responds to the vernal season as in "Now comes spring" with
its blossoming trees and pale green grass." Third in his devotion to the
seasons comes winter, two fine examples being seen in the chilling
"Frozen pond," and "Grey December morning."

His recent exhibition shows more diversified aspects of his feelings for the picturesque in American country life than is usually associated with a "Bruce Crane," as in the lovely "Sunrise—Mohawk Valley."

CROWNINSHIELD, FREDERIC, (P., I., Mural P., and stained-glass designer) b. Boston, Mass., November 27, 1845, d. Capri, Italy, September 13, 1918. Mr. Crowninshield was educated at Harvard and studied art with Rowbotham in London. For a number of years he lived in Italy, and in Rome studied with Jean Achille Bénouville. For three years he lived in Siena where he learned the technical secrets of "buon fresco," almost a lost art. To this period belong many of his delightful water colors. He visited Paris frequently and studied under Cabanel at the Ecole des Beaux Arts and worked with Couture in his studio at Villers-le-Bel, near Paris. Shortly after his return to the United States in 1878 Mr. Crowninshield was appointed instructor of drawing, painting, and decorative art in the school connected with the Boston Museum of Fine Arts. This position he held until 1885, during which time he lectured on artistic anatomy.

After moving to New York he executed a memorable series of stained glass windows. At this time he did his most important mural painting. During the past few years he has developed another side of his talent—landscape painting. Much of his time is devoted to guiding the activities of the art societies in New York. He was president of the Fine Arts Federation of New York 1900-1909; director of the American Academy at Rome, 1909-11, and an associate member of the National Academy of Design. His book, "Mural painting," is a standard work.

As a painter, poet, craftsman, illustrator, teacher, lecturer, after-dinner speaker, organizer, he holds an unique place in the art world of the United States.

CRUNELLE, LEONARD, (S.) b. Lenz, France. His family emigrated to America and found work in the coal mines near Decatur, Ill. Leonard amused himself after work by modeling figures out of coal. Lorado Taft, the sculptor, discovered him and later became his instructor in Chicago.

Mr. Crunelle first won recognition through his models of babies. "The squirrel boy" is perhaps the most popular of his later studies.

Christine Bennett says: "His work has made for itself a permanent place and his future promises a fulfilment that will rank him among the greatest of American sculptors." · (Arts & D 1 :406)

"Crunelle's art," said Lorado Taft, "reminds me of the purity and simplicity of the old Florentines. He rejoices in youth and in the spring-time of life."

CURRAN, CHARLES COURTNEY, (P.) b. Hartford, Ky., February 13, 1861. Began to study art at the Cincinnati School of Design, then became a pupil of the Art Students' League and the National Academy of Design of New York; later studied with Benjamin-Constant and Doucet in Paris. In 1900 he became a member of the American Arts' Commission at the Paris Exposition and was assistant director of fine arts at the Pan-American Exposition. Has taught at the Pratt Institute and Art Students' League. A member of the Society of American Artists and other art associations; elected associate member of the National Academy of Design, 1888; full member, 1904.

In 1888 his picture, "A breezy day," received the third Hallgarten prize and his "Lotus lilies of Lake Erie" won honorable mention in the Paris salon of 1890.

Among his most important canvases are:

"The sirens"   "The enchanted shore"
"The Peris"   "The perfume of roses"
"A deep sea fantasy"   "Catching minnows"
A series of twelve views of the Jungfrau.

"His subjects include domestic genre and outdoor life, ideal groups and figures and compositions in which his imagination takes free play in the depiction of the fanciful realms inhabited by the fairies." (Nat Cyc Am Biog)

"He enacts the doctrine that the truest appeal of oil and canvas should be almost as abstract as that of musical sounds ...... He neither lays an undue emphasis on drawing nor on elaborate or super-refined colorings, though clean and well-controlled in the former direction and clear and as a rule full of sunlight in the latter .... Rather he controls and marks his painting with the needed sentiment of peace and relish in man and nature." (Critic 48:39)

CUSHING, HOWARD GARDINER, (P.) b. Boston, Massachusetts, 1869; d. New York City, April 26, 1916. Studied five years in Paris at the Julian Academy and was a pupil of Laurens, Constant, and Doucet. Associate member of the National Academy of Design, 1906.

The Century Club held in January, 1923, a memorial exhibition of Mr. Cushing's paintings. The correspondent to a Boston daily, in writing up the display of paintings, says: "It is a welcome reminder of a man who was ever a charming and distinguished figure in art circles, who was always the aristocrat in painting, and who by study and consistent development was becoming one of the leading American decorative artists of his time .... His color harmonies are always of the delicacy and refinement that grows out of association with the best of all time." There were portraits, interiors, landscapes, fish, and water plants, and decorative panels (in the Persian manner)—a variety of subjects which gives an idea of the scope of his talent.

Well known works include: "A woman in white," "Woman in a silver dress," and "Sunlight."

He also did a series of mural paintings for the studio of Mrs. Harry Payne Whitney at Roslyn, Long Island.

DABO, LEON, (P.) b. Detroit, Mich., July, 1868, of French parents and educated at Saint Ann's school, Detroit; was also a student at Ecole des Arts Decoratifs and under Daniel Urabietta Vierge, Paris, and received instructions from Galliardi in Rome and Florence; lived in Sicily, Sardinia, and Corsica; returned to the United States in 1892. Is represented in collections at Berlin; Dresden; London National Gallery; New York; Washington; Institute of Arts, Detroit, and other American cities.

The works of this "poet in color" for years were uniformly rejected by the juries of our American exhibitions as regularly as they were sent. But when M. Leonce Bénédite, director of the Luxémbourg Museum, was in this country in 1907 he bore back to Paris in glad triumph for the Luxembourg one of Dabo's pictures that had been uniformly rejected by our exhibitions.

Artists like Edmond Aman-Jean and Auguste Rodin, critics like Paul Vallorbe and Camille Mauclair, poets like Maurice Maeterlinck and Anatol de Braz, and such responsible authorities as M. Leonce Bénédite of the Luxembourg and Alexander D. Goltz, president of the Modern Society of Painters, Vienna, have joined in appreciative praise of this painter. (Craftsm 13 :261)

Most of Dabo's work has been done around New York bay and along the banks of the Hudson river.

"Each picture is made up of a succession of harmonious tones which blend together in pleasing symphonic effects." (Brush & P 17:3)

A few of his works are:

"The Hudson, Fort Lee"	"The Hudson near Kingston"
"The Hudson river"	"The cloud"
"The Hudson in winter"	"The sea"
"The Weehawken basin"	"Early morning, Hudson river"
"Evening on the Hudson"	"Golden days"

"He is a mystic of color. He believes that colors have the power to invoke moods directly and also that by closing one's eyes at any moment one can see the color which is expressive of one's mood at just that time.

"His preference in color is for iridescent shades, for subtle golds and soft blues and for the mystic darks of night. He avoids the garish hours of the day, and all obvious aspects of things; he never wearies of trying to catch on the wing—with sense grown ever finer and keener— those elusive, impalpable, fleeting subleties of color and light which give one the sense of spirituality so characteristic of his best work." (Louise M. Kueffner in Sewanee Review 22:96)

Dabo, Theodore Scott, (P.) b. Detroit, Mich., 1870, of French parents, and educated at Saint Ann's school, Detroit. When his father, Ignace Scott Dabo (himself an artist), died in 1885, the family moved to New York City. Leon, the oldest son, went to work for a decorator, that this gifted brother, T. Scott, might study without turning his talent to commercial profit. For sixteen years the paintings of the brothers Dabo were refused admission to the art exhibitions in this country. Edmond Aman-Jean, the French painter, was the first to recognize the artistic value of their work and took T. Scott to Paris, where his canvases were accepted by the salon and he greeted as an artist of rare individuality and strength.

M. Henri Pene DuBois says: "T. Scott Dabo's works are hymns to nature. They are skies with vermilion mists exhaling praise as from a censer, marshes of melancholy, rivers of peace and forgiveness, fairy spectacles of land and water." Mr. DuBois also suggests Poe as a source of inspiration. Another saw in his work the influence of Mallarme. Octave Mirbeau recently wrote that T. Scott Dabo had the charm of Puvis de Chavannes and the transparency of Carrière.·

Reproductions can give no adequate idea of the depth of light and charm in color in T. Scott Dabo's "Tour St. Jacques in the rain," or his "Evening on the Seine."

"We are the painters of atmospheric conditions," they say: "everything in nature moves, we, therefore, endeavor to paint movement." They make color a vehicle of music-like vibrations. (Int Studio 27:174)

Daingerfield, Elliott, (P., I., Mural P.) b. Harper's Ferry, Va., March 26, 1859. Studied drawing and painting in New York with a private teacher, also at the Art Students' League. First exhibited at National Academy of Design in 1880. Studied in Europe during 1897. Is professor of painting and composition at the Philadelphia School of Design. A member of the National Academy of Design, 1906. A writer on art subjects.

Mr. Daingerfield's productions are largely figure and landscape, and his studies are usually taken from rural life, the toiler of the field being his favorite subject.

In his paintings, color quality and depth of feeling are the dominant features and pervade the rough exteriors in which his characters are dressed.   (Nat Cyc Am Biog)

Among his noted canvases are:

"Two women shall be working in the fields"
"My lady rhododendron"
"Child of Mary"
"A garden of dreams"
"Labor and plenty"
"Planting"

"The lost sheep"
"The mother"
"A madonna of the fields"
"Christ in the wilderness"
"A wood-cutter"
"Story of the madonna"
"The tanagra"

Mr. Daingerfield was commissioned to paint the "Lady Chapel" of the Church of St. Mary the Virgin, New York, in 1902.

"He is an imaginative painter with a strong sense of decorative beauty and he subordinates realistic facts to the effect of the ensemble."

DALLIN, CYRUS EDWIN, (S.) b. Springfield, Utah, November 22, 1861. The first eighteen years of his life were spent in the mountains of Utah. When only seven years of age he attempted to model heads of his favorite Indian chiefs, and at the age of eighteen when sifting ore in the mines he modeled two heads in clay.   These were so admired by the miners that they sent them to a fair in Salt Lake City.   Two wealthy mining men in Utah saw the heads, became interested in the young genius, and made it possible for him to go to Boston where he commenced study with Truman H. Bartlett, the sculptor.   Later he went to Paris and studied under Chapu and Dampt.   While in France he became acquainted with Rosa Bonheur and during the time that Buffalo Bill and his company of Indians were in Paris they—Dallin and the great French artist—worked together, frequently from the same model.

Mr. Dallin has made a remarkable series which tells the story of the Indian's relation to the white man:

First, "Signal of peace"—the welcome
Second, "Medicine man"—the warning
Third, "The protest"—defiance
Fourth, "Appeal to the Great Spirit"—the last hope of the Indian

The fourth of the series—"The appeal to the Great Spirit"—was awarded the gold medal in the Paris salon of 1909.   "This statue is one of the greatest pieces of sculpture in modern art and is comparable with the antique in its simplicity." (Arts & D 4:153)

"This series is an example of the sculptor's synthetic insight and his skillful interpretation of psychological moments."

His bas-relief of Julia Ward Howe is commented on as being "of exquisite sincerity of line, a reticent, self-contained work and an accurate likeness." (New Eng M n. s. 48:408)

A bronze statue of "Don Quixote" was exhibited in the Paris salon and critics refer to it as "one of the most delightfully original and imaginative of American sculptures. .... It is conceived in an absolutely ideal spirit and is enveloped in an atmosphere of romance which is completely in harmony with that of Cervantes."

He modeled the gilded bronze angel which surmounts the spire of the Mormon Temple in Salt Lake City; also modeled the statue of Sir Isaac Newton for the rotunda of the Library of Congress.

His "Despair" is an extremely graceful nude. (New Eng M n. s. 21:196)

DANNAT, WILLIAM T., (P.) b. Hempstead, L. I., July 9, 1853. Going abroad at an early age, he was educated in art at the Royal Academy of Munich; studied also in Italy and Spain, after which he settled in Paris. No foreign painter has ever received greater praise from the French people.

His first picture to attract attention was his celebrated painting entitled "The quartette" exhibited in the salon of 1884. This picture was also exhibited at the Universal Exposition, 1889, and was given a place of honor in the American section. It procured for the artist the rank of chevalier in the Legion of Honor. He was elected officer, 1897; commander, 1900. Mr. Dannat is president of the Paris Society of American Painters and has been the recipient of numerous medals and diplomas.

Popular paintings are:

"After the mass"	"Mariposa"
"Otera"	"Une Saducéenne"; woman in
"Spanish women"	white.
"Aragonese smuggler"	"Un profil blond"; study in red.
"A sacristy in Aragon"	

"Degas is his ideal, and the study of artificial light his field of experiment." (Müther)

"In Mr. Dannat's work we find the qualities of the most gifted artists —a vision of singular acuteness and sensitiveness, a refinement and delicate intelligence, perfect command of the means of drawing and painting, and finally that taste and that aesthetic tact which enables him to avoid every excess whether of commonplace or of eccentricity—these two extremes on the verge of which the masterpiece is conceived and consummated." (Child's "Art and criticism")

Albert Wolff voiced the current opinion when he declared Dannat's "Quartette" to be the best piece of painting in the salon of 1884.

DAVIDSON, Jo (S.) b. New York City, March 30, 1883. Of Russo-Jewish parentage, he grew up on the East Side, experiencing all the vicissitudes of poverty and genius. At fifteen he began to earn his living. When sixteen he won a high school scholarship for drawing and entered the Art Students' League, supporting himself by doing burnt wood drawings. In 1905 he received his first commission for a "David" and two years later sailed to Europe, arriving in Paris with forty dollars in his pocket.

In a short time he broke away from the academic precepts and the accepted form of art, for the subject of light and its effect on sculpture had begun to interest him. He says that the first satisfactory result of his study of the relation of light to form was in a little group he calls "Rapture."

A portrait bust of a Swiss girl was purchased by Mrs. Harry Payne Whitney. This success relieved financial pressure. A short time after this he sent the "Violinist" to the Autumn Salon, 1908, and it was accepted. In 1910 he gave his first exhibition in New York City. He now exhibits in London, Paris, and New York.

Holbrook Jackson, the English author, has a very appreciative article in an English publication (T. P.'s. Magazine) on Davidson and his art. He says: "Davidson's work is impressionistic, but it is not the impressionism of the painter. His art is more allied to impressionism in music than in painting—it has the same reflective emotion, the same self-contained sense of design. Whilst looking at his later work your mind is instinctively swayed by musical rhythm .... In 'Earth' we feel the reawakening of the classical in the modern. The 'Russian dancer' is motion caught on the wing and frozen into bronze."

Huneker said: "This young man is a sculptor born, one who has not allowed his enormous facility to decline into dilettante methods. He models with the plastic, not the literary idea, before him; he is more rhythmic than static; yet he can achieve the effect of rigid ponderousness. His figures are evocations of poetic moods translated into legitimate sculptured terms."

J. P. Collins, English critic, says: "Davidson struck out a line for himself and in ten years' time he acquired breadth and amassed achievements enough to win him the recognition he coveted, not only in Paris, but in America and even London .... By instinct he chooses characters of dominant personality and reproduces his subjects as he sees them. The result is a wonderful interpretation of the mental and the physical."

One of the most interesting and important commissions in the history of portraiture, to make a series of bronze busts of the allied military and political leaders, was given to Mr. Davidson. He sailed for Paris the day after the Armistice was signed and had his first sitting given by Marshal Foch at Senlis, Nov. 24, 1918. Gen. Pershing came next, followed by Marshal Joffre. The King of Belgium, Lloyd George, Marshal Haig, Paderewski, Masaryk, Clemenceau, Col. House, Hon. Robert Lansing, and President Wilson were all included in the famous series.

This great feat was remarkable not only for the execution of the work but for obtaining access to the Peace Makers. So swift and clever was Davidson in his work that he produced the most startling life-like images out of a lump of clay in the briefest time under extremely unfavorable circumstances and conditions.

When in Genoa during the Economic Conference he made busts of the Russian delegates. They are fine examples, showing the revolutionary type of the Russian statesmen of today.

Other characteristic portrait-busts are: John Duncan, the Scotch painter; Joseph Conrad, novelist; Georg Brandes, the Danish critic; the late Lord Northcliffe of the London Times; Rabindranath Tagore, the Bengali poet; Frank Brangwyn, the English artist; Israel Zangwill, the Hebrew novelist; Dr. Abraham Jacobi, the eminent New York physician; Madam Davidson; Miss Flora Whitney; the Countess M. Lillian Shelly; and Beatrice Lovell.

In 1920 a traveling exhibition of the work of this now world-famous sculptor included many of the portrait-busts already mentioned and the following:

Imaginative works—"Eve," "Dawn," "Night," "Le Male," and "La Femelle."

Notable nudes—"A study in repose," "A woman on tiptoe," "Beyond," "L'appel aux armes," "End of the day."

Character sketches—"La danse exotique," "A Russian dancer," "The Indian girl," "Yushinosen," "La femme gargouille," and "Memère."

Mr. Davidson returned from Paris last year after making many portrait busts. The notable were a study in bronze of Gertrude Stein, author of "Tender buttons"; Mabel Dodge, wife of Maurice Sterne; Muriel Draper; and Anatole France.

"To him the surface is the symbol of the soul, a thing written in plain words which go in a definite direction. He is a reporter and an interpreter. The direction he reports is his own interpretation of the sitters."

"Davidson is a type of the eternal fighter. He gives one a sense of fierce enjoyment of life and of the making of life."

Mr. Davidson's latest title is "A philosopher in stone."

DAVIES, ARTHUR B., (P.) b. Utica, N. Y., September 26, 1862. Studied in New York and Chicago.

At the age of seven his drawings attracted the attention of Dwight Williams, who gave him his first lesson in art. In 1886 he went to New York where he made illustrations for magazines. Ten years later two of his paintings appeared in the first International at Carnegie Institute, Pittsburgh, Pa.

An art critic, recently, writing on the American art of the Metropolitan Museum of Art, New York, refers to the strange somnambulistic intensity of his "Dreams." "With an entire absence of color and its great beauty of tone, the sense of slow continuous movement secured not by the drawing of the figure itself, but by the imaginative composition of the background."

William J. Glackens writes enthusiastically of the art of Arthur B. Davies: "He is the most important man in this country. But his art is not national; it is universal. He is a symbolist, a painter of ideas. Davies has felt the influence of the modern Frenchmen or of the old Italians, of Mantegna, for example, and insisted upon harmonious arrangement, upon order, which is the battle-cry of the post-impressionists. He aims straighter, perhaps, than any other man here at beauty." (Arts & D 3:164)

In writing of an exhibition of his paintings recently held at the Montrose Galleries, the New York Times says: "A day of good fortune" is a veritable dance for joy .... In looking at "Whither away" one must listen hardly breathing. The nymph and the tree in "Chrysis in the garden" grow together, helping one another to grow. "Eurydice" is a superb piece of drawing and modeling. Often the figures are manipulated and stretched and turned, not as a clever thing to do, but for the necessary flowing grace of the composition."

His decorative canvas "After-thoughts of earth" won first prize at the twenty-second International at Carnegie Institute in 1923. The distinction carried with it a gold medal and $1,500.

The Boston Transcript says: "Somewhat unreal figures group themselves in an intervale among the hills .... While there is an element of strangeness in the attenuated lines of the figures, there is an utter avoidance of the rectangular shapes the artist has used of later years, and the work apparently executed in glazes is remarkably mellow in tone."

"He is first of all the poet-painter in the sense that Albert Ryder is a painter for those with a fine comprehension of the imagination. . . . . There is no violence in the work of Davies. It is the appreciable relation of harmony and counterpoint in the human heart and mind . . . . It is the condition of music that art in the lyrical state has seemed to suggest." (Touchstone 6:284)

The poetic titles given to some of his canvases are: "Mirrored dreaming," "Sicily—flowering Isle," "Shell of gold," "A portal of the night," "Mystic dalliance."

"Though he paints the unusual and remote and employs at times striking methods in his work, he has achieved a high place among painters in this country and abroad."

Davis, Charles Harold, (P.) b. Amesbury, Mass., January 7, 1856. Very early he displayed marked artistic ability. He was a pupil of Otto Grundmann and the Museum of Fine Arts, Boston, three years; also studied under Lefebvre and Boulanger, Paris, and remained in France ten years, exhibiting in the salons during that time. Mr. Davis has resided at Mystic, Conn., since 1890.

He is represented at Metropolitan Museum, New York; Corcoran Gallery of Art, Washington; Pennsylvania Academy of the Fine Arts, Philadelphia; Art Institute, Chicago; Carnegie Institute, Pittsburgh; and has been awarded prizes and medals at many competitive exhibitions; also received honorable mention in the Paris salon and in 1889 a second-class medal at the Universal Exposition, his works thereby becoming hors de concours. A member of the National Academy since 1906.

Mr. Davis is one of the strongest American landscape painters. He gives the actual tone of the hour, whether it be sunrise, noon, or sunset, in which his own personality, while evident, does not crowd out the personality of nature.

"Conquering light" is one of the most dramatic of his canvases and "September cloud" is quite beautiful.

Among his most famous productions are:

"Winter evening"	"Rocky pasture"
"Summer"	"Oak boughs"
"The brook'	"The hillside"
"Twilight hour"	"Summer breeze"
"The time of the red-wing black-	"Autumn clouds"
bird."	

"The sunny hillside" was awarded the Corcoran silver medal two years ago. "In its subtlety of form and color it was a picture that Twachtman would have liked." "On the west wind" is called a "typical Davis" (clouds and hills). "Blithe June" and "Early summer," "Back of the village" and "Grey brothers" (later paintings) show the many-sidedness of Davis' art.

At an exhibition of Mr. Davis' landscapes held in New York last year, it was a surprise to many to see the variety in subject. The artist is now concerned with other qualities than "cloud effects," for which his early canvases were noted. His later pictures have a higher color-range and a more joyous spirit. One views the delicacies of springtime and the rigors of winter cold and snow.

The pictures of great beauty were the "Little gray house" in a deep rich color scheme of lichen-hued gray and summer green; "The pool," a low bank of yellow clay-rocks overhung with trees of brilliant autumn coloring shading a pool of water; "Summer afternoon"—white cottages showing through trees beside a river bank; "Winter morning" in lovely mauve and white. "In early May" has been described as having the "shy delicacy of a bunch of arbutus, a picture that recalls the lines of Keats as to melancholy abiding in beauty."

"He belongs to no clique, has no pet theories, and is far more concerned about the production of works of art than in a discussion as to the school in which they shall be classified. .... Davis uses his landscape forms entirely as an expression of mood." (Int Studio 75:177)

DEAKIN, EDWIN, (P.) b. Sheffield, England, 1840. Received early education in his native town. From the outset of his career he had a fondness for landscape and architecture. After following his art in England and France he came to America and settled in Berkeley, California, and selected the Spanish missions of California as a specialty.

Mr. Deakin began his work in 1870 and the series, comprising twenty-one missions, was completed in 1899. The series of structures painted by Mr. Deakin was begun under Father Junipero Serra, the leader of the Franciscans, who came to California in 1769. (Brush & P 15:1)

DEARTH, HENRY GOLDEN, (P.) b. Bristol, R. I., April 22, 1863; d. New York City, March 27, 1918. Pupil of Ecole des Beaux Arts; also studied with Morot and Merson. He won the Webb prize, Society American Artists, 1893; bronze medal, Paris Exposition, 1900; silver medal, Pan-American Exposition, Buffalo, 1901; was elected associate member National Academy of Design in 1902; full member in 1906.

Mr. Dearth's specialty is landscapes on the Coast of Normandy. He has a home and a studio at Montreuil-sur-Mer in Pas-de-Calais, along the English Channel, where he works several months each year. The keynote of his work is simplicity. He suggests details. This is most apparent in his "Sunset in Normandy." His pictures have dignity and poetry. (Cent 48:157)

DE CAMP, JOSEPH RODEFER, (P., Mural P.) b. Cincinnati, O., November 5, 1858; d. Baca Grande, Florida, February 11, 1923. Studied art with Frank Duveneck, at the Cincinnati Academy and at the Royal Academy, Munich. Later accompanied Duveneck and Whistler to Florence and Venice. Won first prize in city hall decorative competition, Philadelphia; Temple gold medal, Pennsylvania Academy of the Fine Arts, 1889; received honorable mention at Paris Exposition, 1900; gold medal at St. Louis Exposition, 1904. Member of the society of Ten American Painters. Has been instructor in the Pennsylvania Academy of the Fine Arts and a member of the faculty in the schools of the Boston Museum of Fine Arts.

Mr. De Camp is known chiefly from his portrait and figure painting, although his landscapes are among the finest painted by American artists.

For years he has had steady patronage from soldiers, statesmen, musicians, artists, writers, and educators. His portrait of Col. Roosevelt, which he was commissioned by a committee of the members of the class of 1880 at Harvard to paint and which hangs in Memorial Hall at Cambridge, is considered a wonderful achievement. Mr. De Camp's work is not frequently seen in New York except at exhibitions of the Ten American Painters.

Arthur Hoeber, the art critic, says: "None of the modern painters, either in this country or in Europe, is better equipped technically than is Joseph De Camp .... He draws with academic correctness, has a thorough knowledge of anatomy and construction, and for facility of brush work yields to no one."

Julia de Wolf Addison says that one of the best pictures ever painted by Joseph De Camp is owned by the Boston Museum of Fine Arts— "Guitar player."

Popular figure paintings are:

"The blue cup"   "The window"
"The pink feather"   "The violinist"
"The gray turban"

"Blue kimono" occupied the place of honor in the largest gallery of the Pennsylvania Academy of the Fine Arts latest exhibition. The model has red-gold hair and she wears a purplish-blue kimono with pattern of blue-green; the lining is vivid yellow and there is a golden glow in the face and head, a most delightful play of contrasting color and pattern. "Some way she will always be associated in her sweetness with the funeral wreath which has been hung beneath her frame .... And again the whole is perfect; there is not one discordant note in the brown, bronzed leaves of the wreath and the formal purple velvet bow, which tells without words that De Camp's last picture is painted." (Rose V. S. Barry)

The American Magazine of Art, April, 1923, in a long appreciative article on the late lamented painter says: "His brush work was always interesting and vital, its handling virile. De Camp was what his technique, plus keen insight and discernment (which were frequently uncanny), a love of the beautiful, a respect for truth, an appreciation of the value of color, and a steady growth which was a consistent development made of him—one of America's best painters."

DE HAVEN, FRANK, (P.) b. Bluffton, Ind., December 26, 1856. With money he earned at the age of sixteen he bought his first box of paints. In 1886 he went to New York and became a pupil of George H. Smillie. He won the Inness' prize in 1900; Shaw prize, 1901; and received honorable mention at the Pan-American Exposition, Buffalo, 1901. Elected associate member of National Academy of Design in 1902.

"Moonrise and sunset" he regards as his most important work. It has warm color and a hazy glow—the russet of autumn, lighted by the sinking sun. "Autumn twilight" with its deep clear blue sky, in which the evening star twinkles near the horizon, is full of mystery. "A Maine farm" is a study of early autumn with the neutral atmospheric grays of the waning year. His "Winter night" and "Indian summer" are in direct antithesis.

His versatility is simply another expression for his breadth of interest, and his various tonal schemes for his mastery of color.

"His subjects are simple and poetical, the last glow of the sun, a windy day, a threatening sky, or struggling clouds throwing a stream of light on the plain, furnish the principal themes of his pictures."—Hartmann.

"His chief interest is to manipulate his color so as to make his canvas the means of imparting an emotion .... His scenes are bona fide scenes, simple bits in which he has seen beauty; and the emotion he seeks to arouse is the genuine emotion that he himself has experienced and that he strives to make others feel." (Brush & P 17:179)

DEMING, EDWARD WILLARD, (P., S., I., Mural P.) b. Ashland, Ohio, August 26, 1860. Studied in the Art Students' League and under Boulanger and Lefebvre, Paris.

Mr. Deming's work divides itself into painting, mural decoration principally, and modeling.

It is in his pictures illustrating Indian folk-lore that Mr. Deming takes the greatest interest. "The Hiawatha legends are the subject of his most charming canvases .... he delights in scenes in which there is the mystery of twilight." (Craftsm 10:150)

"Perhaps no one has more exquisitely revealed the first blush of dawn, the majesty of moonlight, the changing gray of twilight, the tragic depths of loneliness in the first daybreak in woods and prairies." (Craftsm 21:456)

"E. W. Deming perhaps as much as any man in sculpture has brought us the very intimate soul of the aboriginal western folk." (Craftsm 28:153)

The buffalo frieze in the residence of Mr. Ernest Thompson Seton, by Mr. Deming, is a transcript of the open plain "under the unappeasable sun of the south west." (Int Studio 27: sup xv)

Mr. Deming has illustrated many stories and books dealing with Indian life. He is now engaged in painting panels of Indian scenes for the American museum of natural history. The panels are eight in number and will illustrate the history of the principal tribes.

DESSAR, LOUIS PAUL, (P.) b. Indianapolis, Ind., 1867. Studied at the National Academy in 1886; later went to Paris and studied under Bouguereau and Robert-Fleury and at the Ecole des Beaux Arts.

Awarded third-class medal at the salon, 1891; received honorable mention, Carnegie Institute, Pittsburgh, 1897; second Hallgarten prize, National Academy, 1900; bronze medal, Paris Exposition, 1900; an associate member National Academy of Design, 1900; full member, 1906.

"An artist with a most delicate color sense. Paints the decorative landscape rather low in key, rich in color, and paint laid on solidly."

It is by his sheep pictures that he is best known in this country. "Evening" was one of the prize pictures at the Columbian Exposition, Chicago, 1893.

Among his well-known works are:

"Going home"	"Nocturne"
"Return of the flock"	"Moonrise"
"The fold in the woods"	"Clearing after the rain"
"Ploughing"	

His wife is the original of the charming subject "Elizabeth."

"He does not seem to care so much for composition or for assimilating the ingredients of the scene and representing them in synthetic form, as for surface play of color in certain portions of the picture." (Artist 24: sup lix)

"He is fond of the atmospheric effects of sunset and moonrise, and often finds an aid to his composition in his interest in animal life." (Int Studio 27 · sup lxvi)

DEWEY, CHARLES MELVILLE, (P.) b. Lowville, New York, July 16, 1851. As a child he displayed artistic talents, earning the money for his first painting materials by building the fire in the country schoolhouse. In 1874 he went to New York and became a pupil in the National Academy; two years later he went to Paris and entered the atelier of Carolus-Duran and was honored in being selected as one of three pupils to assist his master in the decoration of the "Plafond" of the Louvre. He returned to the United States and opened a studio in New York in 1878.

He early became known as a truthful delineator of familiar phases of American landscape.

"His landscapes are synthetic in treatment, for he seeks to interpret, rather than to transcribe an effect." (Nat Cyc Am Biog)

Characteristic paintings are:

"Edge of the forest"	"Gray robe of twilight"
"The close of day"	"River at night"
"The queen of night"	"Return of the hay boats"
"An autumn pastoral"	"The harvest moon"
"The star and the shadows"	

His pictures have a liking for the subdued light of morning and evening, the trees massed dark against the sky, the depth and mistiness of the twilight foliage and the glow of the twilight sky.

DEWING, MARIA OAKLEY, (Mrs. T. W. Dewing), (P., I.) b. New York, October 27, 1857. Pupil of National Academy of Design and John LaFarge in New York; Courtois in Paris. Received bronze medal at Pan-American Exposition, Buffalo, 1901.

Specialty: Figure and flower pieces and portraits.

DEWING, THOMAS WILMER, (P., Mural P.) b. Boston, Mass., May 4, 1851. Pupil of Boulanger and Lefebvre in Paris. Won the Clarke prize, National Academy of Design, 1887; silver medal, Paris Exposition, 1889; Lippincott prize, Pennsylvania Academy of the Fine Arts, 1906; first medal, Carnegie Institute, 1908. Member of Ten American Painters. Elected a member of the National Academy of Design in 1888.

"The exquisite poem 'In the garden' is one of the few perfect master-pieces which American figure painting has produced. 'The south wind' is a very beautiful allegorical conception."

Characteristic paintings are:

"Sorcerers"	"Before sunrise"
"The blue dress"	"The carnation"
"After sunset"	"The garland"
"Yellow tulips"	"The mirror"
"Girl with lute"	"Early portrait of the artist's
"A lady playing the violincello"	daughter"
"The spinet"	

"The quality in Dewing's work which appeals to me [Hartmann] beyond every other, is its personal character; it reflects the man's mind, that of a refined epicureanism, choosing naturally to live among dainty surroundings and beautiful women."

Caffin says: "The technical summary of Thomas W. Deming's work is impressionism, based upon skilful draftsmanship and the facile inter-pretation of a color sense, not catholic, but deeply felt."

Dewing paints amber-toned interiors.

DIELMAN, FREDERICK, (Mural P., I., E.) b. Hanover, Germany, December 25, 1847. Came to the United States in childhood. Graduated at Calvert College. His first artistic work that appeared was entitled "A scene from a confederate raid in Maryland," and this was published when he was sixteen years of age. He studied art under Diez at the Royal Academy, Munich, returned to New York in 1876 and opened a studio there.

Mr. Dielman was one of the founders of the Society of American Artists, and was elected a member of the National Academy of Design in 1883; also was one of the founders of the New York Etching Club; was president of the National Academy of Design, 1889-1909; professor of descriptive geometry and drawing in College of New York since 1903.

He has contributed largely to the illustration of current fiction in leading magazines, and in editions de luxe of the works of Longfellow, Tennyson, Eliot, Hawthorne, and others.

Mr. Dielman is a well-known designer of mosaic and mural work; his panels "Law" and "History" in the Library of Congress, the large mosaic "Thrift" in the Albany Savings Bank and six mosaics in the state capitol at Des Moines, Ia., rank with the best in this line of art in America.

Mr. Dielman also paints in oil, the subjects chosen being usually genre or historical. A few are:

"The marriage of Francis Le Baron"   "Old time favorites"
"The Mora player"   "A girl I know"

His "Pomona," "Gabrielle," and "Christine" are dainty bits of execution.

DILLAYE, BLANCHE, (P., I., E.) b. Syracuse, N. Y. Educated at Ogontz school. Studied art in the Pennsylvania Academy of the Fine Arts and in Paris; a pupil of Stephen Parrish in etching; has exhibited in Paris salons, and in England, as well as at all the principal exhibitions in the United States. Received silver medal for etching at Atlanta Exposition and at Universal Exposition at Lorient, France, 1903. She is represented in the art collection of Syracuse, N. Y.; is vice-president of Philadelphia Water-color Club; member of Women's Art Club, New York, and Women's Art Association in Paris; first president of Plastic Club.

Miss Dillaye has a penchant for odd nooks and narrow alleys—a "Quebec sail loft" being very characteristic.

DIX, EULABEE, (Min. P.) b. Illinois, October 5, 1879. Pupil of St. Louis School of Fine Arts, William J. Whittemore and I. A. Josephi in New York.

"Jewel-like color resembling the earliest stained glass is the effect Miss Dix has most zealously striven for. In the miniature of Mrs. Michael Dreicer the sitter is clothed in emerald green, a color which contrasts most effectively with her reddish brown hair. The miniature of Mark Twain in a gown of an Oxford doctor of letters shows a prevailing tone of gray, the broad red band of the gown lighting the whole picture. The miniature of Mrs. Purdon-Clarke is exceedingly beautiful .... Miss Dix's sense of color values is peculiarly happy."

"Miss Dix thoroughly understands the art of miniature painting as distinct from portrait painting 'in the large.' " (Int Studio 40:sup xciv)

"Eulabee Dix paints in the careful style of the old miniatures."

DIXON, MAYNARD, (P., Mural P.) b. Fresno, California, 1875. A western artist who specializes in scenes from the mountains and desert, having spent many years in the Northwest, Mexico, and Arizona.

One of Mr. Dixon's latest successes is a series of panels for the Indian Hall in the Baldwin home in Santa Anita Canyon, near Pasadena.

There are four panels and they depict the life of the Western Indian. "The victory song" represents savage Indians returning with their captives. "Envoys of peace" is the contrasting panel. The single figure standing in advance of his companions has dignity and repose. "The pool" represents Indian women and children going down to bathe. The fourth panel is "The ghost eagle" and well expresses the fear and superstition of the Indian.

"As a painter, indeed, Mr. Dixon is a remarkable technician. His 'September moonlight' is unlike any such nocturnal effect that has ever come to us from the west .... his 'Cattle range' is another remarkable cloud effect. For dramatic effect his 'Ledges of Sun-land' stands out supreme in its feeling of the bulking mass of red sandstone rising out of the desert with two mounted Indians riding along its base, a truly remarkable piece of color." (Am Art News)

"Mr. Dixon is to be congratulated upon having achieved a signal success in his interpretation of the mystery and silence of the Great Plains and in developing an art which is truly national in that it is distinctly American." (Int Studio 55:sup xcii)

DODGE, WILLIAM DE LEFTWICH, (Mural P.) b. Liberty, Va., March 9, 1867. Studied in Munich and with Gérome in Paris. Received two third class medals and prix d'atelier while studying with Gérome; two medals Cours Yvon; medal at Paris salon, 1888; gold medal, prize fund exhibition, New York, 1886; bronze medal, Paris Exposition, 1889; also medal at Columbian Exposition, 1893. Member Society of Mural Painters.

Mr. Dodge has executed mural paintings in the Library of Congress and in many New York City hotels.

He recently received a commission from the state of New York to paint a series of murals for the flag room in the Capitol at Albany. The general scheme is to show battles in which American troops have taken part with special reference to those participated in by New York troops.

The subjects to be illustrated include five land and four naval battles:

"Battle with the Iroquois Indians at Champlain, 1609"
"The siege of Fort Stanwix in 1777"
"Charge of the 14th New York regiment at Gettysburg, 1863"
"Theodore Roosevelt leading troops in Spanish-American War"
"Smashing of the Hindenburg line in the World War"
"Battle of Lake Champlain, 1812"
"Sinking of the Confederate ram, Albemarle" (Civil War)
"Destruction of Cervera's fleet" (Spanish-American War)
"A submarine attack on an American transport." (World War)

DODSON, SARAH PAXTON BALL, (P.) b. Philadelphia, Pa., 1847; d. Brighton, England, August 8, 1906. First began art studies in the

Pennsylvania Academy schools in 1872. Her training was continued in
Paris where for three years she worked under Evariate Vital Luminais
and afterward under Jules Lefebvre, enjoying also at a later period in
her career the privilege of criticism from Boutet de Monvel. Her first
publicly exhibited work was "L'amour menetrier," shown in the Paris
salon of 1877. Her decorative painting "Pax Patriae" was an especial
feature of the Pennsylvania state building at the Columbian Exposition.
"La dance" is an exemplification of her early style and "Deborah,"
recently acquired by the Corcoran Gallery of Art, Washington, D. C.,
well represents the second period of her art development. Her most
important historical work is "The signing of the Declaration of Independence in the state house, Philadelphia, Fourth of July, 1776," and
"The invocation of Moses" in Saint Bartholomew church, Brighton, England, is her most important decorative work. In her landscapes "there
is a marked delicacy of feeling."

"Her limitations were the limitations of her temperament. In her
painting there can be heard no strident call for recognition, but always
the soft voice of beauty makes last appeal .... Through each suc-
ceeding step of her artistic growth there is a sympathetic intimacy with
the more subtle truths of nature." (Int Studio 45: sup xxxvii)

DOLPH, JOHN H., (P.) b. Fort Ann, N. Y., April 18, 1835; d. New York
City, September 28, 1903. He studied portrait painting with Allen
Smith at Cleveland; began his career by painting portraits in Detroit
in 1857; and went to New York a few years later. Going to Europe he
studied animal painting under Van Kuyck at Antwerp, specializing on
horses. In 1875 he painted a Persian cat which was greatly admired,
and from that time he painted cats and dogs almost exclusively.

He was made an associate member of the National Academy of Design
in 1877, and full member in 1898.

An art critic has written: "Dolph's cat pictures are second only to
Brown's bootblacks though from the technical side Mr. Dolph's work
ranks much higher. In what the painters call qualities—the representation of texture—he is particularly successful. When he puts one of his
cats on a piece of velvet you rather feel that it is velvet."

Dolph's cats are as famous in America as are Ronner's in Europe.

DONOGHUE, JOHN, (S.) b. Chicago, Ill., 1853; d. New Haven, Conn.,
July 3, 1903. Of very humble parentage; had a short period of art study
at the Academy of Design, Chicago; later studied with Jouffroy in the
Ecole des Beaux Arts, Paris. Exhibited a head, "Phaedra," in the salon
of 1880 and returned to Chicago the same year. When Oscar Wilde

visited this country in 1882 he called attention to Donoghue's artistic promise and through his efforts Donoghue was able to return to Europe the following year. Received honorable mention in the Paris salon of 1886. In Rome he produced a number of remarkable works. "Young Sophocles," undoubtedly his highest inspiration, stands among the most perfect examples of ideal sculpture yet produced by an American.

It was Donoghue's dream to be represented in his native city by a great work of art. He conceived the idea for an immense statue to be known as "The spirit." (Milton is said to have been the inspiration.) This colossal statue was intended for the Columbian Exposition, 1893. Arriving too late, no arrangements were made to receive it in New York and it was left on the dock. The artist could not pay the transportation bill. This and the failure to show his work in public caused him grievous disappointment. He lost enthusiasm and ambition and but little was known of him until his dead body was found on the shores of Lake Whitney, near New Haven, Conn., he having committed suicide. (Taft's "History of American sculpture.")

Donoho, Gaines Ruger, (S., P.) b. Church Hill, Miss., 1857. Pupil of Art Students' League of New York and R. Swain Gifford, Lefebvre, and Boulanger. Received silver medal at Paris Exposition, 1889.

Kenyon Cox says: "Mr. Donoho is a painter who has produced too little and exhibited too little of what he has produced, but this picture ["La Marcellerie"] decoratively designed and closely studied shows us a talent at once robust and fine."

Another critic refers to the same picture as fully up to the best salon standards and especially as "being beautifully painted."

Dougherty, Paul, (P.) b. Brooklyn, N. Y., September 6, 1877. Graduated from the New York law school, 1898. Soon after he decided to abandon a legal career and pursue art. He studied perspective and form under Constantin Hertzberg and then traveled; and later studied art five years in Paris, London, Florence, Venice, and Munich. It is by his marines that he won fame. He is a member of leading art clubs; was elected associate of the National Academy of Design, 1906; full member, 1907.

International Studio (36:sup iii) says of him and his art: "Never anecdotal, he is always picturesque .... He would in rock representation show compactness and texture so clearly that its geological history may be read by a scientist. He would in ocean convey a profound impression of its depth, its latent cruelty and its almost resistless and rhythmic power of wave. 'Northern sky' suggests the tremendous speed of a high billow hurled at a towering rock mass with the fury of the whole ocean behind it .... More wave history is told in 'The cleft.' 'The Twisted ledge' is a study in perspective of rock form .... 'The black wave' represents the dynamics of ocean currents .... The nearest approach to impressionism is 'Sun and storm' .... Mr. Dougherty should not be judged entirely as a painter of marine; cloud, mountain, and plain as well as rock, sea, and sky have been depicted by him."

"Better than others has he interpreted atmospheric effects on luminous spray—the evanescent charm of the ever-changing sea." (Art & P 2:7)

His "Land and sea" is in the Corcoran Gallery of Art and his "Sun and mist" is in the National Gallery.

"Paul Dougherty in his 'Rock channel' shows us that he understands the placid beauty of undisturbed blue waters as well as the splendor and terror of Cornwall storms." (Craftsm 24:315)

DUFNER, EDWARD, (P.) b. Buffalo, New York. Received honorable mention in the Paris salon of 1902. Is a member of the Paris American Artists' Association, New York Water-Color Club, and many other leading art clubs. Was elected associate member of the National Academy of Design in 1910. An instructor in the Art Students' League of New York.

As a boy he showed marked artistic talent; was first employed as a messenger for an architect's office; then attended the night school at the Buffalo School of Art where he won a scholarship for one year's study and expenses at the Art Students' League, New York. While in New York he illustrated magazines and finally saved money enough to go to Paris where he became a pupil of Whistler and Laurens.

It was as a painter of spring that he won membership in the National Academy of Design.

"Youth and sunshine," "Summer joys," "Old house in sunlight," and "Joys of spring" are representative works. "In the studio" and a portrait of a young lady in pink are also among his popular canvases.

DUNLAP, MARY STEWART, (P.) b. in Ohio. Now resides in Pasadena, California. Her first art studies were in New York, after which she spent four years in Paris at the academies under Delecluse and Whistler. She sketched and painted in oil and water-color through Brittany and Normandy. Her work in Paris was followed by artistic pilgrimages to Rome and Florence. Returning to the United States she decided to make southern California her home.

"Her delineation is elusive to the point of impressionism; it is rather the spirit of a certain hour of a certain day that she wishes to record

.... Nature in Miss Dunlap's paintings does not necessarily mean a literal representation of natural objects .... Her work suggests rather that the color and the atmospheric transitions of nature are a worthier subject. In Pasadena she found a field for a wider diversity of material she is most desirous of interpreting—the portrayal of transient color effect." (Int Studio 45:sup xxiii)

DUVENECK, FRANK, (P., S., E., Mural P.) b. Covington, Ky., 1848; d. Covington, Ky., January 2, 1919. When eighteen years of age he was employed by a church decorator in Cincinnati and soon became an exceedingly valuable assistant. In 1870 he went to Munich and entered the Royal Academy. After three months' work in the antique class under Strahuber, he was admitted to the painting class of Prof. von Dietz. His progress was looked upon as phenomenal; he took all prizes of the academy from antique drawing to composition. In 1878 he opened a school of painting in Munich which became so popular that when he decided to go to Florence, nearly half of his pupils insisted on going with him; so he continued his classes in Florence and Venice for two years.

He received medals and honors of many kinds. He was elected member of the National Academy of Design, New York, in 1906. After returning to Cincinnati, he devoted much time to teaching a painting class in the Art Museum of that city.

Typical works are:

"Turkish page"   "The woman with forget-me-nots"
"Whistling boy"   "Venetian shrine"
"Man with ruff"   "Interior of St. Marks, Venice"
"Prof. Loefftz"

In addition to painting and etching, he did some remarkable work in sculpture, receiving an award in the salon for a monument he made to his wife. His mural decoration in the new Catholic cathedral, Covington, Ky., is spoken of as being a serious and dignified piece of work.

"Duveneck's works with the paint brush are, with few exceptions, distinctly paintings in the complete and full sense of the word, because they are emphatically made with paint and the paint brush and not drawn and colored. It is the expressive use of the paint brush itself that is a large factor in the artistic value of his work." (Arts & D 1:382)

Mr. Duveneck was awarded the special grand prize at the Panama-Pacific Exposition, 1915.

EAKINS, THOMAS, (P.) b. Philadelphia, Pa., July 25, 1844. Studied art in Philadelphia, at the Ecole des Beaux Arts, the Atelier Bonnat, and under Gérome and Dumont in Paris.

He has received many medals and prizes. Was elected a member of the National Academy of Design, New York, in 1902. Instructor in the Pennsylvania Academy of the Fine Arts.

Since his return to the United States he has taught in life classes, lectured as demonstrator of anatomy, and become professor of painting and director of the Pennsylvania Academy.

His pictures are very varied in their subjects. He has painted many small pictures of domestic scenes in the early days of America, of American sporting and athletic games, studies of the American negro character and also portraits.

"........ Eakins with a like grasp of the personality of his subjects and an even greater enjoyment of the picturesqueness of their attitudes and apparel, yet fails of the popular appreciation that he merits because of his neglect of the beauties and graces of painting— not the beauties and graces of his subjects." (Isham.)

"Cello player" and "Salutat" are finished paintings and better indicate his power as an artist than the "Dancing lesson" and portraits earlier exhibited. (Brush & P 6:130)

EATON, CHARLES HARRY, (P., I.) b. near Akron, O., December 13, 1850; d. Leonia, N. J., August 4, 1901. As a painter and illustrator, was self-taught. First exhibited at the National Academy of Design, New York, 1881. Received silver medal, Boston. Associate member of the National Academy of Design, 1893. Won the Evans prize in 1898 with his painting "The brook," and received the gold medal of the Art Club of Philadelphia for his "Willows" in 1900. "Lily pond" is another popular picture of his.

EATON, WYATT, (P.) b. Philipsburg, Province of Quebec, Canada, May 6, 1849. Studied art in New York at the National Academy of Design before going abroad in 1872. He spent a few weeks in London where he met Whistler, then went to Paris where he worked under Gérome; made the acquaintance of Millet, also Munkaczy. For four years his time was divided between Paris and Barbizon, in the forest of Fontainebleau.

In his "Hay makers" we trace the influence of Millet and Bastien-Lepage.

While in France he painted figure subjects, landscapes, and portraits, exhibiting in the salon of 1874 his "Reverie" and two years later his

"Harvesters at rest." In 1876 he returned to America and became a teacher in the life and antique classes in drawing at Cooper Institute and was active in the formation of the Society of American Artists.

Upon his return to America his first important works were life portraits of Bryant, Longfellow, Emerson, Whittier, and Holmes. His portrait of Mrs. R. W. Gilder and painting entitled "Man and violin" have an undisputed place among the best pictures produced in this country.

"His characteristic note was not strength but rather delicacy of feeling: feeling for tone and color in his "Reflection," feeling for grace in his little classic figures, feeling for character in the crayon heads that he did of Emerson and Holmes and Whittier and others." (Isham.)

EBERLE, ABASTENIA ST. LEGER, (S.) b. in Iowa, April 16, 1878. Studied sculpture with George Grey Barnard and Gutzon Borglum.

Miss Eberle was an accomplished musician, which line of artistic endeavors she abandoned for sculpture. There is a touch of mystery and grace prominent in her small works, as in "The dancer" where the wind of her movements draws her flying draperies against her body. This work was sold at the International exhibition in Venice, 1909. "Windy doorstep" won the Helen Foster Barnett prize. In "L'Isolée" we have the nude; in "Bacchante" a classic theme; and in "Indian Fighting Eagle" we see the aboriginal portrayed in a dramatic manner.

The rendering of motion especially appeals to Miss Eberle. She says: "If I were a painter, I would be an impressionist."

Her collaborations with Miss Anna Vaughn Hyatt have received commendation and praise from those qualified to pass upon their artistic merits.

Giles Edgerton says: "One of the most impersonal of the women sculptors is Miss Abastenia St. Leger Eberle. Her work does not suggest an effort to overcome a feminine point of view or to ape the masculine way of achievement. She just seems to present people, little children, old beggar women, Indians, more absolutely than individually."

She is interested in settlement work and in order to make herself thoroughly familiar with her chosen theme, she took an apartment in the most crowded tenement section of New York City where she could come into close contact with its teeming throng. Thus she is able to produce a host of realistic studies, full of life and charm, for the neighboring children who visit her studio become her unconscious models.

"Tired" has in it the story of a hard day's work. It is sympathetically conceived and powerfully executed.

"Ragpicker" gives the sombre aspect of her work.

"Playing jacks," "Shyness," "Her only brother," and "The little mother" are bits of sculpture that are making Miss Eberle famous.

In the startling realism of the "White slave" is presented all the sordidness and horror of that most hideous traffic. She contrasts youth, innocence, and shame.

"Her studies are based upon accurate and concrete observation. They fearlessly typify those social forces and ideals which are at the very root of society. They are free of thought-compelling power. She has a message for the world and she proclaims it in a way and with a convincing power that cannot fail to render her work immortal." (Art & Archaeol 6:91)

EDGERLY, MIRA (Countess Korzybska), (Min. P.) Although a native of California, the girlhood of this artist was spent in Jackson, Michigan, where her father was a well-known railroad official. The story of her artistic career is most interesting. Very early she showed ability in drawing faces. The hopes of her girlhood were realized when she went abroad to study. Through the advice of Sargent she decided to specialize in painting on ivory. Her success has been unusual for she has become famous as a painter of the royalty, nobility, and aristocracy of Europe and America.

During her early years in England she began to feel the limitations of ivory miniature work and sought another medium. Taking up the matter with Frank Brangwyn, the famous British artist, he said to her: "What matters it if your work is measured by feet or by inches? If your ideals are right you'll win the praise of us all."

As it is impossible to get a sheet of ivory more than five inches wide, Miss Edgerly puts on extensions like the wings of a triptych or border of a stained glass window; and while the painting is all done on ivory and of tiny dimensions, her work cannot be strictly classed as miniature painting.

In 1919 while in Washington, D. C., Miss Edgerly was married to Count Alfred de Skarbek Korzybska, a Polish officer who served as colonel on the staff of Grand Duke Nicholas of Russia.

Besides being a rare artist the countess is a remarkably magnetic woman and charming companion.

ELLIOTT, CHARLES LORING, (P.) b. Scipio, Cayuga Co., N. Y., December, 1812; d. Albany, N. Y., September 20, 1868. Became a pupil of Trumbull and painted portraits while still a young man; opened a studio in New York early in his career. Was elected associate member of the National Academy of Design in 1845, and full member in 1846. Is said to have painted more than seven hundred portraits of eminent people. At the exhibition of the National Academy in 1868-69 many of his paintings were shown, including:

"Don Quixote"
"Falstaff"
"Andrew Van Corlear, the trumpeter"
"The head of Skaneateles Lake" (the only landscape he ever painted)

Tuckerman says: "No one can mistake the rich tints and vigorous expression, the character and color which distinguish Elliott's portraits."

Elliott stands among the first American portrait painters, especially for old and character heads. His portrait of Fletcher Harper is considered by artists and critics to be a masterpiece, and the committee who selected American pictures to be sent to the Paris Exposition unanimously chose it as a typical and clever American portrait.

ELLIOTT, JOHN, (P., I., Mural P.) b. England, April 22, 1858. A student in the Julien Academy; also a pupil of Carolus Duran and of Jose de Villegas at Rome. While in Rome he painted his first important mural decoration, and occupying apartments with Mrs. Elliott's cousin, F. Marion Crawford, who had collected many death masks, he was fascinated with one of Dante. Two pictures of Dante in exile were the result; one of them now hangs in the living room of Queen Margherita of Italy, the other, in the home of Mrs. J. Montgomery Sears of Boston.

A pastel study of Dante thrown into a waste basket and rescued by Mrs. Elliott, is now better known than either of his paintings, and in reproduction has gone all over the world.

His great mural painting, "Diana of the tides," for the National Museum in Washington, D. C., was painted in Rome. "The vintage," frieze and ceilings in the home of Mrs. Potter Palmer, Chicago; and "The triumph of time," ceiling decoration for the children's room in the Boston Public Library, are his most notable mural decorations in America.

Twenty-four pastel drawings made to illustrate Mrs. Anderson's fairy tale "The great sea horse" were exhibited in America.

Of his portrait of Julia Ward Howe, it is said: "The picture is utterly simple .... It is tender, reverential, a sweet and solemn glorification of old age, and of the old age of a distinguished spirit." He said, "I was painting the author of "The battle hymn of the republic."

Mr. Elliott made the well-known silver-point portrait of the late King Humbert which Queen Margherita carries with her on all her journeys.
(Everybody's M 23:95)

Mr. Elliott has been honored with several decorations. (Arts & D 2:359)

ELWELL, FRANK EDWIN, (S.) b. Concord, Mass., June 15, 1859; d. Darien, Conn., January 23, 1922. Adopted by Louisa M. Alcott, with whom he first studied sculpture. Studied in the United States under Daniel Chester French, and in Paris at the Ecole des Beaux Arts under Jean Alexander Falguiere.

Mr. Elwell enjoys the distinction of being the first American sculptor who modeled in America a statue to be erected in Europe.

Best known works are:

"Death of strength," a monument at Edam, Holland
Bust of Lord Provost of Aberdeen at Aberdeen, Scotland
Equestrian statue of General Hancock at Gettysburg .
Monument to Edwin Booth at Mount Auburn, Cambridge, Mass.
Two fountains—"Ceres" and "Kronos"—at Pan-American Exposition
Statue of Dickens and Little Nell, Fairmount Park, Philadelphia
Busts of Levi P. Morton and Garret A. Hobart in the senate chamber at Washington, D. C.

Was associate editor of the Arena magazine and also compiler of the first history of American sculpture.

At an exhibition of the Cincinnati Art Club, of which Mr. Elwell is an honorary member, was shown his bronze statue, "The orchid." "A beautiful young woman in a dancing attitude is gracefully poised on one foot, which hardly seems to touch the earth. The upward action of the arms, the spring of the foot and the suggestive airiness of the drapery all tend to convey the idea that she is of the air, as is the orchid." (Brush & P 6:76)

The honorary title of colonel was bestowed upon him in recognition of his work in creating the statue called "The flag" erected as a monument to the Seventh Rhode Island Infantry at Vicksburg, Miss., and he was also decorated by the King of Belgium.

EMMET, LYDIA FIELD, (Min. P., I.)) b. New Rochelle, N. Y., 1866. Pupil of Bouguereau, Giacomotti, Robert-Fleury, Collin, and MacMonnies in Paris; Chase, Mowbray, Cox, and Robert Reid in New York. Associate member National Academy of Design, 1909. Won many prizes and medals.

"Miss Emmet's color is exquisite and her daring but positive use of vermilion is unusual. Nearly every one of her miniatures might be called a flower of portraiture, for these dainty things suggest gardens of lilies and lilacs." (Brush & P 6:26)

"She is a painter of aristocracy, of the American aristocracy, which is distinct from any other. Her women have intellect, her children health .... Miss Emmet has successfully conquered the matter of grouping before which so many other painters have met with disaster." (Guy du Bois)

"Olivia" won honorable mention at the last exhibition of the Carnegie Institute.

"Her child portraits invariably carry conviction and have pictorial charm .... Her brushwork is strong and her treatment of surfaces and textures adequate."

ENNEKING, JOHN JOSEPH, (P.) b. Minster, O., October 4, 1841; d. Boston, Mass., November 16, 1916. He early showed artistic inclinations although the son of a farmer. After serving in the Civil War he went to Boston and studied lithography. He went abroad in 1873 and studied both figure and landscape in Munich under Lehr. After a trip to Venice he went to Paris and studied for three years with Bonnat and Daubigny. Returning to the United States in 1876 he opened a studio in Boston. He was awarded many medals and prizes.

He excels in depicting New England landscapes and among his best works may be mentioned:

"Summer twilight"   "Calf in the lane"
"Cloudy day in summer" "The clam-digger"
"Indian summer"   "The brook"
"November twilight"   "Sheep and lambs"
"Mill pond, Milton   "After glow"
"December thaw"   "In apple blossom time"
"Red oak"

His earlier but much admired works are:

"Moonlight on the Giudecca"   "Farm yard scene in France"
"Venice"   "The Obersee" (considered by
"Freshly picked"   some to be his best)

"Mr. Enneking is a colorist, but not a riotous colorist. He does not startle, he satisfies .... He is acknowledged to have created, artistically speaking, the "November twilight."

He is one of the most individual of American painters, and withal one of the most developed and rounded of personalities. (Brush & P 10: 335)

Frederick W. Coburn says: "His ideal is the picture that shall be the perfect expression, not of a locality, but of a thought."

A memorial exhibition of Mr. Enneking's paintings was held recently in Boston and the American Art News says in part: "As they hang on the walls the pictures now show individually and as a whole why Enneking was so popular both as an artist and as a man. They are as markedly personal as he was, for in spite of the fact that he studied in Munich, and with Bonnat and Daubigny, there is not the slightest trace in his work of either of these teachers .... "After glow" .... shows the serenity of his outlook on nature, the simplicity of his themes, and the superb glow of his color! .... In "The red oak" he was quite at his best .... This canvas is the peer of "After glow" and "Autumn twilight."

His "Hush of autumn" is one of his most exquisite works and his "Rainy day in New England" is a harmony in pearly grays.

By many he was classed as an impressionist, but he disclaimed this. His paintings are known for their brilliancy of color.

EVANS, RUDULPH, (S.) b. Washington, D. C. A pupil of Falguière and Puech in Paris; is a member of the American Artists' Association of Paris.

Mr. Evans' work is more widely known abroad than at home. The French government has honored him by purchasing a replica of his "Golden hour" for the Luxembourg. The original figure—exhibited at the Paris salon—was cast in bronze to adorn the garden of Mr. F. A. Vanderlip at Scarborough, N. Y. The figure has been repeated again in marble for the Metropolitan Museum of New York.

"It has the repose of the Greek ideal, yet speaks of modernity .... The figure is modeled with deep appreciation of subtlety in curve and texture, and one feels by the eye alone the softness of flesh and the strength of construction. But above all this shines the glowing heart of young womanhood.

"The art of Rudulph Evans is one full of poetry, especially in portraiture. Particularly does he feel the delicate atmosphere of aloofness surrounding childhood, and this he imparts to the portraits." (Int Studio 55: sup lxxxiv)

Two charming busts of children are:

Granddaughter of James Stillman.
Granddaughter of Thomas F. Ryan.

EZEKIEL, MOSES JACOB, (S.) b. Richmond, Va., Oct. 28, 1844; d. Rome, Italy, March 27, 1917. Graduated at the Virginia Military Institute in 1866; studied anatomy at the Medical college of Virginia. In 1869 he went to Europe, entering the Royal Academy of Art in Berlin and remaining there until 1871, working later in the studio of Prof. Albert Wolf.

In 1872 he was admitted into the Society of Artists, Berlin, on the merits of a colossal bust of "Washington," and in 1873 with his "Israel" he gained the Michaelbeer prize, a stipendium for two years study and residence in Italy. He was the first foreigner to win this prize.

The Emperor of Germany and the Grand Duke of Saxe-Meiningen have conferred upon him the cavalier crosses for merit in art and science; the King of Italy bestowed on him the cross of an "Officer of the Crown of Italy"; he won the gold medal of the Royal Association in Palermo; the Raphael medal at Urbino; and was a member of the Societies of Artists in Berlin and Rome, and of the Academy of Raphael in Urbino.

After 1874 he resided in Rome, where his studio itself was a notable place.

Mr. Ezekiel's first important work, a marble group representing "Religious Liberty," is now in Fairmount Park, Philadelphia. His "Thomas Jefferson" is in Louisville, Ky., and a series of eleven statues of famous artists, in Carrara marble, decorate the Corcoran Gallery of Art, Washington, D. C.

The development of patriotic themes was a specialty of this sculptor. "It is probable that in sounding this greatest and best chord of human nature, patriotism, Sir Moses Ezekiel touches and holds his highest level." (W Work 19:12255)

He made many busts of beautiful women scattered throughout Europe and America, but none really so perfect as that of the Dowager Queen of Italy. His "Napoleon" is a notable work. The late F. Marion Crawford called it the history of Napoleon, and Cesareo, the Sicilian poet and art critic, writes of it: "Rarely or never has the tragedy of Napoleon been signified with more severe sorrow, with such intense truth, with more heroic grief, than in the sculpture of Ezekiel."

Liszt, who had a personal acquaintance with all the best artists of Rome, selected Ezekiel to make his portrait-bust for the Academy of Music at Pesth. Cardinal Hohenlohe, an intimate friend of Liszt, also an authority on art, after having viewed the work critically, turned to it again on leaving the room, and said, "Adieu, Liszt! I thus hand thee down to posterity."

An Italian publication, "Publica Opinione," closes a critical review of

Mr. Ezekiel's works with these words: "We conclude this brief notice by expressing our admiration of the great American sculptor in whom we feel Italian pride because his genius was cultured beneath our sky, and was inspired by our great men to become more great."

The statue of Edgar Allan Poe, which stands at the entrance to Wymans Park, Baltimore, and which was unveiled in 1921, was the last work of this sculptor. It is of bronze on a marble base and was completed in his studio at Rome in 1917 but its delivery was delayed on account of the war. On his last visit to his native country Sir Moses was commissioned to execute the Confederate Soldiers' monument in the Arlington National Cemetery which serves in a measure as his tomb, for his request to be buried among his old confederate comrades was granted and with fitting ceremonies his body was placed there on March 30, 1921.

FAIRBANKS, AVARD, (S.) b. Salt Lake, Utah. As a child he camped in the mountains with his father and brother and came to know much about wild animals. He was also much impressed with the stories of pioneer experiences with Indians. He first modeled in clay his pet rabbit, and when fourteen years of age his "Indian scout" and "Pony express" won for him the title, "Boy wonder in sculpture."

Crowds gathered around him in the Zoological Park, New York City, as he placed his modeling stand against the cages to study and model the animals. Before he was fifteen he won two scholarships at the Art Students' League; the first for his "Fighting pumas," and the second for his "Study of fighting panthers." The committee agreed that his drawing was crude and his composition defective, but the *action* reproduced in animals was so lifelike that the prizes were bestowed upon him. At sixteen his ability as a sculptor was recognized by expert critics; and at nineteen he was the sensation of artistic Paris as he studied and worked at the art schools there.

Of his "Pony express" an enthusiastic critic writes: "So lifelike was the figure that one could readily hear in imagination the clatter of the pony's hoof as he leaped in swift bounds along the rocky trail that skirted the base of the mountains." (Tech W 22:204)

FARNHAM, SALLY JAMES (Mrs. Paulding Farnham), (S.) b. Ogdensburg, New York. · Self taught.

As a young girl Sally James traveled extensively with her father in foreign countries. When in Paris she was attracted by certain works of sculpture in the Louvre more than by the gay shops and alluring boulevards, although not inclined to an artistic career. Years later, after marrying and becoming the mother of two children, while convalescing from a serious illness she amused herself (through the suggestion of a friend) with modeling clay. Upon her complete recovery she engaged a studio and took up the profession of sculpture without any instruction or preparation. Frederic Remington encouraged Mrs. Farnham more than any one else. Her first order was for a fountain and it brought her a $5,000 check.

Big public works by Mrs. Farnham which have been highly praised by the critics are fountains in Baltimore, Md.; Soldiers' monument of Ogdensburg, New York; one in Bloomfield, New Jersey; two large monuments in Rochester, New York; a bas-relief of General Chaffee on horseback to be placed at Arlington Cemetery, Washington, D. C.; and the bronze frieze in the Pan-American Building, Washington, D. C., which is regarded as one of the most notable of its kind that has been done in the United States, and has attracted the commendations of the best critics of this country, Europe, and Latin America.

When Venezuela decided to place in Central Park, New York City, a monument to Simon Bolivar, the George Washington of South America, as a gift from that country to the United States, twenty leading sculptors entered into competition for the commission. The model selected by the representatives of the Venezuelan government was the one submitted by Sally James Farnham, this unschooled, self-taught artist, matured in years, married, and the mother of two children before she did her first modeling. The bronze equestrian statue is the largest work by a woman which history anywhere records, and it is the second statue by a woman sculptor to be erected in New York City, the other being the beautiful statue of Joan of Arc on Riverside Drive, by Anna V. Hyatt. On April 19, 1921, the monument was unveiled with fitting ceremony in Central Park, New York City. On the same day at Caracas, Venezuela, two parks were christened Washington and Clay, in honor of George Washington and Henry Clay.

Mrs. Farnham has made a special study of Latin-American history and "has shown in her modeling of the Bolivar statue a sympathy with the spirit of Bolivar's environment and an appreciation of his character and personality."

FARNY, HENRY, (P.) A native of Alsace, he was born in Ribeauville in 1847; d. in Cincinnati, O., December 24, 1916. His family came to this country in 1853, and later took up their home in Cincinnati where his father died in 1865.

His first efforts in art were decorations on water coolers. Afterwards became a designer for lithographs, one of his widely known productions of that period being a caricature of the escape of Jefferson Davis.

In 1867 he went to New York and entered the employ of Harper and Brothers; later he worked his passage to Europe in a sailing vessel. In Rome he met Regnault, who engaged him to make the sketches which appeared in Francis Wey's elaborate work on Rome.

Being a Frenchman by birth, Farny was admitted to fellowship of the French artists in Rome. Went to Düsseldorf, where he became the pupil of Munkaczy. Returning to America in 1870, and being unsuccessful in disposing of his paintings executed abroad, he was compelled to gain support by making designs for the large showbills used by circus companies. Later gained considerable reputation as a cartoonist.

In 1878 in company with Duveneck, Dengler, and Twachtman he again went to Munich and there gained honorable mention in the competition for composition.

For many years he was chiefly engaged in Cincinnati in designing illustrations for school books and magazines.

Farny was most successful in his delineation of Indian life and character; in this field he did pioneer work. A popular specimen is "Song of the talking wire."

"The silent guest" is perhaps the best of his works in oil.

FARRER, HENRY, (E.) b. London, England, March 23, 1843; d. Brooklyn, N. Y., February 24, 1903. He came to America when he was nineteen years of age. His first serious attempts at etching were made about 1868. Necessity compelled him for a time to abandon etching for more lucrative pursuits, but at the formation of the New York Etching Club in 1877, he again took up the work.

In 1879 he became secretary to the American Water Color Society and in 1881 president of the New York Etching Club. Was elected in 1882 a fellow of the Royal Society of Painter-Etchers, London, and in 1885 honorary member of the Philadelphia Society of Painter-Etchers.

Among the best known of Mr. Farrer's earlier works was a series of eleven plates illustrative of "Old New York." These plates have been withdrawn from publication.

His most important and interesting plates are:

"Old oak tree, twilight"	"On the marshes"
"Chickens"	"Twilight"
"The washerwoman"	"October"
"A cloudy day"	"Sunset"
"A November day"	"Winter"
"Twilight on the creek"	"Staten Island shore"

"December"   "On New York Bay"
"Sunset, Coast of Maine"   "Sandy Hook light"
"Winter in the woods"   "A shady spot on a sunny road"
"Old house by the roadside"   "Sunset on East River"
"On the beach at Bay Ridge"
(American Art Review, 1880)

FENN, HARRY, (P., I., E.) b. Richmond, England, September 14, 1845; d. Montclair, N. Y., April 21, 1911. At the age of nineteen he came to America, ostensibly to see Niagara Falls. He remained in this country for six years then went to Italy to study. Shortly after his return to the United States he illustrated his first book, Whittier's "Snowbound," which was soon followed by the "Ballads of New England." These were the first illustrated gift books produced in this country and marked an era in the history of bookmaking. In 1870 he made an extended tour of the United States to gather material for "Picturesque America."

He was one of the founders of the American Water Color Society, a member of the New York Water Color Club, the Society of Illustrators and the Salmagundi Club. (American Art Annual, Vol. 9)

FISHER, HARRISON, (I.) b. Brooklyn, N. Y., July 27, 1875. He manifested artistic inclinations at the age of six and was early instructed in drawing and painting by his father, who was an artist. His family removed to San Francisco and he studied at the Mark Hopkins Institute of Art. At sixteen he did drawing for a San Francisco newspaper. Two sketches accepted by the editor of "Puck" secured him a staff position. Later he did serial work for the "Saturday Evening Post," and went abroad for material to furnish the pictorial part of some articles for McClure's magazine. He has illustrated for "Life," "Ladies' Home Journal," Scribner's, etc.

The creator of the "Fisher girl" it has been estimated has turned out of hand more than a thousand studies of the American girl.

"In a personal way he reflects a boyish sincerity with a philosophic regard to essentials." (Bookm 11:140)

FISHER, (WILLIAM) MARK, (P.) b. Boston, Mass., 1841; d. London, April 29, 1923. Of English and Irish parents, educated in Boston public schools; studied art at Lowell Institute; later was a pupil of George Inness at Medfield. At twenty he went to Paris and studied in Gleyre's atelier. Later he married and returned to his native city but he had small success in Boston and decided to try his fortunes in England. He chose the Essex country for his adopted home and became very distinguished in Great Britain as a landscape and animal painter. Making the peaceful pastures and little villages of this pastoral section of England the subject of his canvases, he exhibited regularly in London and identified himself with the independent group of young artists.

He was a member of the New English Art Club and president of the Essex Art Club. In 1919 he was made full member of the Royal Academy, thus receiving the highest honors an artist can receive in England.

Two of his paintings are now in the Chantrey collection at the Tate Gallery, and four of his paintings have been accepted for this year's Royal Academy exhibition. His works are in the finest public and private collections. He won medals at the Paris, Chicago, and St. Louis expositions.

George Moore in "Modern painting" says: "Mark Fisher's painting is optimistic. His skies are blue, his sunlight dozes in the orchard, his chestnut trees are in bloom. The melodrama of nature never appears in his pictures; his lanes and fields reflect a gentle mind that has found happiness in observing the changes of the seasons."

His best known paintings are:

"The meadows"	"A Scotch hillside"
"On the Cam"	"Early summer"
"Noon"	"Evening"
"A canal jump on the Oise"	"Vision of the sea"

"The human interest meant little if anything except in his portraits .... It was a landscape that absorbed him, but not as a mere background .... The landscape was the thing and if he did introduce figures with it, it was because they belonged just as the cattle and the sheep and fowls belonged .... On no other canvas did the sunlight filter through the trees just as it did in his." (London correspondent.)

FLAGG, JAMES MONTGOMERY, (I., P.) b. Pelham Manor, Westchester Co., N. Y., June 18, 1877. Educated in New York public schools; Dr. Chapin's private school; studied at Art Students' League, New York; four years in Herkomer's Art School, Bushey, England; and also under Victor Maree in Paris. Became illustrator for St. Nicholas magazine, 1890; has been drawing for "Judge" and "Life" since 1892; illustrator for the various magazines. Painted portraits in Paris, 1900; also in St. Louis and New York. Exhibited portraits in the Paris salon of 1900; also portraits in oil and water color in National Academy of Design and New York Water Color Club. Life member of the Lotus Club.

FOOTE, WILL HOWE, (P.) b. Grand Rapids, Michigan, June 29, 1874. Pupil of the Art Institute, Chicago; Art Students' League of New York; Julien Academy under Laurens and Benjamin Constant in Paris. Received honorable mention at the Pan-American Exposition, Buffalo, 1901; third Hallgarten prize, National Academy of Design, 1902; bronze medal at St. Louis Exposition, 1904. Member Paris American Art Association. Instructor at Art Students' League of New York.

FORBES, EDWIN, (P., E.) b. New York, 1839; d. Brooklyn, N. Y., March 6, 1895. Began the study of art in 1857 and two years later became pupil of A. F. Tait. At first devoted himself to animal painting; afterwards gave more attention to genre and landscape. During the Civil War he was a special artist of Frank Leslie's Illustrated newspaper, and his studies of battle scenes were done in etchings, he being the first etcher in America. These etchings, called "Life studies of the great army," have a value as a record of military life during the Civil War. General Sherman bought the first proofs of these sketches for the U. S. government, and they are now in the war department, Washington.

The most noted are:

"The reliable contraband"   "Coming through the lines"
"The sanctuary"   "A night march"
"Returning from picket duty" "The reveille"

In New York in 1865 he produced "Lull in the fight." This picture contains thirty figures and represents a scene in the battle of the wilderness.

In 1878 he established a studio in Brooklyn, N. Y., and devoted himself mainly to landscape and cattle pieces.

Honorary member London Etching Club.

FOSTER, BEN, (P.) b. North Anson, Maine, July 31, 1852. When eighteen years of age he went to New York where he was employed in mercantile business until he was about thirty, when he decided to devote himself to art.

Studied with Abbott Thayer and at the Art Students' League of New York. Went to Paris in 1886 and continued his studies under Olivier Merson and Aime Morot; exhibited in the Paris salon; returned to New York in 1887; regularly represented at the exhibitions. Associate member National Academy of Design, 1901; full member, 1904.

Mr. Foster has given much attention to the painting of landscapes and sheep; his favorite subjects are night effects and woodland scenes.

His compositions are marked by a large feeling of unity. "He treats a morsel of landscape, but as a part of the big mysterious scheme of things." (Artist 29: sup xx)

Among his most important works in oil are:

"A dreary road"   "Fontainebleau forest."
"A Maine hillside"   "First days in spring"
"All in a misty moonshine"   "A windy night"
"The evening star"   "Now the day is over"
"A wet day in the pines"   "Sunset in the Litchfield Hills"
"In the Green Mountains"

Also in water colors:

"The day is done"
"The laggard"
"The shepherd"

His painting, "Lulled by the murmuring stream," exhibited at the Paris Exposition, 1900, was purchased by the French government for the Luxembourg Gallery.

In the autumn of 1900 he was awarded the silver medal and the $1,000 at the Carnegie Institute, Pittsburgh, for "Misty moonlight," and in the spring 1901, at the exhibition of the Society of American Artists, he was awarded the Webb prize for the most meritorious landscape painted by an American.

FOURNIER, ALEXIS JEAN, (P., I.) b. St. Paul, Minn., July 4, 1865. At the age of fifteen, ambitious to accomplish something with brush and color, he found employment in a Minneapolis sign shop; soon after this he engaged to assist in scene-painting. In the fall of 1893 he went to France and entered the Académie Julien, Paris; studied also under Jean Paul Laurens, Benjamin-Constant, Gustav Courtois, and Henri Harpignies.

One of his earliest paintings, "A spring morning near Minnehaha Creek," was exhibited in the salon of 1894. Of his last painting, exhibited in the salon and which was hung next to a Gérome, the Figaro commenting on its merits, said that it was one of the best paintings in the room.

In the summer of 1907 Mr. Fournier went to the village of Barbizon, France, to paint the studios and homes of the great French painters known as the "Men of 1830." These canvases, which are full of the atmosphere and spirit of the place, are:

"Studio of Millet"   "River Oise—Daubigny's house-
"Home of Diaz"   boat"
"Dupre's studio"   "Corot's home"
"Rousseau's cottage"

Other characteristic works are:

"Moonlight on the lagoons"   "Peaceful night, Normandy"
"Old orchard, Normandy"   "Sunset after rain" (particularly
"When golden evening fades"   noteworthy)
"The shepherd's return"

His "Crepuscule" exhibited in the Paris salon is called perfect in tone.

"He is not a painter of ideal scenery but a painter of nature, interpreting her moods with a true poetic feeling. He believes the mission of a painter of out-of-doors is to show Nature in her fine moods—her harmony and music, as it were." (Brush & P 4:243)

FOWLER, FRANK, (P., I.) b. Brooklyn, N. Y., July 12, 1852; d. New Canaan, Conn., August 18, 1910. Pupil of Edwin White in America, and Carolus-Duran and Ecole des Beaux Arts in Paris. Received bronze medal, Paris Exposition, 1889; bronze medal, Pan-American Exposition, 1901. Elected a member of the National Academy of Design, New York, in 1900; member of the Society of American Artists, 1882. Specialty, portraits; among his noteworthy portraits are those of Governor Tilden, Governor Flowers, William Dean Howells, and Madame Modjeska. Mr. Fowler is also a teacher and the author of several works on art, among them being "Portrait and figure painting."

FRASER, JAMES EARLE, (S.) b. Winona, Minn., November 4, 1876. When eighteen years of age he entered the Art Institute at Chicago and six months later went to Paris to enter the Ecole des Beaux Arts. His work in the salon exhibit of 1897-98 not only won the prize offered to American artists but so impressed Saint-Gaudens who was a member of the committee of awards that he wrote to the young sculptor. The result was that Fraser went to Saint-Gaudens, returned to the United States with him in 1900, and worked with him until 1902 when he established himself in New York. At present he has the distinction of being the oldest resident in the artists' colony in Macdougal Alley, and he is an instructor at the Art Students' League. Mr. Fraser is, perhaps, the first among the successful pupils of the late Augustus Saint-Gaudens.

Helen Christine Bennett writes (Arts & D 1:375) : "The relief of the Whitney children upon their horses is particularly attractive .... The bust of Cornelius V. Whitney is that of a very handsome boy to whom the sculptor has done justice. The head of June Evans, especially in profile, shows great delicacy in handling and a certain subdued piquancy of expression which indicates a depth of treatment not shown in the other two."

A relief of Horatio Hathaway Brewster was the first relief portrait done by Mr. Fraser which caught the popular fancy. A bust of Col. Roosevelt shows not only skillful but powerful treatment. The statue of Alexander Hamilton is "a study of character conceived from within." An impression of Mary Garden as "Melisande" reveals a poetic side of the work of the sculptor. "End of the trail"—a memorial to the American Indian—was one of the most popular works on the grounds of the Panama-Pacific Exposition, 1915. It now stands in the Presidio, at San Francisco, at the end of the Lincoln Highway, the great trans-continental trail of the United States. "In a single statue he has perpetuated the pathos, the tragedy, the hopeless end of a vanquished race—the North American Indian."

Mr. Fraser knows the Indian very well, for his early life was spent in the western country.

The memorial to the Swedish-American inventor, John Ericsson, to be erected in Washington, D. C., was given to Mr. Fraser. The design represents Ericsson seated at the square base of the monument, sur-mounting which are three symbolic figures—"Vision," "Adventure," "Labor"—grouped around the Norse mythological tree, "Yggdrasil", typifying the mind and genius of the man.

As a designer of medals Mr. Fraser has few equals in the United States. He also designed the United States five-cent piece known as the "Buffalo nickel."

FRENCH, DANIEL CHESTER, (S.) b. Exeter, N. H., April 20, 1850. Was educated in his native town and at Cambridge, Amherst, and Boston, Mass. At the age of eighteen he began to model and his efforts met with encouragement from Louisa M. Alcott who suggested that he seek sys-tematic instruction. His first subjects were animals, portrait reliefs, and busts of friends. He attended Dr. Rimmer's lectures on artistic anatomy and studied the antique sculptures in the Boston Athenaeum. He is honorary president of the National Sculpture Society; was elected an associate member of the National Academy of Design in 1900; full member in 1901.

Mr. French received his commission for the "Concord Minute-man" when he was twenty-three years of age. This was finished in 1874 and he then went abroad for the first time. He studied two years in Florence with the American sculptor Thomas Ball. In 1886 he again went abroad, this time to Paris where he drew from the models in the class of M. Léon Glaize. Since his return to the United States in 1887 he has permanently resided in New York. Received honorable A. M., Dartmouth, 1898. Associate member National Academy of Design, 1900; full member, 1901.

Busts of Ralph Waldo Emerson and Bronson Alcott, a frieze representing Greeks carrying offerings, and several portraits in the round, low and high reliefs are his early works.

In collaboration with Mr. Edward Clark Potter, Mr. French has produced three equestrian statues of high value: "Washington," presented to France by the Daughters of the Revolution, placed in the Place d'Lena, Paris; "General Grant" in Fairmount Park, Philadelphia; and "General Joseph Hooker" in Boston.

Mr. French's monumental architectural reliefs are distinguished specimens of this new phase of art. "Death and the sculptor"—the Milmore memorial—won him a medal in the Paris salon of 1891. The John Boyle O'Reilly memorial, Boston, is a work of rare strength and beauty. In the "Alice Freeman Palmer memorial," Wellesley College, executed in Carrara marble, the technical details have been rarely wrought. The "Gallaudet group" at Washington, D. C., is one of his most pleasing portrait monuments. His imposing "Alma mater" now adorns the approach of the Library of Columbia University, New York, and he furnished two monumental groups for the Cleveland, Ohio, federal building.

Other important creations are: A. R. Meyer monument, Kansas City; Francis Parkman monument, Boston; Melvin memorial monument, Concord, Mass.; Hunt memorial, New York; Marshall Field memorial, Chicago; "Spirit of life," Trask memorial, Saratoga, N. Y.; statue of Emerson, Concord, Mass.; statues of General Cass, John Harvard, Rufus Choate, and Governor Oglethorpe of Georgia; bust of Phillips Brooks; the well-remembered "Statue of the Republic" at the Columbian Exposition, 1893; and the bronze doors of the Boston Public Library. His statue of Lafayette stands before Lafayette College, Easton, Pennsylvania. It is similar to the one in Prospect Park, Brooklyn, N. Y., but much more effective. At the dedication the degree of LL. D. was bestowed on the sculptor.

The most important object in the Lincoln Memorial at Washington, D. C., is Mr. French's statue of Lincoln. It is colossal in size and yet distinctly personal. Made of Georgia marble, twenty-five feet in height, the statue was cut in marble by the Piccirilli brothers, and it took four years to complete the construction. Mr. French worked personally on the marble.

FRIESEKE, FREDERIC CARL, (P., Mural P.) b. Owosso, Mich., April 7, 1874. Studied at Chicago Art Institute and in Paris under Benjamin-Constant, Laurens, and Whistler. Exhibits in Europe and America. In 1904 one of his pictures, "Before the glass," was purchased by the French government for the Luxembourg Gallery. He is also represented in the Modern Gallery in Vienna; is the possessor of a gold medal from Munich and won a prize from the Corcoran Gallery of Art, Washington, D. C. At the Panama-Pacific Exposition, 1915, was awarded the grand prize for oil painting. In 1908 he was elected sociétarie of the Société Nationale des Beaux Arts, Paris, since which time his works are accepted by the salon without the inspection of a jury. In 1912 he was elected an associate member of the National Academy of Design, New York City; full member in 1914.

Among Mr. Frieseke's figure subjects his decorative canvas "Youth" illustrates the firmness of his modeling, and "The Chinese parasol" and "The girl with bird cage" are also typical examples of his work.

Other popular paintings are:

"The green sash"   "Repose at noonday"
"Misty morn"   "Among the hollyhocks"
"Lady on a gold couch"   "Autumn"
"Breakfast in the garden" "The toilet"
"The yellow room"

"One strong feature, more pleasing in the work of Frieseke than in that of many other members of the American colony in Paris, is his sense of design and balance." (Int Studio 43:273)

Brilliant sunshine has been his particular study for several years. He delights in rendering effects of sunlight upon green foliage.

Clara MacChesney in writing of the work of this artist, says: "The charm of Frieseke is in the light and color of his canvas. His color is purer and higher in key but lacks the mystery of Aman-Jean's. His pictures are more crowded as to composition, but decorative in design like Blanche's. Brilliant garden scenes, palpitating with light and color, landscapes, interiors representing intimate scenes of the toilet or pictures of nude women, and mural decorations form his chief line of work .... He knows nothing about flowers and cares less, nor does he make a careful study of them nor of different kinds of gardens, but his one idea is to portray the dazzle of light and of color of flowers seen in sunlight."

Among Mr. Frieseke's later works are:

"Afternoon tea," recently shown at the Anglo-American exhibition in London; "At the seashore," (painted in the brilliant sunshine of Corsica), one of the fascinating exhibits in the Salon of 1913; "Summer," a marvel of execution (a reclining figure in a blaze of sunlight); "A girl sewing," an interior subject.

As a mural decorator he is best known for his large decorations at John Wanamaker's store in New York. Of his decorations in Hotel Shelbourne, Atlantic City, also of his mural painting in the Rodman Wanamaker Hotel and the Amphitheater of Music, New York, a correspondent and art critic says: "Frieseke's decorations are subdued and harmonious."

One of Frieseke's recently exhibited canvases is called "Morning room." It is a group portrait of two children and a rabbit. The "powdery" dressing room is very interesting and the production takes its own place in the long scroll of twentieth century achievements.

His "Dancer," a small version of the boudoir scenes he treats so delightfully, attracted much attention recently in France, and "Prima della rappresentazione" gained him recognition in Paris as one of the first ten American painters.

He won the grand prize at the Panama-Pacific Exposition in San Francisco in 1915, and in 1920 was made Chevalier of the Legion of Honor, the highest honor that the French government can confer on an artist.

For many years his canvases have hung in the Salon of the Société des Beaux Arts in Paris. Mr. Frieseke lives in France and has a charming home at Giverny.

FRISHMUTH, HARRIET WHITNEY, (S.) b. Philadelphia, Pennsylvania, September 17, 1880. A pupil of Rodin and Injalbert in Paris and Gutzon Borglum in New York.

Miss Frishmuth is a clever sculptor of unusual skill in the modeling of the nude. She has made many very beautiful designs for sundials. Her favorite model, the dancer Desha, posed for her bronze fountain called "The joy of the waters." The "Globe sundial" is one of her finest accomplishments. "Ecstasy" was awarded the National Arts Club prize in 1919, and at the Panama-Pacific Exposition she received honorable mention for her "Saki" sundial. Her "Morning, noon, and night" sundial is at Englewood, N. J.

FROMUTH, CHARLES HENRY, (P.) b. Philadelphia, Pa., February 23, 1861. Pupil of the Pennsylvania Academy of the Fine Arts under Thomas Eakins. Received second class gold medal at the International Exposition of the Fine Arts, Munich, 1897; silver medal, Paris Exposition, 1900; gold medal, St. Louis Exposition, 1904. Associate Société Nationale des Beaux Arts, Paris; Member London Pastel Society; Société des Peintures de Marine, Paris; Berlin Secession Society of Painters. Specialty, marines.

The English Illustrated Magazine for April, 1912, refers to Mr. Fromuth as "an artist of undisputed distinction, recently acknowledged to be the leading pastel painter in the world...."

"The works of this master of pastel are nearly all scenes in harbor and groups of sardine boats painted under varying conditions of light."

"Mr. Fromuth's pictures reveal his extraordinary knowledge of wave movement and cloud form, his sensitiveness to light and shade and his complete mastery of color and effect .... When a painter names his pictures "Fluid water at evening," "The mirror of the storm," "Harbor waters caressed by overhead clouds," "In the jungle of the sardine fleet," etc., we feel that the subjects are chosen for their spiritual meaning as well as their pictorial message."

FROST, ARTHUR BURDETT, (I.) b. Philadelphia, Pa., January 17, 1851. He began his career in a wood-engraver's establishment and later took up lithography, at the same time devoting his evenings to the study of drawing. In 1872 he furnished a number of illustrations for "Out of the hurly-burly" by Charles Heber Clarke, which was very successful, and since then he has illustrated works by various authors. Frank B. Stockton (whose works he illustrated) said of him: "By nature Mr. Frost is essentially a humorist."

In 1877 he went to England to study and work, but preferring American life and atmosphere, returned in 1878.

As a chronicler of phases of American life he has been called the Mark Twain of the illustrators.

"His compositions are apparently done so easily, he realizes his scenes so perfectly himself and is so convincing in his placing of the accent that one has no hesitation in saying that it is that of a cheerful, healthy optimism bred in sunny American country life."

"In his execution, he relies mainly upon sketches on white paper and an equal distribution of parallel-tint and cross-hatch shading."

"How wonderful it is that week in and week out, drawing a hundred landscapes to Ruysdael's one, a hundred tramps to Callot's and Ostade's one, he is able to suggest so vividly the effect of sunlight upon distant meadow, and the homely poses of what, were America the old world, would be called the peasant class." (Knaufft.)

"No one else drawing animals realistically can make them so truly funny." (Ind 59:1397)

FRY, JOHN HENNING, (P.) b. Indiana. Studied with Bouguereau and Lefebvre in Paris; also studied in Rome.

His work is little known in this country but a recent exhibition of his paintings was held in New York.

Mr. Fry has been called a modernizer of the Greek ideal. His subjects are the legends of the classics.

"He paints his women heroically and with a plastic sense that is rare."

"Though avoiding a high-keyed palette, Fry is a strong colorist, obtaining strong dramatic effects by simple untrained methods." (Int Studio 58: sup xi)

Representative works are:

"The eternal drift"	"Seafoam"
"Thetis"	"Oceanites"
"Dryad"	"Paolo and Francesca"

FRY, SHERRY EDMUNDSON, (S.) b. Creston, Ia., September 29, 1879. A pupil of the Art Institute, Chicago, under Taft; also studied with Mac-Monnies in Paris. An associate member of the National Academy of Design, 1914, and the National Sculpture Society.

Mr. Fry received honorable mention at the Paris salon, 1906; medal, salon of 1908; scholarship American Academy at Rome, 1908-11.

Best known works:

"Indian chief," Oskaloosa, Ia.

"Au soliel" fountain, Toledo Museum of Art

"Turtle" fountain, Mount Kisco, N. Y.

"Victory compelling peace," memorial fountain to the late Major Clarence F. Barrett.

"His art is very complete. For sheer beauty of form his sculptures would be difficult to surpass." (Cent 90:198)

All the sculpture on Festival Hall, Panama-Pacific Exposition, 1915, was made by Mr. Fry. The "Boy Pan" was the most popular statue of the many figures symbolizing the moods of music.

Mr. Fry first became famous for his studies of western Indians.

FULLER, GEORGE, (P.) b. Deerfield, Mass., January 16, 1822; d. Boston, Mass., March 21, 1884. Studied in New York, Boston, London, and on the continent of Europe. He was made associate of the National Academy of Design, New York, in 1853; but his painting was unremunerative and on the death of his father he took up farming. After fifteen years of farm life, he went to Boston and found purchasers for his paintings, meeting with success as a professional artist.

"The berry pickers" placed him among the first painters of the world and to his "Romany girl" he owes his greatest renown. Among his best works are: "Winifred Dysart," "Turkey pasture," and "She was a witch."

A memorial exhibition of his works at the Museum of Fine Arts, Boston, 1884, comprised 175 paintings, of which the following are best known:

"Cupid"	"Puritan boy"
"Romany girl"	"Fagot gathering"
"The quadroon"	"Arethusa"
"Nydia"	"Negro nurse with child"
"Turkey pasture"	"Shearing the donkey"
"Pasture with geese"	"Maidenhood"
"Fedalma"	"Driving home the calf"
"Evening—Lorette"	"Priscilla"
"At the bars"	"Twilight on prairie"
"Hannah"	"Girl and calf"
"Psyche"	"Portrait of Henry B. Fuller"
"Berry pickers"	

"He was preeminently an idealist, possessed of a genius for dreamy light effects, somewhat akin to Corot's." (Nat Cyc Am Biog)

"The soul of his art was selection .. He believed the province of art is to call attention to the beauties of nature, not to insist upon the defects, the deformities, and the vulgarities of man or nature .... He never painted a brutal head. If he saw brutality he did not like it and would not represent it." (F. D. Millet, Harper's 69:517)

His "Fedalma," heroine of George Eliot's dramatic poem, "The Spanish gypsy," was sold in 1922 for over $40,000; and a few months later "A gatherer of simples," another famous painting, brought even a higher price. The highest sale record for a work by Fuller previously known was $15,000.

FULLER, LUCIA FAIRCHILD, (Mrs. Henry B. Fuller), (Min. P.) b. Boston, Mass., December 6, 1872. Received bronze medal at the Paris Exposition, 1900; silver medal at Pan-American Exposition, Buffalo, 1901.

Is member of the Society of American Artists. Was elected associate member of the National Academy of Design, New York, 1906.

Mrs. Fuller stands side by side with Miss Laura Coombs Hills in method and in nature of results. "With her women and with her children she swings into play all the tenderness of drawing and all the fascination of transparent flesh tones." (Critic 47:524)

"Her portraits relate to the olden times when the art flourished under the masters who created it and her technique is above reproach."

"Portrait of a child" is in the Metropolitan Museum of New York City. This charming masterpiece is "A little girl standing in her nightgown caressing her doll. In this the color scheme is delicate throughout—in the tender pearly flesh and the pale blue background." (Mentor 4:9)

Her "Mother and child" from a background of blue brocade, beautified by age into faded purple .... recalls the feeling that touches the heart in Della Robbia's babies. (Cent 60:820)

"Mrs. Fuller's achievements are achievements" and her "Portrait of a boy" is splendidly painted, "soft and rich in color and of a simplicity equal to the drawings by Boutet de Monvel, withal of greater depth." (Gardner C. Teall, Brush & P 6:26)

Successful imaginative figure compositions are:

"In the days of King Arthur"
"The Chinese jacket"

Her "Artemidora" at the twelfth annual exhibition of the American Society of Mural Painters, shows a full appreciation of the beauty and purity of the material on which the miniaturist works. Alice T. Searle says: "In this nude study of a woman's figure of classic beauty in an unusual pose, the delicacy and sensitiveness of line in the drawing was suggestive of an etching with a slight staining of color over the whole."

Mrs. Fuller charms and delights the lover of miniature.

FULLER, META VAUX WARRICK, (S.) b. Philadelphia, Pa., June 9, 1877. A descendant of slaves, Mrs. Fuller was a few years ago regarded as the leading woman sculptor in the United States. She is proud of her ancestry. Her great, great grandmother was an African princess who was brought to this country in a slave ship and sold to a wealthy family.

While a pupil in the School of Industrial Art, Philadelphia, Miss Warrick won a scholarship abroad. In Paris she worked three years in the Colarossi Academy and studied with Injalbert in the Ecole des Beaux Arts. She came in contact with Saint-Gaudens who suggested that she join Raphael Collins' life class. After six months with Collins she worked from casts and had Carles criticize her sketches. It was her "Silent sorrow" which caused the great Rodin to say to her after critically examining the figure, "My child, you are a sculptor; you have the sense of form."

A little over twenty years of age, this American negro girl won recognition in the Paris salon, "The wretched," one of her masterpieces, being exhibited in the salon of 1903.

Returning to the United States in 1904 she won a prize for pottery. A fire in 1910 destroyed some of her most valuable works which were stored in Philadelphia.

Her work falls in two divisions, the romantic and the social. The first is represented by "The wretched" and "Secret sorrow," the second by "Immigrant in America" and "The silent appeal."

An art critic in reviewing her work wrote a few years ago: "While Rodin has even outdone Verestchagin in depicting the frightful and the eerie, Miss Warrick has gone a step farther than either and won the pseudonym "sculptor of horrors." When asked how she had acquired her bent for horrors she replied: "Ghost stories did it."

Brawley in his "Negro in literature and art" says of Mrs. Fuller: "Her early work is not delicate or pretty; it is gruesome and terrible, but it is also intense and vital, and from it speaks the very tragedy of the Negro race."

In 1910 Miss Warrick was married to Dr. Solomon C. Fuller, of Framingham, Mass.

GARBER, DANIEL, (P.) Pupil of Cincinnati Art Academy under V. Nowottny and Pennsylvania Academy of the Fine Arts under Anschutz. Won the Cresson scholarship, Pennsylvania Academy of the Fine Arts, 1905; first Hallgarten prize, National Academy of Design, 1909; also the Potter Palmer gold medal carrying with it the sum of $1,000, at a recent exhibition. A member of National Academy of Design, 1913.

Of his "Towering trees," a writer for Art and Progress (3:454) says: "It is an unusual composition, decorative in effect, showing a screen of lofty blue-green pepper trees on the marshy shore of a stream, beyond which one catches a glimpse of a distant landscape and bits of enchanting sky."

GAUL, WILLIAM GILBERT, (P., I.) b. Jersey City, N. J., March 31, 1855; d. New York City, December 21, 1919. Educated in the local schools of

Newark and at Claverack Military Academy. Began the study of art in New York City with J. G. Brown, and is one of our best known illustrators.

In 1872 his first picture was exhibited at the Academy of Design.

"While Mr. Gaul has treated other subjects with sympathy and charm, it is in a painter of battles and soldier life that he is most widely known. .... Many of his paintings represent the picturesque features of army life on the plains of the far west."

He illustrated a number of books and his work in black and white appeared in all the leading magazines.

"Holding the line at all hazards" won a gold medal from the American Art Association in 1881, and "Charging the battery" elected him a member of the National Academy of Design in 1889. At the World's Columbian Exposition, 1893, his illustrations won a medal. (Nat Cyc Am Biog)

"Mr. Gaul's work, often spirited, is always forceful and interesting." ("American Art and Artists," p. 359)

GAY, WALTER, (P.) b. Hingham, Mass., January 22, 1856. His youthful efforts in painting were flower pieces. At the age of nineteen he went to Paris and entered the atelier of Leon Bonnat who chose one of his life studies to be placed on the wall, where it hung for many years, being the only one thus honored. In 1879 he visited Spain and that same year exhibited in the salon of the Champs Elysees his picture entitled "The fencing lesson." It was placed on the line. He is a regular contributor to the Paris salon.

Received honorable mention, Paris salon, 1885; third class medal, salon of 1888; gold medal, Vienna, 1893; gold medals, Antwerp and Munich, 1894; gold medal, Berlin, 1896; silver medal, Paris Exposition, 1900; chevalier of the Legion of Honor, 1894; cross, 1906. Associate member Société Nationale des Beaux Arts; member Société des Amis du Louvre, Paris. His works are hors concours at the Paris salons.

Mr. Gay paints chiefly the peasants of western France.

"Saving grace" was awarded a gold medal of the third class, and this painting and the "Cigarette makers" were purchased by the French government for the Luxembourg.

Other popular paintings are:

"Young girl with a geranium"   "The sewing lesson"
"Plain chant"   "A master stroke"
"Mass in Brittany"   "Knife grinder"
"The spinners"   "Trained pigeons"
"A weaver"   "Conspiracy under Louis XVI"

Mr. Gay is represented in the Tate collection, London; Metropolitan Museum of Art, New York; Museum of Fine Arts, Boston; and in many private collections.

"Through large windows hung with thin curtains, the bright daylight falls into the clean rooms of peasants gleaming, on the boards of the floor, the tops of the tables, and the white caps of the women who sit at their work sewing. It is a familiar problem of light." (Müther.)

GENTH, LILLIAN MATILDE, (P.) b. 1876. Graduate of the School of Design, Philadelphia, Pa., in 1900, (fellowship to Paris); studied under Whistler and at Atelier Colarossi. Won Mary Smith prize, Pennsylvania Academy of the Fine Arts, 1904; Shaw prize, National Academy, 1907; gold medal, American Art Society, Philadelphia, 1907; won Hallgarten prize on "Depth of the woods." Associate member of National Academy of Design, 1908.

The nude figure in a landscape is perhaps the most difficult of all forms of painting, and Miss Genth has won distinction in this, her chosen field.

While studying in France, one day in Brittany she posed a nude figure out in the open, and from that time this became her chosen field. She loves the woods, and she loves to depict human flesh, warm and glowing in the sunshine.

Her delightful country home in the Berkshires, which she named "Hermitcliff," covers seventy acres and places at her command field, forest, and purling pool; here is her studio. Here in the open she poses her models, protected from intruders, among the trees and beside running water, the sunshine filtering through the leaves and producing a singing color of beauty, sunshine, and joy.

Miss Genth is represented in our leading public and private collections. Some of her best known pictures are in the following:

"Springtide," Metropolitan Museum, N. Y.

"Depth of the woods," National Gallery, Washington, D. C.

"Bird song," Carnegie Institute, Pittsburgh, Pa.

"Whirling waters," Museum of Art, Cleveland, Ohio.

"Pastoral," Institute of Arts and Sciences, Brooklyn, N. Y.

"The lark," capably executed and of excellent color, won the Shaw memorial prize. "Golden days" is one of her most characteristic paintings. "Spirit of the earth" and "Sun maiden" are also well known, and "The promenade" is attractive. "A June afternoon"—one of her latest—is an analytical refinement of sunshine.

"Mother and child" is singularly tender and beautiful and painted fearlessly. It is wonderful to think that at last we may enjoy in art as well as in life the impression of kind, generous, beautiful mother-hood without the Puritan streak of horror at facing the real beauty of the thought." (Craftsm 24:315)

GIBSON, CHARLES DANA, (I., P.) b. Roxbury, Mass., September 14, 1867. Began his studies at the Art Students' League of New York at the age of seventeen and continued in that institution during 1883 and 1884. In 1886 he made his debut as an artist for the periodicals, his first draw-ing accepted being "The moon and I" which appeared in "Life." Three years later he gave up work and went to Paris where in 1889 he was enrolled as a student in the Academie Julien. After this period of study he resumed work as an illustrator; he has a studio in New York.

In 1893 he went to Paris, in 1895 to London, and in 1898 to Munich, acquiring material for pictures subsequently published.

"Mr. Gibson is doubtless to be regarded as one of the foremost of mod-ern illustrators. His technique is admirable. He works in three media —pen, chalk, and brush. His versatility, however, is that of ideas and not of types. Few artists have acquired equal reputation with as few distinct characters. His American girls are one American girl—his favorite, and for a certain class of pictures almost his sole female model." (Brush & P 7:277)

The drawings of Gibson have been characterized as genteel pictorial comedy, and probably no happier nor truer phrase could be devised to describe them.

"Charles Dana Gibson is recognized as one of the most distinguished workers in this (illustration) field." (Scrib 72:126)

He has received membership in the Legion of Honor from the French government and the Order of the Crown of Belgium has been bestowed on him by King Albert, both in recognition of Mr. Gibson's work in making posters in the World War.

GIES, JOSEPH W., (P.) b. Detroit, Michigan. Pupil of Bouguereau and Robert-Fleury in Paris; Royal Academy in Munich. Member Society Western Artists. "Lady in pink" and portrait of Robert Hopkin are in the Detroit Museum of Art.

GIFFORD, ROBERT SWAIN, (P., E.) b. Naushon Island, Mass., Decem-ber 23, 1840; d. New York, January 15, 1905. Educated in the public schools of New Bedford, Mass.; studied painting under Albert VanBeest, Rotterdam, Holland; settled in New York in 1866; made sketching tours through California and Oregon in 1869, in Europe and North Africa in 1870-71, and again in 1874-75 in Brittany and other parts of France.

Was elected associate member of the National Academy of Design, New York, in 1867; full member in 1878. Member of the Society of Painter-Etchers, London.

Mr. Gifford's range of landscape is unusually wide; he has painted the heights of the Sierras, the plains of Brittany and coast of New England, as well as Eastern scenes. He is best known through his Eastern pictures in which his rendering of oriental life and atmosphere is peculiarly happy.

In 1867 he sent three marine paintings to the National Academy exhibition,—"Scene at Long Beach," "Cliff scene, Grand Menau," "Vineyard Sound lightship"—and on their merits was elected associate member of the institute.

Oriental paintings:

"An Egyptian caravan"   "Halt in the desert"
"Fountain near Cairo"   "Entrance to a Moorish house in
"On the Nile"   Tangiers"
"View of the Golden Horn"   "The palms of Biskra"
"Evening on the Nile"   "Scene in the Great Square of the
"Rock of Gibraltar"   Rumeyleh, Cairo, Egypt"

His autumn landscapes or sketches of shore are rich in harmonies of tone. Of his "Woodland pastures" Mr. Gifford writes: "The subject is from nature, sketched near my place at Nonquit .... I have painted many of my best pictures in this locality."

"The glen" is an excellent example of his style. His "Near the coast" won the $2,500 prize of the American Art Association in 1885.

"We have stood spell-bound before his drifting October clouds, and the wide expanses of his cold and cheerless skies .... We have wondered how a man could bring before us such a dreary scene and yet force us to bow before it." (New Eng M 14:148)

Mr. Gifford was one of the best of American etchers and his plates have been praised by the most competent critics. Of his "Evening" S. R. Koehler, in his work on "Etching," says: "In my humble opinion, it is about the completest bit of American landscape etching yet accomplished without loss of freedom or breadth."

GLACKENS, WILLIAM J., (P., I.) b. Philadelphia, Pa., March 13, 1870. Received early training in Pennsylvania Academy and studied scenes and types several years in Europe; exhibited at the Paris salon, 1896; Paris Exposition, 1900. McClure's sent him to Cuba during the war with

Spain. He has received medals and honorable mention at the exhibitions of various art societies in this country; was elected associate member of the National Academy of Design, 1906.

A revolutionist in art, he is from an American standpoint the first of illustrators. The art editor of Scribner's has made his work a feature of that magazine's pages.

"His work is distinct and decidedly radical in its purport and inception. He may not please the general public, but has won the unstinted appreciation of his confreres in art, and of those who value originality and forceful thought." (Bookm 11 :244)

"Glacken's paintings are invariably interesting, for the artist is possessed of an exceedingly fresh and engaging point of view. And yet with all its originality the art of Glackens is closely linked with that of Degas and Manet. ......

"Glackens possesses much knowledge of the technique of painting in oils—that most difficult of all media; his composition and his palette are very amusing. His drawings fairly reek with character and his wonderfully expressive line records types in such a truthful and far-seeing manner, his penetrating gaze sees so far beneath the surface of things, that one can only marvel at the simple manner in which he attains his ends." (Int Studio 40: sup lxviii)

"In approaching the slums he does so purely as an artist .... Mr. Glackens is a logical impressionist—one who could never be anything else. He does not see the details at all. He receives simply general impressions." (Bookm 34 :410)

In writing of his recent work, A. E. Gallatin divides them into three classes—beach scenes, portraits, and flower studies.

"In all of them he displays his great color sense, besides a splendid feeling for form and a technique rational and normal." (Am M of Art 7 :262)

GRAFLY, CHARLES, (S.) b. Philadelphia, Pa., December 3, 1862. At the age of seventeen he entered a stone-carving establishment in order to gain practical knowledge of the sculptor's craft; he remained there for five years. Studied modeling and painting under Thomas Eakins at the Pennsylvania Academy of the Fine Arts and in 1888 went to Paris and entered the Académie Julien and studied in the department of sculpture under Chapu; later studied in the Ecole des Beaux Arts.

Received honorable mention in the Paris salon of 1891; honorable mention, Temple Fund, 1892; gold medal of honor, Pennsylvania Academy of the Fine Arts, 1899; gold medal, Paris Exposition, 1900; gold medal, Pan-American Exposition, Buffalo, 1901. Elected associate member of the

National Academy of Design, New York, in 1902; full member in 1905. Mr. Grafly is instructor of sculpture in the Pennsylvania Academy of the Fine Arts: also member of leading art clubs in the United States.

In the salon of 1890 he made his debut with two heads—"Daedalus" and "St. John"; the former was subsequently exhibited in Philadelphia, purchased and cast in bronze by the academy, and is now in the permanent collection. His life-size female nude figure, "Mauvais présage," was accorded honorable mention in the salon of 1891 and is now in the Detroit Institute of Arts. Since 1896 he has resided in Philadelphia.

The most original of his diminutive works is "The symbol of life." In the Paris Exposition of 1900 five of his works—"The vulture of war," "The symbol of life," "From generation to generation," "Portrait of my mother," and portrait of Mrs. Charles Grafly—were exhibited and they were awarded a gold medal.

"The pioneer mother," a statue to motherhood, is a tribute to the pioneer women of California, suggested by the Woman's Board of the Panama-Pacific Exposition. Mr. Grafly was selected as the sculptor after a competition in which ten American sculptors entered designs. After the close of the exposition the monument was placed permanently in the civic center of San Francisco.

He executed the main fountain, "Man," for the Pan-American Exposition, Buffalo, 1901.

Lorado Taft says that there is a leaning towards symbolism in Mr. Grafly's work—"He seems to think that this is what sculpture is for—the expression of one's ideas in form .... Mr. Grafly lost himself for a time in an Egyptian chimera."

GRAYSON, CLIFFORD PROVOST, (P.) b. Philadelphia, Pa., July 14, 1859. Graduated from the University of Pennsylvania in 1878. After studying at the Pennsylvania Academy of the Fine Arts, he went to Paris the same year and studied in the Ecole des Beaux Arts and in the Atelier Gérome. Then he went to Pont Aven and Concarneau where some of his most successful pictures were painted. Subsequently he opened a studio in Paris, and became a regular contributor to the salon.

His first painting shown in the salon of 1882 was "A Breton idyl." This was followed by "Going to market." In 1883 his "Rainy day at Pont Aven" was hung in a most prominent place on the line and received favorable comment. "Ahoy" was exhibited in the salon of 1884, and "Fisherman's family" in 1885. "Midday dreams" won a $2,000 prize in 1886 at an art exhibition in New York.

Mr. Grayson returned from Europe in 1891 to become director of the art department of Drexel Institute. In his work he reminds one of Jules Breton.

GREATOREX, ELIZA, (E.) b. Manor-Hamilton, Ireland; d. Paris, France, 1897. In 1840 she came to New York with her family, and in 1849 married Henry W. Greatorex, a well-known musician and organist. Being early left a widow with three children she made art her profession and went to Paris where she studied under Lambinet for a year and later at the Pinakothek, Munich. After this period of study she returned to New York and in 1869 she was elected an associate member of the National Academy of Design, New York—an honor which at that time only one other woman, Mrs. Bogardus, shared with her; she was the first woman to be elected a member of the Artists' Fund Society of New York.

It is by her pen-and-ink drawings—a series of pictures of old New York—that she is perhaps most widely known.

In 1873 she determined to take up etching and in 1878 settled in Paris and made etching her chief study. In the summer of 1880 she went to the valley of the Chevreuse (Seine et Oise) and at Chevreuse and Cernay-la-Ville etched directly from nature her "Pond at Cernay-le-Ville." Her "Old Dutch church" is most characteristic and attractive. The work of Mrs. Greatorex is delicate rather than strong in its inception as well as in its execution. (Koehler's "American etchings")

She etched her famous plate, "The old Bloomingdale tavern," in 1869.

GREEN, ELIZABETH SHIPPEN (Mrs. Huger Elliott), (I.) Studied at the Pennsylvania Academy of the Fine Arts, also with Howard Pyle; was guided and encouraged in her childhood by her father, a lover of art, who with her mother lived also at the "Red Rose." Studied six years abroad. Began by illustrating for advertisements; then entered the wider field of drawing pictures for children's poems and stories.

"Her love of the dainty mysteries of elves and fays has free expression." Her work appears especially in Harper's.

GROLL, ALBERT LOREY, (P.) b. New York, December 8, 1866. Most of his student years were spent in Munich where he studied at the Royal Academy. He has been a landscape painter since 1895. A member of the National Academy of Design, New York, 1910.

In his student days he gave much attention to figure painting but there came a time when he could not afford models for figure pieces; this forced him to find his models in the trees and rivers, hills and fields. His earlier pictures are studies of the familiar atmospheric effects of dawn, twilight, moonlight, mist, sunrise, and starlight as seen at Cape Cod, Sandy Hook, and in New York City.

Mr. Groll accompanied Prof. Stuart Culin of the Brooklyn Museum of Arts and Sciences on an exploration trip to New Mexico and Arizona and the sketches that he made of the Colorado desert furnished material for his now noted "desert" pictures. His "Arizona" won the gold medal in 1906 at the exhibition of the Pennsylvania Academy of the Fine Arts. "It is only a sketch of desert and sky and low-lying hills, but it glows like a gem with the indescribable never-to-be-forgotten color of the Colorado desert." (Craftsm 9:826) "The sandstorm" is another remarkable production; "The rainbow" still more daring: in "Clouds" he is seen at his best. "Lake Louise" was awarded the Inness gold medal.

He shows the desert in all its moods—placid and savage, bold and mellow. "Groll is the musical dreamer in colors." (Int Studio 27:sup lxvi)

"His art is so completely associated with the deserts of California, Arizona, and New Mexico that his "Temples of New Mexico" comes as something as a surprise. In his "Sand storm" his command of atmospheric effects and wide stretches of waste is well illustrated."

"For pure painter-like quality, Mr. Groll's earlier canvases surpassed his Arizona and New Mexico scenes, is the view of many of his admirers, who have known his work since his Rockaway and Sandy Hook days." (Int Studio 75:496)

His "Milky way"—a representation of a starry night seen from his favorite sand dunes—is referred to as a "profoundly beautiful canvas."

"Kit Carson's house," a drawing in colored crayon, has an historical interest as the house is now established as a museum in memory of that famous Indian scout.

His cloud renderings, of the desert are his most popular paintings.

GROVER, OLIVER DENNETT, (P.) b. Earlville, Ill., January 29, 1861. Studied at Royal Academy, Munich; with Frank Duveneck in Florence; with Boulanger, Lefebvre, and Laurens in Paris. Received the first Yerkes prize, Chicago, 1892, for his painting, "Thy will be done."

"On the Riva"; "Mountain, sea, and cloud"; and "June morning, Lake Orta" are in the Art Institute, Chicago. "A fresh breeze" is owned by the Art Museum, St. Louis, Mo.

GRUPPE, CHARLES PAUL, (P.) b. Pictou, Canada, September 3, 1860. Studied in Holland but is chiefly self-taught. Received gold medal at Rouen; gold medal of American Art Society in 1902; two gold medals in Paris.

Is a member of the Pulchre Studio, The Hague; Arti, Amsterdam; American Water-color Society, New York; Art Club of Philadelphia; New York Water-color Club.

His "Old water wheel" is in the Brooklyn Museum; "Dutch canal" in the Art Institute, Detroit, Michigan; and "Meadow brooks" in the National Gallery, Washington, D. C.

GUERIN, JULES, (P., I., Mural P.) b. St. Louis, Mo., November 18, 1866. Going abroad after preliminary studies, he entered the ateliers of Benjamin-Constant and Jean Paul Laurens in Paris. Received honorable mention at Paris Exposition, 1900; also honorable mention at the Pan-American Exposition, Buffalo, 1901; and silver medal at St. Louis Exposition, 1904. An associate member National Academy of Design, 1916.

Mr. Guerin is an architectural draughtsman, a successful decorative painter, and a well-known illustrator. In recent publications he has collaborated with Robert Hichens, the author, using many of his subjects from Egypt and Palestine.

Among his interesting paintings are a series of French chateaux, Venetian scenes, and public buildings of historic interest in the United States.

In estimating the artistic qualities of Mr. Guerin, the International Studio says: "He studies a building with the trained and informed intelligence, the assured restraint of an architectural draughtsman of the better sort . . . . . . He is careful of design and bold, almost arbitrary, in color, conventionalizing like a decorator."

He has painted six enormous topographical landscapes as mural decorations for the new Pennsylvania Railroad station in New York City. They represent chiefly the country traversed by that railway company.

Mr. Guerin was responsible for the color scheme of the buildings of the Panama Exposition, 1915, and he has the distinction of being the first director of color ever appointed for an international exposition.

"Guerin extended his color treatment to practically everything presenting surface. Nothing could escape his vigilant eyes. Even the sand covering of the asphalted roads is of a peculiarly attractive blend. It seems like a mixture of ordinary sand with a touch of cinnamon. Even that corps of stalwart guards had to submit to a tonal harmony of drabs with touches of yellow melted, warm red puttees and neat little yellow Spanish canes." (Eugen Neuhaus)

The murals in the Lincoln Memorial at Washington, D. C., are the work of Jules Guerin and occupied three years of his time. They represent Emancipation and Reunion. The group above the Gettysburg address typifies Freedom and Liberty; that above the second inaugural address, Unity.

A detailed description of these murals is given by Mr. Guerin in Art and Archaeology, June, 1922.

"As an illustrator, as the author of the charming color scheme of the Panama-Pacific Exposition, and as the artist of numerous architectural drawings in color of unique and delightful type, Mr. Guerin is well known. As a painter of figures and as a mural painter he will step into prominence for the first time when these paintings [Lincoln Memorial murals] are put on view." (Am M of Art 11:130)

GUTHERZ, CARL, (P., Mural P.) b. Schoeftland, Switzerland; d. Washington, D. C., February 7, 1907. Came to this country with his parents in 1851 and settled in Memphis, Tenn. He became a mechanical draughtsman. In 1868 he went to Paris and studied art with Cabason and Pils, and later with Stallaert and Robert in Brussels and Antwerp; finally settled in Rome in 1871 where he studied with Simonetti. There he executed his first important work, "The awakening of spring," and on the strength of this painting he was elected in 1872 a member of the Cercle Artistique Internationale; after spending some time in Munich he returned to the United States in 1873 and became associated with Prof. Halsey G. Ives. In 1880 Mr. Gutherz married an accomplished and cultured lady of a distinguished Alabama family and they soon after removed to Paris where they lived until 1896. While in Paris, Lefebvre, Boulanger, Gabriel Ferrier, Jules Breton, Oliver Merson, and Puvis de Chavannes were among his intimate associates. He exhibited in every salon and in 1876 received a medal from France that rendered his works hors concours in the salon. His work assumed "that dignity and proportion of color symphonies, significant in mystic symbolism." Being awarded the commission for decorating the ceiling of the Representatives' reading room in the Library of Congress, led to his establishing his home in Washington where he was for many years connected with the art department of the Washington University.

His mural paintings in the Library of Congress are seven panels representing "The spectrum of light." He also has a series of mural paintings in the Peoples' Church, St. Paul, Minn., the theme being to represent allegorically life in both the physical and spiritual worlds. In the Courthouse at Fort Wayne, Ind., he has a series of six splendid decorative panels.

In portraiture Mr. Gutherz painted many distinguished men. Among his ideal works are the beautiful "Ad angelis" where two angels are bearing the ethereal body to the realm of light, "The golden legend," "Ecce homo," "Sappho," and "Midsummer night's dream."

Lilian Whiting says: "The story of Carl Gutherz is the story of an ideal embraced in youth and followed in manhood with increasing fidelity. It is the story of a painter whose entire life has been singularly responsive to the artist's vision and the poet's dream." (Int Studio 24: sup lxxxi)

HAGGIN, BEN ALI, (P.) Won third Hallgarten prize of the National Academy of Design, 1909. His technical knowledge was acquired by studying the work of the masters.

"In his portrait of a 'Japanese actress' the fabric of the gown and the manipulation of light is almost Whistlerian, without being in the least like Whistler .... Another thing that Haggin has in common with Whistler is the handling of white. Few contemporary painters get the same quality in the lightness of the heavier white fabrics."

"In his 'Little dancer' the figure stands in the center of a stage, against a golden curtain that blends into the shadows of the dress— shadows that are golden, transparent, and luminous, not dull gray or black. His blacks have the same harmonizing quality, for black is piled on black in a most bewildering fashion."

"He gives to all his portraits a 'dramatic effect'. Perhaps the portrait of Mrs. Wilfred Buckland will be reckoned by a later generation of critics as one of the most essentially brilliant canvases which have ever emanated from his brush."

"His charming portrait of Miss Kitty Gordon is now famous. Otis Skinner as Hajj, the beggar, is considered to be technically the best thing he has handled of late. This characterization was done at one sitting. (Arts & D 2:320)

His portrait of Mary Garden as "Thais" sold for $25,000.

"He is obsessed with a sense of color .... It is in the painting of the nude, however, that Haggin has found his most complete expression .... The flesh is transparent, blue veined, and cooly shadowed."

HALLOWELL, GEORGE H., (Min. P.) b. Boston, Mass., December 5, 1872. Pupil of Benson, Tarbell, and H. B. Warren in painting.

At the tenth annual exhibition of the Society of Miniature Painters Mr. Hallowell showed an interesting group.

"His paintings are representations of a more or less conventionalized nature, and he pays so much attention to the surface of his picture that he produces an effect not unlike the wonderful glaze of the porcelains of the Royal potteries at Copenhagen. His design is always beautiful and his color of an unimpeachable harmony, though purely arbitrary."

HAMMER, TRYGVE, (S.) b. Arendal, Norway, September 6, 1878. He studied decorative painting and modeling for three years in Christiania; then worked in Germany, Austria, and Switzerland until 1904 when he came to the United States. This artist of Norwegian birth was compelled to work at house painting after his arrival in this country, being penniless and friendless. He built himself a little workshop and spent unemployed time in modeling and carving. After a time he was able to study at the Beaux Arts School of Sculpture, the Art Students' League, and the National Academy. In 1917 his work in clay and plaster was for the first time exhibited at the Independent Show; then he began working in stone and marble.

Mr. Hammer's early work was more descriptive than his present work. Like the Gothic sculptors of the Middle Ages, he conventionalizes natural forms. His most impressive examples are "The tree of life" and "The tree of sorrow." These trees are both monumental and expressive. "The tree of sorrow" is a memorial to those dead at sea; "The tree of life" we find in Scandinavian mythology.

"These trees show the mingled spirit of observation and invention that inspires all true art. In them Hammer exhibits a remarkable power of abstracting and adapting natural forms to the needs of design .... Though Hammer's work is especially interesting in its decorative quality, there is much more to it than that. He is best known through his portraits since they have been exhibited most frequently. His 'memorial relief' has been called a 'lithic poem to emotion felt in an after calm.' " (Int Studio 76:104)

HARDING, CHESTER, (P.) b. Conway, Mass., September, 1772; d. in 1866. A remarkable personality. He was noted as an axman—was imprisoned for debt—worked as a house painter—finally became a famous portrait painter.

For a time was a student of art in the Academy in Philadelphia. Finally settled in Boston where he achieved great popularity. Went to England in 1823 where he became popular. Returning to the United States he painted most of the political leaders of his time—Webster, Clay, Calhoun, Marshall, and many more. (Bookm 31:55)

Tuckerman in his "Book of the artists" says: "In 1823 Harding was the fashion in Boston; even Stuart was neglected and used to ask sarcastically, "How goes the Harding fever?"

His portrait of Daniel Webster was much esteemed. His last work was a portrait of General Sherman.

HARDING, GEORGE, (I., P.) b. Philadelphia, Pa., 1882. Studied at Pennsylvania Academy of the Fine Arts and with Howard Pyle. Member of the Philadelphia Water Color Club and Society of Illustrators.

Representative pictures are:

"Coast of Cape Race"   "Busy day at the docks"
"The fisherwoman"   "A wreck on Florida reefs"

HARPER, WILLIAM A., (P.)   Born of colored parents near Cayuga, Canada, December 27, 1873; died in the City of Mexico, March 27, 1910.

In 1895 he entered the Art Institute School, Chicago. Later he taught drawing in the public schools of Houston, Texas. In 1903 and again in 1907 he went to Paris where he was associated with Henry O. Tanner.

The subjects of his paintings were mostly French and American landscapes. Of a memorial exhibition of his paintings held in Chicago soon after his death, a local art critic writes:

"The showing of Harper's work was interesting for the variety of sketching grounds represented, for the dignity of the point of view, and for a consistently high aim in the conception of his pictures."

HARRISON, (LOVELL) BIRGE, (P., I.) b. Philadelphia, Pa., October 28, 1854. Son of Apollos Wolcott and Margaret (Belden) Harrison. Known most widely as a painter of snow. Received an academic education. Went to Paris in 1876; entered the atelier of Carolus-Duran; two years later entered the Ecole des Beaux Arts and studied under Cabanel for four years. Going to Pont-Aven, Brittany, he painted his first important picture, "November," which was exhibited in the salon of 1882 and subsequently purchased by the French government. Associate member National Academy of Design, 1902; full member, 1910.

His work is marked by a love of evanescent effects,—moonrise over a majestic shadowy landscape, winter twilight after snow, the harbor ice in moonlight.

Important works are:

"The return of the Mayflower"   "Moonrise off Santa Barbara"
"Moonlight on the snow"   "Winter sunrise in New England"
"Morning on the Eel river"   "The sentinel"
"Moonlight on the marshes"   "The heights of Levis"
"The Flatiron after rain"   "Woodstock meadows in winter"
"Sunlight and mist"   "Road near Santa Barbara"
"The lower town, Quebec"   "Madison avenue in winter"

"A writer on his art, a teacher and experimenter, he has played with the whole gamut of high and low sunshine on snowy fields." (Innes "Schools of painting" p. 375)

His paintings are hors concours in the Paris salon.

HARRISON, THOMAS ALEXANDER, (P.) b. Philadelphia, Pa., January 17, 1853. Son of Apollos Wolcott and Margaret (Belden) Harrison. In 1879 he studied at the Ecole des Beaux Arts, also under Bastien-Lepage and Gérome, Paris. The same year he joined the colony of artists at Pont-Aven, Brittany, and in 1880 he sent his first marine entitled "The Brittany coast" to the Paris salon. His first popular success came in 1882 when he sent to the salon a charming picture called "Castles in Spain." In the salon of 1884 he again obtained great success with a marine called "Crépuscule" (Twilight). This he followed in the salon of 1885 with "The wave" for which he received honorable mention, and in the salon of 1886 he exhibited "Arcadia" which was later purchased by the French government for the Luxembourg. These four mentioned pictures all figured in the Universal Exhibition of 1889 and represent the artist's greatest and most successful efforts.

Other representative paintings are:

"The River Loing—evening"   "Breton garden"
"Nymph"   "The amateurs"
"Lunar mists"   "Marine"
"Shipwrecked"   "Misty morning"
"Harbor of Concarneau"   "Golden sands"
"Pebbly beach"

Although demonstrating his ability to paint in many directions it is mainly by reason of his great power as a painter of the sea that Mr. Harrison's reputation stands, and in this work none approaches him in the delineation of light and movement and color of wave forms under sky effects. "Very notable is the hue of the foam and curdle, not white but an attenuated tone of the same blue which pervades the mass of water."

"Of all American painters of the sea, Alexander Harrison is .... the most scholarly." (Caffin)

"The key note to Mr. Harrison's art is truth to nature; he is a disciple of the plein-air movement and of the evolution which was determined in French art by Manet."

He has a studio in Paris where he has large classes of students.

His paintings have obtained for him medals and prizes in Paris, Munich, London, New York, and Philadelphia. Is a member of popular art clubs in Paris, Munich, London, New York, and Philadelphia. Was elected associate member of the National Academy of Design in 1898; full member in 1901.

Hassam, Childe, (P., E.) b. Boston, Mass., October 17, 1859. Educated in Boston public schools and studied art in Boston and' Paris, 1886-9. Is the best known follower of Monet in this country—our foremost impressionist since the death of Theodore Robinson.

Has been singularly successful in competition, winning medals in Paris, Munich, Chicago, Philadelphia, Pittsburgh, Buffalo, and St. Louis, and awarded prizes by many American art clubs and societies. He is a member of the Ten American Painters; Société Nationale des Beaux Arts, Paris; The Secessionists, Munich; associate member National Academy of Design, 1902; full member, 1906.

"Subjects," he says, "suggest to me a color scheme, and I just paint; some one else might see a riot of color where I see only whites and drabs and buffs."

"June" is one of his prize paintings. Other well-known works are:

"Improvisation"
"Paris—winter"
"Inner harbor—Gloucester"
"Rue Lafayette on a winter evening"
"The Chinese merchants"
"North shore, moonlight"
"October haze, Manhattan"
"A bowl of nasturtiums"

"The green, New Haven"
"Winter nightfall"
"Plaza Centrale—Havana"
"Cat boats—Newport"
"The abilone shell"
"Summer sea"
"Penelope"
"Lorelei" (prize painting)
"A New York window"

Hassam's "Sun room" won the Altman prize of $500. It is "one of his familiar young women in a rose-colored kimono posed against a French window with a background of lush garden."

"He was one of the first American artists to interpret sunlight with pigments and with pencil. Light and motion are always present in his pictures .... To him Fifth avenue is the most marvelous metropolitan street in the whole world."

At an exhibition of his war work, twenty-two flag pictures were hung —the room was alive with color and motion.

"In his 'April morning' one feels the surging of pedestrians, the pulsing of the air and senses the wind blowing down the wonderful avenue, gently touching the colors into life." (Touchst 5:279)

"He is primarily a great painter of air and soil, sea and sky. He feels the repose and beauty, the strength and immensity of nature in the simplest scenes. He has a definite aim, and every picture brings him nearer the goal." (Int Studio 29:267)

"When Coquelin, the French actor, was in America, he bought two of Hassam's impressionistic canvases to take back with him to France, declaring at the time of purchase that the artist was the most able impressionist painter. The compliment was not ill-advisedly spoken and Hassam will easily maintain the rank assigned him." (Frederick W. Morton)

Mr. Hassam is a designer with a sense of balance and of classic grace almost equal to that of Corot, and he uses the impressionist method to express otherwise the shimmer of delicate foliage that Corot loved.

"Isle of Shoals" series is of recent date. "These water-colors of rocky coast and blue water are glorious in color and even greater interpretations of nature than Sargent's. His concern is with color, not with form." (Arts & D 6:279)

Mr. Hassam has recently taken up etching and an exhibition of sixty of his subjects was held in New York last autumn.

"Mr. Hassam carries over into etching the convictions of a delicate luminist. He refuses consistently the broader and more idiomatic means of expression—the areas of dazzling white paper balancing areas of velvety black, which are common to Rembrandt and the recent English etchers under his domination . . . . In setting himself a definite pictorial ideal identical with that of his painting, Mr. Hassam goes far to asking the impossible of the etched line." (Nation 101:698)

Hassam is not truly a landscape painter. He is not interested in expanse or the mysteries and magic of aerial perspective. His design is purely linear. (Art in Am 8:174)

Aesthetically Hassam is directly related to Whistler, but only in as much as he uses the artistic truths of his philosophy, and this indicates that he is an artistic heir of Japan, the principles of whose art are so clearly manifested in the earlier master.

HAWLEY, MARGARET FOOTE, (Min. P.) Boston, Massachusetts.

Miss Hawley is a thorough craftsman and one of the most talented of the Boston group of miniaturists. At an exhibition of American miniatures held in Boston last year, she had a group of sixteen which formed a most important and interesting assemblage of her work. Her miniature portrait of Alexander Petrunkevitch has been purchased by the Metropolitan Museum of New York City.

"It is one of the most successful likenesses of a man ever painted by a woman, and the force of character there presented would seem to call for a canvas as large as one of Goya's instead of for a space of some three inches by four." (Scrib 67:384)

HAWTHORNE, CHARLES WEBSTER, (P.) b. Maine, 1872. Student of National Academy of Design and Art Students' League, New York. Teacher in New York schools of art; owner and instructor of Cape Cod School of Art, Provincetown, Mass. Associate member National Academy of Design, 1908.

First painted still life, then figures; after a trip to Italy painted landscapes; also paints portraits.

"He is essentially a figure painter, a painter of 'types' surrounded by a jumble of still life. The fishing folk of Cape Cod are his specialty .... In his men with oar and fishing tackle and his Portuguese fisher boys, we feel a whiff of the ocean and their environment is actually dripping with brine .... Hawthorne's art has not yet that expression of joy in expansive life which clings to Winslow Homer's figures, nor has it that anatomical grasp in character which is Eakin's strength. But it is just as vital, natural and wholesome." (Int Studio 26:261)

Arthur Hoeber writes: "'The return' has a sentiment rarely secured by modern men. The expression of the young lad is splendidly caught and is full of youth, hope and courage, while as craftsmanship it is unsurpassed. 'The auctioneer' is a type of the Provincetown fisherman that is to the life, while the painting is a veritable tour de force. One cannot mistake here the man's call to the arts, for the painter is obvious in every brush stroke .... The little Venetian 'Lemon girl' is a gem in its way." (Int Studio 37: sup lxv)

"The trousseau," now owned by the Metropolitan museum, was awarded the Clarke prize in 1911 on the first ballot without a dissenting voice —an unprecedented honor in the history of the National Academy of Design.

Other representative pictures are:

"Fisher boy"
"Fisher children"
"Portuguese fisher boys"
"The fisherman's daughter"
"The boatman"

"Home with the catch"
"The auctioneer"
"The doyen of the fish market"
"Youth"

" 'The first mate' is a wonderful representation of a sea-faring man painted against an imaginative background of sail and fish net and sea and sky in a way which none save Hawthorne himself could do so well— a portrait which one may well believe will be ranked in future years as one of the masterpieces not only of today but of all time."

HEALY, GEORGE PETER ALEXANDER, (P.) b. Boston, Mass., July 15, 1813; d. Chicago, Ill., June 24, 1894. At the age of sixteen he began to copy prints and make likenesses of all who would sit for him. His first success was a copy on canvas of Guido Reni's "Ecce homo" which a Catholic priest purchased for $10 and placed in his church. He studied in Paris in 1836; went to Chicago in 1858; revisited Europe in 1869 and resided long in Rome. While in Rome painted portraits of Longfellow, Pope Pius IX, Princess Oldenberg, and other distinguished persons. He also painted the portraits of Louis Philippe, Guizot, Thier, Gambetta, Webster, Clay, Lincoln, and Grant, and many hundred more distinguished persons. The number of portraits that he painted was enormous.

At his best, his heads are strong, dignified, and characteristic.

He also produced large historic pictures, his "Franklin before Louis XVI" won the third-class medal at the Paris salon in 1840 and his "Webster's reply to Hayne" now hangs in Faneuil Hall, Boston.

HEINIGKE, OTTO, b. Brooklyn, New York, 1851. A mural painter, but makes a specialty of stained glass. Also a writer.

HENRI, ROBERT, (P.) b. Cincinnati, O., June 24, 1865. His first art training was in the Pennsylvania Academy of the Fine Arts, Philadelphia. Later he went to Europe and studied at the Julien Academy and Ecole des Beaux Arts, Paris, and traveled and studied in Spain and Italy. After an absence of about fifteen years he returned to New York. His canvases have been exhibited at the Paris salons and won, many prizes at competitive exhibitions in the United States. He was elected a member of the National Academy of Design in 1906.

Early in his career he concentrated his attention for a considerable time upon the problem of black seen against black and similar problems of value. Now he is reacting in favor of brilliant color, occasionally with loss of sensitiveness to delicate relations of tone.

One of his most popular one-man exhibitions was a collection of fifteen pictures selected by himself. Two were nudes, one a street scene, two views in Ireland, the remainder portraits.

He picks his people from every phase of life—he gathers them from France, Holland, Spain, Ireland, California, New Mexico and the slums of American cities—old and young, happy and sad.

Isham says: "Mr. Robert Henri is the most characteristic of the younger group of painters .:...... his best works are from carefully chosen models .... His girls are modern, complex, and rather mysterious. His workmanship is broad and sure, insistently masterly, with great richness of surface and harmony of tone in the simple scheme of black and white and flesh color."

Hartmann says of Henri: "A street scene painter whose aim is rather to seize the mystery, the passion, the despair as well as the gaiety of a modern metropolis, than to describe its merely topographical features."

"Mr. Henri's Irish types are full of life and color, splendidly characterized and modeled. He would do well to subdue a tendency to overpunctuate with dashes of flesh color of very violent reds and crimsons." (Int Studio 52:sup iii)

"Robert Henri's portrait of Mr. Lloyd Roberts' little daughter Patricia has become so famous in America that she has been nicknamed the Henri baby." (Craftsm 29:256)

"Cathedral woods" is an excellent example of his landscape work. "It possesses the qualities for which his work is known. It is spontaneous, vigorous, forceful, direct. It is painted in bold, brusque manner with a full brush." (Int Studio 69:sup lxxiii)

Some of his best known pictures are in the following collections:

"La neige" (The snow), Luxembourg, Paris.

"Young woman in black," Art Institute, Chicago.

"The equestrian," Carnegie Institute, Pittsburgh.

"Girl with fan," Pennsylvania Academy of the Fine Arts, Philadelphia.

"Spanish gipsy," Metropolitan Museum of Art, New York.

"Tam Gan," Fine Arts Academy, Buffalo, N. Y.

Mr. Henri's Indian is the Indian of tradition, Fenimore Cooper's Indian. His "Indian girl of Santa Clara" is, especially in respect to the rendering of the head, one of the finest portraits of Indians.

"The Indian has turned Henri from realism to mysticism or to, the word may be more exact, idealism .... His Chinese subjects are delightful contrasts to his Indian, a contrast between sublety and arrogance."

"Mr. Henri's brush as it becomes more fluent leads the painter further away from the somewhat narrow path of intimacy. However if he does not give us the soul of the man he does give us the soul of the race."

Oliver S. Tonks, professor of art, Vassar College, in an appreciation of Robert Henri, says: "Mr. Henri in a word stands aloof from the academicians. His style is brusque, direct, and sincere. He is not concerned with types which by the conventional standards are called beautiful. Rather with him the beauty of each work lies in its vitality and the way in which it is handled. And yet, while he thus represents a revolt against the mannerisms and suavity of the academic school, he nevertheless is quite as conscious as the academicians of the value of delicate color."

HERTER, ALBERT, (Mural P.) b. New York, March 2, 1871. He studied art with Carroll Beckwith; also with Laurens and Cormon in Paris. Mr. Herter has won many medals and prizes and received honorable mention in the Paris salon of 1890. In 1910 he was elected an associate member of the National Academy of Design.

Five years ago he brought over from France weavers and looms and established a factory for tapestries and textiles, designing the patterns himself.

His latest achievement has been in mural painting, and among recent wall paintings of note is a series of decorations for the dining room of the St. Francis Hotel, San Francisco, which he painted in his studio in East Hampton, L. I. Seven wall spaces are covered with an allegorical pageant marking the progress of civilization.

"The color effect of the decoration as a whole is remarkably harmonious. In each panel there is brilliant red, considerable blue, and still more green." (House B 37:12)

HIGGINS, EUGENE, (P., E.) b. Kansas City, Mo., February, 1874. Attended the art school in St. Louis, Mo., and later studied in Paris under Laurens, Benjamin-Constant, Gèrome and at the Ecole des Beaux Arts.

Poverty is Mr. Higgins' art inspiration and he is called the Maxim Gorky of painting.

His mother died when he was four years of age and he thenceforth lived in cheap boarding houses with his father who was a stone-cutter by trade. Here "he came in close contact with types of dissolute and luckless humanity, such as he now loves to paint."

When a lad of twelve, an article on Millet gave him his first impulse to be a painter. Millet and Victor Hugo have largely moulded his entire life.

Mr. Higgins paints from memory. He says that a model confuses him. That "people's emotions are more vital to me than their houses and clothes .... When I paint people it is really to use them as symbols, receptacles of emotions."

During his seven years in Paris he chose for his subjects the midnight and dawn of the dark squares of Montmartre.

A few of his works were well hung in the New Salon. He returned to the United States in 1904.

His "Little mother" is in the Carnegie Institute, Pittsburgh; and his etchings are in the New York Public Library, Brooklyn Museum, and Library of Congress, Washington, D. C.

HIGGINS, VICTOR, (P.) b. Shelbyville, Indiana, June 28, 1884. Pupil of Academy of Fine Arts, Chicago; of Réné Ménard and Lucien Simons, Paris; and of Hans von Hyeck, Munich.

Some of his landscapes are immense in size. Among his best known works are the following: "Moorland piper," "Women of Taos," "Juanito and the suspicious cat," "Bread jar," and "A shrine to St. Anthony."

His painting of the Taos mountains has some of the smoothness and color effect of a Maxfield Parrish.

Some of his late paintings are:

"Jews of Poland"   "Girl in the park"
"The road to Jerusalem"   "The soup house"

John Spargo, in the Craftsman (12:141) says: "The question has been raised whether such subjects as Mr. Higgins chooses are suited to the medium of canvas and paint or whether they do not belong rather to literature."

Higgins in defense says: "There is longing, envy, and unrest in the slums and there is feeling, sentiment, and poetry as well."

He portrays the pathetic, the helpless, the ruined, the despised and the rejected of humanity.

HILLS, LAURA COOMBS, (Min. P.) b. Newburyport, Mass., September 7, 1859. Pupil of Helen M. Knowlton, Art Students' League of New York and Cowles Art School in Boston.

Received medal at Paris Exposition, 1900; second Corcoran prize, 1901; silver medal, Pan-American Exposition, Buffalo, 1901; associate member National Academy, 1906; vice president American Society of Miniature Painters; and the first miniature painter to be elected to the Society of American Artists. Although never taught miniature painting, Miss Hills is recognized as a most skilful miniature painter and has gained honors both at home and abroad in this particular form of art.

Her first exhibit was "Seven pretty girls at Newburyport." "The bride," a harmony in 'gray, gold and blue, was one of the most evanescently delicate pieces at a recent exhibition. "The black mantle," "Fire opal," "Butterfly," and "Goldfish" represent the most modern development of all, the essentially pictorial miniature. In these fanciful subjects she takes a place among colorists of the first rank. Her miniature of Alice Brown is full of insight and penetration; the portrait of Mr. Arthur Harlow has all the breadth and dignity of a large portrait with the charm peculiar to the miniature; the charming little head of

Dorothy S. is frank and altogether lovely; the portrait of little Miss Hale is as wholly delightful a child portrait as one could ask. (Int Studio 41:sup xlvi)

Frances Duncan in writing of Miss Hills' work said: "Her portraits are not large portraits done small, but essentially miniature; they have that exquisite jewel-like quality peculiar to the miniature in the hands of the few masters of this exquisite and lovely art, the quality which will make miniature painting a thing apart."

"She understands the emotion of color and by a graceful dexterity masters its adaptation to its subject." (Critic 47:523)

"Her portraits are always big in conception and she appears to be little hampered by the tiny brushes and the elusive quality of the ivory."

The portrait of Master Donald Moffat was the chef d'oeuvre at a recent exhibition of the Miniature Society.

Her masterpiece, "The black hat," is owned by the Metropolitan Museum, New York.

Alice T. Searle says: "Miss Hills is never dull but in the center one of her group of three large ovals [at a recent exhibition], the portrait of Miss Isobel da Costa Green, she outshone her own brilliant past."

In referring to an exhibition of miniature work by American painters held in Boston last year, the Boston Transcript says of Miss Hills' contributions: "A truly remarkable group. In it are outstanding examples of the personal style which is this artist's unique contribution to contemporary practice in miniature painting—the personal style that is so full of elegance and distinction, of such charm and fine taste, and, allowing for the diminutive scale, of such astonishing breadth and decorative character."

"Her painting has some of Sargent's own qualities of dexterous swiftness, her likenesses an assurance and an apparent ease which are his, too. Her mastery of her medium indeed is beyond comparison with any other living painter except with Sargent himself. As John Alexander once said on looking at a miniature of hers, 'Never since Holbein—!' and a silence more eloquent than words finished his sentence." (Scrib 67:384)

Miss Hills is placed in the highest rank among artists who have distinguished themselves in miniature work in the United States.

HITCHCOCK, GEORGE, (P., I.) b. Providence, R. I., September 29, 1850; d. Island of Marken, Netherlands, August 2, 1913. A direct descendant of Roger Williams. Graduated from Brown University in 1872 and from Harvard Law School in 1874; admitted to the bar both in Providence and in New York and practiced law for five years, then gave up jurisprudence for the palette. He went to Europe and became a pupil of Lefebvre and Boulanger in Paris; later went to Holland and studied with Mesdag.

Mr. Hitchcock received honorable mention, gold medals and other coveted prizes. He was a member of the Munich Secessionists, Paris Society of American Painters, the Vienna Academy, and an officer in the Order of Franz Josef; also an associate member of the National Academy of Design, New York, 1909.

France made him a chevalier of the Legion of Honor and he was a regular exhibitor at the Royal Academy, London, salons of Paris and other Continental exhibitions.

It is said that Hitchcock did not discover himself until he found the tulip fields of Egmond, near Amsterdam, on the North Sea. The Egmond School is the result of his painting. While he resided there seventeen studios sprang up and three hundred pupils came to him. The Empress of Austria purchased one of his canvases and this was the beginning of his international success.

Mr. Hitchcock's "Tulip culture" was the foundation of his reputation in the Paris salon of 1887.

"Few artists before him have been impressed as he was by the Haarlem tulip beds and the great brilliant tapestries formed by the variegated hyacinths of the Low Countries."

Mr. Hitchcock prefers Holland in one mood. "Holland flooded in sunlight and covered with a multi-colored floral carpet is the Holland Mr. Hitchcock puts on canvas." "A figure painter quite as unmistakably as a landscape painter, he combines both elements on even terms." (Cent 48:318)

"International interest centers in the fact that George Hitchcock was a pioneer in painting the gentle sunlight and the changing atmosphere of Holland." (Arts & D 14:297)

However it will be noted from the following list of paintings that his art is not limited to Dutch subjects:

"Annunciation"
"Flight into Egypt"
"Mary at the house of Elizabeth"
"Hagar and Ishmael"
"Saint George"

"Saint Genevieve, patron saint of Paris"
"Proserpina"
"Ariadne"
"Sappho"
"Calypso"

Among the most engaging of his Dutch compositions are:

"The mob cap"   "In Brabant"
"Hyacinths"   "Holland morning"
"Maternity"   "Sun-flecked"
"The epitome of Holland"   "Sunday in Zeeland"
"Flower girl in Holland"

In the art galleries of the United States are:

"Hour of vespers," Metropolitan Museum of Art, New York
"Last moments of Sappho," Art Institute, Chicago
"Holland morn," Art Institute, Chicago
"Calypso," Art Institute, Indianapolis

His works have places in private galleries in England, including Blenheim, and the French government has recently acquired for the Luxembourg his painting called "The vanquished."

"The art of George Hitchcock fails to classify with that of any school. One may be tempted because of his subject matter to put him in the 'Modern Dutch School,' but he never looked at Holland through the eyes of a Hollander. He little resembles Israels, the brothers Maris, or Mesdag. Rather is he the pioneer of alien artists who have painted Holland." (Arts & D 14:297)

HITCHCOCK, LUCIUS WOLCOTT, (I.) b. West Williamsfield, O., December 2, 1868. Pupil of Art Students' League of New York; Lefebvre, Benjamin-Constant, Laurens, and Colarossi Academy, Paris. Received honorable mention at Pan-American Exposition, Buffalo, 1901; silver medal for illustration and bronze medal for painting at the St. Louis Exposition, 1904. Also a teacher.

HOFFMAN, MALVINA, (S., P.) b. New York City, June 15, 1887. Pupil of Rodin in Paris and Gutzon Borglum, New York. Awarded first prize for "Russian dancers" at exhibition in Paris; honorable mention for sculpture at Panama-Pacific Exposition, 1915.

Miss Hoffman is the daughter of Richard Hoffman, the musician. She first studied painting for five years with the late John W. Alexander; but, not satisfied with painting, under the encouragement of Gutzon Borglum and Herbert Adams she did a portrait bust of her father in sculpture. Upon seeing this evidence of talent, Mr. Alexander with the sculptors, advised her to continue her training along that line. Taking a trip to Italy and France to study the work of the old masters, Miss

Hoffman met Rodin in Paris. She showed him a photograph of the bust of her father and was accepted as a pupil.

Her studies with Rodin may be divided into three periods; the first, given to drawing; the second, to modeling; the third, to the technique of marble cutting. Returning to New York she studied anatomical drawing and dissecting at the College of Physicians and Surgeons. Thus equipped, her work has an authority of construction and modeling greater than often is found in modern sculpture.

Her "Russian bacchanale" (modeled from Pavlowa and Mordkin in their famous dance) is in the Luxembourg Garden. This is an unusual compliment to this gifted sculptor. The only other sculpture by an American now in the celebrated French garden is the "Bacchante" by Frederick MacMonnies.

Her most ambitious work is a bas-relief, a frieze of twenty-two panels, the subjects of which are the succession of movements in the dance. "In this series of bas-reliefs we come very close to the Greek idea of sculpture as a record of the dance. To the ancient Greek the dance was the expression of thought and feeling through harmonious movement."

The "Modern crusader;" a bronze portrait bust of a Serbian colonel in his knitted helmet, "is an interesting proof of the picturesqueness of modern war costume and the rich character in modern war types." It impresses one with strength and firmness, also expresses dedication, which the title suggests. The Metropolitan Museum of Art, New York, has acquired this fine work of art.

One of her latest works is a group called "The sacrifice." It was presented to Harvard University by Mrs. Robert Bacon in honor of her husband and in memory of the other Harvard men who were killed in the World War. "In this group the sculptor has achieved a work of art which, independent of the sentimental or associational interest, is of the highest esthetic merit. That, in addition, it speaks eloquently of a great sorrow born with high courage and noble pride, gives it place as one of the finest and most sincere memorials that war and its sacrifice have brought into being." (Int Studio 76:235.) "Technically the work shows genuine power and vitality .... The artist's long experience in modeling figures in motion and controlled by muscles trained to extraordinary response in the violence of the Russian dances is a valuable asset .... It should be ranked among the best of the war monuments."

HOMER, WINSLOW, (P.) b. Boston, Mass., February 24, 1836; d. Scarborough, Maine, September 29, 1910. At the age of nineteen he entered the employ of a lithographer in Boston. In 1859 he settled in New

York, studying in the school of the National Academy of Design and under F. Rondel. He was elected associate member of the academy in 1864; full member in 1865.

During the Civil War he was special correspondent and artist for Harper, and his first works in oil which brought him prominently before the public as an artist were "Prisoners from the front," "Home, sweet home," "Zouaves pitching quoits." Then came studies of negro life and character, his "Visit from the old mistress" being one of the best pictures of negro life. Later he painted the landscape of the Adirondacks, then the seafaring people of the New England coast whose life he has interpreted with remarkable poetry and understanding. But it is in his delineation of the ocean, however, that Homer's genius reached its greatest heights.

"It is not the charm of the ocean that he paints. The mood in which he excels is morose,—it is threatening, lowering, savage."

"He is unquestionably the most strictly national painter America has produced, and for that reason he is one of the greatest, if not the greatest. .... His sea is the watery waste, an expression of tremendous force, mystery, peril." His landscapes are redolent of the primeval forests of the new world, its bleak hills, its crags; his men and women are pioneers, fishermen, seafaring folk.

"Cannon rock" is one of his greatest works; "Gulf stream" and "Undertow" are strongly dramatic.

He has made delightful records—joyous and brilliant notes—of his trips to the Bermudas and Bahamas in a group of water colors.

Mr. John W. Beatty of the Carnegie Institute, says of Homer's water colors: "These representations of the spirit and character of the sunlit sea and coast, of the brilliant splendor of the tropic atmosphere are quite without parallel in the history of art. They represent his powerful grasp upon essential qualities and although many of them are painted with unusual breadth, they represent the very essence of truth."

Among his marine masterpieces are:

"A light on the sea"	"On a leeshore"
"The breaker"	"The lookout—All's well"
"The wreck"	"A summer night"
"Watching the breakers—a high sea"	"The fog warning"
	"Kissing the moon"
"The life line"	"A summer squall"
"Sunlight on the coast"	"High cliff, coast of Maine"

Walter Pach, the writer, considers Winslow Homer the greatest American artist. "Homer's renunciation of the joys of color marks him as the stern puritan of the north," he says; and later he compares him to Milton. "Renouncing color, his genius sought consolation in the impressive organization of grand forms, in respect for the individuality of the sea, the sky, and the earth in the almost Tanagra-like grace of human figures."

"Winslow Homer is an absolutely original and national artist; he is the first exponent of pictorial art in the new world. He presents the unique phenomenon of an American painter whose work has in it not the least scintilla or hint of Europe or of Asia." (Brush & P 10:40)

His great marine painting, "Eight bells," recently sold for $50,000, thus establishing the highest recorded price for his canvases. This painting was sold in 1899 for $4,700. In its simplicity and beauty of color, it is one of Homer's greatest achievements.

HOPKIN, ROBERT, (P.) b. Glasgow, Scotland, January 3, 1832; d. Detroit, Michigan, March 21, 1909. Went to Detroit, Michigan, with his parents when eleven years of age and lived there practically all his life.

Mr. Hopkin as a boy grew up on Detroit wharves; received his apprenticeship in mixing colors for decorators and made his living as a scenic artist. For many years he was the leader and patriarch of Detroit artists. At one time was president of the Detroit Association of Arts; also a member of the Society of Western Artists and of the Detroit Water Color Society. His most important work is a series of six paintings for the Cotton Exchange, New Orleans, La. He also painted many drop curtains for Chicago, Denver, Toronto and other cities.

C. Lewis Hind, the English art critic, when in Detroit saw Hopkin's works for the first time and said of them: "No critic could deny to them a place among the very first pictures. They are wonderful, enchanting, powerful, great."

The director of the Museum of Art, Detroit, said: "I believe his modesty, charming as it was, was a great injustice to himself and to the world .... Modesty robbed him of fame due a master's hand."

"His landscapes, figures and interiors are just as suggestive of his poetic power of expression as are his marines." (Detroit Free Press, March 22, 1909)

HOPKINS, EDNA BOIES (Mrs. James R. Hopkins), (E., P.) b. Hudson, Michigan. Studied art in the Cincinnati Art Academy. Mrs. Hopkins is living in France at the present time and is a member of several French art societies.

Her works are in the Library of Congress, Washington, D. C.; Walker Art Gallery, Liverpool; National Museum, Stockholm; Industrial Art Museum, Berlin; and Library of Art and Archaeology, Paris. The Cincinnati Art Gallery has a fine collection of her wood block prints, drawings, and etchings. The subjects range from flowers of Switzerland to Kentucky mountaineers.

"Mrs. Hopkins is of the cosmopolitan type of artist, keenly alive to new ideas and new expressions in art, her own work containing a stimulating feeling of spiritual liveliness that in essence is broadly modern, sanely and beautifully so."

HORNBY, LESTER G., (E.). Began to etch in this country and produced many plates descriptive of New England before he went to Paris in 1906. He has traveled much in foreign lands and has been a regular exhibitor at the Salon des Artistes Francais, and at many of the leading art exhibits held throughout Europe.

Among his most attractive plates are those made in Tunis during the winter of 1908:

"Story teller"   "Passage Arabs"
"Vegetable dealers"   "Marabout tombs"
"The musicians"

His French plates are enthusiastically regarded by those who love Paris:

"Pont Neuf (rainy day)"   "The old court in Rue Vercinge-
"Buildings of the Quai"   torix"
"L'Hiver au Jardin du Luxem-   "St Nicholas des Champs"
   bourg"   "Little balconies"
"Cour des Reines"   "Boulevard de Montparnasse"
                                  "La lettre d'Amour"

Light heartedness of the Paris of the Boulevards, melancholy beauties of the Old Quarter, and the mystery which pervades the life of the far East are interpreted with equal facility.

"It is the life of the city that has attracted Lester G. Hornby .... All seem as parts of a picture of Paris in which houses and streets and people form a characteristic ensemble. Hornby's pictures thus seen and rendered in quiet nooks and corners of Paris, breathe an air of unprejudiced observation recorded with light yet precise indication." (Weiten-kampf.)

HORTON, WILLIAM SAMUEL, (P.) b. Grand Rapids, Michigan, November 16, 1865. Pupil of Art Students' League and National Academy of Design in New York; Laurens and Julien Academy in Paris. Received gold medal at the International Exposition at Nantes, 1904, and medal, second-class, at Orleans, France, 1905. Member of the New York Water Color Club; Cercle Volney and Salon d'Automne, Paris. Also a writer.

HOSMER, HARRIET, (S.) b. Watertown, Mass., October 6, 1830; d. Watertown, Mass., February 21, 1908. She was educated at Lenox, Mass., and displayed a taste for art at an early age; she studied drawing and modeling in Boston. In 1850 she went to St. Louis, Mo., to study anatomy as she could not obtain a course in anatomy from any college in New England because of her sex. Through the influence of friends she was admitted to the medical department of the Missouri State University. In 1852 with her father and Charlotte Cushman she took passage for Italy. In Rome she became the pupil of the English sculptor Gibson, with whom she remained seven years.

Her first works were ideal heads—"Daphne" and "Medusa." They were enthusiastically praised by Gibson and Rauch and were exhibited in Boston in 1853. "Sleeping faun" was exhibited at the Dublin Exhibition of 1865 and was sold on the opening day for $5,000. The London Times said: "In the group of statues are many works of exquisite beauty, but there is one which at once arrests attention and elicits admiration. It is the 'Sleeping faun and satyr' by Miss Hosmer." An Italian publication of the same date contained the following: "The gem of the classic school, in its nobler style of composition is due to an American artist, Harriet Hosmer." Sir Charles Eastlake said: "If it had been discovered among the ruins of Rome or Pompeii it would have been pronounced one of the best Grecian statues," and John Gibson, the sculptor, said, "It is worthy to be an antique."

"Beatrice Cenci" has much grace and beauty of a very intelligible kind; it is now in the Public Library of St. Louis. "Puck" was so popular that thirty replicas were made. The Prince of Wales and the Duke of Hamilton each ordered a copy. Its companion piece, "Will-o'-the-wisp," is pretty and fanciful.

Nathaniel Hawthorne speaks of Miss Hosmer's "Zenobia" as "a very noble and remarkable statue indeed, full of dignity and beauty."

While in Rome she received a commission for a memorial to Madame Falconnet's daughter to be placed in the Church of San Andrea delle

Fratte. This was a great distinction, for she was the first artist other than an Italian to be permitted to place her work in one of the churches of Rome.

Her much criticised statue of Col. Benton in Lafayette Park, St. Louis, Mo., was satisfactory to his daughter, Mrs. Fremont, who at the unveiling said: "She has caught my father's very expression and his attitude."

The "Browning hands" were brought to the United States by Miss Hosmer and presented to her niece although she was offered $5,000 to leave them in England. A cast of these hands was given to the Art Institute, Chicago.

Jarvis, in his "Art idea," says: "She [Miss Hosmer] has no creative power, but has acquired no small degree of dignity and beauty."

Miss Hosmer made a number of discoveries and inventions, including a process of giving Italian limestone the hardness of marble.

HOUSTON, FRANCES C. LYONS, (P.) b. Hudson, Mich., January 17, 1867; d. Windsor, Vt., October, 1906.

Mrs. Houston studied with Lefebvre and Boulanger in Paris; then returned to Boston where she married William C. Houston. She was a member of the Boston Water Color Club, the New York Water Color Club, and the Boston Society of Arts and Crafts.

"The two qualities that gave distinction to Mrs. Houston's work were undoubtedly her sense of style and her sense of beauty .... She worked quietly, satisfied with the joy of creating many forms of beauty in pottery, goldsmith's work, and gardening, in which branches of art she was also an adept. Mrs. Houston's canvases have great technical value." (Cent 75:956)

Her portrait of Ethel Barrymore—her last work—is a charming example of her work as a painter.

HOVENDEN, THOMAS, (P.) b. Dunmanway, Ireland, December 28, 1840; was killed on August 14, 1895, in an unsuccessful effort to save an unknown child from being killed by a railway train. He studied in the Cork School of Design. Came to the United States in 1863, but it was not until 1872 that he began to follow art as a profession. In 1874 he went to Paris and entered the studio of Cabanel, where he remained until 1880 when he returned to the United States. He was elected associate member of the National Academy of Design, New York, in 1881; full member in 1882.

His first notable painting was a "Breton interior of 1793." "Breaking home ties" was one of the most popular paintings at the Columbian

Exposition, 1893. "Last moments of John Brown" which hangs in the Metropolitan Museum of Art, New York, is an especially characteristic canvas. Critics concur in esteeming "Elaine" as his masterpiece. "As a powerful allegorical picture it stands unrivaled among the productions of American genius."

Popular paintings are:

"Jerusalem the golden"   "Thinking of somebody"
"The two lilies"   "News from the conscript"
"A Brittany woman spinning"   "Pride of the old folks"
"Pleasant news"   "Peasant soldiers of La Vendée"
"The image seller"

His is the story-telling picture and the story is told clearly and beautifully.

Howe, William Henry, (P.) b. Ravenna, O., 1846. Pupil of Otto de Thoren and F. de Vuillefroy in Paris. Received honorable mention, New Orleans, 1885; honorable mention, Paris salon, 1886; third-class medal, Paris salon, 1888; silver medal, Paris Exposition, 1889; Temple gold medal, Pennsylvania Academy of the Fine Arts, 1890; grand medal, Crystal Palace, London, 1890; officier d'Acadèmie, Paris, 1896; chevalier Legion of Honor, 1899; member of National Academy of Design, New York, 1897.

Mr Howe has won fame as the painter of landscapes with cattle. His earlier work shows strongly the influence of such masters as Van Marcke and Troyon. His later work is of rare quality and possesses a distinct personal style.

Among his best known paintings are:

"The truants"   "Korten Hof meadows"
"In the orchard"   "Cattle at rest"
"Morning"   "Returning from the heath"

Hubbell, Henry Salem, (P.) b. in the United States. Pupil of Art Institute, Chicago; Whistler, Collin, Laurens, and Benjamin-Constant in Paris. Received honorable mention in the Paris salon, 1901. Is a member of the Paris American Artists' Association and Paris Society of American Painters. Was elected associate member of the National Academy of Design, 1906.

His original training was in illustration, and it was not until 1900, two years after his arrival in Paris, that he "entered upon the study of painting proper" and then visited Spain. In the salon of 1909 he was represented by two canvases—"Caprice" and "Autumn leaves." "Each of these compositions presents a decorative pattern of forms and spaces and a color scheme that is choice and reserved." (Harp 118:289)

Of an exhibition of eleven canvases by this artist at the Art Institute, Chicago, Art and Progress (2:47) writes: "With the exception of an exquisitely painted interior and a study, 'The black fan,' all are portraits. His prize picture, 'The departure,' a life-size portrait of a lady in a long green cloak and a large hat enveloped with a veil, is a harmony in green with a setting of browns. Mr. Hubbell paints with virile and robust temper; and in the portrait of Miss B, a beautiful young woman in pink evening gown, in 'Serena,' a young girl in gray in a shaded room, in 'Sylvia,' another young girl, in 'Winthrop,' a boy, and the extraordinary likeness of 'Aunt Lizzie Aiken,' there is a strength and truth, as well as joyousness of interpretation, which command attention."

HUMPHREYS, MARIE CHAMPNEY, (Min. P.) b. Deerfield, Mass., 1867; d. New Rochelle, N. Y., December 1, 1906. Was married November 22, 1899, to John Sanford Humphreys.

Was a miniature painter. Exhibited in Europe and America.

HUNT, WILLIAM MORRIS, (P., Mural P.) b. Brattleboro, Vt., March 31, 1824; d. Appledore, Isles of Shoals, N. H., September 8, 1879. He began his art studies in the Royal Academy, London, and later went to Düsseldorf. Originally he intended to become a sculptor but abandoned this design and studied under Couture in Paris. While in Paris he was brought into intimate relations with Diaz, and at Barbizon was associated with Millet. In 1855 he returned to the United States and settled in Boston.

The present admiration in this country for modern French art can be directly traced to his advocacy. In his art he liked better to suggest form than to portray it with strong outlines.

He painted many portraits of noted people and also made many original sketches of types of Parisian life; among them, "The street musician," "Girl at the fountain," "Child selling violets."

Among his more important works are:

"The drummer boy"	"Bugle call"
"Boy chasing a butterfly"	"The marguerites"
"The morning star"	"The belated kid"
"Girl reading"	"Girl with cap"

Of Mr. Hunt's "Bathers" a well-known connoisseur has said: "It is one of the three or four paintings of the nude in the nineteenth century which a Greek would have understood and admired."

In 1878 his mural paintings were put up in the Senate Chamber in the Albany state house, and in this work—"Flight of night" and "The discoverer," he had a true conception of mural painting.

Lübke says: "He was the first American to give to the world large mural paintings of artistic importance .... Many of his smaller pictures have great charm, and he is always a forceful technician."

Hunt's place in art can never be overestimated, for his power of personality made him exert tremendous influence on the students that flocked around him.

HUNTINGTON, ANNA V. HYATT (Mrs. Archer M. Huntington) (S.) b. Cambridge, Mass., March 10, 1876. A musician—an artistic performer on the violin—during an attack of nervous prostration, Miss Hyatt found recreation in modeling clay. This diversion was the means of her abandoning her musical career, for upon recovery of health she chose sculpture for her life work, studying with Henry Hudson Kitson and at the Art Students' League, New York. She has been represented in many of the leading exhibitions throughout the country during the past twenty years, and was represented in the salon of 1910. She was elected an associate member of the National Academy of Design in 1916; a full member in 1920.

At an exhibition of her works in New York, 1914, there were displayed forty-three animal subjects. A few were: "The whirlwind" (showing a lioness and crane), "Jaguar," "White horses of the sea," "A yearling colt," "Bull's head," "Rolling bear," "Fox and geese," and "Pigs under fence."

"Her animals are most assertive in character and away from the conventionalized forms we have seen for years by the hundreds .... Miss Hyatt seems to comprehend the psychology of each and every animal she models." (Arts & D 2:106)

In her animal studies she must be classed with Landseer and Bonheur.

Anna V. Hyatt's group of eight plunging horses is a remarkable piece of work and is accorded by critics a place of equality with Borglum's famous "Mares of Diomedes." (Arts & D 2:296)

Among other things Miss Hyatt has restored prehistoric animals for the Brooklyn Museum.

Her most important bronzes are: "Winter," "A steep grade," "Colts playing," "Colts in the storm," "Goats butting," etc.

Miss Hyatt in her early work collaborated with Miss Abastenia St. Leger Eberle, another American young woman who abandoned music for sculpture. Their first group, "Men and bull," was awarded a medal at the St. Louis Exposition; "Boy and goat playing" is another fine group done in collaboration. (Craftsm 8:623)

"In Miss Hyatt we have no doubt the greatest woman exponent of animal life in this country. . . . . She presents the animal to us as only one who knows and understands it can, and reproduces a living thing in all its fullness of strength and natural expression." (Arts & D 4:229)

Miss Hyatt's statue of Joan of Arc, placed on Riverside Drive, New York City, is her most finished work. Several years ago, while in Paris, she executed an equestrian statue of the Maid of Orleans. It was exhibited in the salon of 1910, favorably received, and awarded honorable mention. When a group of American citizens decided to erect a monument to Joan of Arc, this early statue (which was submitted in a competition of designs) was selected by the committee; and it was the first equestrian statue of a woman created by a woman.

Miss Hyatt had much difficulty in her efforts to model the suit of armor historically correct, for experts gave the information that there is not in existence a complete suit of armor of that period. But from fragments of wood, bronze and stone sculpture and old tombs tracings, she worked out the details.

The pedestal is Gothic in design and is particularly appropriate and interesting, for the stones which form the arches were taken from the floor in the cell of the prison in which Joan was confined at Rouen.

In 1917 Miss Hyatt was appointed head of the department of sculpture of the Museum of the French Art Institute in the United States, and has since been assembling in this country examples of French sculpture.

The French government has joined with the Blois municipality in arranging for a replica of Miss Hyatt's Joan of Arc, and she went to France in 1921 to superintend the erection. The town of Blois, the capital of the department of Loire-et-Cher, was the base of Joan of Arc's operations in 1429.

"Whether portraying domestic horse or jungle beast, she gives the impression of a sensitive artist working easily, effectively, and convincingly, stating all the picturesqueness of the animal without overemphasis."

"The breakers" is her most imaginative creation. In the portrayal of life and action she has few, if any, superiors.

Miss Hyatt has received the decoration of the Legion of Honor from the French government.

On March 10, 1923, she was married to Mr. Archer M. Huntington, founder of the Hispanic Society of America.

HUTCHENS, FRANK TOWNSEND, (P.) b. Canandaigua, N. Y., June 7, 1869. Pupil of the Art Students' Institute of New York under Wiles, Dumond, and Mowbray; Julien Academy under Benjamin-Constant and Laurens, and Colarossi Academy in Paris.

"Hutchens is a painter of moods. A peculiar atmospheric condition, a sweep of wind across the landscape, or a sudden luminosity of sky is sufficient to him to lend a simple road or bit of forest land a peculiar and permanent fascination. He is particularly fond of sunlight, and its golden lustre embellishes the simplest objects with a true touch of poetry. But it is the poetry of nature, of contrast and color, or in other words an expression of complete pictorial sanity .... He is an excellent draughtsman—perhaps best shown in his figure work .... Many of his canvases have hung on the walls of the Royal Academy, the New York Academy, and the leading galleries of America." (Int Studio 47:160)

Two of his best known paintings are:

"The marriage column"
"A song in the sky"

HUTT, HENRY, (I.) b. Chicago, Ill., December 18, 1875. After a short season in instruction at the Art Institute of Chicago, he opened a studio in New York City, his commissions warranting the step. His first important undertakings were the illustrations for a continued story for the Saturday Evening Post. He has illustrated many leading magazines and periodicals, books, etc.

Mr. Hutt likes women and children for his subjects, depicting them with finesse and daintiness of execution. His characters suggest spontaneity and human naturalness but they are usually in a setting too decorative for reality.

"His line is quaint and often whimsical with an almost picturesque ensemble, and he conveys his interpretation with sentiment and a redundant sense of beauty."

"He makes clothes tell their portion of the story, but perhaps he is more an apostle of the well-dressed than is Mr. Fisher." (Bkbuyer 22:23)

HUTTY, ALFRED H., (P., E.), b. Grand Haven, Michigan, September, 1877. Pupil of St. Louis School of Fine Arts; also studied with Chase and Birge Harrison.

Mr. Hutty's boyhood was spent in lumbering towns of Michigan and in frontier towns of Kansas at a military post, and although the environment created an atmosphere far from artistic, at the age of fifteen he gained a scholarship to an art school by producing the best original drawing of his school. A few years later he entered a stained glass studio in Kansas City as a designer and painter of figure and landscape windows. After spending some time in St. Louis engaged in similar work, he went east to Woodstock for instructions in landscape painting. During the war he was a member of the camouflage corps. At the close of the war he went south to Charleston, S. C., where he found material for his pencil drawings and etchings which were favorably received at a recent exhibition at the Corcoran Gallery, Washington, D. C.

"To one with an eye for line and a feeling for form, these quaint old houses of an earlier epoch as well as the many charming old gateways, doorways, and vistas down cobbled streets and between high walls, cried aloud for transference to canvas or drawing pad.

"His sense of form and of direction is indeed almost infallible; and even when he is employing the simple formula of cross-hatching to convey the effect of a flat tone or mass of shadow, the direction of the lines is instinctively such as to accentuate the character of the form and its surrounding borders." (Am M of Art 13:479)

HYATT, ANNA VAUGHN. See Mrs. Anna V. H. Huntington.

HYDE, HELEN, (E., P.) b. Lima, N. Y., April 6, 1868; d. Pasadena, Cal., May 16, 1919. Pupil of Emil Carlsen in New York, Raphael Collin in Paris, Skarbïna in Berlin, and Kano Tomanobu in Japan. Specialty: Japanese subjects in colored wood blocks and etching.

It was the enthusiasm of her teacher, Félix Régamey, director of the Musee Guimet in Paris, that first inspired her interest in Japanese art. When her pictures were refused at the salon, she returned home determined to give up her chosen profession.

Taking up her home in San Francisco, the Chinese characteristics interested her; and her sketches, made in Chinatown, became popular. Going to Japan for a few months, she stayed fifteen years; and her experience there brought to this country an interest in Japanese prints.

After a year's study with the last of the famous school of the Kano artists, and acquiring the Japanese method of wielding the brush, she was rewarded when her master asked her to paint a kakemono for the annual exhibition. In competition with the Japanese artists, her picture, "A monarch of Japan," won the first prize.

Later Miss Hyde took up wood engraving and printing, and her color prints in this field of art became famous.

A few of her popular prints are:

"Secrets"	"The bamboo fence"
"The lucky branch"	"Belated"
"The mirror"	"The blossom child"
"Happiness flower"	"Day dreams"
"The greeting"	"Baby San"
"Baby and toy"	"In his father's shoes"
"Rainy evening"	"Child of the people"
"A snowy day in Japan"	"An April evening"
"Winter"	"Going to the fair"
"Red curtain"	

One of Miss Hyde's most successful etchings is "Little Cherry Blossom."

"Perhaps the greatest triumph in Miss Hyde's work lies in the successful rendering of atmosphere which is delicately suggestive of the flower-blossom country .... In "The rainy day" we have this quality at its best." (Int Studio 24:239)

Miss Hyde later painted in Mexico; she also wrote of the "Color lure of Mexico." Several of these paintings are particularly interesting because of the evident Japanese influence upon the artist's style.

Miss Hyde imitated the Japanese only in the method of production. "Her children are real children, sound in body and healthy in disposition. And above all they are children who do something."

She was especially fond of soft pinks and greens and lavenders and yellows. The colors of her prints are their greatest charm.

It has been suggested that as an interpreter of child life she has done for Japan what Boutet de Monvel did for France.

The American Magazine of Art closes its tribute to this late lamented artist as follows: "There is a charm about her rendition of children, whether they be Japanese or Chinese or Mexican or American, which gives token of her sympathy with childhood; and with her passing has gone from the world a life of cheerfulness and courage and high purpose which, like a flower of sweet fragrance, has added beauty to life."

INMAN, HENRY, (P., Min. P.) b. Utica, N. Y., October 20, 1801; d. New York, January 17, 1846. He displayed talent for art as a lad but he inclined to a military career and had secured a commission to enter the West Point Academy when he saw Westmuller's famous "Danaë" in the studio of John Wesley Jarvis in New York. He immediately presented himself as a candidate for artistic instructions, was accepted, and studied with Jarvis several years. For years he executed miniature, cabinet and life-size portraits, practiced lithographic drawing, and sketched scenery with rare assiduity and success. He was one of the founders of the National Academy of Design in 1825 and was elected its first vice-president.

Mr. Inman went to Europe in 1845 and while in England painted the portraits of Wordsworth, Macaulay, Dr. Thomas Chalmers and others; returning to America he also painted the portraits of many distinguished persons.

His landscapes and genre compositions include:

"Scenes from the Bride of Lam-   "The newsboy"
    mermoor"   "The brothers"
"Rydal Falls, England"   "Woodland scene"
"Mumble-the-peg"   "Rip Van Winkle"
"The sisters"   "Boyhood of Washington"
"Ruins of Brambletye house"   "Lake of the Dismal swamp"
"Birnan wood"

"In his happiest efforts at portraiture wherein there was great inequality viewed as a whole, Inman has been compared to Sir Thomas Lawrence; his rapidity of execution was uncommon; a 'delicate mottling' was often admired in his color, a completeness and neatness of style in his landscapes, and skillful manipulation in the works undertaken *con amore*, while it is conceded that he was the first American artist who attempted genre with success." (Tuckerman)

INNESS, GEORGE, (P.) b. Newburg, N. Y., May 1, 1825; d. Bridge of Allan, Scotland, August 3, 1894. At the age of sixteen he began to study engraving in New York and studied art in the studio of Regis Gignoux, New York. In 1846 he began the practice of landscape painting and in 1850 went abroad where he became acquainted with Corot and Rousseau, and enjoyed for a time the close companionship of Millet. He is generally considered our greatest landscape painter. "American sunset" was selected in 1867 by the Paris salon as a representative work of American art. He was elected member of the National Academy of Design, in 1868.

"With him the inspiring idea is principal; form secondary, being the outgrowth of the idea. His pictures illustrate phases of mind and feelings. He uses nature's forms simply as language to express thought." (Tuckerman)

" 'Moonlight' fully represents Inness' idea of the night. He had a strong leaning to the occult and many of his paintings have a spiritual and allegorical significance. Inness' paintings stand in American art where those of Rousseau and Corot do in that of France." (Nat Cyc Am Biog)

"Inness gives with equal felicity the drowsy heat, hot shimmer and languid quiet of a summer noon, or the storm weighed atmosphere; its dark masses of vapor and the wild gathering of thunder clouds with their solemn hush before the tempest breaks. He uses sunlight sparingly, but it glows on his canvas and turns darkness into hope and joy." (Jarvis "Art Idea")

"Delaware valley" is considered by many to be his masterpiece.

Arthur Hoeber says: "At his [Inness'] best he yields to no man in his profession as an interpreter of nature out of doors."

Van Dyke says: "Inness is more allied to Corot than to Meissonier. He never was the perfect master of the brush that we have heard him called, though he was an acceptable and often a very satisfactory technician .... It was with color, light, and air that Inness scored his greatest success."

"His subjects are related to human life and possibly our interest in his pictures is due to the fact that he shows thoughts, emotions and sensations comprehensible of humanity ....

"Inness must be ranked here as the discoverer of the American meadow and woodland—a new realm of beauty. It is possibly his most lasting title to fame .... And Inness .... found all the material he needed within fifty miles of New York. It was the original discovery of this material, his point of view regarding it, what he did with it and what he made us see in it, that gives him high rank in the history of American painting."

Lübke says: "He was like Corot in his indifference to the minute facts of the country before him, and like Corot in his disposition to harmonize sombre foliage and pale distant sky into a lovely harmony, but he was more eager than was Corot to seize the brilliant color of sunset and to use his gray-green trees as a solid frame for those glowing effects."

A list of Inness' principal paintings in public collections, also bibliography and magazine article references are given in "Masters in Art," Vol. 9.

INNESS, GEORGE, JR., (P.) b. Paris, France, January 4, 1854. The son of George Inness. Was a pupil of his father in Rome, 1870-4; studied one year with Bonnat in Paris. Obtained gold medal in Paris salon, 1899; also gold and silver medals at various exhibitions in the United States. Has a studio in New York. Devotes himself to animal painting. Has exhibited at the National Academy of Design, New York, since 1877, when he sent "The ford" and "Patience."

A few of his paintings are:

"Monarch of the farm"   "At the brook"
"The pride of the dairy"   "Abandoned"
"Waiting for the master"   "Maternity"
"New born lamb"

Member of the National Academy of Design, New York, since 1899; and of the French Academy since 1902.

Of his landscapes and atmospheric effects, Müther says: "The younger Inness has a fondness for departing thunder showers, rainbows and misty red sunbeams penetrating in the form of wedges through a sea of mist, and resting upon stony fields."

ISHAM, SAMUEL, (P.) b. New York, May 12, 1855; d. Easthampton, L. I., June 12, 1914. Graduated from Yale College in 1875. Had his first instruction in drawing in the art school under Professor Niemeyer. During a three years' sojourn in Europe he had drawing lessons from Jacquesson de la Chevreuse. On his return to the United States, he took up the study of law and practiced the profession for five years. In 1883 he again took up art and went to Paris and entered the Académie Julien, studying four years under Boulanger and Lefebvre. He was elected a member of the Society of American Artists, 1891; associate member of National Academy of Design, 1900; full member, 1906. He is author of "History of American Painting."

"Mr. Isham both by his brush and pen did work effectively for the prestige of American art." (Outl 107:438)

In reviewing Mr. Isham's "History of American painting," Charles Henry Hart, the art critic, writes: "It is an interesting and invaluable work although it is not a history in the scientific sense of the word as understood today .... It is a most delightfully sane, scholarly, catholic and intelligent criticism of the work of American painters, and as such is entitled to the very first rank in the small library of true art criticism." (Dial 41:86)

IVES, HALSEY COOLEY, (P.) b. Montour Falls, N. Y., October 27, 1847; d. London, England, May 5, 1911. Was a pupil of Alexander Piatowsky. In 1864 he entered the government service as a draughtsman and in 1869 he began a study of decorative art; later he became an instructor in the Polytechnic school of St. Louis. In 1881, at the establishment of the Museum of Fine Arts, St. Louis, he became its director. He was decorated by King Oscar of Sweden with the Order of the Vasa and by King Christian of Denmark with the Dannebrog Cross. He received a silver medal at the St. Louis Exposition for his landscape, "Waste lands," and has received decorations and medals for art services in this country, France, Austria, Japan, China, Portugal, Belgium, Bulgaria, Sweden, and Denmark. A member of the National Sculpture Society, the National Art Club, the Academy of Science and other organizations. (American Art Annual, Vol. 9)

IVES, PERCY, (P.) b. Detroit, Mich., June 5, 1864. At the age of eighteen he entered the Pennsylvania Academy of the Fine Arts. In 1885 he visited Europe, spending six months traveling in Scotland, England, the Netherlands, Germany, and Italy. He studied three years at the Academie Julien, Paris, under Boulanger, Lefebvre, Benjamin-Constant, and Cormon. After a second visit to Paris in 1890 he was appointed dean of the Detroit Institute of Arts. In 1893 he studied at the Ecole des Beaux Arts under Gérome and in the same year exhibited at the salon.

Returning to Detroit in 1895 he resumed his position at the Institute of Arts, since which time he has painted the portraits of many distinguished Americans; has also done some landscape work.

Mr. Ives was one of the organizers of the Society of Western Artists and is an incorporator and trustee of the Detroit Institute of Arts.

JOHANSEN, JOHN CHRISTEN, (P.) b. Copenhagen, Denmark, November 25, 1876. Was brought to this country when an infant and had a course of art study at the Art Institute, Chicago, in early boyhood. He studied under Duveneck, Freer, and Vanderpoel; then went to Paris and continued his art studies with Benjamin-Constant and Jean Paul Laurens; later entered the class of Whistler. In 1901 he returned to the United States to become a member of the faculty of the Art Institute, Chicago, and at about that time identified himself with the Society of Western Artists. Resigned as a teacher that he might devote more time to portrait painting, and in 1906 went to Italy, sojourning long in Venice. On his return, a special exhibition of his Venetian pictures was held in London. Instant recognition came to him and several of the canvases found places in prominent British collections. Arthur Hoeber in writing of this exhibition says: "Mr. Johansen scorned precedent. He depicted Venice in a way entirely his own .... There were pictures of the city at dawn, under golden haze at sunset, in suggestive opal fogs and always there was palpitating color with admirable drawing and construction to her streets, buildings and canals .... And the compositions were so generalized that the spectator delighted in their simplicity, seriousness and beauty. The color which was used generously was piled on in simple masses, broken and vibrating." (Int Studio 42:sup iii)

At a later exhibition of American art held in Chicago, Mr. Johansen had ten canvases. "Each specimen proclaimed its separate personality," writes a critic. "At sundown" is remarkable for its unusual coloring. "The picture book" is a charming arrangement of light. "Autumn afternoon" is riotous in those subdued bright colorings with which Mr. Johansen is so clever. "When the day is done" is a poetic conception. "Evening calm" is a majestic essay of the hour. "Golden mists" demonstrates his skill in rendering.

"Mr. Johansen handles his architectural drawing firmly and well, but in a summary enough fashion to subordinate it to its more fluent, pictorial purpose." (Int Studio 40:sup lxxviii)

"Technique with Mr. Johansen is a medium of expression and in that guise is never employed to excite wonderment."

As an illustrator Mr. Johansen has also been very successful and many consider that in this field he shows as much promise as in his pictorial productions.

His group of paintings of scenes in the United States shipyards during the war are attractive. They are illustrative; also picturesque and artistic.

Mr. Johansen had the distinguished honor of being one of the prominent painters of this country selected by the National Art Committee to paint a group of the leaders of the allies in the World War. He was assigned Premier Orlando, Field Marshal Haig, Marshal Joffre, General Diaz, and "Signing of the Peace Treaty, 1919."

JOHNSON, EASTMAN, (P.) b. Lovell, Maine, July 29, 1824; d. New York, April 5, 1906. As a young man he began the practice of his profession by the execution of portraits in black and white, showing considerable skill and meeting with some success.

In 1849 he went abroad and shared the studio of Emanuel Leutze at Düsseldorf, Prussia. He studied art four years at The Hague and then proceeded to Paris. Returned to the United States in 1856.

His first important works were "Card players" and "Savoyard boy." He opened a studio in New York upon returning to the United States and was made a member of the National Academy of Design in 1860.

Here he painted those pictures of American domestic and Negro life in which he so decidedly excelled. In accurate delineation of character "The old Kentucky home" is hardly surpassed.

Tuckerman says: "In his delineation of the Negro, Eastman Johnson has achieved a peculiar fame. One may find in his best pictures of this class a better insight into the normal character of that unfortunate race than ethnological discussion often yields."

"He was a power in American art life to the very last. He painted a large number of portraits, and his self-painted portrait, painted in 1899, is technically superior to anything executed by him during the first fifty years of his life." (Artists of the Nineteenth Century)

JOHNSON, MARSHALL, (P.) b. Boston, Mass.; pupil of the Lowell Institute; member of the Boston Art Club and Copley Society.

Painter of "United States Frigate Constitution."

JOHNSTON, JOHN HUMPHREYS, (P.) b. New York, November 2, 1857. Studied art under John LaFarge. In 1899 he went to Paris where he studied under Lefebvre and Doucet, and later to Madrid; he has resided mainly in France and Italy since and has a studio in Venice.

One of his pictures, "Domino Rose," is now owned in France, and the portrait of his mother is in the Luxembourg. "Light nights in Norway" and "Mystery of the night" are characteristic paintings.

In 1898 he painted the portrait of Sarah Bernhardt as "Lorenzaccio," and the "Vision of St. Paul at Lystra." Spain and Brittany have furnished many of the subjects he has used.

Mr. Johnston was made a chevalier of the Legion of Honor in 1901; is associate member of the Société Nationale des Beaux Arts, Paris; and of the International Society of Painters, Gravers, etc., London.

JONES, HUGH BOLTON, (P.) b. Baltimore, Md., October 20, 1848. Studied art in France. Received bronze medal at Paris Exposition, 1889; bronze medal at Paris Exposition, 1900; Webb prize, Society American Artists, 1902; Shaw fund prize, 1902; gold medal at St. Louis Exposition, 1904. Is a member of the National Academy. Specialty, landscape.

He visited Europe in 1876 and studied there four years, becoming a member of the artists' colony at Pont Aven in Brittany, and traveling in Spain, France, England, Italy, and Morocco.

Principal paintings are:

"Brittany"	"The road through the poplars"
"October"	"Summer in the Blue Ridge"
"On Herring Run"	"Spring"

Mr. Jones' paintings are in the Metropolitan Museum, New York; Peabody Institute, Baltimore; Erie Art Club; Corcoran Gallery of Art, Washington; Shaw collection, Philadelphia Art Club.

"His work possesses sterling qualities of color and drawing, belongs to the naturalistic school and is widely known at home and abroad." (Nat Cyc Am Biog)

JOSEPHI, ISAAC E., (Min. P.) b. New York City. Pupil of Art Students' League, New York; also of Leon Bonnat in Paris. First president of American Society of Miniature Painters; member Royal Society of Miniature Painters, London. Mr. Josephi is accredited with the conception of the American society. His "Portrait of a lady," shown at the first exhibition of the society, was the subject of much controversy. Some miniaturists insisted that it was far too modern for their art's limitations, while others insisted that their art had no limitations.

KEITH, WILLIAM, (P., I.) b. Aberdeen, Scotland, 1839; d. Berkeley, California, March, 1911. When a lad he came to this country with his parents. Began his career in New York as a wood engraver; afterward worked for Harper.

In 1859 Mr. Keith went to California and began his out of doors painting; he sketched in black and white and also did water color work. In 1869 he went to Düsseldorf, then to Spain.

He was employed by the Northern Pacific Railroad Company to paint some of the characteristic scenes along its route. "Some of his redwood pictures are very beautiful, giving vivid impressions of the magnificent scenery of California, but pastoral scenes with distant mountains are his characteristic subject, and these he has rendered under many varying conditions of light and atmosphere." (Nat Cyc Am Biog)

"He delighted in rich, strong color and in dramatic aspects of nature. His paintings are toneful, poetical and decorative." (Art & P 2:227)

Keith's paintings "deal with emotions aroused or suggested by landscape under certain conditions of light and atmosphere." (Int Studio 33:36)

His paintings are included in the permanent collections of the Chicago Art Institute, the Brooklyn Institute, the Corcoran Gallery of Art and the National Gallery of Art, Washington, as well as in many private collections.

When George Inness visited California in 1890 he made William Keith's studio his headquarters.

KELLER, ARTHUR I., (I.) b. New York, July 4, 1866. Pupil of National Academy of Design under Wilmarth and Ward, and of Loefftz in Munich. Has won many prizes for drawings, water color, illustration, and painting and is a member of leading art clubs.

Of his illustrations shown at an exhibition of the Society of Illustrators, the International Studio for December, 1912, says: "They are so ably executed, so full of technical brilliancy, of learning in the value of accent and contrast, in the animating power of spirited brushwork, that one wonders if he might not make dancing compositions without the introduction of solid figures. He has a sense of color, that intuitive feeling for value that is essentially a painter quality."

Among his best works are:

"At Mass"   "The sisters"
"Lead, kindly light"   "The finishing touches"

Popular books that he has illustrated:

"The first American, George   "Hanging of the crane," Long-
  Washington"   fellow
"A poor man"   "Legend of Sleepy Hollow,"
"Autobiography of a quack"   Irving
"The Virginian"   Bret Hart's stories
"The right of way"

KELLY, JAMES EDWARD, (S., I.) b. New York, July 30, 1855. His first pictures were historical compositions and from his earliest childhood he studied everything he could find touching upon American history. In 1871 he was apprenticed to a wood engraver and studied in the Academy of Design. Also studied with Theodore Robinson and Carl Hirschberg. He assisted in organizing the Art Students' League. Entered the art department of Harper & Brothers in 1873 and opened a studio with Edwin A. Abbey where they began illustrating for magazines. His first statuette was of "Sheridan's ride."

Mr. Kelly was chosen to model the five bas-reliefs around the base of the Monmouth monument. The subjects selected were:

"The council of war at Hopewell"
"Washington rallying his troops"
"Ramsey defending his guns"
"Molly Pitcher"
"Wayne's charge"

Other well known works are:
"Arnold wounded in the trenches"; "Schuyler giving his plans to Gates before the Battle of Saratoga," for the Saratoga monument; statue of General Grant at Donelson, for which the general posed; statue of "Call to arms," for the Troy monument; statue of "General Buford at Gettysburg"; "Knowlton at Harlem Heights," at Columbia College for the Sons of the Revolution.

His later works are an equestrian statue of General Sherman, Col. Roosevelt at San Juan Hill, and the Fitz-John Porter monument for which General Porter selected Mr. Kelly to be the sculptor. (Nat Cyc Am Biog)

KEMBLE, EDWARD WINDSOR, (I.) b. Sacramento, Cal., Jan. 18, 1861. Educated in the public schools of New York. Self-taught in art.

Since 1881 has been connected with various magazines and weekly periodicals as illustrator and cartoonist; specialty, negro characters. Has illustrated many notable books, such as Mark Twain's "Huckleberry Finn" and "Puddin' Head Wilson"; Stowe's "Uncle Tom's Cabin." He is author of books entitled "Rosemary," "Virginia Creeper," "Kemble's Coons," "Kemble's Pickaninnies," "Billy-goat" and other comicali-

He has exhibited in New York, Philadelphia, Chicago, St. Louis, and other cities in the United States.

KEMEYS, EDWARD, (S.) b. Savannah, Ga., January 31, 1843; d. Georgetown Heights, Washington, D. C., May 11, 1907. Received his education in the schools of New York City. Upon leaving school he entered mercantile business which he gave up for federal service during the Civil War; and it was not until after the close of the war and he was employed in the civil engineering corps of Central Park, New York, that he made his début as a sculptor. His specialty is Indians and wild animals of America.

In 1878 he exhibited in the Paris salon his now famous group "Bison and wolves." Returning to New York he produced "Still hunt," "Wolves," "Panther and deer," and "Raven and coyote."

In 1892 he went to Chicago, executing there a number of large groups for the Columbian Exposition. He also modeled the large bronze lions in front of the Chicago Art Institute building.

Julian Hawthorne in 1884 in writing of Mr. Kemeys' art said that we find "not merely, nor chiefly, the accurate representation of the animal's external aspect, but—what is vastly more difficult to seize and portray— the essential animal character or temperament which controls and actuates the animal's movement and behavior .... Here is an artist who understands how to translate pose into meaning, and action into utterance, and to select those poses and actions which convey the broadest and most comprehensive idea of the subject's prevailing traits." (Cent 6:214)

KENDALL, MARGARET STICKNEY (Mrs. William Sergeant Kendall), (Min. P.) b. Staten Island, N. Y., November 29, 1871. Pupil of J. Alden Weir, Julius Rolshoven, and William Sergeant Kendall.

Received bronze medal at St. Louis Exposition, 1904. Member of the American Society of Miniature Painters.

KENDALL, WILLIAM SERGEANT, (P.) b. Spuyten Duyvil, N. Y., January 20, 1869. At the age of fourteen he was painting and modeling with Thomas Eakins in Philadelphia; from seventeen to nineteen he worked in the Art Students' League, New York; then went to Paris where he studied with Luc-Olivier Merson and later at the Ecole des Beaux Arts.

At twenty-one he exhibited in the salon and the next year, 1891, received honorable mention for his "Penitents." This picture has obtained for him several medals and prizes; other paintings have brought him flattering recognition. "Narcissa" won the Harris prize; "Alison" won the Potter Palmer gold medal and $1,000. Is a member of the Society of American Artists; associate member of the National Academy of Design, New York, 1901; full member, 1905.

Mr. Kendall has been called the "painter of children." His own charming children are his models. In his mother and child subjects, he shows the tender joy of motherly love.

Other favorite pictures are:

"A fairy tale"   "The end of day"
"Beatrice"   "The seer"
"An interlude"   "The critic"
"L'Allegro" and "Il Penseroso"   "The green gnome"

"Mr. Kendall is that somewhat rare type of artist, a classical intimist. His vision is eminently classic. All his forms are generalized from repeated observation .... Kendall is not afraid of putting into a picture a good deal that the memory contributes to the eye; he is, one might say, anti-impressionistic." (Arts & D 1:16)

"With ideals unimpaired, Kendall finds himself today the master of a self-evolved technique eminently congenial to their interpretation." (Harper 117:568)

"He is a skilful technician .... Surfaces in his paintings are exquisitely rendered."

KENT, ROCKWELL, (P., I.) b. Tarrytown Heights, N. Y., June 21, 1882. A pupil of Chase and Henri.

Rockwell Kent was one of a group of artists whose pictures were refused admittance to the National Academy exhibition a few years ago. His subjects were snow covered landscapes, rocky coasts, and sea-faring laborers. The late James G. Huneker said of him: "The paint is laid on by an athlete of the truth. Dissonances are dared that make you pull up your coat collar." The critic of the New York Press called them "the finest pictures in their genre ever painted in America." Joseph Chamberlain of the Mail, wrote: "One does not know whether one is in a world of remote antiquity or one of the ideal future, but that does not matter; the pictures themselves are highly beautiful."

Being unsuccessful with his coast of Maine subjects he removed to Newfoundland, but his imaginative paintings and drawings of that country were not popular and he failed to gain recognition. In despair he sailed in the summer of 1918 with his young son for Alaska and remained there, far removed from civilization, until the following spring. His "Wilderness," a journal of his adventures while there, was profusely illustrated with his own drawings.

Lewis Hind describes him as a combination of Walt Whitman and Winslow Homer, and in referring to the sixty drawings which he made while there Hind says, "These Alaskan drawings seem to me very remarkable .... Of course he is a student of Blake and an intense admirer."

The best of these drawings are in series. One called "Autobiography" begins with "Sunrise," includes "Meal time," and closes with "Day's end." Another is "The mad hermit." One of the finest is "Adventure."

"Cain," "Nostalgia," "Foreboding," "Welschmerz," "Ecstasy," "The starlighter victory," and "Prayer" express certain elemental ideas simply and profoundly. His "Prison bars" was the first canvas wherein one could discover the mysticism and largeness of vision characteristic of William Blake. "Winter," a marine of his, is in the Metropolitan Museum of New York City.

Robert Henri, his teacher and sponsor, says: "The very things that he portrays on his canvas are the things that he sees written in the great organization of life; and his painting is a proclamation of the rights of man, of the dignity of man, of the dignity of creation. It is his belief in God. It is what art should mean."

Mr. Kent has recently returned from a ten months' trip to Patagonia, and his thrilling experiences in adventuring about Cape Horn he has related in a series of articles in the Century Magazine (1923). This voyager's log has since been published in book form entitled "Voyaging: south from the Strait of Magellan." The illustrations are original drawings.

KINNEY, MARGARET WEST (Mrs. Troy Kinney), (I.) b. Peoria, Ill. Pupil of Art Students' League of New York; Julien Academy in Paris under Robert-Fleury, Collin, Merson and Lefebvre. Has illustrated many books.

KINNEY, TROY, (I.) b. Kansas City, Mo. Pupil of New York School of Art. Member of Yale Club of New York. Has illustrated "The white Christ" and in collaboration with Margaret W. Kinney "A ladder of swords," "The ward of King Canute," "Barlash of the guard," and other books.

KIRK, MARIA LOUISE, (P., I.) b. Philadelphia, Pa.; daughter of George H. and Harriet (Craig) Kirk; studied at Philadelphia School of Design and Pennsylvania Academy of the Fine Arts, Philadelphia Art Club. Received Mary Smith prize at the Pennsylvania Academy of the Fine Arts, 1894.

Is illustrator of "Alice in Wonderland" and other children's books; also a portrait painter.

Favorite pictures:

"Jack and Jill" "Little Miss Muffett"
"Little Bo Peep" "Mistress Mary"
"Little Boy Blue" "Queen of hearts"
"Little Jack Horner" "This little pig"

KNIGHT, DANIEL RIDGWAY, (P.) b. Philadelphia, Pa., 1839; d. March, 1924; of Quaker parents. Few men who have won distinction with the palette and brush have started under less favorable auspices; a ban was placed under the parental roof on pictures and music. His grandfather was convinced of his artistic talent, and through his influence Ridgway was permitted to enter the classes of the Pennsylvania Academy of the Fine Arts. Later, with parental sanction and support, he was settled in Paris. He studied in the atelier Gleyre, then spent three years at the Ecole des Beaux Arts; later studied at the British Academy, Rome; returned to the United States and took a studio in Philadelphia for a time painting portraits and genre pictures and teaching.

In 1871 went to Paris and in 1873 with his family moved to Poissy where he met Meissonier. This acquaintance ripened into warm friendship, and Mr. Knight ever afterward acknowledged the great French painter as his master.

He received honorable mention at the Paris salon of 1884; third-class gold medal, Paris salon, 1888; was honored with the Cross of the Legion of Honor, France, 1889; and with the Cross of Saint Michael of Bavaria, 1892.

To the salon of 1873 he sent "The fugitives" and to the salon of 1875, "Washerwomen."

"The Shepherdess of Rolleboise," "A summer evening," "On the terrace." "The gardener's daughter," "July morning," "Quietude," and "Curiosity" are all salon pictures and give a fair idea of the character of his work.

"Those familiar with Knight's paintings will recognize in them a sort of family resemblance, due to likeness of models and similarity of landscape backgrounds."

He is for the most part the painter of a single class of models—demure little peasant girls with their wooden shoes and picturesque costumes.

"He glories in the fact .... that he is a painter of popular pictures, in which happy conceptions successfully worked out meet public approval and command public patronage." (Brush & P 7:193)

At the age of eighty-four, this dean of the American painters in France was still painting at his home on the Seine, near Paris.

KNOX, SUSAN RICKER, (P.) b. Portsmouth, N. H. Received her art training in the art schools of Philadelphia and New York; also studied in Europe; is a member of several art societies and her paintings have been exhibited in the larger cities of the United States.

Miss Knox is known as a painter of portraits and especially the portraits of children.

"In the painting of hair, Miss Knox is particularly happy ....
Miss Knox has been at work for a number of years on a series of canvases depicting some special phase of motherhood where the spiritual
relation is expressed as well as the physical .... 'The usurper' is a
charming example of Miss Knox's art." (Int Studio 49 :sup lxxvii)

Miss Knox recently exhibited a series of paintings of the European
emigrants at Ellis Island. The painting is admirably done and engaging in quality. The pictures were exhibited in the Capitol at Washington, D. C., to help the passage of the Immigration bill.

KONTI, ISIDORE, (S.) b. Vienna, Austria, July 2, 1862, of Hungarian
parents. Entered the Imperial Academy at the age of sixteen; won
several scholarships and finished his studies at Meisterschule of Prof.
Karl Kundmann, Vienna. After two years in Rome he returned to
Vienna and executed numerous works, including a marble bust of
Emperor Francis Joseph. Came to the United States in 1890.

Associate member of the National Academy in 1906; full member in
1909. Vice president of the National Sculpture Society; one of the
directors of the Architectural League and a member of the leading art
societies of the United States.

Decorative monumental and ideal work is his specialty.

Among the more important works which Mr. Konti has executed is
"The despotic age," a monumental marble group in the Metropolitan
Museum, N. Y. Another beautiful work, the "Edward Beale and Kit
Carson" monument, is now in the National Museum in Washington, D.
C. The McKinley monument in Philadelphia was executed in collabora-
tion with the late Charles Lopez. (Int Studio 45 :197)

Among Mr. Konti's ideal works may be mentioned the figures "Inspiration" and "Orpheus," the groups "Pan and Cupid," "Awakening of
Spring," and a fountain symbolizing "The brook."

"Mr. Konti is always refined, but this coy figure, 'The brook,' is a
veritable embodiment of sinuous grace." (Taft)

His "Mother and Child" has been purchased by the mayor of Boston
for Fenway Garden, on the recommendation of the Boston Art Commission and the Metropolitan Improvement Association.

KOOPMAN, AUGUSTUS, (P.) Born Charlotte, North Carolina, in 1869;
died Etaples, France, January 30, 1914. He studied art in Pennsylvania
Academy of the Fine Arts, Philadelphia; later in Paris at the Ecole des
Beaux Arts; also under Bouguereau and Robert Fleury.

Mr. Koopman belonged to the American colony of artists in France,
wintering in Paris and spending the spring and summer at Etaples. He
was elected an associé of the Société Nationale des Beaux Arts in 1912.

In 1913 he had a successful exhibition in the United States and while here painted in the Grand Canyon, Arizona.

"In much of his early work his color and composition had many of the qualities characteristic of the modern Dutch artists." Some of his later pictures gained a unique popularity for their impressionism.

Koopman loved the sea but he was not essentially a marine painter for he rarely painted it except as seen from the shore. His pictures that he valued highest were figure subjects—his own children being his models.

A few of his paintings are known as:

"Launching the boat"   "The parting word"
"With might and main"   "Winter"
"After the storm"   "Hoisting sails"

(Int Studio 52:215)

KOST, FREDERICK W., (P.) b: New York, May 15, 1861. Pupil National Academy of Design. Received honorable mention at Paris Exposition, 1900; bronze medal at Pan-American Exposition, Buffalo, 1901; silver medal at St. Louis Exposition, 1904. Associate member of National Academy of Design, 1900; full member in 1906. . Member Society Landscape Painters, Brooklyn, N. Y.

Specialty: landscapes and marines.

LACHMAN, HARRY B., (P.) b. La Salle, Ill., June 29, 1886. His studio is in Paris where he is a member of the Societé Internationale des Artistes et Sculpteurs and of the Societé Paris Moderne. Mr. Lachman is an American landscape painter better known in France than in 'his native land.

The Roman newspapers gave favorable comments on his paintings recently exhibited in Rome, and as a result the Modern Museum in Rome purchased one of his canvases.

The French government has purchased his "The Valley of Grand Andely," the landscape rejected by the International Exhibition of the Carnegie Institute. When invited to exhibit at the Carnegie, M. Leonce Benedité, director of the Luxembourg, was in his studio and helped him select this picture.

His "St. Nicholas du Chardonnet," "Uzerdie," and "Antibes" are now in the Luxembourg and his "Printemp Parisien" is in the Musée du Petit Palais.

LADD, ANNA COLEMAN (Mrs. Maynard Ladd), (S.) Received her art education in Europe. She first exhibited in Boston, Philadelphia, and New York in 1907. Since then her work has been included in every American exhibit of sculpture.

Mrs. Ladd prefers imaginative subjects but she has modeled a number of successful portrait-busts and reliefs.

"The American," which first attracted thoughtful artists, stands for the universal human qualities of strength, determination, and moral force. "Beasts of prey" portrays the low earth side of man. "Pan" and "Youth" personify the American spirit of the woods. "Human instrument" has a personified 'cello, awakened to life by a master. "The sword" is a human figure standing on a victim.

Among Mrs. Ladd's later works is a bronze portrait-bust of Eleanor Duse. The famous Italian actress is also the owner of the "Wind and spray" fountain.

Mrs. Ladd explains her "Wind and spray" fountain: "I wanted a fountain that would have simply what I saw when I watched the wind blowing the spray about—the wild wind whose voice is always sad seeking the unattainable; blowing before him the driving, leaping, dancing, falling spray." A replica is in the Borghese palace, Rome.

In the Italian garden of Mrs. W. Scott Fitz, Manchester-by-the-Sea, are two exceedingly fine examples of Mrs. Ladd's work. "The bird fountain" has a charm in the figure of St. Francis who holds a bird in his hand as others gather around him. In the "Sundial" the figures, grouped around the Greek pillar surmounted by the dial, represent youth, manhood, and age; the first, the dreamer; the second, the man of action; the third, the thinker.

The "Rock and the flower" (exhibited at the Panama-Pacific Exposition) is one of her most beautiful groups. "It suggests the American flower garden, flowers and rocks, slenderness and strength, and demonstrates subtly and beautifully the vital line, one of the most essential qualities in sculpture."

The fine bronze portrait bust of Mrs. Andrew Robeson Sargent is in the Fenway Court collection, Boston.

"Triton babies," one of her latest groups, has been placed in the Public Garden, Boston.

While in France, during the war, Mrs. Ladd rendered extraordinary service in making masks for the permanently disfigured. She made some seventy masks while there and organized the work under French sculptors and mechanics so it could be continued.

"She has the 'second sight' of imagination that feels as well as sees, and interprets as well as grasps."

"Her work has not only originality but strength and unusual significance. While it stirs the emotions it also provokes thought." (Anna Seaton-Schmidt in Art & P 2:251)

Her sculpture ranks high in Europe as well as in the United States.

LA FARGE, JOHN, (P. Mural P., Stained-glass designer) b. New York, March 13, 1835; d. Providence, R. I., November 14, 1910. His boyhood was spent in Newport, R. I., where his environment was such as to foster and develop his strong sense of color. From his earliest youth flowers were his intimate and loving companions, and from them he learned the secret of delicate gradation and harmony of color. At the age of twenty-one he went to Paris and entered the studio of Couture.

Mr. La Farge's work is so varied in subject, in feeling, in scale, it is executed in so many different mediums (he worked in oil, in water-color, and on wood; was a mural decorator, a painter in stained glass and a sculptor) that generalization is impossible.

A member of the National Academy of Design since 1869.

He received the honorary degree, M.A., Yale, 1896; LL.D., Yale, 1901; Princeton, 1904. He was an art critic and lecturer, as well as the most learned painter of our times. From the mystics of early China to those of Barbizon, the history of painting was an open book to him. It was one of his strongest convictions that color symbolizes character and can be made to express the hidden meaning of things.

In his purely imaginative works in oil, he drew from the realm of fairyland and witchcraft for subjects: "The pied piper of Hamelin," "The wolf charmer," "The sorceress," "The fisherman and the genii," "The siren's song."

At a London exhibition one of his landscapes was hung between a Rousseau and a Delacroix, and the French government bestowed the insignia of the Legion of Honor upon him when he exhibited the Watson memorial window at the Paris Exposition in 1889.

A triumph in mural decoration are his four paintings in the Supreme Court room in the Minnesota state house; and his "Ascension" in the Church of the Ascension, New York, is one of the most beautiful things done in modern religious mural painting.

It was his color again that proclaimed his authority in glass, and recalls the richness and splendor of the old masters. He invented the "opaline glass" and his new method for making stained glass windows changed the entire art of glass stainer. His masterpiece in glass work is the famous Peacock window now preserved in the Art Museum at Worcester, Mass.

"A great colorist who expressed in the language of color all the emotion of the human soul. He has placed an indelible mark upon American art." (Jarves "Art idea")

"With his mastery of color he created new forms of devotional beauty unsurpassed since the renaissance." (Art and P 3:379)

"He had probably the most complex nature in our artistic history, and indeed he had in this respect no parallel among the masters of his time abroad." (Cortissoz)

LAMB, CHARLES ROLLISON, (Stained-glass designer) b. New York. Studied art at the Art Students' League of New York. Specialty: religious and municipal art.

The artistic decoration of the Sage Memorial Chapel at Cornell University was designed by Mr. Lamb. The lower wall surface in mosaic— a processional—expresses the idea of education; the center subject is that of life and character, and the ceiling that of religion.

The paintings and studies of detail in the processional were made by his wife, Ella Condie Lamb, and the mural paintings on the ceiling in the groined arches, by his brother, Frederick Stymatz Lamb.

In describing this work, the Outlook (70:571) says: "This mosaic is one of the most important in size and character of anything executed in the United States. It ranks in this regard with that recently undertaken by William B. Richmond, of the Royal Academy in St. Paul's Cathedral in London, the great processional in the Madeleine Church of Paris by Charles Lehmair, the panels on the new facade of the Cathedral at Florence, or what has been wrought by the late Sir Edward Burne-Jones in the American Church at Rome."

Mr. Charles Rollison Lamb has unusual quality as an artist-decorator. "He sees things 'in the whole,' with rare judgment and art feeling." (Craftsm 13:420)

LAMB, ELLA CONDIE (Mrs. Charles R. Lamb), (Mural P., S., I.) b. New York. Pupil of William M. Chase, C. Y. Turner, Walter Shirlaw in New York, Courtois and Collin in Paris, and Herkomer in England; has received many prizes and medals for her work shown at various exhibitions in this country.

Mrs. Lamb specializes in decorative designs for public edifices. Among her works are "The Advent angel;" "The Christ child," for the Conrad memorial (in mosaic), St. Mary's church, Wayne, Pa.; and "The Arts" and "The Sciences" for the memorial chapel at Cornell University in collaboration with her husband, Mr. Charles Rollison Lamb, who designed the elaborate interior decoration of this marvelous art tribute to Henry W. Sage and wife.

LAMB, FREDERICK STYMATZ, (Mural P., Stained-glass designer) b. New York, June 24, 1863. Pupil of Art Students' League of New York; also studied under Lefebvre and Boulanger in Paris. Specialty: stained-glass.

Received honorable mention at the Columbian Exposition, Chicago, 1893; medal from the French government for a window at Paris Exposition, 1900; and was one of the four glass workers invited to represent the United States at that exposition.

He has received commissions for important mural decorations, among them a large canvas for the Bethlehem Presbyterian Church, Philadelphia, Pa.; work for the Bethesda Church, Saratoga, New York; and St. Peter's Church, New York. Designed the window in Emerson Memorial Chapel, Titusville, Pa.—"Friendship" (David and Jonathan). "Religion" is an especially fine window in the Jones Memorial Library, Lynchburg, Va., as is also "Gloria in excelsis," his mural painting in the Sage Memorial Chapel at Cornell University.

His most important recent design is a series of eight windows in the old Plymouth Church, Brooklyn, N. Y.:

"Hampden and Pym appealing for the Bill of Rights before Charles I"
"Milton writing the plea for the liberty of the press"
"John Robinson's prayer on the Speedwell—Departure of the Pilgrims from Delfshaven"
"The signing of the Compact on board the Mayflower"
"The landing of the Pilgrims"
"Founding Harvard College"
"John Eliot preaching to the Indians"
"Cromwell announcing to George Fox personal liberty of worship"

Besides these, there are three other windows, showing in the central one, Abraham Lincoln as president; on one side, Henry Ward Beecher speaking on the platform of Exeter Hall, London, in favor of the anti-slavery bill; on the other, Harriet Beecher Stowe in a group of women prominent in the movement for the higher education of women. This work is gorgeous in color and beautifully harmonizes with the architecture and decorative scheme of the church.

"There is a human quality in the art of this artist and even where the utmost conventionality of form has to be respected, there is a story with picturesque surroundings." (Craftsm 13:420)

LATHROP, FRANCIS, (Mural P., Stained-glass designer) b. at sea near the Hawaiian Islands, June 22, 1849; d. Woodcliffe Lake, N. Y., October 18, 1909.

In 1862 he went to Dresden, Germany, and studied painting at the Royal Academy of Fine Arts; afterwards studied in London with Ford Madox-Brown and Sir Edward Burne-Jones and acted as assistant to R. Spencer Stanhope and William Morris, devoting special attention to stained-glass work. After 1873 was engaged in portrait and decorative painting.

Among his chief decorative works are the mural paintings entitled: "The Light of the world" over the altar of St. Bartholomew's Church; "Apollo" over the proscenium of the Metropolitan opera house, New York; "Moses with the tablets of the Lord," a wall-painting in the Bowdoin chapel, Brunswick, Me.

For the Marquard memorial window in Princeton college chapel, he received a gold medal in 1889.

Mr. Lathrop executed many mural paintings and much stained-glass work for numerous churches and residences in New York, Albany, Boston, Baltimore, and other cities.

A member of the National Academy of Design, 1906; also a member of the leading art societies and clubs.

LAUBER, JOSEPH, (P., S., E., Mural P., and Stained-glass designer) b. Westphalia, Germany, August 31, 1856. Pupil of Walter Shirlaw and William M. Chase in painting. He assisted John La Farge in the sculptural decorations of Cornelius Vanderbilt's residence, 1882; executed a number of etchings, 1887-94; and has painted a conception of the Christ which has been widely noticed.

Among the best known mural paintings and stained-glass work are:

"Redemption" window, Westminster Presbyterian church, Bloomfield, N. J.

"The pilgrimage of life," First Congregational church, Montclair, N. J.

"Christ's admonition to Thomas" window, Church of the Ascension, New York.

"Christ before the doctors," Lutheran Church, New York.

"Christ as the True Vine" window, Church of Transfiguration, New York.

"The Spirit of Grace and the Spirit Triumphant" window, Trinity Church, Lancaster, Pa.

"Hope," Presbyterian Church, Lafayette avenue, Brooklyn, N. Y.

"St. Agnes," St. Andrew's Methodist Episcopal Church, West 76th St., New York.

"Te Deum" window, St. Paul's church, Richmond, Va.

"Adoration" (painting) over the altar, Trinity Church, Ossining, N. Y.

"Virtues of the upright judiciary," panels in court room, appellate court building, New York.

"Psyche at the spring" window in the library of J. P. Morgan.

"Greek dance" mural painting in the library of Whitelaw Reid, New York.

LAWSON, ERNEST, (P.) b. California, 1873. He studied art in France and has won many prizes for his paintings. In 1908 he was elected an associate member of the National Academy of Design; full member in 1917.

Mr. Lawson's work is distinctly impressionistic.

"No American painter of the day contains more of the qualities, such qualities as are pictured with charm and light, admired by the order of connoisseur in preponderance ...... Mr. Lawson is a painter of the order of Rembrandt and Monticelli—a traditional colorist and in no sense an inventor ...... He is nearer to the Renaissance than to the moderns ...... He has added quality ...... to the color of Manet and done it because his love of air, or of light is combined with a sensuous realization of the weight of materials ...... If he is not the greatest, he is one of the greatest American landscape painters." (Arts & D 6:240)

"Lawson has a very good impressionistic canvas, at times metallically inharmonious, at others competently imitative of nature." (Forum 55: 333)

"Winter" is in the Metropolitan Museum of Art, New York; "Boat-house, Harlem river, winter" in the Corcoran Gallery, Washington, D. C.; "An abandoned farm" in the National Gallery, Washington. D. C.

While spending the summer on Long Island, Mr. Lawson found many picturesque subjects. The sea gulls interested him and they appear in a number of his new canvases. In his "Incoming tide" the birds are modelled in paint and stand out from the surface in low relief. His canvas, "Black ducks—dawn," is notable. This is due to the elements of motion in the flying ducks and the power in its dark color scheme.

"He is one of the most original, individual of American landscape painters of today. ...... Though a poor draughtsman and a not very proficient technician, he is nevertheless a master of landscape painting in a very real sense. ...... Awkward, uncouth features of a landscape he does not eliminate, for he is a robust realist of a downright sort." (F. F. Sherman—Art in Am 8:32)

LEIGH, WILLIAM ROBINSON, (P., I.) b. Berkeley county, W. Va., September 23, 1866. He studied art at the Maryland Institute, Baltimore, and in Munich. His paintings received honorable mention in the Paris salon of 1892 and silver and bronze medals from the Munich Academy.

Mr. Leigh depicts scenes of ranch life in the west and desert episodes. A reproduction in colors of "Poisoned pool" appeared in the American Magazine, March, 1913, and without seeing the original, the directors of the Munich galleries cabled their agent in the United States to secure it for their exhibition. As a representative of the western type of art for the Anglo-American exhibition at London last year, "The stampede" was selected by Mr. Hugo Reisinger. "The Great Spirit" also attracted much interest at exhibitions.

Other notable scenes of western life are:

"An argument with the sheriff" "Sacred Mountain of Zuni"
"Sunset over the Badlands"   "The old story"
"Roping"

"Mr. Leigh's canvases give an impression of immense space and possess a deep feeling for the finer romance of nature."

"His work is almost invariably compared or contrasted, as may be the conviction of the critic, with that of Frederic Remington." (Cur Opin 57:269)

His paintings of the west increase in interest every year. Among his late pictures are two in which the figure lying prone on the ground is beautifully modeled, showing intimate knowledge of the essential anatomy on the part of the artist. Excellent characterization is in the figure of the mother in the composition called "Morning."

"These qualities, ... make him seem a painter from whom may be expected more than he has yet accomplished in the way of artistic achievement."

LE ROY, ANITA, (P., I.). Studied at the Pennsylvania Academy of the Fine Arts, Philadelphia, and under Whistler in Paris. Has exhibited in the large cities of the United States. Member of the Plastic Club, Philadelphia.

A few popular paintings are:

"Dutch canal and boat"   "Dutch woman sweeping snow"
"Dutch children"   "Dutch fisherman"

Leutze, Emanual, (P.) b. Emingen, near Reuthingen, in Wurtemberg, Bavaria, May 24, 1816; d. Washington, D. C., July 18, 1868. When a child came to Philadelphia with his parents. By the sale of numerous drawings he realized enough money to carry him to Europe in 1841. He went to Düsseldorf and entered the academy there, and as a pupil of Lessing soon acquired a name in historical art—a branch to which all his tastes and talent inclined. Elected a member of the National Academy of Design, New York, in 1860.

In 1860 he received a commission from Congress to decorate a stairway in the national capitol building, and painted the "Star of empire." "This painting stands quite alone in this country as an example of German decorative work." (Isham.)

He painted a long series of historical compositions, many of American subjects.

Among his most dramatic and elaborate pictures which have won popular favor are:

"Washington crossing the Delaware"
"The settlement of Maryland"
"An Indian contemplating the setting sun"
"The flight of the Puritans"
"Henry VIII and Anne Boleyn"

"Knox and Mary Stuart"
"First mass of Mary Stuart in Scotland"
"Landing of the Norsemen"
"Columbus before the queen"
"Cromwell and his daughter"

Among his portraits of eminent men, that of General Grant is a fine example.

"In all his works, Leutze shows himself a typical Düsseldorfian, with the enthusiasm and admirations of the German romantic period, expressed in a smooth, dull technique."

He represents the culmination of a certain type of historical painting in America—that besides the story told, the picture shall have a moral significance.

Leutze resembles Carlyle—both teach hero worship. (Tuckerman.)

Lewis, Edmonia, (S.) b. in the state of New York. Descended from both Indian and African ancestors. Comparatively untaught, she displayed a natural genius for sculpture and in 1865 exhibited in Boston a portrait-bust of Colonel Shaw which attracted much attention. In 1867 she exhibited a statue called "The freed-woman." Soon after she went to Rome where she has since resided. She sent to the Centennial Exhibition in 1876 the "Death of Cleopatra" in marble. Her "Old arrowmaker and his daughter," "Asleep," and terra-cotta busts of Sumner,

Longfellow, John Brown, and others are well known to visitors of her studio in Rome. The Marquis of Bute bought her "Madonna with the Infant Christ," an altarpiece. Her groups illustrating Longfellow's poem of "Hiawatha" are charming bits, poetic, simple, and natural, and "no happier illustrations of Longfellow's most original poem, were ever made than by the Indian sculptor." (Revolution, April, 1871)

LIE, JONAS, (P.) b. Norway, April 29, 1880. Comes from a family noted for genius in one form or another.

When twelve years of age his father died and after spending a year with his famous uncle in Paris, he came to America to join his mother who was an American and he has resided here ever since.

He attended evening classes of the Academy of Design and also did hard work in the night school of the Art Students' League. While still a student at the academy he sent a canvas, "The gray day," to the jury. The picture was accepted and well hung. Three years later he sent a painting to the exhibition of the Pennsylvania Academy and it was not only accepted but purchased by William M. Chase. He was awarded a silver medal at the St. Louis Exposition for his "Mill race" and is now represented in many of the best private and public galleries in America.

"He likes best to paint a snow-covered hillside with a gray leaden sky ...... There is a force about his work, a mastery of composition which goes far to atone for an occasional artificiality of expression or crudity of coloring ...... He likes nature in motion ...... he likes the whirl of wind and storm through his pictures ...... Jonas Lie has found out the secret of his art which sends a gale across canvas from frame to frame." (Craftsm 13:135)

This painter knows how to handle bridges.

The International Studio (53:sup lv), in commenting on American art in an exhibition at Shepherd's Bush, said: "Jonas Lie gives a glorious rendering of New York's skyscrapers after dark. It comes near to justifying the claims of the artist's friends. It is majestic and highly romantic. Look at the original at six o'clock on a winter evening from the North river and you will see like majesty in a line that no other part of the world can compete in."

A recent exhibition of Mr. Lie's oil paintings displayed seventeen subjects the treatment of which is described as remarkably effective. "To meet the day" has a brilliant crimson sky over a wide stretch of blue and green sea. There were fishing scenes, near shore, landscapes, and flower compositions.

"Jonas Lie has the real painter's vision in his picture 'Lower Bay, ice-bound.' A flower composition of his, too, is remarkably strong in color and pleasing in arrangement." (Int Studio 54: sup cxii)

The American Art News, in writing of his notable group of paintings of the Panama Canal, says that he has succeeded in portraying the material side of the canal with the same convincing force as he has his landscapes. His "Heavenly host" is dramatic; "The conquerors," a valuable record; "Across the canal" has bigness and breadth; "Palms in the wind," grace and movement; "Gatun Hill," true artistic quality; and "Culebra Slide" is painted from an original and interesting view point.

His Panama Canal canvases are bits of artistic history. Of late, winter and summer scenes have occupied him.

"Frosty morning" is brilliant with glittering snow on birch trees.

"Maidens of the forest," a decorative canvas, is tree shadows on snow in intricate pattern.

"Silver morn" is a very distinguished winter landscape in white and blue.

"The ice harvest" is owned by the Luxembourg, Paris.

LINDE, OSSIP L., (P.) b. Russia, but for many years a naturalized citizen of the United States. A pupil of the Art Institute, Chicago, he also studied with Laurens in Paris and received honorable mention in the Paris Salon. Has won many medals and prizes.

As a child in Russia he painted war pictures on strips of paper and made statuettes of soldiers out of soft stone and sold them to boy friends for military buttons of which he accumulated a fine assortment.

In 1902 he purchased his first box of oils from a fellow-student in Bruges; with these he painted his first picture in oils in the market place. It was accepted by the salon judges and well hung; in 1910 he received the gold medal.

Mr. Linde has been called the "eulogist of Bruges and Venice."

"His color is luscious but restricted, his technique free and unfatigued ...... Added to gem-like quality of color, his shadows are luminous, his figures well drawn and modeled, his houses solidly painted." (Int Studio 55: sup xiv)

LINDER, HENRY, (S.) b. Brooklyn, N. Y., September 26, 1854; d. Brooklyn, N. Y., February 7, 1910. At fifteen he was apprenticed to a marble firm, and when seventeen went with his mother to Germany. He studied art with Adam Bock of Lauterecken, then went to Munich and studied three years with Prof. Knabel, director of the Munich Academy. A year's study in Rome followed; he returned to New York in 1878. A member of the National Sculpture Society, National Society of Craftsmen, and of the Albrecht Dürer Verein.

Mr. Linder was eminently successful in child figures. A memorial exhibition of his works was held at the American Fine Arts' Building under the auspices of the National Sculpture Society in April, 1910.

LITTLE, J. WESLEY, (P.) b. Forkville, Pa., August 24, 1867, d. Williamsport, Pa., 1923. Studied art at the National Academy of Design, New York, and with Leonard Ochtman; also studied in Europe in 1899 and in 1905. Is a member of the Washington Water Color Club, Philadelphia Sketch Club, Philadelphia Water Color Club, and Chicago Water Color Club. Specialty: landscapes.

Some of his best known pictures are:

"A Dartmoor border"   "Green and gold"
"Westman's wood"   "Parting day"
"A Devonshire lane"   "Under autumn skies"
"Late pasture"   "Threshold of night"
"Breakfast"

LOEB, LOUIS, (P., I., E.) b. Cleveland, O., November 7, 1866; d. Canterbury, N. H., July 12, 1909. An illustrator, etcher, and figure painter. Studied under Gérome in Paris. Exhibited in the Paris salon of 1895 and received honorable mention; also third medal in 1897; Hallgarten prize of the National Academy of Design, 1902; and Webb prize of the Society of American Artists, 1903. Was elected associate member of the National Academy of Design, in 1901; full member in 1906.

In his "Temple of the winds, sunset," a work of distinction, the drawing is full of spirit, and the pure coloring and sense of air and sunset light are very fascinating. "The breeze" was more of a success and "Morning" won the Carnegie prize in 1905.

Other pictures are:

"Blossoming"
"The siren"
"The gift shawl"

He painted symbolical pictures in which the landscape plays a great part.

LONGMAN, MARY EVELYN BEATRICE. See Mrs. Evelyn B. Longman Batchelder.

LONGPRE, PAUL DE, (P.) b. Lyons, France, April 18, 1855; d. Hollywood, Los Angeles, California, June 29, 1911.

At twelve years of age he was in Paris painting flowers on fans, and at twenty-one his first oil painting was accepted at the salon. He came to the United States in 1890 and in 1896 gave his first exhibition in New York which consisted entirely of floral subjects. Three acres of flowers surrounded his home in Hollywood. His father and two brothers were also painters. Although Mr. De Longpre's proper title was Marquis Paul Mancherat de Longpré, closely related to the ducal houses of De Luynes and De Chevreuse and descendant of the celebrated statesman, the Marquis de Mesmer, he desired to be known as a plain American citizen.

LOPEZ, CHARLES ALBERT, (S.) b. Metamora, Mexico, October 19, 1869; d. New York, May 18, 1906. Came to New York when a youth. Studied in the studio of J. Q. A. Ward in New York; later studied with Falguière and at the Ecole des Beaux Arts, Paris.

He received first prize in a sun dial competition; first prize in a flag staff competition in New York; and first prize for the McKinley monument at Fairmount Park, Philadelphia. He was a member of the Society of American Artists and was elected an associate member of the National Academy of Design in 1906.

Mr. Lopez had just completed the working models for the McKinley memorial when he died from an operation. This work was done in collaboration with the sculptor, Isidore Konti.

LOW, WILL HICOK, (P., I., Mural P., Stained-glass designer) b. Albany, N. Y., May 13, 1853. Pupil of Ecole des Beaux Arts under Gérome and Carolus-Duran in Paris. His pictures in oil were exhibited in the Paris salon. In 1881 he became a teacher in the antique and life classes of the Woman's Art School of Cooper Union. Was elected a member of the National Academy of Design, 1890. His illustrations of Keats' poems were exhibited at the Paris Universal Exposition in 1889, and won a medal. In 1910 he gave the Scammon lectures at the Chicago Art Institute.

Mr. Low acquired his first knowledge of stained-glass from John LaFarge and has since furnished cartoons for stained-glass windows for many churches and public edifices. He is also one of the best exponents of the art of mural painting, his ceiling decorations of the ladies' reception room in the Waldorf-Astoria hotel, New York, gracefully entitled "Homage to woman" being most noteworthy.

His painting, "The maids of Cashmere," has for its subject the Feast of Roses, a charming oriental fete which Moore has pictured in "Lalla Rookh."

At a recent Chicago Art Exhibition Mr. Low made a thoroughly representative display of his work—one hundred and forty drawings, sketches, cartoons, and easel-pictures. Features of the display were the monochrome illustrations for Keats' "Lamia" and "The odes and sonnets," and the original studies for the celebrated decorations of the ball-room of the Waldorf-Astoria hotel in New York.

Mr. Low's most extensive decorative work, which consists of thirty-two panels, is in the New York Education Building at Albany, N. Y.

Mr. Low has also achieved success in literary pursuits.

LUCAS, ALBERT PIKE, (P., S.) b. Jersey City, N. J. As a child he drew plants and animals and modeled in clay. He studied at the Ecole des Beaux Arts, Paris, under Hébert and Boulanger during the years 1882-8, and was also a pupil of Courtois and Dagnan-Bouveret. Later he traveled in Holland, Belgium, and Italy, studying the representative masters of each country. Returning to France he made that country his home for twenty years, exhibiting regularly in the Paris salon. He was made a member of the Societé Nationale des Beaux Arts, and his well known painting, "The call," held one of the places of honor. It was later awarded a medal at the Pan-American Exposition.

His bronze bust, "Sambo, a native of Alabama," was exhibited at the Paris Exposition, 1900; "Extaze," a beautifully chiselled head of a woman, also in bronze, is in the Metropolitan Museum, New York City; "Laughing faun" is one of his recent sculptured works.

"Golden madonna" is so called from the wonderful golden light. "Susette" is a charming delineation of childish character. "The red shawl," now in the Boston Museum of Fine Arts, was placed in the "honor circle" in the Paris salon a few years ago.

"The marvel of all this artist's work [painting] is his management of diffused light. There is never a sense of the light streaming on the canvas reflecting from wall or mirror; it comes out through the painting and radiates beyond it ...... It is always the lyric note in Mr. Lucas' work, never the dramatic, the tragic, the morbid." (Craftsm 19:284)

"To a lover of lyric poetry, of fairy stories, of MacDowell music, the art of Albert Lucas will most strongly appeal." (Int Studio 54: sup xxiii)

LUKEMAN, (HENRY) AUGUSTUS, (S.) b. Richmond, Va., January 28, 1871. His parents took up their residence in New York City when he was a boy. He supplemented his art studies at the National Academy of Design with a course in anatomy at Bellevue Hospital. After this technical preparation he became a pupil and later an assistant of Daniel Chester French, doing some of the group work at the World's Columbian Exposition; he also studied in Paris under Falguiere in the Ecole des Beaux Arts. Preparatory to his architectural collaboration he had a course in architecture. His earliest work in this line was two groups —"Peace" and "Power"—on the Memorial bridge at the Pan-American Exposition. This was followed by designs for the group "Music" and the figures "Speed," "Heat," "Light," and "Power" at the St. Louis Exposition.

His architectural sculpture for buildings in Pittsburgh, Boston, and New York are well known. The statue of "Manu," the lawgiver of India, on the appellate court building, New York, is a remarkable conception and strikingly effective as an example of architectural sculpture. Mr. Lukeman is exceedingly versatile as a sculptor, doing equally well portrait busts, bas-reliefs, memorials, and monuments.

"Mr. Lukeman has practically mastered the sculptor's chief problem of distributing broad, simple masses in their true relation to the smaller and more decorative parts." (Arch Rec 35:415)

A memorial to the early leader of the Methodists in this country, Bishop Francis Asbury, is an admirable example of Mr. Lukeman's equestrian work and of his ability to interpret character.

His model for the monument to the Women of the Confederacy, to be erected in bronze at Raleigh, North Carolina, ranks high among the works of American sculpture.

LUKS, GEORGE BENJAMIN, (P.) b. Williamsport, Pa., August 13, 1867. His father, a physician, was a clever draughtsman and his mother a painter of talent. He studied art at the Pennsylvania Academy of the Fine Arts and in Düsseldorf, Paris, and London.

A radical worker in art, he has a disdain for art schools and consequently has little or no academic training. He is a natural draughtsman, however, and the charm of accuracy and poise distinguish his work. Most of his work has been of the city types. He finds his subjects in the debris of the human struggle. He is the painter of the East Side of New York. Luks sees artistic possibilities in the dock laborers—both man and animal. "The patient waiting horses, the gray overcast river and the straining movements of the men as they work are registered upon the canvas with astonishing rapidity and fidelity." (Craftsm 12:599)

In 1907 the National Academy of Design refused at its annual exhibition to accept a canvas of Mr. Luks, notwithstanding Robert Henri made a spirited appeal for recognition of this artist's work.

"With a grim and appalling psychologic power of a Gorky he paints creatures such as Higgins paints, but without Higgins' dramatic effects."

"As a painter he uses his palette with a riotous disposition of tone ...... He sees nature with warmth and vitality, and his work is full of light and shade."

"His method, perhaps, resembles Millet's. It is likely that if Millet painted streets and cafés instead of meadows and peasants' huts, he would have painted them very much as Luks paints them."

His most admired picture is "The spielers"—a joyous canvas-movement, the dominating note.

"Old clothes man" is impressive for "its dignity of composition, its lustre of color and above all for its character." (Int Studio 56:241)

His recent Parisian sketches have been referred to as "pencil biographies" of Parisian types, and as quite superior to his earlier work. "Paris seems to have made George Luks more quick of eye and more certain of hand than he has ever been before. There is nothing maudlin or sentimental about his drawings. He never pities or patronizes the rich or poor. No nice little socialistic sermon is tucked away in any of his studies. They never suggest the posed model of the studio. His personages are caught—working or playing—haphazard in the street or in the café."

"George Luks knows the slums and his canvases are vibrant with that knowledge." (Bookm 34:400)

"The thing perhaps that impresses me most about Mr. Luks' work is his profound intimacy with children. ...... All the people in the vicinity where Mr. Luks lives are his friends, the policemen and the ragged children. ...... He loves life in the same simple, unselfconscious, intense way that Whitman did; and he paints it the way Whitman wrote about it." (Mary Fanton Roberts)

MacCAMERON, ROBERT LEE, (P.) b. Chicago, Ill., January 14, 1866; d. New York City, December 29, 1912. His early boyhood was passed in the wild forests of Wisconsin where he played with Indian children and became an expert rifle shot. At fourteen years of age he worked in the log drive, earning a man's wages—$2.50 a day and board—and was able to save sufficient money to commence an art career, taking lessons in the Y. M. C. A. of Chicago. Going to New York he studied painting under William M. Chase. In 1888 he went to London where he found employment on the staff of a paper called "Boys' own," published in the interests of youth. Later he continued his art studies at the Ecole des Beaux Arts in Paris under Gérome and Collin, also studied with Whistler. Received gold medals in the Paris salon of 1905 and his works have been hors concours since 1907. He was made a member of the

National Academy of Design in 1910 and a chevalier of the Legion of Honor of France in 1912.

Since 1908 when his picture which is popularly known as "The absinthe drinkers" was shown in the Paris salon, Mr. MacCameron has been accorded recognition as one of the most original artists of the day.

"Not satisfied to be merely a clever painter, he aims at an interpretation of abstract aesthetic qualities. He believes that art should be an interpretation of mental spiritual impressions."

The recent presentation by J. P. Morgan to the Metropolitan Museum of New York of the painter's "August Rodin" speaks for the distinction in which his work is held. He has painted portraits of many prominent persons.

"Les habitués" is owned by the Memorial Museum of Philadelphia.

"The absinthe drinkers" was bought for the Corcoran Gallery of Art, Washington, D. C.

"Daughter's return" is in the Whistler room of the Metropolitan Museum of Art, New York.

A memorial exhibition of his paintings was held in New York on January 28, 1913.

McCARTER, HENRY, (I.) b. Norristown, Pa., July 5, 1865. Began expressing himself as an illustrator when a boy student at the Pennsylvania Academy of the Fine Arts. The Century and the Magazine of Art accepted his first work. Later he studied in Paris under Puvis de Chavannes and also came under the influence of Rixens, Bonnat, and Alexander **Harrison.**

The "Lourdes" of Zola was the beginning of his important book illustrations; he also furnished notable drawings to illustrate the poems of Paul Verlaine.

"Mr. McCarter seems essentially equipped for the pictorial interpretation of poetry; he has the most sentient appreciation of both delicacy and strength and a love of nature that is almost archaic. To these qualities he adds a psychology of beauty that is vividly real and through them all he gets the dramatic and forceful with still a persuasive grace and elusiveness." (Bookm 11:244)

"A colorist of exquisite clarity of tone, the value of which is apparent in his black and white medium."

"He does not so much suggest a pronounced individuality as he conveys a pervasive identity, a conscious medium of nature and life."

His illustrations of Verlaine's poems, notably "Claire de Lune" and "Le piano" are veritable triumphs of suggestiveness in the sense that the

French symbolist poets apply the word. Of special technical interest was also his "Easter hymn."

MacDonald, James Alexander Wilson, (S.) b. Steubenville, Ohio, August 25, 1824; d. Yonkers, N. Y., August 14, 1908.

A St. Louis publisher, at the age of thirty, he devoted himself to art. He made the first portrait-bust cut in marble west of the Mississippi—that of Senator James T. Benton of Missouri. After the Civil War he came to New York and his bust of Charles O'Connor is in the appellate court and that of James T. Brady is in the law library, while his bronze statue of Fitz-Greene Halleck is in Central Park and his Washington Irving in Prospect Park, Brooklyn. (American art annual, vol. 7)

MacEwen, Walter, (P., Mural P.) b. Chicago, Ill., February 13, 1860. Pupil of Cormon and Robert-Fleury in Paris. Received honorable mention in Paris salon of 1886; silver medal, Paris Exposition, 1889; silver medal, London, 1890; gold medal from city of Berlin, 1891; medal of honor, Antwerp, 1894; small gold medal, Munich, 1897; large gold medal, Munich, 1901; medal, Vienna, 1902; Lippincott prize, Philadelphia, 1902; gold medal, Liege, Belgium; chevalier of Legion of Honor of France; officer, 1908; chevalier Order of St. Michael, Bavaria; officer Order of Leopold, Belgium, 1909. Associate member of National Academy of Design, New York, 1903. First vice-president of the Paris Society of American Painters.

"Paints interiors with delicate light, moist sea air and monotonous dunes with laborers returning in the evening from their work." (Müther)

Successful in the lighting of his subjects drawn from the private life of the Dutch bourgeoisie, while his portraits are excellent—well drawn and well painted.

"Woman of the empire" exhibited in the Paris salon of 1903 is remarkable for its unusual finish rather than for originality or force of conception. "Holland interior" and "The secret" are two popular works. "Phyllis" is a prize picture.

Other paintings are:
"The yellow robe"
"The betrothed"
"The secretary"
"Judgment of Paris"
"Idyl of summer"
"The shepherdess"

"At the window"
"The letter"
"Confidences"
"Head of young Dutch girl"
"At the burgomaster's"

"It is MacEwen's consummate ability to represent textures and to produce a soft harmonious effect that imparts charm to the canvas." (Brush & P 11:301)

His mural decorations in the Library of Congress are a series illustrating the stories of Greek heroes. (Brush & P 19:21)

MacKay, Edwin Murray, (P.) b. Sebewaing, Michigan.   He first studied art on an iron ore barge; then at the Detroit Museum of Art; the Art Students' League, New York; in Paris at the Julien Academy under Jean Paul Laurens; and at the Vitti Academy under Jacques E. Blanche.   This period was followed by extensive travel in Europe studying various schools of portrait painting.

Mr. MacKay has exhibited his paintings at the Paris salon; in provinces of France; National Academy of Design, New York; Pennsylvania Academy of the Fine Arts; and Carnegie Institute.

His portraits are listed in private collections in Holland, England, France, and the United States; and his drawings are in a collection at the New York Public Library.   Some of Mr. MacKay's finest portraits were painted in Michigan, among the most notable being those of former Governor Sleeper of Michigan and Justices Brooks, Fellows, McAlvay, Moore, Ostrander, and Steere of the Michigan Supreme Court.   Other portraits are of Monsieur Nettlement, former French consul general to Petrograd; Flavia, daughter of Lady Angela Forbes of England; and Mildred Aldrich, the American writer.

McKenzie, Robert Tait, (S.) b. Almonte, Ontario, Canada, May 26, 1867.   A member of the faculty of the University of Pennsylvania.

His father died and left the family in straitened circumstances; but the youth, encouraged by his mother, surmounted all obstacles, and made his way through college; then he entered a medical school.   He became ship's surgeon, a lecturer on anatomy, and later house physician to the governor-general of Canada.   He also specialized in the treatment of physical deformities.   From his early youth he was an enthusiastic football player and had keen interest in all athletics and gymnastics. He believed that team sports were among the classics of physical education and that jumping, climbing, and swimming were the grammar of athletics.   Dr. McKenzie was one of the first to advocate compulsory physical training in schools and colleges.   As a youth he drew and painted, and later made remarkable plaster casts in his medical and surgical work.   While teaching anatomy in Canada he conceived the idea of constructing a model athlete whose physical proportions should be a sort of American Doryphorus. After several attempts he success-fully modeled "The sprinter" which won congratulations and placed him in a new field—that of a sculptor.

Dr. McKenzie has been called the "sporting sculptor." "The sprinter" was exhibited in the United States, London, and Paris and is now the property of the Fitzwilliam Museum, Cambridge, England.

In 1904 he was appointed professor of physical education and director of all athletics and gymnastics in the University of Pennsylvania. Since that time he has combined two careers—the work of a scientist and the work of an artist. His book "Exercise and education" dealing with medical examination and prescriptions of exercises is accepted as an authority by both aspiring athletes and student sculptors.

Dr. McKenzie's sculptural work covers low relief, the round, portrait busts, and medals. To immortalize the American athlete is his ideal.

One of his finest achievements in low relief is "The joy of effort" set in the wall of the stadium at Stockholm by the order of the King of Sweden. "The athlete," "The competitor," "The supple juggler," "The relay," and "The onslaught" (football group) emphasize the American athlete's physical traits.

"From the beginning he aimed to realize the esthetically perfect by working up to it from absolute physical accuracy."

The World War called forth a new phase of his work, two of the most impressive works being "Blighty," and "Guy Drummond," a Scotch Canadian killed in action. He also did work with other English and American and French sculptors in making masks for disfigured faces of soldiers. His "Homecoming," a memorial to the men of Cambridge-shire, England, was unveiled in 1922 and the artist went to England to be present at the dedication.

McLane, Myrtle Jean (Mrs. John C. Johansen), (P., I.) b. Chicago, September 14, 1878. Studied in the Art Institute, Chicago, and under Duveneck and Chase. Has illustrated for Harper's and Scribner's magazines. Studio residence is in New York City.

Her "Mother and child" was awarded the Shaw prize and given a place of honor at the annual exhibition of the National Academy of Design, New York; she has also won several other prizes.

"Her work is strong, colorful and convincing." (Art & P 3:612)

"On the hilltop," exhibited at the Paris salon, was particularly attractive. "It was a buoyant canvas, alert with the abounding wholesomeness and spacious exhilaration of the upper air."

"The impression that her art creates is of breadth of vision and clear comprehension. These qualities are felt in her standing portrait "Girl in gray," with which she first attracted particular notice."

"Wholesomeness is a distinguishing quality of her art." (Harper 118:291)

Mrs. Johansen had the honor of being the second woman artist selected (Cecilia Beaux was the first) to be one of eight American artists to paint the portraits of the leaders of the allies in the World War. She was assigned Elizabeth, queen of Belgium, Premier Venizelos of Greece, and Premier Hughes of Australia.

MacLaughlan, Donald Shaw, (E.) b. Boston, Mass., November 9, 1876. Studied art with W. D. Hamilton, later went to Paris to continue his studies.

Received silver medal for etching at the Pan-American Exposition, Buffalo, 1901; medal of honor, Limoges, 1903; bronze medal at St. Louis Exposition, 1904. A member of the Paris American Artists' Society.

Mr. Frederick Wedmore, in a lecture on "Etching" delivered January 23, 1911, before the Royal Society of Arts, said: "America, since Whistler, has given us one etcher of importance, Mr. MacLaughlan."

In the short period of Mr. McLaughlan's activity he has catalogued about one hundred etchings and dry-points.

One of the International Studio's critics writes: "Looking at the etchings now reproduced one is quickly convinced of this truth—that even coming after the greatest among the masters .... such as Dürer, Rembrandt, Callot, Méryon, Whistler, Seymour-Haden, Flameng and Buhot, an artist endowed as MacLaughlan is endowed with the feeling of modernity and strong in his impeccable craftsmanship, may yet be able to add a personal page to the history of engraving."

Minuteness added to a broad and sure sense of general effects; here in few words is the essence of his art.

His "Lauterbrunnen" was found by one critic to be "one of the few pictures that realize the vastness of the mountains .... Space, sweep, grandeur, rudeness, and power are found in this remarkable plate which also is beautifully obedient to the canons of the art." (Weitenkampf)

Mr. MacLaughlan has found his principal subjects in the streets of Paris, although Parma, Pavia, Bologna, Tuscany, the Roman Campagna, Tivoli and the Neapolitan district all in turn have attracted him.

MacMonnies, Frederick William, (S., P.) b. Brooklyn, N. Y., September 28, 1863. At the age of sixteen he attracted the attention of Augustus Saint-Gaudens who received him as an apprentice in his studio; later he went to Paris and Munich where he spent some time studying painting which he considered so closely allied to sculpture as to be a necessary preparation. On a second trip to Europe he entered the atelier Falguière in the Ecole des Beaux Arts, and also worked in the private studio of Antonio Mercié.

In Paris he speedily achieved the most gratifying success, carrying off for two successive years the prix d'atelier, the highest award for which foreigners in France may compete. Among the many flattering recognitions of his gifts are decorations of the Legion of Honor of France, and the cross of Saint Michael of Bavaria; he has also won the first prize of the National School of Fine Arts. A member of the National Academy of Design, 1906.

In 1889 his first exhibit, a "Diana," obtained honorable mention from the Paris salon. He exhibited in the salon of 1891 the statues of Nathan Hale and James S. T. Stronahan and was awarded a second gold medal, this being the first and only time that an American sculptor has attained that honor.

These were followed by "Pan of Rohallion" and "Faun with heron" which obtained for him such a reputation in the United States that he was chosen to execute the colossal fountain of the Columbian Exposition, containing twenty-seven gigantic figures.

His "Bacchante" was purchased by the French government for the Luxembourg gallery, he being the first American sculptor to be so honored. A copy was rejected by the Boston Public Library and is now in the Metropolitan Museum, New York.

"Daphne" is in the Luxembourg garden; "Winged Victory" at the United States Military Academy at Annapolis.

The statue by which the "Pioneer monument" at Denver, Colorado, is surmounted, is a portrait of Kit Carson, that intrepid pioneer. The groups at the base are allegorical; the ornamental details symbolic. "Profoundly significant, it is at the same time extremely decorative—a notable work of art and a valuable asset to the city." (Art & P 2:330)

"Wisdom" and "Inspiration"—an elderly man and young woman— statues of heroic size, have been placed at the entrance to the New York Public Library.

A group for Princeton College, the "Battle of Princeton," to commemorate the Revolutionary battle, having Washington as one of the principal figures; a monument with figure typifying French courage at the Marne (a gift of the United States) ; and the "Civic virtue" fountain for the New York City Hall Park are his latest works.

The last, "Civic Virtue," after much controversy has been accepted by the city committee and erected in the place originally selected. "Civic Virtue" is represented by a youth carrying a huge club. Two alluring sirens have besieged him but lie overcome at his feet. The statue is the largest ever designed by an American sculptor, and is said to have been made from the largest single block of marble carved since the days of Michelangelo's figure of David. The block of Georgia marble from which it was carved weighed fifty-five tons. The carving was done by the Piccirilli **brothers.**

Mr. MacMonnies' latest work is a bust of Whistler to be placed among the memorials to great American artists in the reading room of the Gould Memorial Library, New York University. He was selected to make the bust (the third ever made) by a committee of which Mr. Pennell, who is a recognized authority on Whistler, was a leading member.

Mr. MacMonnies' studio at Giverny, France, was turned into a hospital for French soldiers after the battle of the Marne.

MacNeil, Carol Brooks (Mrs. H. A. MacNeil), (S.) b. Chicago, Ill., January 15, 1871. Pupil of Art Institute, Chicago, under Lorado Taft; MacMonnies and Injalbert in Paris. Member of N. Y. Woman's Art Club; National Sculpture Society.

"She might be called a miniature sculptor, if there is such a phrase, for her creations are not of statuesque proportions. Portrait busts she has done and they are well done; but her originality has run rather to unique designs for vases, inkstands, fountains and other articles of practical utility." (W Work 14:9403)

MacNeil, Hermon Atkins, (S.) b. Everett, Mass., February 27, 1866. Pupil of the Massachusetts Normal Art School in Boston, Chapu at Julien Academy, and Falguière at Ecole des Beaux Arts in Paris. On his return from Paris he went immediately to the Northwest where he sojourned with the Indians making sketches for the four bronze reliefs that now adorn the Marquette building in Chicago. These reliefs symbolize four dramatic incidents in the life of Pere Marquette.

Mr. MacNeil taught in the Art Institute, Chicago, for a time; then he won the Rinehart scholarship and studied in Rome for four years. He was the first instructor in drawing and modeling at Cornell University, also serving as instructor in Pratt Institute, Brooklyn, in the Art Students' League, and the Academy of Design in New York. He has won many medals and prizes; was elected associate National Academy of Design, 1905; full member, 1906.

"The coming of the white man" is perhaps the best known of Mr. Mac-Neil's Indian groups, and the McKinley statue at Columbus, Ohio, is the first masterpiece of the kind that he has produced." (W Work 14:9403)

In 1888 he went to Paris and in 1890 exhibited a bust in the salon. While living in Rome and working in the Villa dell'Aurora, he produced:

"The moqui runner"   "From chaos came light"
"A primitive chant"   "The sun vow"

The "Sun vow" is regarded by critics as Mr. MacNeil's most perfect production. An old Indian seated watches a boy who shoots an arrow at the sun.

Taft says: "There are few American sculptors who manipulate the clay as charmingly as does Mr. MacNeil. His work is full of delightful touches and felicitous passages, yet the firm construction is never sacrificed to the superficial graces ...... Two busts of women modeled by him are among the finest works yet produced by an American—Herbert Adams alone has surpassed the 'Agnese' ...... 'Beatrice' is less beautiful in execution."

In the Court of the Universe at the Panama-Pacific Exposition was the first sculpture column at any exposition called the Column of Progress, and it was crowned by MacNeil's very daring group "Adventurous bowman."

"The effect of the column as seen from any point is inspiring in its monumental grandeur. The group on top, the Bowman, represents man's supreme effort in life. He is supported on the left by his fellow-man adding strength and steadiness to his aim, while on the right the crouching figure of a woman watches anxiously the sureness of his aim. She holds ready in her hand the laurel wreath which she confidently feels will be his just reward." (Art of the Exposition, Neuhaus)

MACOMBER, MARY L., (P.) b. Fall River, Mass., August 21, 1861; d. Boston, Mass., February 4, 1916. Pupil of Duveneck and Boston Museum of Fine Arts. Specialty, ideal figures.

With the exception of a few weeks in England, France, and Holland her life was spent in the United States.

Her ancestors were New England orthodox with direct and easily traceable line from the Plymouth Pilgrims. She was shocked because the religious atmosphere of her earliest creations caused some to think her a Roman Catholic and she gave up the religious subjects of the old masters and began the delineation of her ideals by means of winged figures representing allegories of love. This style giving rise to the charge of sentimentality, she abandoned the winged figures for her present types.

Many of her pictures in recent years have been in the panel form, and as decorations have proven highly satisfactory. Her "Hour of grace," "An Easter carol," and "The magdalen" are among such works.

Miss Macomber's early work shows the influence of the Burne-Jones-Rossetti-Watts school and in such of her early creations as "Memory comforting Sorrow," "Night and her daughter Sleep" her partiality to this group of idealists is plainly traceable.

In more recent years, however, her originality of subject is unquestioned in such as:

"Springtime"   "The nightingale"
"Life"   "Kissed fruit"
"Singing stars"   "Spring"
(Charles A. Parker in Int Studio 47: sup lxi)

MALBONE, EDWARD GREENE, (Min. P.) b. Newport, R. I., August, 1777; d. May 7, 1807. "What Gilbert Stuart was to the larger portraiture of America, such was Edward Greene Malbone to the miniature work of his native land."

From childhood he was ambitious to become an artist, and at the age of seventeen he was working professionally drawing heads in miniature; and in the spring of 1796 he was fairly established as a miniature painter in Boston. Meeting Washington Allston, a strong friendship was formed which lasted during the life of the younger artist. In 1800 Malbone and Allston went south where the former painted many miniatures. Later they went to London where Benjamin West, then president of the Royal Academy, gave them a cordial reception. Here Malbone painted his celebrated picture known as "The hours." It is upon ivory and is exquisite in composition and color. It is now owned by the Athenaeum at Providence, R. I. Of this achievement Benjamin West said: "I have seen a picture painted by a young man named Malbone which no man in England could excel."

This picture remained for nearly a hundred years an isolated example of American art, when its influence was worthily carried out by Mr. W. J. Baers' "Aurora" and "Golden hour," and the interesting figure pieces by Lucia Fairchild Fuller. "He had the happy talent," writes Allston, "of elevating the character without impairing the likeness. (Heirlooms in miniatures" Anne Hollingsworth Wharton)

"Malbone was easily at his best in portraiture. His famous composition, "The hours," now owned by the Athenaeum at Providence is remarkable for its brilliancy and harmony of coloring and execution.

Malbone's reputation rests on the correct drawing and acute discernment of character always present in his portraits, coupled with harmony
and truth in coloring." (Scrib 47:564)

MANSHIP, PAUL, (S.) b. St. Paul, Minnesota, December 25, 1885.
While attending school in his native city he became interested in model
ing and decided to be a sculptor. Later he had instructions from
Charles Grafly, the sculptor, and won in 1909 the Roman prize of the
American Academy which gave him three years' study in Rome and also
travel in Greece. In 1913 he returned to the United States and his
bronzes at once became the most attractive feature of art exhibits; since
that time he has won increasing prominence until he is now recognized
as one of our most conspicuous and distinguished sculptors. He was
elected associate member of the National Academy of Design in 1914, and
full member in 1916. In 1922 he was appointed annual professor for
the academic year 1922-23 in the American Academy in Rome.

His "Centaur and nymph" is in the Metropolitan Museum, New York;
"Duck girl" (bronze fountain), Fairmount Park, Philadelphia; "Centaur
and dryad" and "Flight of night," Detroit Institute of Art; "Indian
and pronghorn antelope," Art Institute, Chicago; "Dancing girls and
fauns," Art Institute, Chicago; "Playfulness," Art Institute, Minneapolis,
Minnesota; "Dancers and gazelles" in Cleveland, Ohio; and another
version purchased by the Luxembourg Gallery, Paris.

"What impresses the observer of Mr. Manship's work is the combination in it of classic precision with western virility and reality ......
The bronze at the academy which drew most comments from the artists
was the one entitled "The awakening of spring." (Outl 106:335)

During the month of December, 1915, an exhibition of forty-four
pieces of sculpture by Mr. Manship was held in the Detroit Art Institute.
The following excerpts are taken from the bulletin issued by the museum
in January, 1916:

"The exhibition covers a wide range of themes, the treatment of which
shows Mr. Manship to be a man of ideas and versatility. ...... Four
panels in relief symbolizing the elements, 'Fire,' 'Water,' 'Earth,' and
'Air' show the quality of the sculptor at his best. ...... One finds in the
'Salome' of Manship a charm of line and a verve seldom encountered in
a representation of this subject. ...... The 'Portrait of a baby three
weeks old,' a high relief in colored marble, is as decorative and plastic
as the best thing of the Italian Renaissance. ...... Through the work
of Manship one finds him fascinated with the animal kingdom, and in
using beasts and birds as the motives of his decoration he gives them a
conventional quality, yet they are expressive of life."

His groups, "Dance" and "Music," were placed in the Court of the Universe at the Panama-Pacific Exposition. "These are typical examples of Manship's power to combine classic restraint, sculptural dignity, and grace of line with complete freedom and untrammeled ease of method."

Mr. Manship shows a fondness for color on sculpture and he applies copper, gold, and green very liberally to his works. He has been called a meticulous craftsman, as his work many times suggests the jeweler's art before the sculptor's.

The London Times in reviewing the work of this influential young American sculptor in an exhibition at Leicester Galleries, London, says: "Manship is eclectic; now he shows clearly the influence of archaic Greek sculpture. . . . . . Elsewhere he reminds one of the small bronzes of the Renaissance; elsewhere he is modern in the style of Bakst's design for the Russian ballet."

No piece of sculpture exhibited in recent years in New York City has aroused so much interest and discussion as his bust of John D. Rockefeller. "Paul Manship brings the whole man before us. He dramatizes in marble the whole life of John D. Rockefeller. . . . . . The test of the artist's power comes in his appreciation of the traits and characteristics which have been instrumental in producing the whole man."

The New York Times says of the bust: "It is great sculpture, as cruel as science and as pathetic as life."

In 1921 the Athenaeum gave an estimate of Mr. Manship from an English point of view. "He is a curiously unequal artist; some of his exhibits (such as "Nude reclining") are about as bad as sculpture can possibly be; others again, such as the bronze "Dancer and gazelles," are perfectly charming in feeling and design, and most delicately executed.

"Above all, he has assimilated the clear-cut linear stylization of the Greek vase painters, and it is this influence more than any other, which controls his production. . . . . . The beauty of his successful works is essentially the beauty of line. And this beauty is contained in one view only. In other words, his bronzes have no three dimensional existence."

During the war he did efficient work for the American Red Cross in Italy and has designed a series of notable medals commemorative of the war.

MARIN, JOHN, (E., P.) b. Rutherford, N. J., 1875. A pupil of the Pennsylvania Academy of the Fine Arts, and Art Students' League, New York. He studied etching in Paris.

Of an exhibition of his water colors, a critic writes: "No matter how harshly we may criticize him for not having finally found himself and with himself, something vital, he has nevertheless undoubtedly made an excellent start along little trodden lines. The influences one deduces are of the Chinese and Cézanne, although there are no symbols common to either of them ...... Marin's color in his later works is pale and not always complete, but his sensitivity is such that as he progresses, a desire for the complete chromatic gamut will instinctively be felt by him, and his color will no doubt become strengthened ...... Marin is a man to watch and buy and to encourage." (Forum 55:331)

In an article on some masters of the water color, Arts and Decoration (6:279) is: "Cézanne is another master, as is John Marin, who has been so influenced by him ...... Very abstract in character, impossible at times to follow them, their art is nevertheless pregnant with beauty, selection, taste; these are the virtues that count in art."

"Marin's personality stands forth healthy and strong, not dependent on the crutches of second-hand inspiration ...... From the very simplest types of order (such as a slight block form of objects) he has attained to a rhythmic conception of his subject matter until it has become almost abstract. In this sense he at times reveals a certain inevitable Chinese aspect." (Int Studio 58: sup xviii)

Mr. Marin belongs to the Post-impressionist movement in Paris.

"He has achieved brilliant success in etching, showing much originality and power in his flexibility of line and depth of color."

One observed at a recent exhibition that his color is richer and deeper, more sonorous, especially in his painting of tossing waves. Where he was once lyric he is now dramatic. Noticeable was a series of pictures of schooners.

"Mills of Meaux" is now owned by the French government.

It was suggested that the title, "The complete John Marin," be given to a recent exhibition of his work on view in the Montrose gallery. There were one hundred ten water colors from date as early as 1908, thirty-one etchings from 1906 to 1915, and four oils dated 1921.

"As a colorist Mr. Marin stands exceedingly high."

MARSH, ALICE RANDALL (Mrs. Fred Dana Marsh), (Min. P.) b. Coldwater, Michigan. A pupil of the Art Institute, Chicago, she later studied with Merson, Collin, Whistler, and MacMonnies in Paris.

Mrs. Marsh is a member of the American Society of Miniature Painters, and her work in this line of painting has been very favorably received.

MARSH, FRED DANA, (Mural P.) b. Chicago, Ill., April 6, 1872. Pupil of Art Institute, Chicago. Won bronze medal, Paris Exposition, 1900; silver medal, Pan-American Exposition, Buffalo, 1901; bronze medal, St. Louis Exposition, 1904. Member Society American Artists. Associate member of National Academy of Design, 1906.

His most notable work is a series of mural paintings symbolic of modern progress in engineering, executed for the New York Engineers' Club.

MARTIN, HOMER DODGE, (P.) b. Albany, N. Y., October 28, 1836; d. St. Paul, Minn., February 12, 1897. Established a studio in New York in 1862. Was elected member of the National Academy of Design in 1874. His first trip to Europe was made in 1876 when he met Whistler who promptly recognized his qualities as a painter and invited him to work in his studio; he resided in France during 1882-6.

Among his most important works are:

"White Mountains from Randolph hill"
"Lake Sanford"
"Honfleur lights"
"Source of the Hudson"
"Old Normandy Manor"
"The mussel gatherers"
"On the Seine" (Harp of the winds)

"Morning on the Saranac"
"A fire-slash lookout"
"A lake in the wilderness"
"Evening on the Thames"
"Sand dunes of Lake Ontario"
"The sun worshippers"
"Golden sands"

"Winchester hills" and "Adirondack scenery" are considered his masterpieces. His painting "The old church at Criqueboeuf"—Normandy landscape—was called by M. Boutet de Monvel, the late well known French painter, "The greatest landscape ever painted in America." He further declared that it was equal to the best of Rousseau's work, and yet was unlike anything that Rousseau had done.

During his lifetime his pictures did not sell or were purchased by admiring friends, among whom were artists, critics, editors, poets, musicians, physicians, and bankers; but now it is practically impossible to buy a really important example of his work.

"The harp of the winds," "The Normandy farm," and "The Adirondacks" were painted after he was practically blind; the optic nerve of one eye was dead and a cataract partly clouded the other. The story of his failure to interest the buying public, together with ill-health and approaching blindness, is most pathetic. He never looked with bitterness on the success of men far inferior to himself.

"His work is that of a poet painter, but of one who felt more deeply the grandeur of mountain scenery than he did the pastoral beauty of simple scenes." "More than one critic has accorded to Martin the highest rank among the poet painters of American landscape." (Nat Cyc Am Biog)

Hartmann says: "He was one of the men who brought our landscape art to its highest pinnacle of perfection."

Lübke says: "It was in his study that his composition was made and it was there that he produced those astonishing pieces of truth in the anatomy of hillside and rocky cliff in which no landscape painter has ever surpassed him."

MAYNARD, GEORGE W., (P., Mural P., I.) b. Washington, D. C., March 5, 1843; d. New York City, April 5, 1923. A student at the National Academy of Design in 1868. A year later he went to Antwerp where in company with Francis D. Millet he entered the Royal Academy of Fine Arts and studied under Van Lerius. After four years in the academy and the museums of Belgium, he and his friend made a trip through central and southern Europe, returning to New York in the spring of 1874. The following year he became assistant to John LaFarge in company with Saint-Gaudens, Millet, and Lathrop in the interior decoration of Trinity Church, Boston, the first important work of this character done in America, the merit of which has hardly been excelled.

In 1877 he again visited Europe, making a special study of mural painting. He was elected associate member of the National Academy of Design in 1881, full member in 1885, and taught drawing for many years in the schools of Cooper Institute and at the Academy.

In 1884 he won the Temple gold medal at Philadelphia, and in 1888 the American Art Association medal of honor was awarded to him by the artist exhibitors. His picture "Sappho" was purchased by the Pennsylvania Academy of the Fine Arts in 1889 and "Sirens" won the Evan prize.

For many years he was librarian of the National Academy of Design.

Among his numerous pictures are:

"The angelus"   "Strange gods"
"Water carriers of Venice"   "Old and rare"
"An ancient mariner"

"He is a decorator in the truest sense. He is broader than a regiment of studio men, for he brings to his canvas a born colorist's palette, and a style and comprehension of what is purely beautiful beyond the mere prettiness of ordinary drawing room motives. His picture entitled "In strange seas" is a captivating group of sportive sirens gamboling amid the blue billows of the real ocean, an almost possible vision, attractively mingling the poetic and the actual." (New Eng M 14:148)

Mr. Maynard was noted for his decorations, the best known being the Metropolitan Opera House ceiling and frieze; and in the court house of the appellate division, Madison Square. His "Discovery," "Conquest," "Civilization," and "The virtues" are panels in the Library of Congress in Washington, D. C.

MEARS, HELEN FARNSWORTH, (S.) b. Oshkosh, Wis., 1876; d. 1916. Studied art in New York and Paris; later was an assistant of Augustus Saint-Gaudens.

Her first success was "Genius of war." This was followed by "The fountain of life" and busts of George Rogers Clark and Dr. William L. G. Morton and portrait reliefs of Augustus Saint-Gaudens, Louise Collier Wilcox and Edward A. MacDowell.

Miss Mears' most notable work was the execution of the statue of the late Frances E. Willard placed in the Hall of Statues in the capitol at Washington, and unveiled on February 17, 1908. This is the first statue of a woman by a woman to be placed in the building.

MELCHERS, J. GARI, (P., Mural P.) b. Detroit, Mich., August 11, 1860. At the age of seventeen he went to Germany, studying art in Düsseldorf under Van Gebhardt; later he studied under Lefebvre and Boulanger, also at the Cour Yvon (famous class at Ecole des Beaux Arts), Paris; after this he took up his residence in Holland and has a studio at Egmondaan-Zee.

Mr. Melchers has received many honors in recognition of his fine artistic ability. He is a chevalier of the Legion of Honor of France; Knight of the Order of St. Michael, Bavaria; Knight of the Red Eagle, Germany; and has received honorable mention in the Paris salon; also won medals of honor from Amsterdam, Antwerp, Munich, and Vienna. He is a member of the International Society of Artists, London; The Secessionists, Munich; Société Nationale des Beaux Arts, Paris; and professor at the Grand-Ducal Academy of Art in Weimar; was elected associate member of the National Academy of Design, New York, in 1904; full member in 1906; was first vice-president of the Paris Society of American Painters.

Mr. Melchers' first effort in Dutch painting, "The sermon," won honorable mention in the Paris salon in 1886. In 1889, when twenty-eight years old he received the blue ribbon of art—a medal of honor in Paris. Up to 1917, only three American painters had won this coveted distinction—Whistler, Sargent, and Melchers.

His "Family" hangs in Berlin; "Maternity" in the Luxembourg; "The ship builder" in Dresden; "Man with the cloak" in Rome; "Supper at Emmaus" owned by the Krupp family; "Girl in church" is in the Royal Gallery, Munich; and nearly every art gallery and museum of note in the United States has fine examples of Mr. Melchers' work.

Brinton says in "Modern artists": "It is not alone the homely picturesqueness of peasant or fisherman, the vast mottled skies, or the play of constantly diffused light which attract him to Holland. It was also the sterling artistic tradition of the country itself."

His frescoes "Peace" and "War" in the Library of Congress at Washington share with Sargent's frieze "The prophets" in the Boston Public Library, the distinction of being the finest frescoes in America.

Landscape painting is Mr. Melchers' relaxation—"Green summer," "The arbor," "Winter," "Under the trees" are studies in sunlight and reflection.

Melchers was the first artist to apply for permission to copy the Botticelli frescoes when they were put in the Louvre.

He has painted a great many portraits in America and abroad. Caffin says: "Melchers is a searching analyst, stating without comment of his own, exactly what he sees, but—he sees below the surface."

Among his finest works are:

"Married"
"Sainte Gudule"
"The communion"
"Stevedore"
"The skaters"
"A Holland lady"
"A fencer"
"Audrey"
"The nativity"
"The bride"
"The wedding"
"Little Constance"

"Penelope"
"Child in church"
"The green mantle"
"Mother and child"
"Pilots"
"Young mother"
"The kiss"
"Sailor and his sweetheart"
"The China closet"
"The Delft horse"
"Vespers"

After many years in Europe with studio in Holland, Mr. Melchers has returned to the United States and has been doing very notable mural work.

Detroit has the satisfaction of seeing its finest building—the new public library—decorated, in part, by a native artist, Mr. Melchers having been commissioned to paint three murals in the delivery hall. The themes are taken from the city's early history.

The central panel symbolizes the "Spirit of the Northwest": two figures, the "Pathfinder" and the "Trapper," are in the foreground; Saint Claire in grey robe and lilies in hand is poised above.

The panel on the right illustrates the "Conspiracy of Pontiac;" the one on the left represents the "Landing of Cadillac's wife" at Detroit.

The murals are brilliant in color and very decorative.

Mr. Melchers is engaged on panels to decorate the governor's reception room in the Missouri state capitol. The subjects are four famous Missourians: Mark Twain, humorist; Eugene Field, poet; Major S. S. Rollins, founder of the Missouri State University; and Susan Blow who introduced the kindergarten to the United States. The panels will be six by twelve feet, and the sum to be paid is said to be $20,000.

Mr. Melchers' work has found favor through the years "with discriminating lovers of art throughout the world."

MERRITT, ANNA LEA (Mrs. Henry Merritt,), (E.) b. Philadelphia, Pa., September 13, 1844. Began painting at the age of twenty-one but never had the advantage of academic training. She traveled four years on the continent with her parents and sisters and in 1871 exhibited her first picture, a portrait, at the Royal Academy, London. Since then she has been a constant exhibitor at that institution, and is a member of the Society of Painter-Etchers, London. She married Henry Merritt, artist and author, London, who died within a few months; and it was to furnish by her own hand etchings for a memorial work to her husband that she learned to etch.

Mrs. Merritt is one of the few women in this country who have etched the human figure. Her portraits of her husband, Sir Gilbert Scott, the celebrated architect, Louis Agassiz, Lady Dufferin, Oliver Wendell Holmes, and others rank among the best of modern etched portraits.

"She has executed many charming plates, principally portraits of distinguished men and women of the time, with an occasional plate of river scenery, landscape, or interpretation of her own paintings. Her vigorous portraits of Miss Ellen Terry and a large head of Mr. Leslie Stephens are striking examples of good etching."

Mrs. Merritt was the first woman painter whose work was purchased by the Chantrey fund. "Love locked out" was the subject. The picture is now in the Chantrey collection of the Tate Gallery, London.

METCALF, WILLARD LeROY, (P., Mural P.) b. Lowell, Mass., July 1, 1858. Educated in the public schools of Massachusetts; apprenticed to a wood engraver of Boston in 1875; then to George L. Brown, a landscape painter, Boston, 1876-7. Student in Lowell Institute, Boston Normal Art School, Boston Art Museum School, Académie Julien, Paris; also studied under Boulanger and Lefebvre in 1883. He is represented in the leading art galleries of the United States; received the Webb prize, Society of American Artists, 1896; and was awarded the Temple gold medal, Pennsylvania Academy of the Fine Arts; also Corcoran gold medal; member of the Ten American Painters.

Mr. Metcalf is numbered among the foremost of the American land-scape painters. During his six years' study in Paris his most successful picture was the "Arab market" which received honorable mention in the Paris salon in 1889. Most of his painting is portrait work; taught antique and life classes at the Cooper Institute; traveled in the west two years with Frank Cushing, getting the benefit of his profound knowledge of the Indians.

Well known works are:

"A family of birches"	"Golden screen"
"May night"	"Mid-winter"
"Unfolding buds"	"The snow bearers"
"Spring fields"	"Green canopy"
"Ice bound"	"The white veil"

"Light and air are to him matters of serious concern, but also are form and motion. Unlike the majority of those who follow the impression-ists' teaching, he cares not merely for the effect of sunlight but for the object upon which the sunlight falls, and paints now always in a high key." (Int Studio 39:8)

Mr. Metcalf is quite remarkable in the field of flower painting.

By general consent Mr. Metcalf's "Trembling leaves" has been labeled notable.

Mr. Metcalf recently held an exhibition in New York of fifteen canvases painted in the last two years. They represent scenes taken from Ver-mont, chiefly in autumn and winter. The best example of his later work is "Indian summer." "It has all the austere beauty of the American landscape in its simple pattern of stream and valley and nobly outlined hill." In "The coming festival" the slender trees with frost-touched yellow and crimson leaves blaze with hot autumn sunshine. "His winter scenes have the same graces, the whole exhibition being almost the last word in the perfection of American landscape painting." "October carnival" is a splendidly brilliant canvas—the sort he painted in the days when the Society of Ten was in full power.

"He is an expert on the quality of light. The allure of the coming of day, midday's frank revelations, and the quaint mysteries of evening flood his canvases at will and never fail to charm." (Country L 38:37 June)

MIELATZ, CHARLES FREDERICK WILLIAM, (E.) b. Buddin, Germany, May 24, 1864; d. New York City, June 2, 1919. A pupil of the National Academy of Design and of F. Rondel.

Member of the International Jury of Awards, St. Louis Exposition, 1904; member of New York Etching Club; was elected associate member of National Academy of Design, 1906; a teacher of etching in the academy.

A. L. Baldry says in "Modern etching" that Mr. Mielatz "possesses a power of rendering a great variety of subject-matter with success. Bulk and masses of architecture, characteristics of street people and buildings, he sets down always with grace and conviction."

"Mr. Mielatz's etchings are more interesting from the historical point of view than considered purely as works of art." (Arts 2:178)

MILLER, RICHARD E., (P.) b. St. Louis, Mo., March 22, 1875. A pupil of the St. Louis School of Fine Arts, he later studied with Benjamin-Constant and Laurens in Paris. In 1900 he received the third-class medal in the Paris salon, and in 1904, the second-class medal. Since 1905 his paintings have been hors concours in the salon of the Société des Artistes, France. He is a member of the Legion of Honor and has been second vice-president of the Paris Society of American Painters.

Mr. Miller lives in France and has been for many years prominent in the American colony in Paris. He has had very many artistic honors bestowed upon him, both in France and in the United States.

Two of his paintings, "The mother" and "The puppet," are hung in the permanent collection of the Luxembourg, Paris, and another has been placed in the Petit Palais. "The dressing table" (a portrait of Mrs. Miller) has been purchased by the Italian government; "Lady with fan" is in the Gallery of Modern Art, Rome; "The Chinese statuette," Metropolitan Museum, New York; "The boudoir," Corcoran Gallery of Art, Washington, D. C. Examples of his work are also in the Royal Museum of Christiana, King of Italy's private collection; Museum of Fine Arts, Antwerp, and Modern Gallery of Venice.

"The open window" (also called "Spring") was shown in the Salon des Artistes Français in 1914. A nude exhibited at the Chicago Art

Institute Annual Exhibition a few years ago was awarded the Potter Palmer prize. It has been pronounced one of his best works.

Other popular paintings are:

"In the garden"	"The green parasol"
"The mirror"	"Lady with red hair"
"The Chinese coat"	"The cafe"

The play of light on objects whether indoors or out presents innumerable problems of alluring interest. It is in the solution of these that Mr. Miller has found special delight and success.

"Art's mission," he says, "is not literary, the telling of a story, but decorative, the conveying of a pleasant optical sensation."

"His exteriors are vividly if pleasingly green, relieved always by the presence of flesh and light summer gowns, and invariably somewhere a touch of red."

"The Miller pictures, to analyze their popularity, are all suggestive and broad in treatment ...... Everything is selective, but harmonious through a clear general concept of values."

Among his latest works are two panels in the senate chamber of the Missouri state capitol. One is the Benton panel; the other shows the return of Clark and Lewis from their western expedition.

MILLET, FRANCIS DAVIS, (P., I., Mural P.) b. Mattapoisett, Mass., November 3, 1846. Lost his life in the S. S. Titanic disaster, April 15, 1912. Pupil of the Royal Academy of Arts in Antwerp under Van Lerius and De Keyser.

Received silver and gold medals of honor, 1872 and 1873, at the Royal Academy, Antwerp; silver medal, Paris Exposition, 1889; chevalier of the Legion of Honor of France. He was special correspondent for the "Daily News" during the Russo-Turkish war, 1877. For this work he received the Roumanian Iron Cross and the Order of Chevalier St. Anne and of St. Stanislaus from the Russian government; was also special correspondent of the "London Times" at Manila during the Spanish War. Director of decorations, Columbian Exposition, Chicago, 1893. Member of the National Academy of Design since 1885.

He was vice-chairman of the Federal Committee of Fine Arts as well as secretary and executive officer of the American Academy in Rome. He organized the American Federation of Arts and was its secretary from the beginning.

Mr. Millet painted a number of portraits, the most important being those of Charles Francis Adams, Jr. and Samuel L. Clemens (Mark Twain) both exhibited at the National Academy of Design, New York, in 1877.

A few of his paintings in oil are:

"Off duty"   "A cozy corner"
"How the gossip grew"   "A handmaiden"
"A difficult duet"   "Piping times of peace"
"Love letter"   "The black sheep"
"Wandering thoughts"   "Between two fires"
"Fireside companions"   "Rook and pigeon"
"Lucky at cards, unlucky in love"

"Mr. Millet does not revel in painting considered as being by itself one of the fine arts; his intention is almost as much literary as it is artistic; an episode of life, an anecdote, a state of soul rendered manifest in a pleasing manner and in the midst of curious amusing accessories, studied with the minuteness and neatness of touch of the later Old Dutch masters—such is Millet's conception of his art." (Child's "Art and criticism")

"In his pictures of episode he reveals the situation, not by acting but by suggesting it; therefore they have the charm of repose. His canvases have incipient or completed action—rarely the suspended motion that tires us by its arrest or vehemence."

His "Thesmophoria" or harvest feast, in a Pittsburgh bank, is a fine piece of mural painting.

"Fine as his easel pictures are, it is as a great mural painter that his fame will last. His masterpiece is his monumental work for the Baltimore custom house—"The evolution of navigation." (Art & P 3:635)

MINOR, ROBERT CRANNELL, (P.) b. New York City, 1840; d. Waterford, Conn., August 3, 1904.

First entered a business career but later decided to become a painter. He studied painting for two years under Alfred C. Howland, then went to Europe, studying with Van Luppen and Boulanger in Holland and Belgium. After three years in Paris he joined the colony at Barbizon where he was more or less under the personal influence of Diaz and Corot. In 1872 he exhibited "The silent lake" in the Paris salon, then spent two years in England during which time he exhibited at the Royal Academy and Grosvenor Gallery.

"Moonlight" secured honorable mention at the Paris Exposition and "Close of a day" won a bronze medal.

Among his best known paintings are:

"Studio of Corot"	"Under the oaks"
"Wold of Kent"	"Cradle of the Hudson"
"Mountain path"	"Gray day in September"

Coffin wrote of his work: "Poetic sentiment with fine resonant color effects are found in the landscapes of Robert C. Minor who is an avowed 'Barbizon man' ...... Simplicity of subject and completeness of composition are the main factors in his creations and particularly in sunset and in twilight effects does he appear as a sympathetic interpreter of nature's subtle changes."

Mr. Minor was vice-president of the Société Artistique Litteraire of Antwerp, president of the Salmagundi Club in 1898, and elected a member of the National Academy of Design in 1897.

MITCHELL, JOHN JAMES, (E., P.) b. New York, 1845. Lived abroad from 1867-70, studying architecture, which profession he practiced in Boston until 1876. In that year he again went to Europe and devoted himself to the study of drawing and painting under Boulanger and Lefebvre and Albert Maigman until his return in September, 1880. His first efforts in etching were made in Boston but he did not begin the practice of this art until 1876 when he received instruction from Brunet-Dehaines, one of the best French etchers of our day; he learned from him a delicacy and refinement in the management of his tools which stood him in good stead in several series of small figure subjects published some time ago in Paris. "He is especially clever, if at times a bit theatrical, in his management of strong floods of light." (Cent o.s. 25:497)

MONKS, JOHN AUSTIN SANDS, (P., E.) b. Cold Springs-on-Hudson, N. Y., November 7, 1850; d. Chicago, Ill., March, 1917. Pupil of George N. Cass and George Inness.

As a young man he was an engraver, but after a trip to Boston he took up landscape painting. Inness saw his study of an old willow tree, sent for him to come to his studio, and later invited him to become his pupil. "Not only has he painted sheep indoors and out, at play, sleeping in sunshine, in twilight, but he has modeled them in clay." He has also painted the sheep of the various localities in this country until he has become known as America's painter of sheep." (Craftsm 22:619)

"Mr. Monks studied his sheep from the standpoint of a practical farmer as well as a poet and painter, hence the solid construction of his pictures, and the convincing reality of every incident and detail of their action and environment."

"As a painter of sheep this finely trained artist has attained a mastery that allows him to speak the whole art language through the vehicle of the simple life incidents of these most humanly suggestive of our domestic animals." (New Eng M 42:755)

MORA, FRANCIS LUIS, (P., I., Mural P.) b. Montevideo, Uruguay, July 27, 1874. He received his art education in the School of the Boston Museum under Benson and Tarbell and at the Art Students' League of New York under Mowbray. Beginning about 1892 he did illustrating work for all the leading magazines and periodicals. He has won many prizes and medals and is a member of the leading art organizations; an associate member of the National Academy of Design, 1904, a full member, 1906. For nine years was a teacher in drawing and painting classes of the New York School of Art.

Mr. Mora's father was a Spanish painter, his mother a Frenchwoman and his early life was spent in South America. "Perhaps it is these very conflicting conditions in the life of Mr. Luis Mora that has evolved the unusual quality of his art, an art essentially Spanish in subject and feeling and wholly modern and American in expression .... The quality of Mr. Mora's paintings of gardens is a thing one returns to again and again in memory as one likes to see them over and over again in his studio .... In these gardens there is Spain's past magnificence .... The women are slow-moving and graceful, the children joyous, and behind all the radiance of these fine silent gardens hovers the shadow of a tragic, barbaric nation." (Craftsm 17:402)

"Picnic on the beach" is a most affirmative picture, capital in fresh white and blue, composed with utmost wisdom of technique, but efflorescent with nature both in composition and in gaiety of spirit." (Int Studio 35: sup lii)

MORAN, EDWARD, (P.) b. Bolton, Lancashire, England, August 19, 1829; d. New York, June 9, 1901. Elder brother of Peter and Thomas Moran. He arrived in Philadelphia in 1844 and was a pupil of James Hamilton, marine painter, and of Paul Weber, landscape painter. In 1862 he went abroad, studying in the Royal Academy of London for a few months. In 1869 he settled in New York, going to Paris in 1877 where he lived some time. He was a member of Pennsylvania Academy of the Fine Arts and elected associate member of the National Academy of Design in 1873.

His first pictures were exhibited in Philadelphia in 1853. The Baltimore Gazette, July 1, 1873, in commenting on Mr. Moran's painting entitled "In the narrows," said: "The great charm of the picture is motion."

He printed in 1872 the first illustrated catalog printed in this country. He worked chiefly in marines, in both oil and water-color.

A series of historical paintings, thirteen in number, was completed in 1899. These represent thirteen epochs in the marine history of America from the landing of Leif Erickson in 1001 to the return of Admiral Dewey in 1899.

MORAN, MARY NIMMO, (E., P.) b. Strathaven near Glasgow, Scotland, 1842; d. September, 1899. Came when a child with her family to the United States. In 1863 she married Thomas Moran, the well known landscape painter; in 1867 accompanied him to England, France and Italy and in 1874 traveled with him in the far west. Her work was principally water-color until 1879 when she made her first attempts in etching as a pastime during her husband's absence on an extended trip.

Mrs. Schuyler Van Rensselaer says Mrs. Moran found her true artistic voice only when she took up the etching needle. In 1887 an exhibition of the work of the women etchers in America was held at the Museum of Fine Arts, Boston, and while Miss Gabrielle D. Clements, Miss Mary Cummings Brown, Mrs. Edith Loring Peirce Getchell, Mrs. Eliza Greatorex, Mrs. Anna Lea Merritt, Miss Margaret M. Taylor, and sixteen other talented women were represented, Mrs. Mary Nimmo Moran took rank both in number and quality of plates. This position she held until the time of her death.

Her "Twilight" is a plate of extraordinary power and beauty. "Easthampton Barren" which possesses a poetic charm, and "Bridge over the Delaware" (her first plate) are two of the four original etchings made in 1879 that were sent to the New York Etching Club and which gained her recognition as a master of the needle. "Solitude" is one of her best, as it is one of her strongest etchings. "Goose pond" was the diploma etching that secured her election to the Society of Painter-Etchers, London. (Brush & P 8:3)

"In etching, Mrs. Moran finds a language that accords entirely with her ideas and modes of expression. She treats her subjects with poetical disdain of detail, but with a firm grasp of the leading truths that give force and character to her work. While her etchings do not display the smoothness that comes from great mechanical dexterity, her touch is essentially that of the true etcher." (Koehler's "American Etchings")

"Her etchings are marked by energetic emphasis and bold directness rather than delicacy or smoothness." (Scrib 46:731)

MORAN, PETER, (E., P.) b. Bolton, Lancashire, England, March 4, 1842; d. Philadelphia, Pa., November 13, 1914. He was brought to America by his parents when three years of age. When sixteen he was apprenticed by his father to learn the trade of lithographic printing in Philadelphia. Later devoted himself to painting, becoming in 1859 the pupil of his brothers—landscape, with Thomas, and marine, with Edward. He studied the works of Lambinet and those of Troyon and Rosa Bonheur for annual painting, which subject chiefly attracted him. His plate called "The return of the herd" may possibly be called his best.

From 1875 he devoted much time to etching, and reached the first rank in that branch of art. His etching, "Chariot race in the Circus Maximus," is a masterpiece and is considered one of the most important of the kind produced in America.

A few of his original plates are:

"Low tide on the Schuylkill"   "An old New England orchard"
"A burro train"   "Passing storm"
"An August day"   "A summer afternoon"

Of the last three, Mrs. Schuyler Van Rensselaer, the distinguished art-critic, wrote: "If we will ask for pictures from our etchers, we should rejoice when they give them to us of so complete a kind and yet with so much of the intrusive charm of etching, properly so-called, as does Mr. Peter Moran."

To Peter Moran and his brother, Thomas, belong the honor of having been the first among the artists to recognize the picturesque qualities of the scenery of the southwest, and of the life of its aboriginal inhabitants —the Pueblo Indians.

Jules Breton, the distinguished French painter, on seeing some of Mr. Moran's etchings exhibited in Paris, exclaimed: "The man who etched those plates, is a master!"

MORAN, THOMAS, (P., E., I.) b. Bolton, Lancashire, England, January 12, 1837. Came with his family to America in 1844. Of the talented Moran family, he displayed artistic tastes at an early age and was apprenticed to a wood-engraver in Philadelphia, remaining with him for two years. At twenty-three he painted a scene from Shelley's "Alastor" and from 1866-71 studied the masters of France, Italy, and Germany. Returning to America in 1871, he sought subjects of the most impressive character, and joined the exploring expedition of that year to the Yellowstone country, making sketches for his two great works, "The great canyon of the Yellowstone" and "The chasm of the Colorado." These were bought by Congress for $10,000 each and are now in the Capitol at Washington. ,

Noted paintings are:

"The mountain of the Holy Cross"

"The cliffs of the Green river"

"Ponce De Leon in Florida"

"The last arrow"

"The groves were God's .first temples"

"A dream of the Orient"

"The children of the mountain"

He made a series of remarkably fine designs in illustration of Longfellow's "Hiawatha" and original water-color drawings of the Yellowstone National Park.

In etching his achievements have been both numerous and valuable. Among his most excellent plates are: "Sounding sea," "The gate of Venice," "Harbor of Vera Cruz, Mexico," "Venice," "Dordrecht."

"His knowledge of form and constructive ability is quite remarkable, and his skill in composition reveals itself best in the black and white reproductions of his works." (Hartmann)

"He has found congenial themes in the wierd scenery of the Yellowstone, he has dreamed of Turner in his dreams of the Orient and has painted us lovely mornings in the harbor scenes for which he brought home his sketches from Cuba and Mexico." (Koehler)

For some time, in addition to his many paintings and etchings, he designed 250 illustrations annually. His etchings won hearty praise from John Ruskin. Associate member National Academy of Design 1881, full member, 1884.

Thomas Moran was the forerunner and frontiersman in mountain landscape, and had much to do with drawing the attention of the American public to the beauties of the great West. He is still painting at the age of 86.

MOSLER, HENRY, (P.) b. New York, June 6, 1841; d. New York City, April 21, 1920. Removed to Cincinnati in 1851 and to Nashville, Tenn., in 1854; studied wood-engraving and painting without much outside aid; was draughtsman on "The Omnibus," a Cincinnati comic weekly in 1855. Pupil of James H. Beard, 1862-3. Appointed on staff of Gen. R. W. Johnson. Studied art in Düsseldorf and Paris, 1863-6.

In 1874 he again went to Europe, going to Munich where he studied under Wagner and also received private and special criticism from Piloty. When in Munich he won the medal of the Royal Academy. In 1877 he removed to Paris, and the following year "The quadroon girl" and "Early cares" were exhibited in the salon. His "La retour," better known as "The return of the prodigal son," received honorable mention in the salon of 1879 and was purchased by the French government for the Luxembourg. This was the first picture that France purchased from an American artist. Mr. Mosler has never surpassed the technical skill displayed in this Luxembourg picture.

His "Harvest dance," a Brittany scene, received the gold medal in the salon of 1888, which placed his works hors concours in the salon. "The last moments" won the only gold medal awarded to a foreign artist by the Arch-Duke Carl Ludwig of Austria at an Exhibition in Vienna. He received in 1892 the titles Chevalier de la Legion d'Honneur and Officier d'Académie. In 1894 he returned to New York. He was a member of the National Academy of Design.

"The qualities of Mr. Mosler are homely sentiment, a talent for telling an obvious story such as ordinary people can comprehend and enjoy, and an execution which is always adequate and often excellent, so far as it goes." (Child's "Art and criticism")

The number of his works is considerable. Their titles like the subjects treated are generally anecdotic, such as:

"The return of the prodigal son"   "Visit to the marchioness"
"The village clockmaker"   "Breton harvest dawn"
"The coming storm"   "The birth of the flag"
"Forging the cross"   "Ring, ring for liberty"
"The wedding gown"

Mowbray, Henry Siddons, (Mural P.) b. Alexandria, Egypt, August 5, 1858, of English parents. In 1875 he received an appointment to the U. S. Military Academy but remained there less than a year; took up chemistry; in 1879 following a preference for art, he went to Paris and entered the school of Leon Bonnat. For three years occupied himself with genre subjects, of which the best known perhaps is "Aladdin." Settled in New York in 1885. Since 1886 has been an instructor in the Art Students' League.

Has won many prizes and medals. "His Evening breeze" won the Clark prize in 1888 and he was made full academician in 1891.

"In many of his works, Mr. Mowbray gives pictorial form to the romantic days of Florentine chateau life during the renaissance; in others he has chosen oriental subjects ...... other paintings are purely fanciful, of these an excellent example is found in "Floreal" with its graceful maidens treading a measure to the sound of the pipe and tambourine." (Nat Cyc Am Biog)

"In H. Siddons Mowbray we have a colorist and man of imagination, a wonderful narrator of fanciful tales with ample knowledge and manual skill in the practice of his craft." (New Eng M 14:143)

He also paints portraits of women with sympathetic interpretation and exquisite technique. Of late years has given much time to mural painting, and among his most recent achievements in this branch of art is "The transmission of the law" in the appellate court building, New York.

"It is a beautiful decoration; very individual and refined, with a purity of color and general spontaneity of feeling and execution most captivating." (Artist 27: sup ix)

MURPHY, JOHN FRANCIS, (P.) b. Oswego, N. Y., December 11, 1853; d. New York City, January 29, 1921. Went to New York City to live in 1875. First exhibited at the National Academy of Design in 1876. In 1885 he was elected an associate and two years later a full member of the National Academy of Design.

"Tints of a vanished past" won the Hallgarten prize of the National Academy in 1885, "Brook and fields" won the Webb prize of the Society of American Artists in 1887, and "Under gray skies" won a prize in 1894.

Mr. Murphy is one of America's simplest and at the same time most poetic landscape painters.

At an exhibition in 1910 he contributed the following:

"The opal sunset"	"The music boats"
"A twilight in Venice"	"The path to the village"
"An upland cornfield"	"After the frosts"
"Edge of the pond"	"Stony fields"
"Sunny slopes"	"April weather"
"The brook"	"Approach to an old farm"
"Sunset"	"An October day"
"The charcoal burners"	"Landscape"
"Early fall"	"Sundown"
"A cloudy afternoon"	"The yellow leaf"
"A gray morning"	"Neglected lands"

He is represented by "October" in the Corcoran Gallery, Washington, D. C.; "Neglected lands," Museum of Fine Arts, Buffalo, N. Y.; "The clearing," Art Museum, Worcester, Mass.; "Path to the village" and "Indian summer," National Gallery, Washington, D. C.; "Hill top," Art Institute, Chicago; "The old barn," Metropolitan Museum of Art, New York City; "Afternoon lights on the hill," Carnegie Institute, Pittsburgh, Pa.; "After the rain" and "Landscape," Museum of Art Institute, Brooklyn, N. Y.

"Simple in the selection of his themes, unpretentious in his compositions, synthetic in his treatment, not given to sharp contrasts of form or color, he has relied for his effects on simple straightforward rendering, told in plain terms of personal interpretation." (Brush & P 10:205)

"Others have sounded stronger, deeper notes, others have possessed an infinitely wider range of expression; no one of his countrymen has surpassed Murphy in the accuracy of his touch, his mastery of values."

"Murphy is a painter last and primarily a lover of the open, a kind of unmethodical naturalist, with something ineradicably primitive and rural in his blood." (Int Studio 53: sup vi, viii)

"This typically American artist worked out his own style through a synthesis of two methods—that of impressionists who placed pure colors side by side to create vibration, and that of the old masters whose radiance of tone was the result of placing one color over another. The effect in Murphy's case was to gain the richness of tone and depth of atmosphere that are his distinguishing characteristics."

"Murphy was never a colorist in the fullest sense of the term. His color is always related to values, and his values express light. Thus his problem like Wyant's, is closely associated with chiaroscuro, the gradation of light and dark which subtly relates the contrasts of the composition." (Art in Am 6:167)

A memorial exhibition last year, given by the Lotus Club, comprised seventy-five examples of his work. Autumn was his favorite subject and it is interesting to compare the various pictures he painted of this season of the year.

MYERS, JEROME, (P., E.) b. Petersburg, Va., March 20, 1867. Studied at Cooper Union and the Art Students' League, New York.

"Mr. Myers, whose crayon and pastel and pencil and water color drawings have for a long time been the subject of general admiration, has recently turned his hand to the biting of the copper plate. The result surpasses the most roseate expectation ...... Not one of our draughtsmen has more individuality of line and design. Not one has a deeper, truer love of life or a more solid philosophy."

"Usually the first delight one secures from an etching is the quality of the man's technique, his lightness of line or column, the richness or scantiness, but from Mr. Myers' etching, as in all his work, there is the joy of receiving his knowledge of humanity, his kindness, his humor, his understanding of all the great and small tragedies of humble life ...... His sketches are never rounded into a picture; they are frag- ments of life—you feel some one coming into the picture at one side; and at the others, some one moving out."

"Mr. Myers' work ...... presents the ebb and flow of the vital life of the common people—the alien on the East Side, the shop folks and their babies in the Luxembourg Gardens." (Craftsm 29:32)

"There is stability and character in his work and his slightest sketches evince a depth and aesthetic sensitiveness rare in a generation so ap- pallingly devoted to the superficial and the trivial." (Bookm 34:404)

Of American etchers, John Sloan, Eugene Higgins, and Jerome Myers alone are interested in life as life, says Arts and Decoration.

NADELMAN, ELI, (S.) b. Warsaw, Poland, and studied in the art schools of his native country, then went to Paris where he lived for twelve years. When the European war broke out he was one of the first foreign artists to come to the United States.

While Mr. Nadelman can hardly be classed as an American artist, his presence has been felt in artistic circles and his works are exhibited in American art exhibits; his recent exhibition of drawings and sculpture brought forth much comment from our art critics.

"His treatment of draperies is at times distinctly oriental; and while the pure Archaic Greek and Phidian era have influenced him, there are works of his which show a development not unlike Chinese art just after the dissemination of Greek ideals ...... In his lightness of touch and the ethereality of his inventions he expresses a genuine poetic spirit ...... He is at all times a serious artist. His work is as purely beauti- ful as a Watteau, but not so profound as a good Picasso." (Forum 55:215)

Another critic writes: "He may indeed arouse your feelings, but primarily plastic art is not concerned with love or patriotism ...... His art savors indeed of mathematical formulae ...... At times it is almost pure architecture in miniature ...... He is for the private study and the glass cabinet, rather than for the open air. The intellect- ual note and aloofness is intensified by the extraordinarily high polish which he gives to his surfaces."

Some of his heads "fixed forever in marble meditation display a beauty of rare delicacy, a kind of spirituality which forever disposes of those detractors who believe that he is an apostle of ugliness." (Int Studio 57: sup lv)

NAST, THOMAS, (P., I.) b. Landau, Bavaria, September 27, 1840; d. Guayaquil, Ecuador, December 7, 1902.   Came with his parents to America in 1846; was educated in the New York public schools and displayed a decided talent for art.   At the age of fourteen began the study of art with Theodore Kaufman and at the age of fifteen furnished sketches and drawings for Frank Leslie's Illustrated Newspaper, his first assignment being the illustration of an account of a prize fight. Later he went to England to make sketches for the New York Illustrated News.   He followed Garibaldi's army through Sicily and Calabria and contributed numerous battle pieces to the illustrated press of New York. He returned to the United States in 1861 and became a member of Harper's staff in the following year.

Mr. Nast was first to introduce caricature work into America and his pictures of war scenes, of Andrew Johnson, and of the Tweed Ring had great influence on the politics of his time.   His war pictures for Harper's Weekly are among his most notable works.

"A particular feature of Mr. Nast's work apart from his wonderful portraits was the ability to portray the individuality of his subject by some characteristic pose or peculiarity of apparel."

His historical paintings in oil hold high rank in America for beauty of conception and execution.   The most notable of these are:

"Peace again"   "Appomattox"
"Lincoln entering Richmond"   "The day before the surrender"
"Saving the flag"   "Garibaldi"
"During the Civil War"
"The seventh regiment going to
   war"

"Mr. Nast's reputation will probably rest on his cartoon work, but it was his ardent desire that his name should be handed down as a great painter of historical scenes."   (Brush & P 11:470)

NEANDROSS, SIGURD, (S.) Born of Norwegian parents on the Pacific ocean, while they were en route to the United States.   With his nativity the ocean, ancestry Scandinavian, a Greek sounding name, and having lived several years in Denmark, Sigurd Neandross classes himself with American sculptors.

One of his earliest works, "The sound of the sea," was made for a monument at Copenhagen.

Two groups representing contrasting views of life are his "Mother and child"—the happiness of life, and "The Egyptian widow"—hopeless sorrow.

"He belongs to that rarer kind of sculptor who makes one think ...... He is a sculptor with temperament who goes his own way endeavoring to express lovely and innocent and poetic feelings to the best of his ability through his chosen art." (Int Studio 52: sup xxi)

NEWCOMB, MARIA GUISE, (P.) b. New Jersey. Pupil of Edourd Detaille in Paris. She studied horses and dogs under Schenck, the animal painter, and sheep with Chialiva and traveled in Algeria and the Sahara, studying the Arab and his horses. "Very few artists can be compared with Mrs. Newcomb in representing horses. She has a genius for portraying this animal and understands its anatomy as few painters have done ...... Her studies in Paris were comprehensive and her work shows the results and places her among the distinguished painters of animals." (Women in the Fine Arts, p. 248)

The first picture that Miss Guise (Mrs. Newcomb) sent to the Paris salon was a golden haying scene with farmers and Brittany horses; it was accepted and well hung. Her greatest work, as she considers it, is entitled "The work horses need"—the heads of four horses drinking from a street fountain. (American art and artists, p. 13)

NEWELL, GEORGE GLENN, (P.) b. Berrien county, Michigan, 1870. Pupil of the National Academy of Design under Ward and of Teachers' College, New York, under Will S. Robinson. Member Salmagundi Club. Specialty, landscapes and cattle.

His best known paintings are:

"Mists of the morning"
"The toilers"
"Through shower and sun"

NEWELL, PETER, (I.) b. McDonough Co., Ill., March 5, 1862. His childhood was spent in Bushnell, Ill., and at the age of seventeen he went to work in a cigar factory. Later did pencil work and crayon enlargements of photographs. A student at the Art Students' League, New York, for three months, then made drawings which were used by illustrators on Harper's magazine.

Mr. Newell is an author as well as an illustrator and gives pictorial interpretations of his writings. He won his reputation with his book—"Peter Newell's pictures and rhymes."

"While Mr. Newell's art is so distinctive and individual as to make it conspicuously personal, he has not found the interpretation of another's text a difficult task."

Popular books having Newell illustrations are:

John Kendricks Bangs' "House boat on the Styx," "Pursuit of the house boat," and "The enchanted typewriter"
Guy Wetmore Carryl's "Fables of the frivolous"
Frank B. Stockton's "Great stone of Sardis"
Albert Lee's "Tommy Toddles"
Lewis Carroll's "Alice in Wonderland"

"He has .... evolved his own technique—a technique, by the way, that suffers nothing by comparison in its adroitness and direct charm with the illustrations of the day." (Bookm 11:335)

"Mr. Newell is a painter as well as an illustrator and he cares most for the qualities of tone in his studies and compositions."

NEY, ELIZABETH, (S.) b. in Westphalia, Germany, in 1830; d. Austin, Texas, June 30, 1907. Studied art in Berlin and Munich under Christian Rauch. She lived for a time in Georgia, then settled in Texas.

"Miss Ney was one of the most interesting characters as she was one of the best equipped of women sculptors. Nothing could be more romantic than the life of this gifted woman who was patronized by the 'mad king' Ludwig II of Bavaria."

Among the great men who sat to Miss Ney were von Humboldt, von Liebig, Jacob Grimm, Schopenhauer, Joachim, Garibaldi, and Bismark. She also executed statues of Sam Houston and other noted Texan characters.

Of her memorial to General Albert Sidney Johnston for the cemetery of Austin: "The conception is vivid ...... This is a work of high order, ... one of the most expressive and eminently sculptural conceptions among recent American ideals." (Lorado Taft's "History of American Sculpture," p. 214)

NICHOLLS, RHODA HOLMES, (P., I.) b. Coventry England. Pupil of Bloomsbury School of Art, London. Studied landscape in Rome with Vertunni, and the human figure with Cannerano. While living in Italy her work attracted the attention of the queen who summoned her to receive compliments on her attainments. Three years later, she went to South Africa and returned to England with many canvases. Previous to this she had received recognition in England, her pictures having been hung on the line in Royal Academy exhibitions. In 1884 Miss Holmes married Mr. Burr H. Nicholls and immediately came to America.

Her pictures are chiefly figure subjects, among which are "Those evening bells," "The scarlet letter," "A daughter of Eve," "Indian after the chase," "Searching the Scriptures."

In the Studio, March 1901, in writing of the exhibition of the American Water-color Society, the critic says: "In her two works, "Cherries" and "A rose," Mrs. Rhoda Holmes Nicholls shows us a true water-color executed by a master hand."

Mrs. Nicholls is also known as an illustrator; her work ranges all along the line of oil painting, water-colors, wash drawings, crayons, pastels. As a colorist she has few rivals and her acute knowledge of drawing and genius for composition are apparent in everything she does.

"Quickness of conception, bold treatment and fine color mark all her work, while the wide reach of her subjects is remarkable."

Mrs. Nicholls has been vice-president of the New York Water Color Club, member Women's Art Club, New York, also of Canada; member of Aquarelle Club, Rome.

At a recent exhibition held in Knoedler Galleries, New York, two canvases of Mrs. Nicholls' attracted attention. One was a slender girl holding a bowl of roses; the other, a Venetian water-color sketch, "Gamins," lightly and delicately painted, yet full of expression and vivid effect of tones." (Giles Edgerton)

Niehaus, Charles Henry, (S.) b. Cincinnati, O., January 24, 1855. Pupil of McMicken School in Cincinnati, also Royal Academy in Munich. He received a gold medal at Pan-American Exposition, Buffalo, 1901; was elected associate member of the National Academy of Design in 1902; full member in 1906.

While at the McMicken School he won the distinction of obtaining at the time of his matriculation a first prize, medal and diploma, for a composition entitled "Fleeting time." After studying at the Munich Royal Academy he returned to Cincinnati and received commissions for statues of Garfield; one for Cincinnati, the other to be placed in the rotunda of the Capitol, Washington, in the name of the State of Ohio. After successfully executing these commissions he returned to Italy, establishing a studio in Rome. Merit of the work done there brought about his election as a Fellow L'Associazione della Artistica Internationale di Roma. He has been a resident of New York since 1885.

Mr. Niehaus has a pronounced leaning toward classic subjects. "The Greek athlete using a strigil" is considered his best study of the nude. This work is known to the artist world as "The scraper" and is undoubtedly, says Taft, "one of the few good nude figures in American sculpture."

He has made statues of many distinguished citizens of the United States, the most celebrated being the bronze statue of McKinley in front of the stately mausoleum at Canton, Ohio; a pair of doors for Trinity Church, New York, done in high relief; equestrian statue of General Forrest for Forrest Park, Memphis, Tenn. He contributed to the Library of Congress two figures, "Moses" and "Gibbon." Among his latest undertakings is a large nude figure, "The driller," an important feature of a monument at Titusville, Pa., to the memory of Col. Edwin L. Drake, who sank the first oil well in Pennsylvania in 1859.

Several critics have remarked that "the admirable breadth and smoothness of his treatment recalls the antique draperies in which the Greeks found delight." (Taft's History of American Sculpture")

NOBLE, JOHN, (P.) His early life was spent in the Osage Indian Reservation, now a part of Kansas. After many adventures as a sheepherder he found his way to the Cincinnati Academy to study art. From there he went to Paris and studied under Laurens at Julien's. For nearly ten years he has lived in Brittany and painted the fisher-folk; he is a member of the art colony near Etaples in the north of France.

Clara T. MacChesney says: "He generally sees nature in a mist of blue and rose ...... He sometimes advances far into the field of the impressionist and gives us bold, crude, decorative effects in direct contrast to his more finished pictures."

Of his "Moonlight on the sea," enveloped in a fog, a French critic says: "An artist must be both painter and poet to bathe his pictures in an atmosphere so poetic and true. He has given with an infinite delicacy the pale, unreal light of the morning fog ...... His technique is marvelously suited to the subjects he treats."

NORDFELDT, BROR J. OLSSON, (P., E.) b. Scania in the south of Sweden, 1878. When thirteen years of age his parents came to America and settled in Chicago. He was put to work as printer's devil on a Swedish newspaper. At nineteen he took up the study of art in the classes of Frederick Richardson at the Art Institute; also studied drawing under John H. Vanderpoel. He became assistant of Albert Herter in painting mural decorations, and in 1900 went to Paris to study. His first effort was hung in the Paris salon of 1901. Also in the same year he had a product on the line at the Royal Academy, London.

Mr. Nordfeldt was awarded a silver medal by the Italian government for an exhibit at the Milan Exhibition, 1906.

"He works directly from nature, composing his etchings or his canvas with the scene before him." His etchings "have been a surprise to his friends who have known his portraits, his landscapes, and woodblock prints."

The Provincetown series takes us among the boats along the water side with reflections out at sea. "Mothers" is an excellent composition including many figures and nursemaids in Washington Square; it recalls groups familiar to that locality.

NOURSE, ELIZABETH, (P.) b. Mount Pleasant, Cincinnati, O., 1860. At the age of thirteen she showed remarkable talent for painting and her parents sent her to the Cincinnati Art School. Later the family fortune was lost in a financial panic and she earned money to continue her studies in Paris by designing and decorating the interiors of homes in Cincinnati. At the age of eighteen she entered the Académie Julien. Her drawing was so good that Boulanger advised her to take a studio and work alone, that her style might develop uninfluenced by academic training. She followed his advice and the same year her painting, "A mother and child" was accepted in the salon and hung on the line, an unprecedented honor for a new-comer. Today she is one of the strongest American painters in Paris.

When Puvis de Chavannes, Dagnan-Bouveret, and others formed the Société Nationale des Beaux Arts, Miss Nourse sent her pictures to the New Salon. They were received "with acclamation" and three years later she was made an associée. Puvis de Chavannes was the first to congratulate her; and when she was made a sociétaire in 1901, Dagnan-Bouveret, Cazin, Besnard, Rodin, and others showered upon her congratulations. Miss Nourse was the first American woman on whom this coveted honor was conferred.

One of her happiest interpretations of a mother's joy in her children is her "Happy days" (owned by Detroit Museum of Art), and one of the most appealing canvases is "Thirst," now in a gallery in Rouen, France. "Closed shutters" has been purchased by the French government for the Luxembourg.

A. Dubuisson, a French art critic, says: "There is no painter who has reproduced better than Miss Nourse the naiveté of a baby's attitude and the tenderness of motherly love ......"

Other characteristic paintings are:

"On the dyke"
"Evening"
"The Madeleine chapel at Pen-
  march"
"In the sheepfold"
"Good Friday in Rome"
"Morning toilet"
"The first communion"
"Little sister"
"The children of Penmarch"
"The family repast"

"Among neighbors"
"In the country"
"The pardon of St. Francis
  d'Assisi"
"In the fields"
"The procession of Our Lady of
  Joy, Penmarch"
"The close of the day"
"Grandfather's feast"
"Consolation"

Her pictures are not portraits of models, but types of human character. Some of her most beautiful pictures are landscapes of Brittany or bits in the old forest of Rambouillet, where she has spent many summers. In the oriental exhibition held in Paris in 1905, her sketches of the African desert of Tunis held a place of honor. Years of study in Paris have broadened her technique—her brushwork has become more firm, her color more beautiful, but the character of her painting remains unaltered. "She believes in art not alone for art's sake, but also for the sake of a humanity which it can uplift and spiritualize." (Int Studio 27:247)

Her goodness to her models is well known in Paris. A profound sympathy exists between her and the humble people whom she paints.

At the Paris salon last year Miss Nourse's "Consolation" attracted unusual interest.

OAKLEY, VIOLET, (Mural P., I.) b. New Jersey, 1874. Began her studies at the Art Student's League in New York; after studying a year with Carroll Beckwith she went to Paris and became the pupil of Aman-Jean; she also was a pupil of Charles Lasar in England. Upon her return to the United States she settled in Philadelphia where she received instructions from Cecilia Beaux and others. As her work led naturally toward illustration, she entered the class of Howard Pyle.

In the illustrations for "Evangeline" published by Houghton, Mifflin & Co. in 1897 she and Jessie Willcox Smith were collaborators, and in that color work came the first suggestion for stained-glass.

In 1898 she executed mural decorations, a mosaic reredos, and five stained-glass windows in the Church of All Saints, New York; has also designed and decorated a window in the Convent of the Holy Child at Sharon Hill, Pa.

She has been a frequent exhibitor at the academy in Philadelphia with studies and compositions in color and in black and white and her window for the Church of the Epiphany in Boston was exhibited in New York before being placed.

In 1893 Miss Oakley was commissioned to decorate the walls of the governor's reception room in the capitol at Harrisburg, Pa. This is the first work of its kind to be confided to an American woman. The decorations consist of thirteen decorative panels forming a frieze of heroic size. Under the title of "The founding of the state of liberty spiritual" they impressively record events in the life of William Penn. These designs were exhibited at the Pennsylvania Academy of the Fine Arts and they won for her a special gold medal from the academy. An art critic writing of this work, now completed, says that her grasp of the subject in union with great technical skill has placed Miss Oakley in the foremost rank of American artists.

Miss Oakley was chosen to complete the important mural decorations in the capitol that the late Edwin A. Abbey had been commissioned to do. The work was successfully executed by her, the decorations being entirely her own creation.

She has completed her $20,000 painting, "The Constitutional Convention," for the new Cuyhoga county court house, Cleveland, Ohio; and also executed nine panels in the senate chamber of the Harrisburg capitol entitled, "The creation and preservation of the Union."

Miss Oakley designed the "Philadelphia award" medal, an annual gift of Edward W. Bok, which carries with it $10,000 to the citizen of Philadelphia "who has performed an act or a service calculated to advance the best and largest interest of that city." The medal measures three inches in diameter. The obverse shows the figure of Christ washing the feet of the disciple John and the text "I am among you as he that serveth."

At the St. George Gallery, Hanover Square, London, Miss Oakley recently exhibited her preliminary studies and drawings for her famous murals in the capitol at Harrisburg, Pa.

A London correspondent says: "Although Miss Oakley is in a sense the successor of Edwin Abbey, R.A., it cannot be said that her work is reminiscent of his—rather is it the outcome of long comparative study of the best in mural decoration with an acknowledgment of its architectural demands. She has always before her the problem of scale and never does she allow it to baffle her ...... Miss Oakley has a grand style, illustrative yet decorative, while possessing an imaginative feeling and the immense driving force of the message these decorations bear."

O'CONNOR, ANDREW, Jr., (S.) b. Worcester, Mass., June 7, 1874. At the age of fourteen he was working with his father at the occupation of producing designs and monuments for cemeteries. While still a youth he went to Chicago and was employed in the studio of William Ordway Partridge. Later he went to New York where he became the pupil of Daniel Chester French. Going to London he studied under the direction of Sargent; then to Paris where he lived and worked for many years, being much influenced by Rodin who accepted him as a pupil.

"Sea dream," a relief of a head, was exhibited in the Royal Academy of London in his early period, and it is said to have been praised by Leighton and Whistler. A bust of Robert L. Newman, exhibited in Paris at one of the salons of the Société des Artistes Francais, was purchased and placed in the Luxembourg Gallery. "The owl," a most remarkable achievement during his Paris sojourn, was pronounced by M. Guillemot, a distinguished art critic, an extraordinary piece of monumental sculpture. It is a sort of Egyptian phantasy. "Inspiration," an allegorical study, also evoked the praise of several French art critics. It was shown in the Fine Arts Building at the St. Louis Exposition, 1904. His bronze statue of General Lawton, with heroic figure carrying shield and palm on the pedestal, completed in Paris, is now at Indianapolis, Ind.

A relief panel for the bronze door of a tomb was his first commission. It interested Stanford White who afterwards was instrumental in O'Connor receiving several important commissions.

Mr. O'Connor designed the statues and reliefs which embellish the Essex county court house at Newark, N. J. "Justice" adorns the gable, while on the cornice of the porch are ranged eight statues of heroic size: on the right, "Adam" and "Eve"; on the left, "Cain" and "Thais"; extreme right, "Wisdom" and "Learning"; extreme left, "Maternity" and "Light." These groups are suggestive of the Rodin influence.

His "Boy scouts of America," a fountain group at the Glen View Golf Club, Chicago (a memorial to Theodore Roosevelt), is a popular work. This symbol of youth represents four boys with dog standing on a pedestal at the head of a pool. These boys were modeled from the sons of the sculptor.

The Lincoln statue was dedicated at the celebration of the centenary of Springfield, Ill., and stands before the state house.

"Often his work is conceived with the most exquisite elegance and again he creates subjects shrouded in a phenomenal and impressive gloom. This artist's expression is eloquent without emphasis, without melodramatic tendency. He gives and absorbs the best that American life stands for." (Arts & D 12:85)

OCHTMAN, LEONARD, (P.) b. Zonnenmaire, Zeeland, Netherlands, October 21, 1854. Came with his family to this country and settled at Albany, N. Y., in 1866. At the age of sixteen he entered an engraving office as a draughtsman. A winter course at the Art Students' League of New York was practically the extent of his art education. His specialty—landscape—was entirely self-taught. He first exhibited at the National Academy of Design in 1882 and has since that time been a regular exhibitor at the art institutes and associations in the United States.

In 1885 he traveled in England, France, and Holland.

Frederick W. Morton writes: "He is the exponent of home—a home that he knows intimately and deeply loves ...... He sees broadly and paints simply and sympathetically ...... The scenes he loves to depict are essentially idyllic."

His "Night on the Mianus river," a prize picture, holds the spectator in a sense spellbound, as do his "The light of night," "An autumn moonlight," "Moonlight night," and other night scenes. "The enchanted vale" is one of his typical canvases—painted in the reds and yellows of early autumn. The same qualities are found in "In the mountains," "Views from Woodwild," "Seaside farm," "Buds and blossoms."

"If they [his pictures] could be translated into words, as expressive as are the artists' pigments, they would all have the simple rhythm, the grace and beauty of lyrics ...... He has approached nature like an Inness." (Brush & P 9:65)

Associate member of National Academy of Design, 1898; full member, 1904.

OSTHAUS, EDMUND HENRY, (P.) b. Hildesheim, Germany, August 5, 1858. Studied art in the Royal Academy of Arts, Düsseldorf, 1874-82; pupil of Andreas Muller, Peter Janser, E. V. Gebhardt, E. Deger, and C. Kroner (a noted landscape painter). Came to the United States in 1883; was principal of the Toledo Academy of Fine Arts in 1886; now devotes his time to painting principally pictures of shooting and fishing, hunters and dogs.

"A born sportsman and a student of animals, explains his adoption of a specialty, and his study and life explain his art."

"One of the most successful painters of animals. He paints animals as they are in a natural environment. His dogs are in action or in characteristic attitudes; his canvases are for the most part skilful combinations of landscape and animal figure painting '.... A careful draughtsman and a good colorist ...... His works are documents of dog life."

It is related that he commenced to draw as soon as he could grasp a pencil, and that he used the white pine floors (his mother's pride and despair) as material on which to express his youthful inspiration.

The action and postures of his animals are those that can be properly termed characteristic.

Favorite paintings are:

"Slow music"   "A first effort"
"Stumped"   "My old coon dog"
"Full cry"   "On the bay farm"
"The dog's glory"   (Brush & P 18:81)
"The leaders"

OTIS, AMY, (Min. P.) b. Sherwood, N. Y. Pupil of Philadelphia School of Design and Pennsylvania Academy of the Fine Arts; also studied under Courtois and Garrido in the Colarossi Academy in Paris. Member Plastic Club, Philadelphia Water Color Club, Pennsylvania Society Miniature Painters, Fellowship Pennsylvania Academy of the Fine Arts.

Miss Otis has either drawn or painted portraits of many prominent persons, those of Dr. Horace Howard Furness, Prof. Corson of Cornell University, and Mrs. Julia Ward Howe being her best work. She has also done much in the line of landscape.

PAEFF, BASHKA, (S.) b. Minsk, Russia, August 12, 1893. Her parents came to this country when she was an infant, and Boston has been her home ever since. She was educated in the public schools, studied art in the Normal Art School, and sculpture under Bela Pratt in the Boston Museum of Fine Arts, reaping honors as she went. The art world of Boston knows that for years while studying at the museum she was employed as a ticket taker at the Park street subway. Miss Paeff comes from a talented family; one sister is a distinguished pianist, another has produced some notable musical compositions.

Miss Paeff's studio is over a carpenter's shop on River street, Boston.

The John E. Warren memorial fountain (a drinking fountain for man and beast), erected at Westbrook, Maine, is one of Miss Paeff's most important works. The conception is original. Another fountain group —mother and child composition—is for the sun parlor of the Julius Rosenwald mansion, near Chicago.

An exhibition of Miss Paeff's work featured relief portraits; portrait busts in marble, bronze, and plaster; dog portraits; ideal pieces; and fountain designs.

The following are among her best known works in relief: "Two daughters of Mr. and Mrs. J. Macy Willets," "Little Peter," "Portrait of Dean James Barr Ames of the Harvard law school," and "Portrait of Mr. Arthur Foote." Among portrait heads that of Miss Nancy Cox, young daughter of the governor of Massachusetts, is notably intimate and delightful in characterization. Another beautiful portrait is that of the young son of Mr. and Mrs. J. Macy Willets.

"There is a refinement, taste, and distinction in the best of these reliefs which are truly admirable; and they are wrought with adequate skill."

She has a well-earned reputation as a sculptor of animal portraits, French bulldogs and Irish terriers being fine examples of her talent in the delineation of canine character.

"Spirit of 1918" immortalizes the service man, and is one of the many exquisite pieces of work that have brought fame to the young sculptor.

In the Massachusetts Hall of Fame is a memorial to the Massachusetts chaplains who lost their lives in military or naval service in the World War, designed and executed by this Russian girl. It is a tablet of appealing beauty. The soldier's face is the artist's conception of the representative type of the Massachusetts service man.

Her latest work is a sculptured portrait of Laddie Boy, the famous White House airedale. The statue, which is to be presented to Mrs. Harding, will be cast in metal obtained by melting down the pennies which the newsboys have given for this tribute to the late president.

PAGE, WALTER GILMAN, (P.) b. Boston, Mass., October 13, 1862. Was educated in the private schools of Boston. Studied art in Paris at the Académie Julien. Exhibited three years in the salons, also at leading art exhibitions in United States.

Mr. Page was one of the founders of the first public school art league in the United States.

PALMER, WALTER LAUNT, (P.) b. Albany, N. Y., August 1, 1854. Pupil of F. E. Church in Hudson, N. Y., of Carolus-Duran in Paris. Received second Hallgarten prize, National Academy of Design, 1887, and many medals and prizes since that time. Member National Academy of Design, 1897. Specialty, winter landscapes.

Charles C. Curran, former instructor at the Art Students' League, N. Y., writes: "In Mr. Palmers' 'White world' we have a remarkable example of the transformation of a homely spot behind the old farm barn ...... The sky is a story in itself, thin vapors taking on the color of the delicate morning sunlight ......"

Rhoda Holmes Nicholls comments on the same painting: "Exquisite and tender as Walter Palmer's snow pieces always are, this one is perhaps more subtle than the rest. Its extreme simplicity is its most appealing quality."

Other fine examples of his paintings are:

"Morning light"   "November snow"
"Red barn"   "The snow mantle"
"Evening star"

PAPE, ERIC, (P., I.) b. San Francisco, Cal., October 17, 1870. Pupil of Ecole des Beaux Arts, and of Gérome, Laurens, Blanc, Lefebvre, Boulanger, and Delance in Paris. The list of honors and medals and decorations that have come to Mr. Pape is said to be overpowering.

Under the age of twenty, he entered the Académie Julien, Paris, and in his examination for admission to the Ecole des Beaux Arts his drawing was marked "No. 3," the competitors numbering several hundred. His first salon picture—"Zevener Spinnerin"—was exhibited when he was nineteen; the following year he had three pictures and a bas-relief medallion at the same salon; has been a frequent exhibitor since. His largest and most important picture, "The two eras," shared with another the chief attention in the salon of 1893. His first work in the illustration line was executed for the Century Company when he was still in Paris. Upon his return to the United States in 1894 he made a large number of drawings for the "Life of Napoleon" published by the same firm. Perhaps the most important single commission that he has performed was for Houghton, Mifflin & Co., in their exquisite edition of General Lew Wallace's "Fair God." His series of thirty-five water-color drawings made in illustration of "The life of Mahomet" in 1900 is well remembered, as are the illustrations for an edition de luxe of Hawthorne's "Scarlet letter" published in 1905. "The romaunt of the oak" is one of a group of paintings to adorn a five-volume edition de luxe of the poems of his personal friend, Madison Cawein.

Mr. Pape spent several years in Egypt studying the ancient people and typical architecture. "The romantic, the archaic, and the mediæval are attractive to him, the sumptuous, the oriental and the pageantry of barbaric splendor."

He conducts the Eric Pape Art School, Boston, and his wife who was Miss Alice Monroe, a skilful artist, was his assistant in this school until her death May 17, 1911. (New Eng M 39:455)

PARKER, EDGAR, (P.) b. Framingham, Mass., 1840. Spent his professional life in Boston. Had no instruction in painting. Three of his portraits are in Faneuil Hall—Charles Sumner, Henry Wilson, and Rear Admiral John A. Winslow.

Whittier gave him sittings in 1875 for a portrait which is the only original likeness of that great poet in existence, excepting one by Hoyt, painted in Whittier's youth.

He painted the popular "Embarkation of the pilgrims" after a painting by Robert Weir.

PARKER, LAWTON S., (P.) b. Fairfield, Michigan, August 7, 1868. When a young boy he won a prize offered for the best drawing by a person who had no artistic instruction, and a member of the jury was so impressed by the effort that he offered young Parker free instructions if he would come to Chicago. The boy eagerly accepted the offer and soon won a scholarship at the Art Institute. In Paris he was instructed by Gérome, Laurens, Benjamin-Constant, Besnard, and Whistler. Mr. Parker became director of art at Beloit College in 1893, president of the New York School of Art in 1898, and president of the Chicago Academy of Fine Arts in 1903. An associate member of the National Academy of Design, 1916.

While studying in Paris Mr. Parker received honorable mention in the salon of 1900; two years later he won the third medal and in 1905, the gold medal at the International Exposition at Munich.

A great distinguishing honor came to Mr. Parker when in 1913 the Société des Artistes Francais awarded him the gold medal. This is the highest award of the Old Salon and he is the first foreigner upon whom it has ever been bestowed—an American, and a western American at that.

"The quality in his work which has called forth particular praise from critics is its luminousness; it is emphatically what the French call *plein-air,* full of the atmosphere of summer months spent near the little village of Giverny, of its opalescence and shimmering greens against which the figure stands." (Outl 107:55)

PARRISH, MAXFIELD, (I., Mural P.) b. Philadelphia, Pa., July 25, 1870. Son of Stephen Parrish who is a painter and etcher of ability. Graduated at Heverford College and then entered the Pennsylvania Academy of the Fine Arts; after this he studied under Howard Pyle at Drexel Institute. Received honorable mention at the Paris Exposition, 1900; silver medal for drawing at the Pan-American Exposition, 1901. Member of Society of American Artists, 1897; associate member of the National Academy of Design, New York, 1905; full member in 1906.

After living in England and France for several years he returned to the United States. Mr. Parrish has become celebrated as an illustrator but his first productions were of a decorative character. The first work to bring him into prominence was a cover design for the Christmas number of Harper's Weekly, 1895. In 1894 he was elected a member of the Society of American Artists on his pictures, "The sandman" and "The bulletin board." He has contributed designs for Century Magazine, Harper's Weekly, the Round Table, Scribner's Magazine, and the Book Buyer; illustrated Kenneth Grahame's "Golden age," Irving's "History of New York," Eugene Field's "Poems of childhood," Edith Wharton's "Italian villas and their gardens," R. Stannard Baker's "Great northwest" and "Great southwest."

"Mr. Parrish is at his best in color. His palette is rich and full; his use of color strikingly effective, both as a means of artistic and of poetic expression .... His imagination finds expression not only in warm, rich tones and a glow of color, but when other ends are sought it employs the most subdued effects, and at times it rests on empty space .... Mr. Parrish is one of those rare illustrators who never disappoint. There is always something to admire in his work, and in most of his pictures a cause for genuine delight ...... His pictures and decoration have a distinct place of their own in modern American art." (Outl 78:839)

"A calm completeness and faultless finality are in everything he does. His color schemes are as synthetic and clearly understood as his architectural settings." (Ind 59:1398)

"Decorative it is to exaggeration and whimsical and quaint and so individual as to be personal—but withal so full of humor and sentiment as to make genial its Gothic spirit."

Mr. Parrish has made the mural decorations for the Curtis Publishing Company of Philadelphia in their new building. This series is on the top floor and is by far the finest thing he has ever done. There are seventeen paintings. "Sixteen of these occupy the space between the windows, and form a sequence of glimpses of an architectural garden-terrace and above the terrace may be seen vistas of a wonderful turquoise sky, through the branches of venerable and fantastically gnarled cedars .... A carnival is depicted in the last panel and shows the loggia of an Italian palace ...... The drawing is at once masterful and exquisite ...... Each figure is a study in itself ...... Of the color what can be said other that what has been said above—that it is like a painting of Maxfield Parrish." (Int Studio 47: sup xxv)

His mural painting, "Old King Cole," designed for the Knickerbocker Hotel, New York City, and purchased by Vincent Astor was shown in the exhibition by the Society of American Mural Painters at the Chicago

Art Institute in 1922. It is in three panels and one of the best examples of Mr. Parrish's work in spirit and in execution. "Old King Cole enthroned" is the central panel, the "Call for pipe and bowl" another, and the "Fiddlers three" is the third. The subjects are treated with simplicity, and the reds and blues enter into an unusual and beautiful color scheme.

PARRISH, STEPHEN, (E., P.) b. Philadelphia, Pa., July 9, 1846. After the age of thirty-one he applied himself to art, studying under a local teacher; took up etching and produced his first plate in 1879. Has exhibited in New York, Boston, Philadelphia, Vienna, and Dresden. Is a member of the Royal Society of Painter-Etchers, London.

Mr. Parrish takes the very first rank in American etching. He has experimented widely with his art, especially in the matter of sky treatment.

Exhibited "Evening, low tide" in the salon of 1885, and "On the Rance, Brittany" in 1886. Koehler says that Stephen Parrish's "Annisquam" is a convincing argument that the etching process is fitted to express broad sunlight as well as twilight effects.

Among his best prints are:

"The shepherd's Christmas eve"   "Fishermen's houses, Cape Ann"
"Old fish-house"   **"Coast of New Brunswick"**
"Low tide, Bay of Fundy"   "Midsummer twilight"

PARTON, ARTHUR, (P.) b. Hudson, N. Y., March 26, 1842. Began to draw and paint while still a schoolboy and early entered the studio of William T. Richards in Philadelphia; also attended the Pennsylvania Academy of the Fine Arts. Spent a year in travel and study in Europe in 1869. Returned to New York. Associate member National Academy of Design, 1872; full member, 1884.

The works that brought him prominently before the public were "On the road to Mount Marcy," "A mountain brook," "Sycamores of old Shokan," "Delaware river near Milford," "Nightfall," "The morning ride," "Winter on the Hudson," "Evening, Harlem river."

His "November," "Loch Lomond," "Solitude," and "Stirling Castle" (four splendid pictures) attracted much attention at the Centennial Exhibition of 1876. It was this group that gave a national scope to his reputation.

PARTRIDGE, WILLIAM ORDWAY, (S.) b. Paris, France, April 11, 1861, of American parents. A pupil of Elwell in New York and of Pio Welonski in Paris; is a member of the National Sculptural Society.

Taft says: "His general culture has broadened the range of his interests, and one is not surprised to find him at his best in picturing the great poets .... The expressions of his 'Shelley,' 'Tennyson,' 'Burns,' 'Whittiers,' etc., are those of inherent refinement, not untouched with the deeper glow of creative fire."

Of his "Alexander Hamilton" in Brooklyn, N. Y., Prof. Goodyear says: "As the ideal of an orator, it appeals to me the most successful work in modern art."

Before beginning his statue of Shakespeare (which is in Lincoln Park, Chicago,) Mr. Partridge went to England to gather information upon the subject. "Henry Irving introduced him to Seymore Lucas, who later designed the costume used for this statue, the costume being made by Mr. Irving's costumer. Mr. Lucas claimed that it is the first accurate costume made for any statue of Shakespeare. The time of life at which he is represented is the period of James I, rather than the Elizabethan period, which was fifteen or twenty years before Shakespeare died. The site chosen is near the greenhouse, surrounded by flowers where Shakespeare is represented sitting in his garden, at his ease, with a book in one hand, as if reading, his face turned toward the sunset."

"There is a place left on the statue for two bas-reliefs, one of Henry Irving, and one of Edwin Booth." (Int Studio 58: sup xiviii)

PAULUS, FRANCIS PETRUS, (P., E.) b. Detroit, Michigan, 1862. Studied first at the Pennsylvania Academy of the Fine Arts in Philadelphia, then under Bonnat in the Ecole des Beaux Arts, Paris, and Prof. Loefftz in Munich; finally traveled and studied in Italy, Portugal, Holland, and Belgium. He is a member of the Internationale Société de la Gravure Originale en Noir of Paris, Munich Society of Etchers, and was one of the founders of the Society of Western Artists; has received recognition and honors at the salons in Brussels, Antwerp, Ghent, and Paris, and his works are equally well known in America.

. Mr. Paulus was a teacher of art in Detroit for some years, but a few years ago he, with his charming wife, took up residence in the old city of Bruges, where he has made great use of the material there offered.

"Mr. Paulus finds a special fascination in sunlight, moonlight, and fire-light, and perhaps he is never better than when he introduces the conflicting lights of sunlight and artificial light as in his clever picture called 'The forge' in which he reveals himself as a master."

"In his love of light he resembles Rembrandt. Mr. Paulus is frankly an impressionist, and a believer in the supremacy of a great idea over technique."

A portrait of Mrs. Paulus won great praise when exhibited in the salon of 1904. The most interesting portrait he has ever painted—that of his friend, Alfred Gilbert, the English sculptor—hangs in his studio. One of the finest pictures Mr. Paulus has painted is "The house of the lowly." "The golden curtain" is a homely subject exquisitely treated, showing a group of busy peasant women working at the washtub. The light coming through the yellow curtain illuminates the clouds of steaming vapor and the women intent upon their work.

On "The old market," I. G. McAllister comments: "It is a grand example of what Mr. Paulus delights in painting, a subject vibrating with life and movement."

"Work and gossip" gleams with the brilliant life of southern latitudes. The entire scale of color is given in remarkable gradations of tone.

Mr. Paulus is wide in his range of subjects from portraits to charming interiors, landscapes, subject pictures, and pastels.

He has never chosen the hackneyed sensational subjects likely to appeal to the public. (English Ill M 47:411)

"He has an unusual gift of the power of penetration into the deeper meaning and poetical side of his subjects so that the homeliest theme is invested with a dignity and grace under his hand and realism is never allowed to master refinement of treatment." (Int Studio 46:141)

Mr. Paulus has been painting in Belgium and France for some years and showed in his studio at Detroit last spring some of his own work and also several old masters which have come into his possession since the World War—many of which he uncovered himself under other pictures painted over them.

PAXTON, WILLIAM McGREGOR, (P.) b. Baltimore, Md., June 22, 1869. Pupil of Ecole des Beaux Arts under Gérome in Paris; Denis M. Bunker in New York.

Received honorable mention at Pan-American Exposition, Buffalo, 1901; bronze medal at St. Louis Exposition, 1904. A teacher.

"Woman sewing" by popular vote was the overwhelming choice of the visitors at the annual exhibition at Detroit last year. A little later the Corcoran Gallery, Washington, D. C., announced that Mr. Paxton's "Girl arranging flowers" had won the popular prize of two hundred dollars.

Among other notable works are:

"A string of pearls"   "At the telephone"
"The white sunshade"   "The huntsman"
"The bride"

Frederick W. Coburn, New England Magazine (39:37), says: "Mr. Paxton became an interesting figure in American art a few years ago when it was announced that he takes account in his painting of the facts of binocular vision. It was observed during his large exhibition at the St. Botolph Club, Boston, in the winter of 1905, that he had undertaken to render nature as seen with both eyes, instead of as nearly every other painter has done, as seen with only one eye. A certain doubling of vertical lines, in other words, that are visible just outside of the visual focus has ordinarily been presented, if at all, simply by a device of blurring or lowering the tone of accessories. Mr. Paxton, so far as I know, was the first painter to render naturalistically this overlapping of images in such a manner as largely to increase the optical illusion ...."

"Velasquez, Vermeer, Gainsborough, and Ingres seem to be Paxton's masters so far as he is indebted to the past. As to affiliation with present day artists he stands somewhat aloof, although generally accepted as one of the 'Boston impressionists.'"

PEALE, CHARLES WILSON, (P.) b. Chestertown, Md., April 16, 1741; d. Philadelphia, Pa., February 22, 1827. At thirteen he was apprenticed to a saddler and afterwards established himself in the business. Becoming interested in art he took lessons from a German painter to whom he gave a saddle for the privilege of seeing him paint. Influential friends provided the funds necessary for him to go to England to continue his art studies. He studied under John Singleton Copley at Boston and in 1770 went to London and became a pupil of Benjamin West. Returning to the United States he established himself in Philadelphia in 1776. He commanded a corps of volunteers in the Revolutionary War, became interested in politics, and later lectured on natural history. He was one of the founders of the Pennsylvania Academy of the Fine Arts at Philadelphia in 1805.

His fame rests mainly on his achievements as a portrait painter and the circumstances of his association with Washington, who gave him fourteen sittings. "He was the only portrait painter at that time and his genius was in great demand."

The first of the fourteen portraits of Washington by Peale was in the uniform of a Virginia colonel and is the only one now extant of those painted before the revolution and is highly valued as the first authentic likeness of him.

His portraits gathered in Independence Hall, Philadelphia—one hundred and seventeen—include most of the celebrities, native and foreign, associated with American history and society.

"His likenesses," says his son Rembrandt, "were strong but never flattered; in execution spirited and natural."

PEARCE, CHARLES SPRAGUE, (P., Mural P.) b. Boston, Mass., October 13, 1851; d. Paris, May 18, 1914. Certain success as an amateur painter led him to, regard art as a possible profession and after five years in mercantile business he took up painting as a profession. He went to Paris in 1873 and entered the school of Léon Bonnat, where he remained three years.

Ill-health made it advisable for him to pass the winters in a warmer climate and he visited Egypt, Nubia, Algeria, Italy, and southern France. Afterwards he lived at Auvers-sur-Oise. His first' painting publicly exhibited was shown at the Paris salon of 1876.

He has received prizes and medals from exhibitions and salons in the United States and Europe and been accorded the distinction of an election as a member of the Order of Dannebrog, Denmark; Order of the Red Eagle, Prussia; Order of Leopold, Belgium; and chevalier of the Legion of Honor, France; is a member of the Paris Society of American Artists and of the National Academy of Design, New York.

He has painted portraits and figure subjects but has made his greatest success picturing the rustic landscape and the peasants of northern France.

"His shepherdesses, peasant girls and women chopping wood or minding their herds are the work of a man who acquired forcible technique under Bonnat and studied Bastien-Lepage with understanding." (Müther.)

"The shepherdess" is probably his masterpiece.

Other works are:

"Across the common"	"Abraham's sacrifice"
"Death of the first born"	"Pet of the harem"
"Beheading of Saint John"	":Water carrier"
"Prelude"	"Toiler of the sea"
"Return of the flock"	"Evening"
"Saint Genevieve"	"The shawl"
"Un chemin a Auvers-sur-Oise"	

PEIXOTTO, ERNEST CLIFFORD, (P., I., Min. and Mural P.) b. San Francisco, Cal., 1869. Pupil of Benjamin-Constant, Lefebvre and Doucet in Paris. Received honorable mention in the Paris salon of 1895. Elected associate member of the National Academy 1909. Instructor in the Art Institute, Chicago, 1907-8.

Has illustrated Henry Cabot Lodge's "Story of the Rebellion;" Roosevelt's "Life of Cromwell," Hemstreet's "Nooks and corners of old New York" and numerous articles and stories in current magazines.

Mr. Peixotto was one of the eight official artists sent to France in 1918 by the war department to make sketches of the American soldiers while in action. His war landscapes are of historic as well as artistic value, many of them being sketched while under fire. They have been given permanent place in the National Museum.

In 1921 the Ministry of Fine Arts in France authorized the use of the Palace of Fontainebleau as an American academy of music. Since then a school of fine arts has been established in connection with the school of music, and the French government has placed Mr. Peixotto in charge of the department of painting and sculpture.

PENFOLD, FRANK C., (P.) b. Buffalo, N. Y. Received honorable mention in the Paris salon of 1889 and honorable mention at the Pan-American Exposition, Buffalo, 1901.

A good specimen of his work is "Stormy weather, North Sea."

PENNELL, JOSEPH, (I., E.) b. Philadelphia, Pa., July 4, 1860. He was a pupil in the Pennsylvania Academy of the Fine Arts and his unusual ability in etching was early recognized by his instructor, James L. Claghorn. He has won honorable mention and medals at Philadelphia, Chicago, Paris and elsewhere and has acquired no small measure of fame as a public lecturer and as a critic and author. Associate member National Academy of Design, 1907; full member, 1909.

Mr. Pennell is represented in the Luxembourg Gallery, Paris, Cabinet des Estamps, France, Uffizi Gallery, Florence, Modern Gallery, Venice, Berlin National Gallery, Dresden, Buda-Pesth, South Kensington galleries and in many collections in the United States.

As an illustrator for a time he worked in New Orleans in collaboration with Cable, the novelist; in 1881 he went to Europe to illustrate some of the Italian writings of W. D. Howells. Here he received recognition from Philip Gilbert Hamerton who secured his services in illustrating a book on a tour along the River Saone. "The fame of his work soon brought him all the commissions he wished, and he collaborated with Henry James, Justin McCarthy, and Sir Walter Besant in illustrating the picturesque streets and buildings of London; with Andrew Lang in doing the same service for Edinburgh; with Mrs. Schuyler Van Rensselaer in portraying the majesty and beauty of the English cathedrals; with his wife Elizabeth Robbins Pennell in recording the charms of European travel ...... His drawings are legion in number and must be seen to be appreciated. His etchings (he has destroyed all his early plates to prevent inferior prints from worn-out plates finding their way into the market), run up into the hundreds and have an average excellence rarely maintained by a devotee of the needle; his Philadelphia, New Orleans, Italian, and London series, all have their own charm and their own excellence."

"No American illustrator has won for himself a more enviable fame than Joseph Pennell. His art is unique, peculiarly his own. As a draughtsman the world has produced few equals and no superior. With rare exception everything he has done has in an eminent degree, the quality of the artistic." (Brush & P 12:81)

Mr. Pennell's series of twenty-three lithographs of the Panama Canal are famous, and the Italian government has purchased for the Uffizi Gallery the originals, also his lithographs of the Grand Canyon and the Yosemite. It is the first time lithographs have been acquired for the Uffizi and confers distinction upon this talented American artist.

His lithographs of war work commissioned by the United States government and Great Britain during the war were high-class artistic propaganda—to stir the war spirit and to stimulate national pride. His subjects were the iron and coal mines, blast furnaces, ship building, airplanes and hydroplanes, great machines, shell factories, and training camps. Exhibitions of these lithographs were held in the United States and England and were a liberal education. This master-etcher and lithographer sees beauty in great machines and an artistic appeal in the wonder of work. Referring to his lithograph entitled "Forging shells" he says of this scene: "No composition could be finer, no movement more expressive, no grouping more perfect, and yet all this was happening every day and all day in an oily, dirty, smoky shell factory, and the workmen, black men, were turning the big shell under the big hammer to the big capstan wheel that held it."

"Mr. Pennell invests every one of his drawings with rare mood. His skies of dawn, noon, sunset, storm, and sunshine are chosen and painted with supreme skill, making pictures of high emotional value."

As an etcher Mr. Pennell is without a peer.

Since returning to the United States he has put up a strenuous fight against unsightly bill boards.

PERRAULT, I. MARIE, (P.) b. Detroit, Mich. Studied at the Detroit Museum of Art School and for the past seven years in Paris, The Hague and Brussels.

Mrs. Perrault's work is very well thought of in Holland and she is well represented in the collections of that country. She is pre-eminently a painter of children, her later work being influenced by Carriére. Member of several art clubs abroad.

Her best works are:

"Maternite"   "The dream"
"Springtime"   "The yellow flower"

At a special exhibition of her paintings and sketches held in Detroit, Michigan, October, 1911, Mrs. Perrault was represented by thirty-five interesting and characteristic canvases.

After living in Paris twenty-one years Madame Perrault is again a resident of her native city.

When the war came on she was known in Paris as a painter of children's portraits. The privations of war forced her to abandon her profession and she took up the novel and fascinating work of making manikins. She molds the little bodies out of clay and they represent characters from old myths, from history, and little children of modern days. Madame Perrault has become quite famous as the maker of these quaint and delightful dolls.

PICCIRILLI, ATTILIO, (S.) b. Massa, Italy, May 16, 1866. Pupil of the Accademia San Luca, Rome. Came to the United States in 1888. Associate member of the National Academy of Design in 1909.

No more interesting family has ever come from foreign lands to make the United States its home than that of Giuseppe Piccirilli, an Italian marble worker, and his six gifted sons from the famous Carrara marble center of Tuscany. From a few rooms on the East Side, their first location, to their present comfortable, commodious workshops and studios in the Bronx, their industry and artistic talents have placed them. Here the gifts of the six brothers are harmoniously combined. Giutolio, the youngest, is the business manager and handles the large contracts which come to the firm; Orazio is the accomplished master of animal form as well as of sculptured ornaments; Maso and Ferruccio are general assistants; while Attilio and Furio are now classed with our best sculptors.

It was in the Piccirilli studios that the great statue of Lincoln by Daniel Chester French, now in the Lincoln Memorial at Washington, D. C., was developed and completed through the services of the famous marble cutters.

In collaboration with Mr. Magonigle as architect, Attilio has created two of New York's most imposing monuments: the Maine monument at the southwest entrance to Central Park and the Firemen's Memorial on Riverside Drive. "In both these works the sculptured groups are conceived in genuine emotion and carried out with the skill of a virtuoso ...... An unusual and a picturesque feature of the Firemen's Memorial is the spirited relief that pays a tribute to the horses as well as to the men."

"The spirit of the Alps," a beautiful symbolic figure, is now regarded as one of the great statues. "Outcast" was shown at the Panama-Pacific Exposition in 1915.

PICCIRILLI, FURIO, (S.) b. Massa, Italy, March 14, 1868. Pupil of the Accademia San Luca, Rome. Came to the United States in 1888. Elected associate member of the National Academy of Design in 1907.

In the Court of the Four Seasons at the Panama-Pacific Exposition, San Francisco, 1915, Furio was represented by four groups—"Spring," "Summer," "Autumn," and "Winter." The most effective group was "Winter." "The severe rigidity of the lovely central standing figure expresses well that feeling of suspended activity which we associate with the conventional conceptions of the season of dormant life; the kneeling figures are in full harmony of expression with the central figure." In "Spring" we see the "very fine psychological quality of the standing figure in giving expression in a very graceful fashion to that invigorating and reviving quality of our loveliest season." "Autumn" in its decorative scheme suggests peace and plenty. The naturalistic modeling in "Summer" is not expressed so well.

Furio has created many lovely ornamental designs as well as heroic statues and groups. His colossal statue of Pierre Gautier de la Varenne is, with several others, to adorn the new parliament building at Winnipeg, Canada.

PICKNELL, WILLIAM LAMB, (P.) b. Hinesburg, Vt., October 23, 1854; d. Marblehead, Mass., August 9, 1897. Went to Europe in 1874, studying with George Inness in Rome, later for a few months under Gérome in Paris. From France he went to England and for a number of years was an exhibitor at the Royal Academy, London; also lived and painted in Brittany, working under Robert Wylie until the death of that artist.

Received honorable mention in the Paris salon of 1880; awarded medals in Boston, Mass., 1881 and 1884; won Lippincott prize, Pennsylvania Academy of the Fine Arts, 1896.

Member of the Society of American Artists, New York, and the Society of British Artists, London; associate member of the National Academy of Design, New York, 1891.

Mr. Picknell is represented in the Luxembourg, Paris; Institute of Arts and Sciences, Brooklyn; Metropolitan Museum of Art, New York; Boston Museum of Art; and Carnegie Art Gallery, Pittsburgh.

The first picture to bring him recognition and standing as a painter was his "Route de Concarneau" painted at Pont Aven, Brittany. His "Breton peasant girl feeding ducks" was exhibited at the Royal Academy, London, 1877, and "The fields of Kerren" received honorable mention in the salon of 1878. "Wintry March" was purchased for the Walker Art Gallery of Liverpool and hung in the apartment occupied by Queen Victoria on her visit to that city. "On the borders of the marsh" was one of the first pictures purchased by the Pennsylvania Academy of the Fine Arts and "A toiler of the sea" was the first picture bought for the Carnegie Art Gallery, Pittsburgh. His marine "Plowing deep while others sleep" won the £100 prize of the Society of British Artists.

The French and English critics gave unstinted praise to the strength and distinction of his pictures.

"Art to him was holy; there must be no hypocrisy, no shirking, no secrets. All his knowledge he was eager to impart without price......"

An Italian gentleman and painter paid this tribute to him: "It is the sad privilege and prerogative of such natures to leave darkness where their spirit threw light, for he was one of those enthusiasts in the etymological sense of the word, possessed, carrying with them a power— a god if you like—and such guests are felt even in ordinary surround- ings." (Cent o. s. 62:710)

Notable examples of his art are:

"A stormy day"	"Among the olives"
"Coast of Ipswich"	"A gray morning, Moret"
"Sunshine and drifting sand"	"Late afternoon, Moret"
"A sultry day"	"Morning on the Loing"
"After the storm"	"Morning on the Mediterranean"
"The edge of winter"	"Twilight on the Mediterranean"
"Where broad ocean leans against the land"	"Mid-winter on the Litorel"

"Picknell does not compose pretty scenes, but he drives home the facts of his subjects with sledgehammer blows. He is a sort of second Courbet in his strength and in his virility." (New Eng M 14:148)

"Picknell made extensive use of the palette knife, gaining thus some- thing of the purity of tone, the vibration and the marvelous amount of atmosphere that distinguished many of his canvases."

PITTS, LENDALL, (E.) b. Detroit, Michigan, November, 1875. Pupil of Jean Paul Laurens in Paris.

E. A. Taylor in writing of American etchers (Studio special number), says: "In color, American etchers with but few exceptions have not shown any notable examples, the most distinctly personal and interest- ing results yet attained being those by Lendall Pitts, who exhibited some remarkable results of his experimental achievements in the St. Louis Museum of Fine Arts in 1908. In his studio in Paris he works heedless of recognized methods and public appreciation, producing many little masterpieces with delightful simplicity. "Sunset on the lake," "Castle of Sigüenza, Spain," and "The cascade" are unique illustrations of his color-etching and aquatint."

"He has chosen the most difficult subject in landscape art—the mountain—and he has rendered it with fidelity which has lost none of the majesty and grandeur of this vast phase of nature ...... With his technical preparation and his high color sense one feels that he is fully able to cope with his problems.

"He treats them en masse rather than in detail, and there is usually some note in his pictures by which the magnitude of the mountains and the spaciousness of his pictures may be measured." (Bulletin Detroit Institute of Arts)

A special correspondent writing of the American art colony in Paris says: "Lendall Pitts may be taken as the ablest aquafortist in color to be found in Paris. His decorative sense, his good taste have saved him from falling into vulgarity—a fault often found in colored etchings."

PLATT, ALETHEA HILL, (P.) b. Scarsdale, N. Y. A pupil of Henry B. Snell, Ben Foster, and Art Students' League, New York. She received first prize for water color, New York Woman's Art Club, 1903; and is a member New York Woman's Art Club, Pen & Brush Club, National Arts Club, and New York Water Color Club.

In writing of the exhibition of the New York Water Color Club, Palette and Bench, February, 1910, has this: "The 'scrub method' originated by Mr. Henry B. Snell was well represented by one of his ablest pupils, Miss Alethea H. Platt in her fine interior, 'An old world kitchen' ...... There are some delicious bits of color in this old kitchen scene."

The art critic of one of the New York papers writes: "One of the most interesting displays is made up of thirty paintings by Miss Alethea Hill Platt in the Powell gallery. The artist presents scenes from the fair land of Devon and from the coast of Brittany. Charming interiors showing the homely life of the peasantry on both sides of the channel, of which Miss Platt has made a specialty in her European sojourns, are already well known.

"There is something entirely new, however, in several landscapes which she shows. They are brilliant in tone but true to the colors found in sky and plain and vale. Those familiar with her earlier work will be deeply interested in the new departure as revealed in 'The sunlit moor' and 'Tors on Dartmoor' which are bathed in the soft airs of England. A water color, 'A Moorland shepherd,' represents a herdsman returning at eventide to his cottage and there is wonderful charm and feeling in this peaceful bit of rural England, which includes his cottage and its surroundings."

PLOWMAN, GEORGE TAYLOR, (I., E.) b. Le Sueur, Minn., October 19, 1869, and studied architecture in Paris and elsewhere; studied in the Royal College of Engraving at South Kensington, London, under Sir Frank Short; also traveled and etched on the continent. Although young in etching he is represented in the permanent collection of Royal College and Crystal Palace, London; Art Museum, Boston; Public Library, New York; and Congressional Library, Washington, D. C.

The Berlin Photographic Company has reproduced many of Mr. Plowman's etchings.

Mr. Plowman has written a book on etching which explains the methods of Sir Frank Short. (Int Studio 51: sup cxxxiv)

POLASEK, ALBIN, (S.) b. Frenstat, Czechoslovakia.

For more than twenty years the United States has been his home of adoption. His early art training was under Charles Grafly in the Pennsylvania Academy of the Fine Arts. While studying there he won a scholarship which entitled him to three years study in Rome at the American Academy. After his sojourn in Italy he settled in New York City and later took up his residence in Chicago. He is now head of the sculpture department in the Art Institute.

Mr. Polasek's sculptural work is chiefly portrait busts and single figures.

"Fantasy" is in the Metropolitan Museum, New York; "F. D. Millet" (bust) in the Pennsylvania Academy of the Fine Arts, Philadelphia; and "Sower" in the Art Institute, Chicago.

POPE, ALEXANDER, (P., S.) b. Boston, Mass., March 25, 1849. At the age of seven he did creditable work in sketching animals, and was self-taught with the exception of instruction in perspective drawing and anatomy from Dr. Rimmer. At twenty he was a devotee of wood-carving and modeling. He originated painted game birds carved out of pine wood, two of them being purchased by the Czar of Russia. Later he was ambitious to become a sculptor. His first notable canvas was "Calling out the hounds," and his two most noted pictures are his "Martyrdom of St. Euphemia" and his "Glaucus and the lion" (taken from Bulwer's "Last days of Pompeii").

One of his most realistic productions is the painting of a white swan hanging to a door. "Just from town" shows two peacocks and is one of his simplest and most pleasing paintings. (Brush & P 8:105)

Mr. Pope's portraits of dogs have won for him the title "American Landseer," and his lions and horses have brought him an even wider reputation.

Supplementing the fundamental grounding he received from Dr. Rimmer by individual study and constant practice, he haunted stables, aviaries, and kennels and spent much time in the zoological gardens of New York and Philadelphia; also at Bridgeport, Conn., when Barnum's winter headquarters were there, where he especially studied and sketched lions.

Mr. Pope has published a series of game bird plates entitled "Upland game birds and water fowls of the United States," also "Celebrated dogs of America."

POTTER, EDWARD CLARK, (S.) b. New London, Conn., November 26, 1857; d. New London, Conn., June 21, 1923. He was educated at Amherst College; studied sculpture under Mercié and Fremiet, Paris, 1888-9; has been a member of the National Academy of Design, New York, since 1906.

Mr. Potter's first prominence was due to his collaboration with Mr. Daniel Chester French at Chicago in 1893 where their Columbus Quadriga and other groups were among the most admired of the many decorations.

Lorado Taft says it is probable that no American sculptor knows the horse quite so well structurally, as does Mr. Potter.

Mr. Potter has not restricted himself, however, to animal sculpture nor to partnership enterprises. His delightful little "Sleeping faun" is in the Art Institute of Chicago; his Governor Blair of Michigan stands in an admirable repose before the state capitol at Lansing. His equestrian statue of General Slocum on the battlefield of Gettysburg is considered a striking portrait. "There is no more impressive sculpture upon the famous battlefield." (Taft's "History of American sculpture")

Mr. Potter has also executed two noteworthy bas-reliefs of Dante and Savonarola.

Mr. Potter designed the bronze statue of Colonel R. C. Bolling, U.S.A., who was the first American high officer to lose his life in the World War. The statue is erected on the school grounds in Greenwich, Conn.

POTTER, LOUIS, (S., E.) b. Troy, N. Y., November 14, 1873; d. Seattle, Wash., August 29, 1912. He graduated at Trinity College, Hartford, in 1896; and received first instructions in art from Charles Noel Flagg. In 1896 he went to Paris and remained there for three years, studying painting under Luc-Olivier Merson and modeling under Jean Dampt. His first exhibition was a bust of Boutet de Monvel.

Mr. Potter spent some time in Tunis and while there was commissioned to represent Arab life at the Exposition. For this service the Bey conferred upon him a decoration of Officer du Nicham Iftikar or "Order of Renown." After his return to the United States he devoted himself to distinctively American subjects. The Indians, particularly, both Alaskan and American, became one of his favorite subjects.

Mr. Potter took up the investigation of the occult science for the purpose of arriving at some higher spiritual insight. This he abandoned, declaring the practice of no value, possibly harmful.

"The earth man" and "The earth's unfoldment" were accepted unanimously by the French salon of 1912. "The man" is groping for light; this is realized in the "Earth unfoldment"—the spiritual awakening of the woman.

POTTHAST, EDWARD HENRY, (P., I., Mural P.) b. Cincinnati, O., June 11, 1857. Pupil Cincinnati School of Fine Arts. Studied in Antwerp, Munich, and Paris. Won Clarke prize National Academy of Design, 1899; also several gold and silver medals. Member Society American Artists; associate member National Academy of Design, 1899; full member, 1906.

POWELL, WILLIAM HENRY, (P.) b. New York, February 14, 1823; d. New York, October 6, 1879.

He began the study of art under Henry Inman in New York City in 1843 and continued his studies in Paris and Florence. He first exhibited at the National Academy of Design, New York, in 1838; was elected an associate member of the academy in 1854.

Probably no historical work of art is more familiar to the American people than his painting, "The battle of Lake Erie." It was originally executed for the state of Ohio at a cost of $10,000. In 1873 Mr. Powell reproduced the work on a larger canvas for the national government and this painting now hangs in the senate wing of the capitol at Washington, D. C.

Other historical paintings are:

"De Soto discovering the   "Landing of the Pilgrims"
   Mississippi"   "Washington at Valley Forge"
"Siege of Vera Cruz"

He also produced famous portraits of Albert Gallatin, Peter Cooper, and Washington Irving. His portrait of General McClellan and that of Major Anderson are in the city hall, New York.

Pratt, Bela L., (S.) b. Norwich, Conn., December 11, 1867; d. Boston, Mass., May 18, 1917. At the age of sixteen he entered the Yale School of Fine Arts where he studied under Professors Neimeyer and Weir. In 1887 he entered the Art Students' League of New York, continuing his studies under Saint-Gaudens, Elwell, Chase, and Kenyon Cox. He went to Paris in 1890 where he studied under Chapu and Falguiére. While in the Ecole des Beaux Arts he received three medals and two prizes. In 1892 he returned to the United States; was commissioned for two colossal groups 'on the water gate of the Peristyle at the Columbian Exposition, 1893; and in 1895 and 1896 he shared in the decorations of the Library of Congress, Washington, D. C. Mr. Pratt's contributions to the Pan-American Exposition were numerous and certain of them of great beauty. In 1900 he was made an associate member of the National Academy of Design.

Mr. Pratt has produced many works in sculpture, including statues, memorials, groups, tablets, medallions, and portrait busts of many eminent personages identified with the history of New England.

His best known memorial and monumental groups are:

"General Stevenson" and "Army nurses" memorials in State House; colossal bronze statues, "Art" and "Science," at the entrance of the public library; and "Edward Everett Hale," Public Gardens, Boston, Mass.

"Soldiers and sailors monument," Malden, Mass.

"Barefoot boy" mounted on a native boulder, Ashburnham, Mass.

"Peace and war" for the Butler memorial, Lowell, Mass.

"Andersonville prisoner boy," erected at Andersonville, Ga.

"Spanish War soldier boy," St. Paul's school, Concord, N. H.

Six spandrel figures, a figure of "Philosophy," and a series of four medallions—"The seasons"—in library of Congress, Washington, D. C.

"Dancer" (marble relief) in Brooklyn Museum, Brooklyn, N. Y.

"Nathan Hale," Yale University, New Haven, Conn.

"The whaleman" is also for the monument to native seafarers erected at New Bedford, Mass., in 1913. The Architectural Record (35:508) says of this work: "Spirit and action characterize the stalwart figure of a New Bedford whaleman who is portrayed with long harpoon poised in the air, and standing in a whale boat dashing through the surf, in pursuit of some great leviathan of the deep ...... The sculptor is revealed at his best in the full-length figure of 'Youth' fraught with charm and the naiveté of tender years ...... He is gifted with unusual feeling for his subjects, has imagination, and is a subtle draughtsman. His art accords him a foremost place with illustrious American sculptors of today."

Three large decorative panels for the facade of the Opera House, Boston, are interesting examples of Mr. Pratt's art. They are molded in blue and white terra cotta, after the Della Robbias, and form a frieze just beneath the cornice. The subjects are "Music," "Drama," and "The dance." "Music" is one of the most effective panels in the series and is poetic in conception and subtle in modeling.

His series of nudes along with the portrait busts and the low relief works will constitute his most valid title to fame. His small nudes are very beautiful and interesting. "Blind Cupid," one of his most beautiful creations, and his exquisite "Water nymph" are in the Metropolitan Museum, New York City.

"His portraits in bas relief and his medals show a singularly fine sentiment for graceful movement of line and the subtle play of light and shade."

At a memorial exhibition of his works, held by the Guild of Boston Artists, some thirty-four were shown in marble, bronze, and plaster. In the collection were two of Mr. Pratt's latest works in marble, "The archer" and "Blind Cupid;" and the most notable among the portrait sculpture was the marble head of the artist's mother.

"The supreme test of a sculptor's ability, that of the treatment of the human form in all its undraped beauty [his nudes], is here met with signal success ...... Few things of its kind in modern sculpture are more perfect than the 'Eros and Psyche.' "

Since 1893 Mr. Pratt had been instructor in modeling in the school of the Museum of Fine Arts, Boston, and at the time of his death he was regarded as the head of his profession in that city.

PRELLWITZ, EDITH MITCHELL (Mrs. Henry Prellwitz), (P.) b. South Orange, N. J., 1865. Pupil of Art Students' League of New York under George de Forest Brush and Kenyon Cox; Académie Julien in Paris under Bouguereau, Robert-Fleury, and Courtois.

Received second Hallgarten prize in 1894 for her "Hagar and Ishmael;" Dodge prize in 1895; bronze medal at Pan-American Exposition, Buffalo, 1901. Elected associate member of the National Academy of Design, New York, in 1906.

PRELLWITZ, HENRY, (P.) b. New York, 1865. Pupil of T. W. Dewing and Art Students' League of New York; Académié Julien in Paris.

Received third Hallgarten prize, National Academy of Design, 1893; bronze medal, Pan-American Exposition, Buffalo, 1901; medal, St. Louis Exposition, 1904; Clark prize, National Academy of Design, 1907.

Member of the Society of American Artists, 1906. Instructor in life drawing and painting at Pratt Institute, Brooklyn, N. Y.

Elected associate member of the National Academy of Design, New York, 1906.

PRESTON, MARY WILSON (Mrs. James Preston), (I.) b. New York, August 11, 1873. Educated at Oberlin College. Studied art in New York art schools, 1896-7; Whistler School, Paris, 1899-1900. Began illustrating for magazines in 1902. Has illustrated:

"Seeing France with Uncle John"   "The incubator baby"
"The smugglers"   "The diary of Delia"

PROCTOR, ALEXANDER PHIMISTER, (S., P.) b. Bozanquit, Ont., Canada, September 27, 1862. Pupil of National Academy of Design and Art Students' League in New York; Puech and Injalbert in Paris.

Received gold medal for sculpture and bronze medal for painting at St. Louis Exposition, 1904. Elected member of the National Academy of Design, 1904.

For years Mr. Proctor was a huntsman, living in the Rocky Mountains where he made a study of wild animals. Realizing that he needed better training, in 1887 he went to New York and entered the classes of the National Academy. Being awarded the Rinehart scholarship he went to Paris for five years' study in technique.

At the Paris Exposition, 1900, Mr. Proctor's well known panthers kept guard at the entrance on the Place de la Concorde. His "Bison" shows evidence of the sculptor's close observation and acute sense of the animal character, as do his "Fawn," "Bear," and "Striding panther."

Of his famous bison, Mr. William Walton says: "To the formidable bulk and weight and strength which are this animal's obvious monumental qualities the sculptor adds an action, an alertness, head and tail up, also founded on truth, which gives him that air of power and menace necessary to symbolic animals." (Scrib M 55:666)

Mr. Proctor is represented in public parks in New York, Denver, Pittsburgh, Buffalo and other cities of the United States. These various groups have brought him recognition and success.

An old wolf-trapper posed for the sketch which resulted in the heroic figure, "The pioneer," on the campus of the University of Oregon.

During the two years spent in the west from 1914, he made a number of figures and animals—Indians with broncos and buffaloes, decorative bas-reliefs of lions and elks—but the cowboy did not interest him as a subject as he did Remington or Solon Borglum.

When Roosevelt was president he decided that the lion heads in the state dining room were out of place in the American white house and that bison heads were more appropriate. Mr. Proctor was called in and modeled a pair of buffalo heads to take their places.

His bronze statue of an Indian astride a rock, reaching toward a stream of water, has been placed in the State Park overlooking Lake George. The statue is in memory of the tribes of Indians who once had their home in the Adirondacks. It was the gift of George D. Pratt and was dedicated by the New York Historical Society. Chief Beaver, a Blackfoot Indian whom Proctor brought to New York with him, was the model.

PYLE, HOWARD, (P., I., Mural P.) b. Wilmington, Delaware, March 5, 1853; d. Florence, Italy, November 9, 1911. Was educated in private schools and in the Art Students' League of New York; an instructor at the Drexel Institute, Philadelphia; a member of the National Institute of Arts and Letters; associate member of the National Academy of Design, 1905, full member, 1907.

At first being unsuccessful in art he went into business, but some of his drawings finally being accepted by a magazine he again took up the profession of his choice.·

His first assignment in illustration—a picture called "Wreck in the offing"—brought him steady employment in the field of art. His most important work was done in periodical illustration.

Mr. Pyle ranked as our foremost American illustrator. Both in his stories (he was an author as well as an artist) he exhibited a well-defined style, characterized by vigorous and sustained imagination and a certain charming quaintness eminently adapted to tales of fairyland or olden days.

His principal publications are:

"The merry adventures of Robin Hood"
"Pepper and salt"
"Within the capes"
"The wonder clock"
"The rose of Paradise"
"Otto of the silver hand"
"A modern Aladdin"
"Men of iron"
"Jack Ballister's fortunes"
"The stolen treasure"

"Twilight land"
"The garden behind the moon"
"Semper idem"
"Rejected of men"
"The story of Arthur and his knights"
"The story of the champions of the Round Table"
"The story of Launcelot and his companions"

"His plates, rich and often gorgeous in color as they were, pictorial in intent and spirited in movement, showed the hand that was acquainted with the shortcomings as well as the successes of the reproductive process."

"Throughout his career he held pronounced views as to the disadvantage of foreign training and association." (Nation 93:479)

"Nowhere have I seen text better idealized or illustrations better described than in that series of articles by Pyle on the 'Buccaneers.'" (F. Hopkinson Smith)

"Surely never before were pirates so satisfactorily bloody-minded offered for the delectation of youth." (Isham)

Isham says: "Howard Pyle is the only man who seems to know thoroughly the colonial and revolutionary epoch."

"He liked to draw for the accompaniment of text, and did much to dignify the practice. His later work generally shows him the complete artist-writer, decorator, illustrator, and spiritual thinker as in the imaginative "Travels of the soul" and in the "Fate of a treasure town" so different in character."

Several creditable paintings bear his signature: "One hoss shay," "Old violin," "Trotting match;" these are well known.

Arthur Hoeber in the International Studio for January, 1912, says: "There was something convincing about Pyle's work; his knights and ladies, his revolutionary soldiers and his men and women of colonial times were to the manor born and not posed models dressed up for the occasion ...... The death of Mr. Pyle leaves a distinct void and his place will in all probability never be filled, for his work was entirely personal, full of the liveliest interest with great literary as well as artistic charm."

"In Howard Pyle America had one of the great illustrators of modern times. His genius was remarkably varied in expression and everything he did was marked by distinction ...... With a fine technical equipment he united the literary faculty to give dramatic significance and historical accuracy to his figures and scenes. His influence for good upon American illustration has been incalculable, and he developed a number of pupils whose careers have done him honor." (Scrib 72:126)

QUINN, EDMOND T., (S., P.) b. Philadelphia, Pa., December 20, 1868. A pupil of the Pennsylvania Academy of the Fine Arts, also studied under Injalbert in Paris. A member of the National Sculpture Society and Architectural League of America.

The following comments are taken from the International Studio (55:sup x): "Mr. Edmond T. Quinn's work is besides all its other qualities, eminently unaffected. It is this attribute of his work—this lack of straining and the power of being subjective rather than objective in the carrying out of it—that earned for him the honor of being given in competition with seven other sculptors the Booth Memorial statue to be placed in Gramercy Park by the Players Club."

"Quinn's well-known bust of Edgar Allan Poe is a complete, vital rendition of the fantastic poet."

"Great picturesqueness has been attained in the bust of Allan Pollock, the actor."

"In the bust of Mr. Francis Wilson, all the alert, intelligent, inherent humor of that well-known actor has been used admirably as a motive for a striking character study."

Best known works are:

John Howard, portrait statue, Williamsport, Pa.
Battle monument reliefs, King's Mountain, S. C.
Zoroaster statue, Brooklyn Institute of Arts and Sciences
Swanström Memorial, Borough Hall, Brooklyn

Busts: Edwin Markham, Francis Wilson, Albert Sterner, Miss Donez Halstead, C. H. Chavant.

Mr. Quinn did the decoration of the Pittsburgh Athletic Club and also paints portraits.

RANGER, HENRY WARD, (P.) b. near Rochester, N. Y., January, 1858; d. New York City, November 7, 1916. Practically self-taught. Went to New York and took a studio in the early seventies where he became acquainted with the works of the Barbizon men by which he has ever since been influenced. He studied many years in England, France, and Holland where he enjoyed an intimacy with Israels, Mauve, and other leaders of the Dutch school. He was elected associate member of the National Academy of Design in 1901; a full member in 1906.

Although the artistic public knows little of Henry W. Ranger, yet he was unquestionably one of the few great artists America has produced. This is largely because he rarely exhibited in public displays. He was opposed to competition for honor of any sort, objecting on principle to distinctions other than came from the ability of his canvases to attract serious attention.

In viewing Mr. Ranger's pictures one feels the presence of a single dominating idea. This dominating central idea is the mastery of tone. This tonal quality is defined as "a close and sympathetic adjustment of

the hues and values of a picture to its dominating key—which is the
index of its emotional meaning." (Brush & P 16:39)

This tonal quality in Mr. Ranger's work is joined with a strong sense
of structure and rhythmical composition.

Among his best known works are:

"Autumn woods"   "Hawk's nest pool"
"Golden evening—Noank"   "On Mason's island"
"Bow bridge"   "Sentinel rock"
"Bradbury's mill-pond No. 2"   "Noank shipyard"
"Spring woods"   "Noank street"
"September gale—Noank"   "Flying point"
"Peaceful moonlight reveries"   "The edge of the woods"
"The last of spring"   "Willows"
"Spring pastures"   "Entrance to the harbor"
"A gray day"   "Top of the hill"
"Saunders' hollow"   "High bridge"
"Connecticut woods"   "Sea and sky"

"These are ample to show that underlying all this wide range is one
perfectly definite personality that is itself throughout able to command
moods that range from the tender and persuasive to the vigorous and
powerful." (Int Studio 29:33)

"His art is based on a profound and sympathetic appreciation of
nature. An artistic selection from her various and at times conflicting
moods, it is with all its science, emotional." (Brush & P 16:41)

"He was a painter of the forest—not the impressionistic forest, or
the gentle, delicate forest, or the merely decorative forests of other
artists, but the bold, emphatic, forceful, rugged Connecticut woods,
generally those near Noank, his summer home, and with usually one
dominant rich color."

His canvases are to be seen in the galleries in New York City, Washington, Philadelphia, Pittsburgh, Toledo, Buffalo and Syracuse, his native city.

READ, THOMAS BUCHANAN, (P.) b. in Chester county, Pa., March 12,
1822; d. New York, May 11, 1872.

Mr. Read is better known as a poet than a painter. At the age of
seventeen he removed to Cincinnati and studied sculpture, then took up
painting. In 1841 he established himself as a portrait painter in New
York. In 1850 he went to Europe and resided several years in Rome and
Florence. Of his ideal pictures the "Lost Pleiad" and the "Water
Sprite" are the most characteristic.

"The tone of mind of this artist is essentially poetical." (Tuckerman's "Book of the artists" p. 460)

"With the exception of a few historical and fancy pieces he has confined himself to portrait painting." (Nat M 6:292)

REDFIELD, EDWARD WILLIS, (P.) b. Bridgeville, Delaware, December 19, 1868. At an early age he developed a love for art and was sent to a local academy where he was instructed in free-hand drawing; later studied in the Pennsylvania Academy of the Fine Arts and under Bouguereau and Robert-Fleury, Paris. He is a member of the Society of American Artists; was elected associate member of the National Academy of Design, New York, in 1904; full member in 1906.

Mr. Redfield has received many competitive medals.

Winter is his constant theme. He is a pioneer in this country in the realistic painting of winter, in which field he has few equals today. The French government has purchased his "February" for the Luxembourg Gallery. "The valley of Springtime" won the Carnegie prize.

A few characteristic landscapes are:

"Grey days"	"The crest"
"Landscape in April"	"The red barn"
"Brook in winter"	"December"
"Hill and valley"	"The briar patch"
"The road to center bridge"	"Cedar hills"
"Foothills of the Blue Ridge"	"The canal"
"The hemlocks"	"The old bridge"
"Surf"	"The fallen tree"
"Winter"	"On the banks of a river"
"The three boats"	"Center bridge"

"He is the standard bearer of that progressive, one might almost say aggressive, group of painters who are glorifying American landscape painting with a veracity and force that is astonishing the eyes of the Old World, long accustomed to a servile aping of its standards ...... While the greater part of his work celebrates the glories of winter, his whole output reveals a comprehensive diversity of subjects." (J. N. Laurvik)

"A village of France" is one of Mr. Redfield's most delightful canvases and is not a winter scene. The time of the year is spring and the time of day high noon.

"Energy and devotion to American art—a wise devotion—these are characteristic of the man. No strife of schools for him. He stands unyielding before the political storms of art and bends his back to help each movement, unmoved by selfish aims." (Int Studio 75:410)

"Redfield aims at illusion, and no painter has succeeded better in producing it. His color is brilliant, active, and glowing. He works in the key of nature and does not seek to force the effect beyond its natural appearance. He is assuredly one of the foremost realists of his time." (Scrib 72:766)

"In his manner and method of painting, his work is a reflection of the methods of impressionists, which he has adapted to his own use." (Int Studio 41 sup xxix)

His "Canal in winter" hangs in the Luxembourg Gallery, Paris.

REDFIELD, HELOÏSE GUILLOU, (Min. P.) b. Philadelphia, Pa., 1883. Pupil of Martha S. Baker, William M. Chase, and Cecilia Beaux; Madame LaForge and Delecluse in Paris.

Mrs. Redfield's miniatures "are remarkable for their 'paint quality' and a carrying force equal to that of life-size painting."

"She has developed a form of expression which is really painting although the medium is water color and the scale miniature.

"Her work shows that she has a strong mental conception at the outset, virile enough to bend the means of expression to serve the artist's will." (Int Studio 48: sup xix)

REED, EARL H., (E., S.) b. Geneva, Ill., July 5, 1863. Studied art at the Art Institute, Chicago, and later specialized in etching.

At the annual exhibition of American etchers held in New York, 1913, Mr. Reed's group of ten plates was very popular; four of these—"Voices of the dunes," "Among the sandhills," "Marsh haystacks," and "Edge of the forest"—had previously been seen in the Paris salon.

"The poetry of the sea, the shore, a flight of birds, an oncoming storm, the driven sand, the play of the winds, a tangled root, the light waning through the trees are subjects which arrest his attention." (Int Studio 51: sup lxxxi)

It was mainly owing to the initiative of Mr. Reed that the Chicago Society of Etchers came into existence in 1910, and he was its president until recently.

Mr. Reed has recently taken up sculpture.

REID, ROBERT, (P., Mural P.) b. Stockbridge, Mass., July 29, 1862. Studied at the Museum of Fine Arts, Boston, 1880, and for three years was assistant instructor. From 1885 to 1889 he studied in the Art Students' League, New York; later went to Paris and studied in the Académie Julien under Boulanger and Lefebvre. Exhibited in the salon of 1889; had a studio for the summer in Etaples-pas-de-Calais; returned to New York in 1889. He is a member of the Ten American Painters and one of the eight American artists who painted frescoes on the dome of the Liberal Arts Building at the Columbian Exposition, 1893. Mr. Reid has been instructor of painting in the Art Students' League and in Cooper Institute and was elected member of the National Academy of Design, New York, in 1906. He has received many medals and prizes.

In the decoration of the Library of Congress five octagons on the ceiling of the second floor and four circular panels on the wall are his work.

His decorations for the International Navigation Company mark a new line of work in marine architecture and decoration.

"Autumn" is considered by some critics the best picture he has ever painted.

A few characteristic paintings are:

"Gládiola"
"Canna"
"Tiger lily"
"Pink carnation"
"Vine"
"Fleur de lys"
"Azalea"
"Yellow flower"
"Goldfish"

"White parasol"
"Water sprite"
"Tennis girl"
"Butterfly"
"Village Juno"
"The mirror"
"Little country girl"
"Meditation"

His work is devoid of any spiritual, philosophical, or philanthropic pretensions. It exists for itself alone, and persistently sings of youth, sunlight, flowers and supple rhythmic forms and contours. (Brinton, Arts and Decoration 2:13)

Many titles of his pictures are chosen from the particular flower which is given prominence in the composition.

Royal Cortissoz writes of Mr. Reid's work: "His paintings have a durable charm. The liveliness of his flower-laden girls does not fade; his windows and his mural decorations are as persistently persuasive. The reason, I think, is that he has a true perception of beauty and never wearies in his pursuit of technical excellence."

"He has secured from impressionism, what could be of service to himself—the delicate discrimination of color and the subtleties of various kinds of light and assimilated these facts into his own vigorous personality." (Artist 24: sup lxiv)

Mr. Reid is one of the leading impressionists.

REINHART, CHARLES STANLEY, (I.) b. Pittsburgh, Pa., May 16, 1844; d. New York, August 30, 1897. Served in the Civil War; later engaged in

mercantile business four years.   In 1868 went to Europe to begin a sys-
tematic study of art.   He spent one year in Atelier Suisse, Paris, and
then became the pupil of Professors Echter and Otto, Munich; returned
to the United States in 1870 and began illustrating for various publishers; regularly employed by Harper & Bro. from 1871-7.   He was an
associate member of the National Academy of Design, New York.

Mr. Reinhart was best known for his excellent work in black and white,
in which he is without peer.   He is equally effective in color work, and
was a regular contributor to the Paris salon during the ten years he
resided at the French capital.

He was one of the first to introduce "painter qualities" into illustrative work.

REMINGTON, FREDERIC, (P., I., S.) b. Canton, N. Y., October 4, 1861; d.
Ridgeville, Conn., December 26, 1909.   He was educated at Yale Art
School (and it is said that his eminence at college was on the football
field rather than in the art classes) ; also studied at the Art Students'
League of New York.   He was clerk in a business office, then cowboy and
stockman on a ranch in the west; subsequently illustrator for magazines
treating military and American subjects and during 1897-8, Cuban
scenes.   Associate member of National Academy of Design, 1891.   Mr.
Remington was the most eminent and successful of a half dozen painters
who have made the field of Indian warfare and cowboy adventure their
own.   Essentially an illustrator, he never became a "painter's painter"
but he was the people's favorite through the subjects he chose.   "The
Indian appealed to him not in any histrionic way .... but just as a
human creature."

Cortissoz says: "His night scenes are both veracious and beautiful
...... and they exert a very original charm.   He knows how the light
of the moon or of the stars is diffused, how softly and magically it
envelops the landscape.   His picture 'The gossips' is one of the hand-
somest and most convincing Indian studies ever painted."

Familiar paintings are:

"The luckless hunter"
"The moose country"
"The buffalo runners"
"The fall of the cowboy"
"Coming to call"
"An Indian trapper"
"Downing the nigh leader"
"Advance guard"

"Trailing Texas cattle"
"The chieftain"
"Picture writing"
"The winter campaign"
"Among the led horses"
"Driving cattle on the plains"
"Indian runner"

In writing of an exhibition of his pictures, an eminent art critic says: "Two aspects of his ability as a painter of life were brought out in sharp relief by this collection of pictures—his authentic interpretation of the Indian, and his fidelity to things as they are amongst our soldiers and cowboys."

His ponies are full of "horse character" and connoisseurs agree that in the painting of the horse, Remington surpassed Meissonier, Fromentin, and Detaille. His equestrian bronzes are picturesque and spirited. He approaches sculpture from the pictorial rather than the monumental side.

Lorado Taft says: "Mr. Remington is not an interpreter, nor is he likely ever to conceive a theme sculpturally."

His "Bronco buster" and "Wounded bunkie" are his leading sculpture.

REUTERDAHL, HENRY, (I., P.) b. Malmo, Sweden, August 30, 1871. Member Society of Illustrators and American Water Color Society. Represented at the 45th annual exhibition of the American Water Color Society.

"Henry Reuterdahl stands alone in his wonderful realistic paintings of steamships laboring in tempestuous waters. He has dramatized the warship, the destroyer, the liner and the 'tramp' as no other painter and shows in his exhibition pictures a high indication of his attainment as an illustrator—and vice versa."

RHIND, J. MASSEY, (S.) b. Edinburgh, Scotland, July 9, 1860. From his earliest childhood Mr. Rhind has modeled in clay. His father, John Rhind, R. S. A., gave him instructions in art and while still very young he was sent to an art school in Lambeth where he became a pupil of Delau, the French sculptor, at that time a political exile. Later Rhind studied at the Royal Academy. He took three gold medals in one year at South Kensington, being the first student who ever scored such a success. Later he went to Paris, then back to England and came to the United States in 1889.

When he submitted the design for the bronze doors of Trinity church, the world in general recognized him as a powerful sculptor. His design for a fountain in Washington Park, Albany, to be erected as a memorial to Senator Rufus King, was accepted. "For originality and dramatic effect, there is nothing in America to surpass it."

Mr. Rhind's work is to be seen in several of the great business buildings erected in New York City and in the decorative figures on the front of the Alexander Commencement Hall at Princeton. One of his latest works is the Calhoun statue, and one of his finest examples of interior decorative work is the mantel in the great hall of the Yerkes' New York house. (Munsey 14:671)

His heroic bronze statue of "The scout" is a strikingly vigorous figure, magnificent in a wonderfully wrought war bonnet.

His most famous work is a fountain in Bushnell Park, Hartford, Conn. The figures are of heroic size and illustrate four epochs of Indian history.

He has executed the equestrian statue of George Washington in Newark; the statue of Stephen Girard in Philadelphia; that of Peter Stuyvesant in Jersey City; one of Robert Burns in Pittsburgh; and the McKinley memorial in Niles, Ohio.

New York sculptors say that the eighteen symbolic figures in the frieze of the Farmers' Deposit Building in Pittsburgh, are the finest examples of architectural sculpture in the United States.

Mr. Rhind was chosen by the Wanamaker memorial committee to execute the statue of John Wanamaker.

RICHARDS, WILLIAM TROST, (P.) b. Philadelphia, Pa., November 14, 1833; d. Newport, R. I., November 8, 1905. At an early age he turned his attention to the study of art and received his first instructions from Paul Weber. In 1855 he went to Europe, studying in Florence, Rome, and Paris. He was an exhibitor in the Paris salon; the Royal Academy and Grosvenor Gallery, London; and was an honorary member of the National Academy of Design, New York.

A painter of landscapes and marines, his best works in oil are:

"The Wissahickon"   "Mid-ocean"
"New England coast"   "At Atlantic City" (Paris salon,
"Mid-summer"   1873)
"June woods"   "Wood scene"
"Spring"   "Summer afternoon"
"Ebbtide"   "Old orchard at Newport"
"The inlet near Newport"   "Out in the country"
"Tulip trees"   "Sea and sky"
"Land's end"

"So carefully painted in some of Richard's landscapes are the leaves, grasses, grain-stalks, weeds, stones, and flowers, that we seem not to be looking at a distant prospect, but lying on the ground with herbage and blossoms directly under our eyes." (Tuckerman)

"Richards was one of the first American painters who adopted the pre-Raphaelite style of treatment in their pictures; this was in 1858, and since that time no artist in this country has achieved greater success in the profession. His drawing is never at fault and the crispness of his touch is charming." (Art Journal, Aug., 1877)

In writing of the art of William T. Richards in "Masterpieces of the sea," Harrison S. Morris says: "He was a realist ...... the things he painted, the sea, the sky, all outdoors—these things were real to him and were not things to play tricks with. He did not paint a sunrise effect, he painted 'Sunrise.' He did not paint 'Fog—an impression—' he painted fog an actuality."

ROBINSON, BOARDMAN, (I.). A member of the Society of illustrators since 1909, and has ·taken an active part in the new movement—a sort of renaissance of the art of the cartoon.

"Of all the newspaper artists in this country," says William Marion Reedy of the St. Louis Mirror, "Boardman Robinson has the finest, freeest, swashing stroke, the greatest daring in massing his black and letting in the white."

The editor of Cartoons, says: "His ideas are refreshing, the spirit of his work being attack on sham and on things, animate or not—customs, habits, individuals, corporations, and so forth—that obstruct the path of progress."

"Mr. Robinson is no unworthy successor of the French masters of caricature, Gavarni and Daumier, and his work shows kinship with that of Forain, the brilliant artist of the Figaro." (Cur Lit 53:461)

Herbert Adams, the sculptor, also pays a tribute to the art of Mr. Robinson.

ROBINSON, THEODORE, (P., I.) b. Irasburg, Vt., June 3, 1852; d. April 2, 1896. Studied art in Paris under Carolus-Duran and Gèrome. He spent the years 1884-88 with Monet at Giverny, then returned to this country and devoted himself to the Delaware and Hudson River Canal scenery. In earlier years he did a great deal of mural painting in New York, and he was well known as an illustrator.

"He accepted the impressionist theory that the first consciousness we receive of an object consists of a confusion of color dots. But he painted merely in prismatic color strokes, varying in size according to the subject." (Hartmann)

"In many of his works, especially in 'The girl and cow' he shows the real benefit the impressionist doctrine may convey to those whose individual strength repels ill-digested imitation. He revelled in light and

analyzed it with subtle intuition growing emotional at every sunburst."
He was strictly a neo-impressionist.

"Robinson had the faculty to impress one with the spontaneity of his
expression. His work always seems to be done *au premier coup.* He
possesses the true tonality of nature." The same tone of nature is found
in his "Winter landscape" as in his "The girl and cow."

While studying under Carolus-Duran and Gèrome he painted his
"Study of a girl," the first of his pictures to be accepted by the Paris
salon. In 1890 "Winter landscape" was awarded the Webb prize as the
best landscape by an artist under forty years of age. In 1892 he won the
Shaw prize of $1,000 for the figure painting in his "In the sun."

Soon after his death in 1896 one of his pictures was offered as a gift
to the Metropolitan Museum, New York, and the gift was declined.
Within the last four years the museum has acquired three of his pictures
and exhibits a fourth which is loaned.

Cox writes of the "cold and intellectual gaiety" of Robinson's views
of Giverny.

ROGERS, JOHN, (S.) b. Salem, Mass., October 30, 1829; d. New Canaan,
Conn., July 26, 1904.

He was compelled to abandon the profession of civil engineering on
account of weak eyes and entered a machine shop and modeled in clay
during his leisure moments. With the exception of three months in
Rome in 1850 when he worked in the studio of Mr. Spencer, an English-
man, he was self taught. In 1859 he executed the first of his small plaster
groups which met with such popular success. He sent twenty-nine
"Rogers groups" to the Centennial Exhibition in Philadelphia in 1876,
and received the highest award at the Columbian Exposition in 1893 for
his dignified seated figure of Lincoln.

Mr. Rogers was elected a member of the National Academy in 1863,
and belonged to the National Sculpture Society. (American Art Annual, Vol. 5)

ROLSHOVEN, JULIUS, (P.) b. Detroit, Mich., October 28, 1858. Studied
art in Düsseldorf and Munich where he met Frank Duveneck with whom
he also studied, accompanying him to Italy. In 1882 he went to Paris
and worked in the studio of Robert-Fleury. He has exhibited in Paris,
Munich, Berlin, London, Brussels, Vienna, and Florence and in the
principal cities of the United States and received honors and medals
and artistic recognition from these exhibitions.

Mr. Rolshoven has instructed art classes in Paris, London, and
Florence; is a member of the Munich Secessionists; the Société Nationale

des Beaux Arts; Paris; the Chelsea Art Club, London; and the Taos Society of Artists, New Mexico.

Drawing is perhaps the most noticeable strength of Mr. Rolshoven's work. He is also noted for the poetic way in which he treats interior and out-of-door scenes.

His beautiful nude, "La Venere bruna," an echo of his Paris period, done in pastel, was given the place of honor in the first pastel exhibition in London. His work has of late years rebuilt itself upon a stronger and finer line. This the discriminating critic finds in "The girl with the kitten."

In 1906 the Art Institute, Chicago, had on exhibition two of Mr. Rolshoven's paintings that are particularly interesting: "The cloister, church of St. Francis d'Assisi" and "The prayer." The first gives the interior, peaceful but radiant in sparkling sunlight, while the second is bathed in the cool, pale evening light.

His Venetian pictures have strong, green-blue tones—no sunny play of light.

The Rome correspondent writing on American artists at the exposition of 1911, says: "One of the best portraits of women in the exhibition is that by Julius Rolshoven. This fine painting is rich in color and delightful in its treatment."

The Paris edition of the New York Herald contained a flattering comment on his works displayed at an exhibition there, mentioning particularly "Expectancy," "The three Graces," "The dancer in white," and the "Salon of Mona Lisa."

Following a sojourn in Tunis and Algeria, Mr. Rolshoven brought to Detroit for exhibition in his native city a collection of eighty works. There was a series of studies in light (African paintings), also groups of Venetian life, scenes of Tuscany, and nude subjects. The interiors were of his Florentine villa, the thirteenth century Castello del Diavolo (his home in Italy). These interiors are painted in the charming low tones for which the artist has a wide reputation.

"All in all it is a most versatile one man show, in which every touch is aesthetic and every subject satisfying to one's sense of the beautiful." (Bulletin of the Detroit Institute of Arts, January, 1912.)

"The masquerade," one of the finest pieces of work ever done by Mr. Rolshoven, is loaned to the Detroit Museum of Art. The figures were painted from models in England and the back-ground finished in Italy.

Returning to the United States in 1914 Mr. Rolshoven visited San Diego during the Panama-Pacific Exposition, 1915. He was impressed with the unusual architecture of one of the buildings, and upon investigation he learned that it was a replica of an old mission in northern New

Mexico. Curiosity prompted him to seek it out and he found himself with a group of old-time artist friends among the Taos Indians. He became one of the ten men who make up the now famous Taos group.

For years Mr. Rolshoven's ideas had been concerned with the mysticism of Italian art, and the deep religious feeling and profound reverence for ceremonial in the life of the Taos Indians so impressed him that a departure from his old style became his favorite mood in production.

His "Land of Sip-o-phey" (the shadow world—the hereafter) is one of his finest achievements. It is 12 x 16 feet in size, and shows a wonderful mastery of conception and brilliance of color.

His Indian pictures make a long list; those best known are:

"The Taos town council"   "War chief, Sun Arrow"
"Cochite Buck"   "Chief White Sun"
"The scarlet blanket"   "Indian devotion"
"Tesuque boy with Olla"   "The call to the dance"
"Taos Indian maiden"   "War cloud and deer path"
"Little chief coming"   "The aristocrat"
"Rain Cloud"   "Summer deer"

An exhibition of Mr. Rolshoven's recent paintings was held in Detroit in the spring of 1923. The New Mexican pictures were painted in Italy after his sojourn in the southwest of this country. And the sunshine of these pictures is more the restful, comforting suffusions of Italy than the harsh garish sunlight of New Mexico.

Several other subjects have as the background his own Florentine villa or portions of the enchanting grounds about the ancient castle. His nudes are sculpturesque. The portraits have backgrounds of tapestry and velvet that are effective color combinations. Those with Florentine background seem of greater artistic worth than his Indian delineation.

RoTH, ERNEST DAVID, (E.) b. Stuttgart, Germany, January 17, 1879. Came to America with his parents when he was very young. Being obliged to work by day he attended the evening classes at the National Academy of Design, studying etching with the late James David Smillie.

For a number of years Mr. Roth exhibited his paintings in New York and Philadelphia. Not meeting with success he went to Europe and worked exclusively at etching. Locating in Italy, he fell under the spell of Florence, and so caught the spirit of Old Florence that the director of Uffizi Gallery purchased a series of his Florentine etchings for the Uffizi print department—a distinguishing honor.

"In developing his plates he does not make use of the three baths in customary use among etchers. His method is to apply the acid, touch by touch, with a feather, blotting paper at hand. By this method, involving almost infinite labor, he is sometimes able to secure as many as twelve values.

"Mr. Roth's work has been welcomed in America as promising well for the future of the art." (Int Studio 54:13)

Roth, Frederick George Richard, (S.) b. Brooklyn, N. Y., April 28, 1872. A pupil of Hellman in Vienna, 1892, and Academy of Fine Arts, Berlin, 1894. He received silver medal at St. Louis Exposition, 1904, and was elected full member of the National Academy of Design in 1906. A member of the National Sculpture Society and has exhibited in Europe and the United States.

Mr. Roth works in clay, glazed porcelain, bronze, and marble. His group of polar bears won his election to the National Academy. He designed the architectural tigers for one of the gates of Princeton University.

"He is capable of producing a portrait of an individual creature as well as a symbol of the species." (Arts & D 2:222)

Ruckstuhl, Frederick Wellington, (S.) b. Breitenbach, Alsace, Germany, May 22, 1853; came to America when one year old. Pupil of Academie Julien under Mercié, Boulanger, and Lefebvre. He received honorable mention in the Paris salon, 1889. For many years was secretary of the National Sculpture Society.

"Without question Mr. Ruckstuhl's most beautiful work is his marble figure, 'Evening,' which he modeled in Paris and which won him an honorable mention at the salon of 1888 and a medal at the Columbian Exposition. It is a poetic conception very simply expressed in a pose of unusual grace, and reveals a close study of nature." (Taft)

Other well known works of his are:

"Mercury teasing the eagle of Jupiter," in St. Louis

"Solon," in the Library of Congress

"Wisdom" and "Force," the two seated figures which guard the entrance of the appellate court in New York City.

One of his latest and most popular works is "The spirit of the confederacy." (Taft)

Rungius, Carl, (I., P.) b. Berlin, Germany, August 18, 1869. Came to the United States when twenty-five years old. Elected associate member of the National Academy of Design in 1913.

Last year his "Fall round-up" was awarded the first Altman prize of $1,000, when it was discovered that his being of foreign birth barred him from the competition, as one condition of the will of Mr. Altman was that the prize could not be given to other than "an American-born artist." So the name of Ernest Blumenschein who was born in this country was substituted, his prize winning picture being "Superstition."

Mr. Rungius' painting "Fall round-up" is a fine picture and thoroughly American in subject and treatment. Two cattlemen are in their saddles on a hill overlooking a valley with spots of vegetation and cattle in the distance and a blue sky over all.

Carl Rungius, E. Irving Couse, Albert L. Groll, and Ernest L. Blumenschein are called the "big four" who depict the decorative delights of Taosian half-breeds.

"There is in his paintings a hearty invigorating message of nature on a big scale."

Ryder, Albert Pinkham, (P.) b, New Bedford, Mass., March 19, 1847; d. Elmhurst, N. Y., March 28, 1917. Studied art under William E. Marshall and at the National Academy of Design, New York. Practically self-taught. Member of the National Academy of Design, New York, since 1906.

The titles of some of his characteristic works give an idea of the scope of his subjects:

"Jonah and the whale"   "The old mill"
"Christ appearing unto Mary"   "The wandering cow"
"The story of the cross"   "The race"
"Charity"   "Chase"
"The forest of Arden"   "The passing song"
"The little maid of Arcady"   "Siegfried"
"The two lovers"   "Flying Dutchman"
"Constance"   "The temple of the mind"
"The sisters"   "The tempest"
"Desdemona"   "Poet on Pegasus visiting the
"Macbeth on horseback"   muses"
"Meeting the three witches"   "The horseman"
"Autumn landscape"   "Twilight"
"Moonlight"

Charles DeKay, the art critic, who really discovered Ryder, writes of him as "a colorist quite apart from schools and masters who, like Homer D. Martin, is what might be called an instructive colorist ...."

Generally small in size, often jewel-like, inwardly more glowing and charming than Limoges enamels, his pictures deal in color as the works of a great born composer deal in music.

"His moonlight scenes are imbued with the witchery and mystery of night, as perhaps no one else has presented it .... His is that obscure illusive quality that is to painting what Browning is to poetry."

Isham, in his "History of American Painting," says: "Ryder's pictures differ from Whistler's as well as from Fuller's in being not transcriptions from nature but creations of the imagination, and in striving to convey ideas, vague but poetic."

Walter Pach, the writer, in the L'art et les Artistes, names Ryder as one of the three great American painters and says: "His art is like the playing of some master violinist, color and form and other painters' harmonies being the strings of his fine instrument .... He chooses his subjects from the poets .... and out of them he produces pictures of profound and poignant beauty, intensely personal expressions of his own rare spirit."

"We know of no living artist who fills us with such rare and charming poetical thoughts, none who transports us into such a mysterious, delightful unreal, fairy realm of the fancy." (New Eng M 14:150)

"Ryder's astonishing ability as a draughtsman, his unerring instinct for the very lines of truth in drawing horses, sheep, and other animals as well as domestic fowls and birds is seen in many canvases in which they are chief if not the only interest. His horses are as fine as Géricault's and his sheep as fine as Jacque's when he wishes them to be .... His landscapes are the least successful of his works and yet even in landscape he has done some fine things." (Art in Am 5:161)

"Structurally and technically they [small marines] represent the artist at his best." (Art in Am 8:28)

"The insistent charm of Ryder's painting lies in the subtlety of his manipulation of values in the few colors in which he worked."

Four paintings which cover several periods of his development are named by Francis Fairchild Sherman as:

"Childe Harold's pilgrimage," owned by Mr. Warren P. King
"Landscape with cattle," owned by Mr. Gellatly
"Arcadia," owned by Mrs. Julia Munson Sherman
"Pastoral," owned by Mr. Salvator Guarino.

Saint-Gaudens, Augustus, (S.) b. Dublin, Ireland, March 1, 1848; d. Cornish, N. H., August 3, 1907. At the age of six months he came with his family to America. When thirteen he was apprenticed to Louis Avet, a cameo cutter. From 1864-7 he studied drawing at night at Cooper Union and at the National Academy of Design, and in 1867 went to Paris to study sculpture. In 1869 he entered Jouffroy's studio in the Ecole des Beaux Arts. While in Rome, 1870-2, he produced the statues of "Hiawatha" and "Silence"; also experimented in painting, making studies of the Campagna. He returned to the United States in 1874. An associate member of National Academy of Design, 1888; full member, 1889.

His five monuments in the remarkable series of memorials to Civil War heroes are the Farragut statue and the equestrian statue of Sherman in New York, Shaw memorial in Boston, and the statues of Lincoln and Logan in Chicago.

The "Head of Christ" for the Phillips Brooks memorial was one of the last things that Saint-Gaudens did with his own hands.

An eminent critic has called the Sherman monument the third greatest equestrian statue in the world, placing only the "Colleoni" of Verrocchio and the "Gattamelata" of Donatello before it. His "Deacon Chapin" is probably the finest embodiment of Puritanism in our art.

Kenyon Cox says: "I believe Saint-Gaudens is the most complete master of relief since the fifteenth century." His technical perfection in this rare art is best seen in the relief-portraits of the "Butler children," "Sarah Redwood Lee," and the "Schiff children."

Of the "Adams memorial" now placed in Rock Creek cemetery near Washington, D. C., the above mentioned critic writes: "One knows of nothing since the tombs of the Medici that fills one with the same hushed awe as this shrouded, hooded, deeply brooding figure, rigid with contemplation, still with an eternal stillness, her soul rapt from the body on some distant quest ...... Her meaning is mystery; she is the everlasting enigma."

"France made him an officer of the Legion of Honor and the art societies of France elected him to the highest position within their gift. But the honors which he valued most of all were the degrees conferred upon him by Harvard and Princeton—the gratifying token of recognition by great centers of learning of the fact that he had done notable work in raising American sculpture to its present heights." (Craftsm 13:59)

Sargent, John Singer, (P., Mural P.) b. Florence, Italy, January 12, 1856, of American parents. From his infancy he breathed an atmosphere of culture and art. He began his art studies at the Academy of Fine

Arts in Florence and continued them in the studio of Carolus-Duran, Paris. At the age of twenty-two he received honorable mention in the Paris salon for his "Fishing excursion." In 1879 he sprang into notoriety with his portrait of his master, Carolus-Duran. His "El Jaelo," a dancing girl, created a sensation in 1882; Madame Gauthereau's portrait made him famous and "Carmencita" was purchased by France for the Luxembourg Gallery. His charming "Carnation, lily, lily, rose" was purchased for the Royal Academy, London, and his great canvas "The four doctors" was presented to the Johns Hopkins University in 1907.

Mr. Sargent is a member of the Royal Academy, London; the Société des Beaux Arts, Paris; National Academy of Design, New York; a chevalier of the Legion of Honor, France; and his works are hors concours in the Paris salon.

The highest honor of artistic distinction came to him in 1897 when he was invited to paint a portrait of himself to be hung in the famous portrait gallery of the Uffizi, Florence, Italy. As none but truly great and world-famous artists are thus honored, this compliment ensures to him undying fame.

His portrait painting has given him world-fame. Isham says: "With all limitations and reserves made, he has talents manifest and unmistakable that give him securely his position as the first portrait painter since Reynolds and Gainsborough."

The portrait of John D. Rockefeller was the first portrait done by Sargent after several years of painting landscapes. The Rockefeller portrait was followed by his much discussed portrait of former-President Wilson which was painted under the following interesting circumstances:.

Shortly after the outbreak of the World War, Mr. Sargent generously offered to paint a picture by commission of the highest bidder and to donate the purchase price to the Red Cross. The offer of this unpainted canvas was auctioned at a public sale in London and Sir Hugh Lane was the highest bidder, buying the proposed picture for $50,000. Before the choice of the subject to be painted was made, Sir Hugh Lane was lost on the Lusitania and the privilege passed to the National Gallery of Ireland, to which his art collection was bequeathed. The trustees selected President Wilson as the subject of the painting. Mr. Sargent was in the United States at the time painting the Rockefeller portrait and Mr. Wilson consented to give him sittings.

The portrait of Manuel Garcia, famous music teacher, at the age of one hundred years, is justly considered one of Sargent's most extraordinary interpretations of character.

A sensation of the Royal Academy exhibition in London last year was when Sargent and Charles Sims (English painter) both displayed portraits of Lady Rocksavage.

"Gassed," sketched while at the front, has been called by many critics, the foremost of all war paintings. It held the place of honor in the Royal Academy exhibition in 1919.

Sargent has completed his series of murals on the "Triumph of Religion" in the Boston Public Library. The frieze of the prophets—18 figures—the third great division of the work, is a magnificent series of portraits that has brought him great popularity in the United States.

"This frieze has a character much like that of a Greek chorus interpreting and supporting the movement of a great drama." On the left of Moses are the prophets of despair; on the right, those of hope. It has been said that Sargent's favorite figure in the frieze is Hosea.

"These murals are as splendid an exhibition of artistic power as any painter living could make them. The color is beautiful enough to carry them into the first rank for that merit alone; and while never transgressing the rules that govern the art of mural painting, they do not appear to be limited by them in any way." (King's American Mural Painting, p. 124)

"Church triumphant" and "Synagogue defeated" were chosen by the artist to complete the series. The state legislature, supreme court and attorney general of Massachusetts were called upon to pass upon the fitness of the one representing Judaism—the "Synagogue"—which offends the people of the Jewish faith. The offending panel is represented as a despairing, gray haired woman with tragic expression, seated on the broken steps of a wrecked temple; blindfolded she is losing her crown. She has saved from the ruins nothing but a broken sceptre and the Table of the Law.

In 1916 the trustees of the Boston Museum of Fine Arts commissioned Mr. Sargent to paint the mural decorations for the dome of the building, and after five years devoted to this monumental work it was unveiled in November, 1921. These and his murals in the Boston Public Library are considered Mr. Sargent's crown and glory. He repudiates modernism and follows the neo-classic style. The design comprises four large and four small canvases, twelve bas-reliefs and many architectural ornaments, and every part of the whole was executed by his own hand. The color scheme is blue and white and gold. There is no connected story. He takes mythological divinities who symbolize the various arts. The message is the glory of art and the compulsion of beauty. "Nowhere is there any hint of heaviness, of laborious effort, of the burning of the mid-night oil. The entire impression is gay, limpid, buoyant, free." (Lit Digest 71:26)

The murals for the Widener Memorial Library at Harvard College were recently unveiled. They are a memorial to the Harvard men who fought and died in the World War. They are two upright panels placed on either side of the wall facing the main staircase. The panel at the left represents a soldier desperately wounded supported by the figures of "Death" and "Victory." The panel on the right is called "Marching soldiers," representing the departure of the Harvardmen to the World War.

Sargent's famous nine portraits of the Wertheimer family have been bequeathed to England, and the National Gallery has accepted them, although there is a rule which precludes it from hanging modern work. Frank Rutter, one of England's leading art critics, says in discussing the hanging of Sargent's Wertheimer portraits that his "Asher Werth-eimer" is worthy to hang beside a Hals or a Velasquez; and also, "I am tempted to wonder whether since the time of Rembrandt there has been any more striking rendering in paint of what J. T. Grein has called the jew with a capital "J."

"Possibly the feature of Mr. Sargent's work that excites the greatest admiration in his fellow-artists is his facile handling of the brush. The final result of it gives one the impression of work done easily—in fact rather improvised than premeditated. But the impression is somewhat misleading, every stroke is calmly calculated, every touch is coolly de-signed." (John C. Van Dyke)

SARTAIN, WILLIAM, (P.) b. Philadelphia, Pa., November 21, 1843. A pupil of Pennsylvania Academy of the Fine Arts, of Bonnat and Ecole des Beaux Arts in Paris, he also studied in Italy and Spain; won silver medal in Boston; received honorable mention Pennsylvania Academy of the Fine Arts and bronze medal Pan-American Exposition, Buffalo, 1901. He is an associate member of the National Academy of Design; was one of the founders of the Society of American Artists; president New York Art Club; and taught life classes in Art Students' League, New York.

"There is in Mr. Sartain's work a delicacy of tone in the simple masses not striking at first, but whose absolute justness is recognized on longer acquaintance. Some of his Moorish street scenes have a depth of lumi-nous atmosphere enveloping the figures in a way comparable to that of Pieter de Hooge." (Isham)

Cox writes of the romantic feeling and deep golden tone of Sartain's "Kasba."

SCHILLE, ALICE, (P., Min. P.) b. Columbus, Ohio. Pupil of Columbus Art School, Art Students' League, and New York School of Art under William M. Chase; and Prinet, Collin, and Courtois in Paris. Won the New York Woman's Art Club prize in 1908.

"Sufficiently an impressionist to be clever and not sufficiently pledged to impressionism to run into the amazing technical vagaries of that cult." (Int Studio 45: sup xliii)

SCHNEIDER, OTTO J., (P., E.) b. 1875, and spent his childhood in Atlanta, Ill., moving to Chicago at the age of twelve. He received instructions at the Chicago Art Institute; was employed as an illustrator for a number of years in the art departments of various metropolitan newspapers; and later took up etching.

Mr. Schneider's portraits of men exhibit his strongest work. The profile portrait of Ralph Waldo Emerson has the idealistic qualities of a great portrait. The portrait of the late President McKinley in the calm dignity that was part of the man, inspired a memorial etching. Again power is shown in the analysis and presentment of the unique personality of Elbert Hubbard; in the dry-point of Dr. Quinn the musician, in profile; in the full face of Mr. A. F. Brooks, the painter; and again in the portrait of Bror J. Olsson-Nordfeldt, the etcher and painter. In each the salient characteristic are portrayed in their true light. "His portraits of women are fantasies on the motif of grace; those of men penetrate character and are documents of human endeavor; the street study opens to another impersonal interest and in the landscape Mr. Schneider has reached a point worthy of the highest appreciation. Into his picture 'A quiet nook' there is reflection of the artist's own consciousness and his belief 'that nature never did betray the heart that loved her.'" (Lena M. McCauley)

"Schneider's swing and easy mastery of line has produced direct and virile characterizations of notabilities: Lincoln, Emerson, Mark Twain. In contrast to these free and vigorous character studies are his graceful female portraits with a suggestion of Helleu, but individual nevertheless." (Weitenkampf)

SCHOFIELD, W. ELMER, (P.) b. Philadelphia, Pa., September 9, 1867. Pupil of the Pennsylvania Academy of the Fine Arts and under Bouguereau, Doucet, Ferrier, and Edmond Aman-Jean in Paris. Received. honorable mention at exhibition of Art Club of Philadelphia in 1898, also at Paris Exposition, 1900; Webb prize, Society of American Artists, 1900; first Hallgarten prize, National Academy of Design, New York; honorable mention, Carnegie Institute, Pittsburgh; Sesnan gold medal

of honor, Carnegie Institute, Pittsburgh, 1904.   Member of the National
Academy of Design, New York, since 1907.

Represented in permanent collections in Buffalo Museum of Art; Pennsylvania Academy of the Fine Arts, Cincinnati Museum; Carnegie Institute, Pittsburgh; John Herron Art Gallery, Indianapolis; and Corcoran
Gallery of Art, Washington.

Best known paintings are:

"January evening"   "Sand dunes near Lelant"
"Winter—snow study"   "The packet boat"
"Winter in Picardy"   "Early evening, Boulogne"
"The wood road"   "Below the lock"
"February morning"   "Early days of spring"
"Midwinter thaw"   "March snow"

"Mr. Schofield is a landscape painter who favors snowscapes; he paints
his landscapes after the fashion of the Manet impressionism—of seeing
things flat, as broad masses."

"Schofield lays on his pigment in broad touches, and the picture has
a tendency to lie on the surface of the canvas as a decorative pattern.
His subjects have the quality of a tapestry of delicate gray and buff
spots." (Isham)

"Essentially a man of the open, Mr. Schofield makes the spectator conscious of a rugged quality dominating his canvases wherein detail is
subordinated to mass and general effect .... To his excellent draughtsmanship Mr. Schofield added a distinguished feeling for tone and color,
and always he had an innate sense of the pictorial, grasping intuitively
the possibilities of the picturesque in a composition way." (Arthur
Hoeber)

"He is a painter of power, virility, and verve. A brilliant craftsman,
broad and firm in handling, he has a sure sense of the carrying power of
pigment and the illusion produced at a given distance ...... In subject
he is versatile, but he is most happy in rendering snow which allows of
sweeping brush strokes and simple effective masses." (Scrib 72:766)

The French government has purchased his "Morning light" which will
hang in the Luxembourg Gallery, Paris.

SCHULER, HANS, (S.) b. Alsace-Lorraine in 1874. When five years of
age he came with his parents to the United States. Living in Baltimore,
he attended the Maryland Institute and studied with the Charcoal Club.
When the Rinehart School of Sculpture was opened he was one of the
original four students who received instructions. Here he studied for

three years, then went to Paris in 1898 and studied at the Academie Julien under Raoul Verlet. During the year he was in Paris he won two class medals, and in 1899 the Prix Honoraire. Saint-Gaudens became interested in the young sculptor and through his influence he was awarded the Rinehart Scholarship for Paris.

His "Ariadne" was sent to the salon in 1901 and it was awarded the coveted Gold Medal; "Paradise lost" was exhibited in the salon of 1903; and "Memory," a tomb figure in bronze, was completed in 1904. Returning to the United States in 1905 he received many commissions for portrait busts of distinguished people.

One of his most beautiful works is "Aphrodite" springing from the sea foam.

"Schuler's work is strong. His ideas are original, his conceptions are inspiring, lifelike—almost human." (Int Studio 53: sup xxix)

SCOTT, EMILY MARIA SPAFORD, (P.) b. Springwater, N. Y., August 27, 1832. Mrs. Scott's first attempt at drawing was in the copying of fashion plates, because when she was young pictures in the family were few and far between and even chromos were scarce. She was educated in the public schools of Springwater and at Ann Arbor, Michigan. In 1871 she went to New York City to study at the National Academy of Design and later entered the Art Students' League. In 1872 she went to Europe, spending two years in study in Paris and in the cities of Italy and other countries. Since 1876 her home has been in New York City. March 1, 1853, Miss Spaford was married to Charles Scott of Ann Arbor, Michigan.

"Roses have been Mrs. Scott's favorite study and she paints them with a tenderness and sentiment rarely seen in flower pictures."

SCUDDER, JANET, (S.) b. Terre Haute, Ind. A pupil of Rebisso in Cincinnati and Lorado Taft in Chicago; in Paris she studied first in the Vitti Academie and Colarossi's night school, then under MacMonnies. After an absence of three years, Miss Scudder returned to the United States and opened a studio in New York. Her first commission was for a lamp post design and her second, the seal for the Bar Association of New York. After receiving commissions for several memorial tablets and portraits in relief, she again went to Paris and from there to Florence, Italy, where she had a studio for several years.

Miss Scudder has been honored in Paris, five of her medallion portraits having been purchased by the French government, and these are the first work of an American woman sculptor to be admitted to the Luxembourg. These medallions are in bas-relief in marble, framed in bronze; casts of them have been made in gold and silver. One is said to be the largest medallion ever made in gold, being about four inches long. (Clements "Women in Fine Arts")

Her portrait medallion of Bishop Hare is especially notable. Delightful also is the portrait of Master Billy Fahnestock. Her "Sun goddess" for the Brooklyn Institute of Arts and Sciences, representing Japanese Art, is a gravely dignified and significant sculptural creation.

Miss Scudder is preeminently the creator of beautiful fountains. While residing in Italy she became interested in fountains and in this line of work she has made her largest contribution to contemporary art. She has not less than thirty fountains to her credit.

"It is these which give the keynote to her art, establishing its individuality and to a degree measuring its worth. Her theory is that sculpture can be at the same time both gay and serious, enlivening and uplifting ...... In her figures of children she has embodied the very essence of childish glee while keeping invariably in mind the prerogatives of plastic expression ...... While her fountains are merry, they are in nowise trivial." (Int Studio 39: sup lxxxi)

Miss Scudder has been selected to design a decorative memorial fountain to the late D. B. Burnham, the architect, to be placed in Burnham Green, Manila, Philippines.

Several of Miss Scudder's charming fountain centers were displayed at and became a part of the decorative exhibits at the Panama-Pacific Exposition.

"Her fountains and garden pieces are small and sportive, but intensely sincere and never trivial."

The favorite subjects are:

"Young Diana"
"Little lady of the sea"
"Young Pan"
"Flying cupid"
"Frog" fountain, Metropolitan Museum, New York.
"Fighting boys" fountain, Art Institute, Chicago.

Her most noteworthy one is the National Suffrage fountain, "Femina victrix,"· erected in Washington, D. C. A beautiful female figure is poised on a globe and holds the emblem of victory aloft. "For subtle curvature and grace of line, this lovely creation has few equals." (Art and Archaeol 6:314)

SEARS, TABER, (Mural P.) b. Boston, Mass., 1870. Pupil Academie Julien in Paris under Benjamin-Constant and Laurens; also studied with Merson in Paris, and in Florence and Rome.

Mural paintings:

"Spirit of Niagara," in Buffalo historical society.
"New York among the nations," New York city hall.
Frieze of the apostles, Epiphany church, Pittsburgh, Pa.
Stained glass window: "Presentation in the temple." (Art & P 2:315)

SETON, ERNEST THOMPSON, (I.) b. South Shields, England, August 14, 1860. Lived in the backwoods of Canada, 1866-70; on the western plains, 1882-7; educated at Toronto Collegiate Institute and Royal Academy, London; studied art in Paris in 1890 and again in 1894, a pupil of Gérome, Bouguereau, and Ferrier. Exhibited in the salons paintings and drawings of wolves, his favorite subject.

He was one of the chief illustrators of the Century Dictionary, contributing fully a thousand drawings of animals and birds; was also official naturalist to the government of Manitoba, and is well known as an artist, author, and lecturer.

SEWELL, ROBERT V. V., (Mural P.) b. New York, 1860. Pupil of Lefebvre and Boulanger in Paris. Received first Hallgarten prize National Academy of Design, 1889; also won many medals. Elected associate member of National Academy, 1902. Member of leading art clubs.

His mural painting "The Canterbury Pilgrims" in the great hall of Georgian court, Lakewood, and several others are widely known.

SHANNON, JAMES JEBUSA, (P.) b. Auburn, N. Y., February 3, 1862. Spent early boyhood at St. Catherines, Ont. First painted bill posters for agricultural fairs; at the age of fifteen he went to London. Worked three years in South Kensington School where he took gold medal for figure painting; has also taken medals for portraits at expositions in Paris, Berlin, Vienna, and Chicago. He was one of the first members of the New English Art Club. In 1897 he was elected associate member of the Royal Academy, London; full member in 1909; associate member of the National Academy of Design, New York, in 1908.

While a student he painted by command of Queen Victoria the portrait of Miss Horatia Stopford, one of the maids of honor, after which time he was overrun with commissions.

In 1887 his portrait of Henry Vigne, in hunting costume, not only attracted attention at the academy exhibition but obtained medals at

Paris, Berlin, and Vienna.   He soon became one of the leading portrait painters of England.

Among his notable works are his portraits of the young Duchess of Portland, Marchioness of Granby, Lady Marjorie Manners, Duchess of Sutherland, "Miss Kitty," Lady Carbery and children, Miss Clough, and Sir Alfred Lyall. His "Iris," a portrait of his wife, has won high praise and was, together with "War" and "Flower girl," purchased for the Tate Gallery.

"The portrait which J. J. Shannon paints may be designated as pictorial ...... Shannon belongs to those who will first and last see an object and render it with reference to its value as a picture. This priceless quality of the art to which Shannon and his colleagues are the heirs is its ability to suggest the special atmosphere and environment of a given period." (Brinton's "Modern Artists.")

In England Mr. Shannon enjoyed a popularity as a portrait painter second to John Singer Sargent.

Commenting on his portrait of Princess Mary, a London art correspondent says: "The artist has done full justice to his subject in the delightful freshness and simplicity of style which he has brought to bear on it, skilfully avoiding the usual stiffness and conventionality of the average royal portrait."

He is represented by "Girl in brown" in the Corcoran Gallery, "Miss Kitty" in the Carnegie Institute, and "Fairy tales" and "Magnolia" in the Metropolitan Museum, New York City.

Mr. Shannon received the unique distinction of a "médaille d'honneur" for his portrait of Phil May, exhibited at the International Exposition of Fine Arts at Barcelona, Spain, 1911.

The honor of knighthood was bestowed on Mr. Shannon on New Year's day, 1922.

While his last work, "Flora and the silver cup," was on the way to the 22nd International Exhibition at Pittsburgh, he died in London. Nine years before he fell from a horse and it was from the effects of this accident that his illness resulted.

SHARP, JOSEPH HENRY, (P.) b. Bridgeport, Ohio, September 27, 1859. Studied in Munich under Marr, in Paris under Laurens and Benjamin-Constant, in Antwerp with Verlat, and in Spain with Duveneck.

Mr. Sharp is the veteran Indian painter who first gave the Taos Indian prominence in the art world.

About twenty years ago while prospecting in the Southwest he accidentally came upon the little adobe town of Taos, New Mexico, thirty-five miles from the nearest railroad. Struck by the splendid type of

Indians found there he remained some time and painted them. Later in Paris he told such glowing tales of this region and its people that Bert Phillips and Ernest Blumenschein decided to return to the United States and investigate this new field of art. They painted during the summer; then Blumenschein went to Mexico, but Phillips remained. Blumenschein returned as did Sharp; then Couse who had been painting Indians in Oregon moved to Taos and from these four grew the Taos Society, one of the most unique and interesting colonies in the art world, now famous at home and abroad. The little group of painters gather each year at the Indian reservation just outside Taos to perpetuate on canvas types of the fast disappearing red man who is found at his best here. Membership is not bestowed by favor but because of performance. One of the requirements is that the artist spend three consecutive seasons painting at Taos; all pictures must be of Taos and the surrounding country and its aboriginal inhabitants. While artists now flock by hundreds to this locality, the members of the Taos Society are: E. Irving Couse, Bert G. Phillips, Ernest L. Blumenschein, J. H. Sharp, W. Herbert Dunton, O. E. Berninghaus, Victor Higgins, Walter Ufer (now president of the society), and Julius Rolshoven.

Eleven of Mr. Sharp's Indian pictures are in the Smithsonian Institution, and nearly a hundred of his portraits and pictures of Indians are in the University of California.

"Harvest dance—Pueblo Indians," "Old Dog—Crow Indian chief," and "Strikes his enemy pretty" are in the Cincinnati Art Museum.

SHERWOOD, ROSINA EMMET (Mrs. Arthur M. Sherwood), (Min. P., I.) b. New York City, December 13, 1857. Pupil of William M. Chase in New York; Academie Julien in Paris.

Mrs. Sherwood has received many prizes and medals for drawing and miniature work, and was elected associate member of National Academy, 1906.

SHINN, EVERETT, (P., I., Mural P.) b. Woodstown, N. Y., November 6, 1873. Studied art at the Pennsylvania Academy of the Fine Arts for five years. Mr. Shinn did illustrating for Philadelphia newspapers and for two years furnished drawings for the New York Press. He has been represented in all leading magazines, and the Boussod, Valadon Company sent him abroad to make pictures of the street scenes and typical life in Paris, exclusively for their trade.

"Shinn is a master of the pastel; he knows thoroughly the possibilities and the limitations of his medium." (Int Studio 30:84)

"Matinée crowd, Broadway;" "French music hall;" and "Outdoor stage, France," are admirable examples of his work in this medium.

In his mural decorations he revives the eighteenth century French painting, copying the style of Watteau, Fragonard, and Boucher.

Mr. Gallatin says of Shinn's decorations: "We have very charming souvenirs of the joyous days when Louis XVI sat upon the throne of France." His latest and most successful effort in this line is a series of panels painted for W. M. Salisbury's house at Pittsfield, Mass.

Mr. Shinn has been greatly influenced by Degas with whom he studied drawing.

SHINN, FLORENCE SCOVEL, (I.) b. Camden, N. Y. Studied art at the Pennsylvania Academy of the Fine Arts; an illustrator since 1897.

Her keen sense of humor crops out in every group, and the turn of a line gives a comical effect. The peculiar gift that Mrs. Shinn is endowed with is that she can draw the most pitiful little figures and yet infuse into the picture a happy, healthy atmosphere that impresses us with the worth and joy of living. Her characters are never caricatures; they are appealing and provoke the laughter that bears no malice.

SHIRLAW, WALTER, (P., Mural P.) b. Paisley, Scotland, August 6, 1838; d. Madrid, Spain, December 29, 1909. Began his career as an engraver and illustrator; was thirty-two years of age when he went abroad to study. After seven years in the school in Munich under the instruction of Wagner and Kaulbach, he returned to this country and devoted himself to the interests and advancement of national art. He was one of the first instructors at the Art Students' League, New York. One of the founders, and the first president of the Society of American Artists.

Earlier pictures are:

"Toning of the bell"   "A study of a head"
"Sheep-shearing in the Bavarian   "Feeding the poultry"
    highlands"   "Good morning"
"The young patrician"   "Sheep"

Other works:

"Capelmeister"   "Indian girl"
"The fiddler"   "Eager for the fray"
"Very old"   "Autumn"
"Sleep"   "Brittany"
"Gathering seaweed"   "Among the old poets"
"Roses"   "Rhubarb green"
"The dancer"   "Checker players"
"Marble quarry

Mr. Shirlaw received medal of the Royal Academy, Munich; honorable mention at the Paris Exposition in 1889; was elected associate member. of the National Academy of Design, New York, 1878; full member, 1888.

"The name and fame of Walter Shirlaw will, however, be more certainly perpetuated through his gifts as a master of decorative arts and by the influence and effect of his rare personality and noble character on contemporaneous art development." (Int Studio 43: sup lxx)

"Shirlaw's strong point is not color; he shows a decided leaning to sculpture." (Innes "School of painting")

In the Morgan Memorial Art Gallery at Hartford, Conn., there has recently been hung one of Mr. Shirlaw's important canvases—"The marble quarry." It is an Italian landscape. "This landscape more than holds its own in proximity to an exquisite Corot, as well as in close association with worthy examples of Daubigny, Troyon, and Jules Dupre."

SHRADY, HENRY MERWIN, (S.) b. New York, October 24, 1871; d. New York City, April 12, 1922. A son of Dr. George F. Shrady, one of General Grant's physicians, he graduated from the law department of Columbia College, but never took up the profession. Recovering from an illness he engaged in mercantile business until 1900 when a financial failure caused him to take up drawing and modeling. His first effort was the painting of a mouse. His wife offered it to the National Academy of Design for exhibition. It was accepted and hung and later sold for $50. A study of kittens followed—this brought a fair price. Sketching at the Zoological Gardens he interested Karl Bitter, the sculptor, who invited him to share his studio; here he modeled the colossal figures which decorated the bridges in the grounds of the Pan-American Exposition at Buffalo, 1901.

In 1909 he was elected an associate member of the National Academy of Design.

Designs by thirty-four competitors were submitted for the Grant Memorial to be erected in Washington, D. C. Mr. Shrady was awarded the commission—$50,000. He had previously won the commission for the Washington statue, Brooklyn, N. Y., and also had been commissioned by the Holland Society of New York to make an equestrian statue of William the Silent.

Writing of the Grant Memorial, a critic says of the artillery group: "Nothing in monumental sculpture could well be more spirited and imposing than the view from the front of these three great artillery horses ...... Mr. Shrady ...... again illustrated his intimate knowledge and anatomical familiarity with his subjects in seizing upon and arresting the happy moment which presents less stress and strain in conveying the spirit of life and motion." (Jour of Am Hist 7:1013)

Other statues are General Lee, Charlottesville, Va.; General Williams, Detroit, Mich.; and Jay Cooke, Duluth, Minn.

SHULZ, ADOLPH ROBERT, (P.) b. Delavan, Wisconsin, June 12, 1869. Studied abroad at the Academie Julien under Lefebvre, Benjamin-Constant, Laurens, and others. Specialty: landscapes. Also a teacher.

At an early age Mr. Shulz became interested in the study of trees, their formation and color. He also became familiar with their individual aspect, while the moods of the sky were his delight.

Among his best works are:

"Autumn fog"
"Spring song"
"Frost and fog"
(Arts & D 2:332)

SIMMONS, EDWARD EMERSON, (P., Mural P.) b. Concord, Mass., October 27, 1852; a nephew of Ralph Waldo Emerson; graduated from Harvard in 1874. Studied art in Boston, then went to Paris and studied under Boulanger and Lefebvre in the Académie Julien, winning the gold medal of the studio at the end of his first season. He has been a professional painter since 1879. Is a member of the Ten American Painters. Has lived much abroad in Brittany, France, and in Cornwall, England, but since 1893 has lived chiefly in New York.

It was from Brittany that he sent to the Paris salon of 1882 his painting, "The washerwoman," which brought him honorable mention. This model was rendered famous by serving as the heroine for Blanche Willis Howard's novel, "Guenn," which was written that year at Concarneau.

Mr. Simmons painted Breton themes exclusively until he took up his residence in St. Ives, Cornwall. Here he became associated with a colony of English artists and here he painted his successful "Mother and child" and a splendid marine of the Bay of Lelant. His pictures of the Bay of St. Ives are among the most beautiful and poetic works of the kind that we owe to any modern artist. They have been exhibited at the Royal Academy, London. (Brush & P 5:241)

Among other popular paintings may be mentioned:

"Study at Concarneau"

"Corner of the market"

"Summer"

"Breakfast"

"The winnowers"

"Bout de la cour"

"Low tide"

"The carpenter's son" (considered one of his best works)

His mural decorations have been highly praised by critics. Of those in the Library of Congress, Washington, D. C. (a series of nine paintings representing the Muses) Arthur Hoeber says: "The work is thoughtful, serious, and able; and besides the admirable technical excellence displayed there is felt the intellectual power behind the composition."

"His decorations of the Astor gallery of the Astoria, New York, rank among the finest artistic achievements that the country can boast; and the artist has never surpassed the standard that he has here set for himself." (King's "American mural painting")

"Mr. Simmons is a painter of remarkable versatility and his work is distinguished by freedom of execution, exquisite drawing, repose, and much charm of color."

At the Panama-Pacific Exposition in 1915 Mr. Simmons had two very charming murals full of great refinement and delicacy. One, particularly attractive, tells of the dreams which led to the exploring and exploiting of the great West. Carefully designed figures of great refinement represent "Hope" and "Illusory Hope" scattering tempting bubbles, heading the procession of stately women. They are followed by "Adventure," "Art," "Imagination," "Truth," and "Religion."

In Mr. Simmons' autobiography "From Seven to Seventy" he gives a very interesting explanation of the symbolism of his three panels, "Justice of the law," in the Criminal Courts Building, New York. It is quite different from that commonly given now as the symbolic meaning of these noted murals.

SINGER, WILLIAM H., JR., (P.) b. Pittsburgh, Pa., July 5, 1868. Mr. Singer had very little instruction in the art schools. In 1900 he went to Paris and studied for a short time at the Académie Julien; then went to Laren, Holland, and later to Norway. The following year his first exhibition was made in the Old Salon in Paris; later he exhibited in the New Salon. Elected an associate member of the National Academy of Design, 1916.

Mr. Singer paints from nature and does not retouch his work, maintaining that "he cannot in the quiet of his studio obtain any of the thrills produced by the open."

"In the matter of color, the man is entirely personal. He sees the tenderness of tones, the poetry and charm of atmosphere, the envelopment and the harmony of the open ...... The movement of his 'Salmon river,' the dignity of his 'Birches,' the refinement and subtlety of his snow in 'My garden' and the delicate analysis of his 'The falls,' are all refreshing and novel, presaging much for the future and giving satisfaction in the present accomplishment." (Int Studio 54: sup cxxiv)

SLADE, C. ARNOLD, (P.). Studied under Laurens and sketched in the East as well as in Italy and France. One of the few American painters who are specializing in religious subjects. Some of his canvases remind one of Tanner's. They have found their way into several famous collections. His "Christ on the mountain" is considered to be a masterpiece— "full of the spell of the East and the solemnity of the occasion."

William R. Lester writes that Slade's viewpoints are original and pictorially interesting; that his pictures "have the distinctive note of the modern French school—vibrant, clear, luminous, and imaginative." (Int Studio 51: sup cxxxi)

SLOAN, JOHN, (P., I., E.,) b. Lock Haven, Pa., August 2, 1871. Studied in the evenings for a short time at the Pennsylvania Academy of the Fine Arts, Philadelphia, but in general he may be said to be self-taught.

For several years he was staff artist on the Philadelphia Press; later was instructor in Art Students' League, Philadelphia.

The following extracts are from an article which appeared in Craftsman 15:559:

"He early learned to handle the etcher's needle with a measure of distinction, but he did not take up painting until about ten years ago.

"In 1904 he left Philadelphia and made his home in New York City, just outside the Tenderloin district.

John Sloan has been classed as a member of what is known in our academic art circles as the Revolutionary gang, or the Black school.

"One finds a literary analogy to Sloan's art in the works of both Dickens and Balzac ...... John Sloan, both in his paintings and in the brilliant relentless little etchings which give such vivid glimpses of New York life, shows no tendency to grasp human wretchedness in the mass but rather to show here and there a detached bit of life which has the power of suggesting the whole turbid current.

"The coffee line" received honorable mention at the Carnegie Institute, 1905, and was the most talked of picture of the entire exhibition. The scene of "The coffee line" is Madison Square on a bitter, blustery night in winter where the shivering unemployed are forming a ragged waiting line at the rear of a hot coffee wagon. Startling in its fidelity, the picture displays Sloan in one of his most tense and dramatic moods."

Of late Mr. Sloan has been making Indian scenes the subjects of his canvases, having taken up his residence in Santa Fé, New Mexico.

"The eagle dance" is his latest study of Indian life in its ceremonial phase. The Taos eagle dance is performed as a religious festival and cameras and easels are never permitted. This painting is done from memory.

"There is a certain flashing beauty in the background, and in front and below it, the half deserted pueblo and the few old men solemnly treasuring their old beliefs. Sunlight streams over the mesa and over the dancers . . . . . . In spite of some touches of vivid color, the painting is a record of remote old figures moving sadly out of the world's history." (Arts 2:94)

"He paints largely, as George Moore writes. Whatever the subject, whatever the occupation, Moore so handles his medium that you get the bigness and splendor of life itself in his stories, and John Sloan does this with canvases . . . . . . His color is not pretty—it has the sterner quality of beauty."

SMEDLEY, WILLIAM THOMAS, (P., I.) b. Chester county, Pa., March 26, 1858; d. Bronxville N. Y., March 26, 1920. Entered newspaper office at fifteen; studied engraving in Philadelphia and art in Pennsylvania Academy of the Fine Arts; went to New York in 1878, and later to Paris where he studied under Jean Paul Laurens. He opened a studio in New York in 1880 and has since been actively engaged as illustrator for Harper's and other standard periodicals. In 1883 he was engaged by publishers of "Picturesque Canada" to travel with the Marquis of Lorne through the west and northwest Canada and illustrate the work; has since made several sketching tours in the United States and in 1890 around the world.

In 1881 he made his first contribution to the National Academy of Design, New York; and in 1888 was represented, for the first time, in the Paris salon. In 1890 he won the William T. Evans prize with "A Thanksgiving dinner."

As an illustrator, Mr. Smedley depicted high and low life with equal skill.

His illustrations of Warner's "Golden house" and Howell's "Their silver wedding journey" may be cited as examples of his success in one direction, and those of T. A. Janvier's "Casa Napoleon" and Miss Murfree's "Strange peoples' country" of his success in the other.

Elected member of the National Academy of Design, New York, in 1905.

Burlington magazine says: "Smedley seems like an American Ghirlandajo."

"His pen execution, free and unrestrained, displays the habit of the sketcher."

SMILLIE, JAMES D., (P., E.) b. New York, July 16, 1833; d. September 14, 1909. The son of a jeweler and silversmith, he did etching before he was eight years old. The sentimental bias of early years is shown in a weeping willow and tombstone, while a struggle to break the bonds of conventionality is evident in a processional line of six or eight black-looking buffaloes. He says: "If I remember rightly, sun, moon and stars appeared in the firmament." At fourteen years of age he made ambitious illustrations of Milton's "Paradise lost."

In 1862 he went abroad to study, having previously been employed in bank-note engraving. In 1864 he abandoned engraving and took up painting. In 1865 he was elected an associate member of the National Academy of Design and a full member in 1876. Was the founder of the American Water-color Society, serving as president and treasurer. It was to the efforts of Mr. Smillie and Dr. L. M. Yale, an amateur etcher of merit, that the organization of the New York Etching Club was effected.

He etched almost the entire work on the large plates, "Childhood," "Manhood," and "Old age" after Cole's painting entitled "Voyage of life."

Upon the formation of the Painter-Etchers Society of London in 1860, (Sir Francis Seymour-Haden, president), he was made one of the "original" fellows. Representing American etchers, he made a collection of their productions and sent them to the first exhibition of that society in London.

"He is possessed not only of the qualities needed by an original etcher, but the powers of adaptation."

SMITH, FRANCIS HOPKINSON, (P., I.) b. Baltimore, Md., October 23, 1838; d. New York City, April 7, 1915. He belonged to a family of artists, his great grandfather, Francis Hopkinson, a signer of the Declaration of Independence, being an amateur in water color and his grandfather, Judge Joseph Hopkinson, the first president of the Pennsylvania Academy of the Fine Arts. When a boy Mr. Smith began to paint and has made thousands of sketches and studies in the open air. He not only seems at his strongest in charcoal but he prefers it to lead, to oils, or to water-colors; as an artist he is substantially self-taught.

His paintings are all of a summer-like character. "Franconia Notch" is remarkably successful in the delineation of falling water and the moss-covered rocks which line the ravine.

Of his views of Venice, Isham says: "They are not emotional, they are not subtle, they are not tonal, but they are very charming with their delicately colored skies, their luminous air, their soft sunlit marbles, and clear cool shadows."

"His water-color sketches have a softened brilliancy, a breadth of treatment and a simplicity that gives evidence of practical skill and carrying the idea that the effort was one of expression and that he has portrayed the scene just as it was at the time he sketched it." (Nat Cyc Am Biog)

"In his cloud effects and in his representation of limpid water Mr. Smith shows very exceptional ability."

He achieved distinction as an artist, author, lecturer, critic, playwright, engineer, and expert bridge constructor.

SMITH, JESSIE WILLCOX, (P., I.) b. Philadelphia, Pa. Educated in private schools; studied art at the Pennsylvania Academy of the Fine Arts and under Howard Pyle at Drexel Institute.

Miss Smith was a kindergarten teacher until her health failed; she has been engaged as an artist and as an illustrator since 1890 and her work is seen in all the leading American magazines. Her first actual work was in the advertising department of the Ladies' Home Journal.

"Jessie Willcox Smith's particularity is the decorative use of everyday subjects. She paints or draws in broad flat masses and is almost Japanesque in her use of the planes of her composition." (Bkbuyer 24:201.)

"Her gardens smell of roses and old fashioned blooms."

The series of her pictures entitled "A mother's day" is an idyll of American motherhood: "Morning," "In the garden," "Checkers," "Bedtime."

"Miss Smith's aim is definite and frank, her method vital and strong, and she is also a colorist of charm."

In critically viewing the paintings in the American exhibit at the Roman Exposition of 1911, the dowager queen of Italy (herself a skillful painter) expressed special delight with the picture entitled "The dark," the work of this talented artist.

Jessie Willcox Smith is best known by her illustrations for Robert Louis Stevenson's "A child's garden of verses;" "A child's book of old verses;" "A book of old stories;" series of pictures: "Five senses," "Children of Dickens," "Seven ages of childhood," and "Child calendar."

SMITH, LETTA CRAPO, (P.) b. Flint, Mich., July 4, 1862; d. Boston, Mass., March 17, 1921. Studied art at the Académie Julien, Paris; also a pupil of Julius Rolshoven and George Hitchcock.

Received bronze medal at St. Louis Exposition, 1904, for "The first birthday."

This painting is now in the Detroit Institute of Arts. Other works have been exhibited in Philadelphia, New York, and Chicago.

SONNTAG, WILLIAM LOUIS, (P.) b. Pittsburgh, Pa., March 2, 1822; d. New York, January 22, 1900. Went to Cincinnati to study art in his boyhood; also studied in Europe. Made his home in New York City in 1854. Associate member of the National Academy, 1860; full member, 1861.

"Some of his best landscapes illustrate the picturesque scenery of Western Virginia."

SOUTHWICK, ELSIE WHITMORE, (Min. P.) b. Providence, R. I. Pupil of Prinet, Dauchez, and Madame Chennevières, Paris.

Besides interesting miniatures that are purely pictorial, Miss Southwick has been unusually successful with her portraits.

"Her nudes are wonderfully delicate in line and color, subtle shades of pink and rose predominating.

"Vividness of color is characteristic of Miss Southwick's work. She loves vermilion—gay blues and yellows and violet she likes ...... maroon and brown and the other dull tones are almost tabooed in her work.

"The peasants of Brittany are a source of interest to her as subject matter"

She also paints in oil and pastel and sketches in crayon. In all her work she shows the firm and direct drawing, the vigorous and gay coloring, the strong character that are evident in her miniatures. (Arts & D 1:205)

SPEICHER, EUGENE E., (P.) b. in Buffalo, N. Y., April 5, 1883. Studied art there and in New York City; later spent three years abroad.

In 1921 at the twentieth International Exhibition he was awarded third prize for his painting, "Girl with green hat." At the twenty-second International Exhibition, 1923, his "The hunter" won second prize, a silver medal and $1,000.

"The hunter" .... is a canvas that is conspicuous because of merit and proportion and takes an authoritative place on the line. A youth who sits by a table on which is cap and pipe holds a gun; he is roughly clad in leather vest, blue shirt, and coarse trousers while

the background is a gray-green curtain .... Here is a strong work
ably conceived and realized to which few will begrudge an award."
(Boston Transcript)

"Morning light" is in the Metropolitan Museum, New York City; and
"Mountain landscape" is in the Art League, Galveston, Texas.

A critic says of him, "He is a distinguished and vigorous figure among
the younger American painters. His art is of a robust, full-blooded,
and decidedly American type."

SPERRY, EDWARD PECK, (Mural P., Stained-glass designer). Member
of American Society of Mural Painters, and New York Architectural
League. Specialty, stained glass.

STANLEY, JAMES M., (P.) b. Canandaigua, N. Y., January 17, 1814; d.
April 10, 1872.

In 1834 he removed to Michigan and in 1835 commenced the profession
of portrait painting in Detroit. Went to Chicago in 1837 and for the
following two years he painted portraits of Indians and took sketches of
the Indian country in the region of Ft. Snelling, Minn. Subsequently he
followed his profession in New York City, Philadelphia, Baltimore and
Troy, N. Y. In 1842 he traveled extensively over the western prairie,
painting the portraits of the leading warriors (in full costume) around
Fort Gibson, Ark., and in Texas and New Mexico. After spending some
time in the Hawaiian Islands he returned and lived in Washington, D.
C., then took up his permanent residence in Detroit, Michigan.

Mr. Stanley placed a valuable collection of portraits of the Indian
chiefs of America in the Smithsonian Institution; these were destroyed
by fire in 1865; there were 152 paintings. One of the most important
paintings, "The trial of Red Jacket," was exhibited in all the principal
cities of America and Europe and finally placed in Detroit. Valuable
both historically and artistically it was appraised at $30,000. His por-
traits of distinguished men from all parts of the United States won him
deserved renown.

Mr. Stanley was the organizer of the Western Art Association and one
of the founders of a gallery of painting that in later years became a
permanent and valuable acquisition to Detroit. (Nat Cyc Am Biog
6:467)

STANTON, LUCY MAY, (Min. P.) b. Atlanta, Ga., May 22, 1875. Pupil
of Colarossi Academy, Simon, Blanche, Gandara, and A. Koopman in
Paris. Member Pa. Society of Miniature Painters. Specialty: portraits.
Also teacher.

Miss Stanton's name is included in a group of miniature painters whose work is commented on as follows: "Their miniatures are executed in a broad, free style, difficult to attain on ivory, but very delightful when done with the spontaneity and freshness of color exhibited in the work of these artists. The color in these is spread on the ivory like a stain and is left untouched save for a few accenting touches here and there."

Her group at the American miniaturists exhibition in Boston last year was one of the most original and varied in the collection. These miniatures illustrated the life of the colored people of Georgia, with portraits of negro types of character in the south.

STEELE, HELEN McKAY (Mrs. Brandt T. Steele), (P., I., Stained glass designer) b. Indianapolis, Ind. Pupil of T. C. Steele and William Forsyth. Specialty: portrait sketches and designs for stained glass.

STEPHENS, ALICE BARBER, (I.) b. Salem, N. Y., 1858. Was educated in the public schools of Philadelphia; received her art education in the Philadelphia School of Design for Women and in the Pennsylvania Academy of the Fine Arts. She has been wood-engraver for Scribner's and illustrator for Harper's, Century, and other magazines; has also illustrated for the Ladies' Home Journal, and taught portrait and life classes in the Philadelphia School of Design for Women. Although Mrs. Stephens has studied in Paris in the Académie Julien and at Colarossi's she regards her development due to her Philadelphia instruction and experience in her own studio.

There is a peculiar tenderness in her conception of childhood, entirely free from prettiness and sentimentality.

"Alice Barber Stephens has a talent somewhat akin to Sterner. She is known for her imagination and facile powers of expression." (Hartmann)

"Although nearly all of her pictorial compositions are constructed and executed with understanding, they are seldom spontaneously dramatic and it is therefore in pictures of quiet scenes and rural incidents that Mrs. Stephens excels." She regards the illustrations for "Fishin' Jimmy" as among her most satisfactory achievements. The Bret Harte pictures and the illustrations for "John Halifax, gentleman," and "Middlemarch," are in another vein and one in which Mrs. Stephens is not quite so convincing.

The beautiful illustrations for James Lane Allen's "In Arcady" were made by her for that story at the author's own request. She was Conan Doyle's selection, also, of an illustrator for his "Stark Monroe" papers. (Brush & P 6:241)

STERNE, MAURICE, (P., E.) b. Libau, Russia, 1877. When fourteen years of age emigrated with his widowed mother to New York. He attended night school; later joined a class at the old Academy of Design and attended other art schools in the city. He won prizes with ease. William M. Chase encouraged and honored him by purchasing one of his canvases for a substantial sum of money. He also achieved local fame by making a series of etchings, chief among them the Coney Island set; he assisted the late James D. Smillie as instructor of etching. He went to Europe in 1904, and studied in Greece and the Orient.

"Sterne's plates are notable for their sincerity, freshness, and novelty, and they received special and very favorable mention when they were afterwards exhibited in the Paris salons."

"In balance and color, transition of tones, and in their savage nudity they resemble the work of Matisse, but Sterne is not a reflection of the French so-called post-impressionistic movement." (Int Studio 46: sup iii)

"Rockaway beach" and "Harbor scene" are probably his most important plates, though "Maggie" was a prize winner, and many of his portraits, particularly "The reader" and "A profile," are especially delicate, and finely etched." (Brush & P 10:99)

STERNER, ALBERT EDWARD, (P., I.) b. London, England, November 8, 1863. At the age of eleven, his family went to Birmingham, England, to live and he entered King Edward's School at the head of a competitive list of seven hundred students; took the prize in drawing and after studying at the Birmingham Art Institute, where he won a scholarship, went to Germany in his fifteenth year. When he was eighteen he came to his parents who had preceded him to Chicago. Here he took up lithography, scene painting, and drafting on wood for engravers and designers.

In 1885 he took up his residence in New York, where he illustrated for "Life," "St. Nicholas," and "Harper." Three years later went to Paris and studied at the Ecole des Beaux Arts and at Académie Julien under Boulanger and Lefebvre. Received honorable mention in 1891 for a painting in oil, "The bachelor," exhibited in the salon, to which he was a regular contributor. Associate member National Academy of Design, 1910.

He has illustrated "Prue and I" by George William Curtis, works of Edgar Allan Poe and "Eleanor" by Mrs. Humphrey Ward.

"He is an admirable painter, a soft, rich, and brilliant colorist. This quality of color finds its way into his black and white. His chief quality is his artisticness. He is a conservative radical in art." (Quarterly Illustrator, Vol. 2)

Mr. Sterner has recently appeared in a new role—that of making portraits in red chalk—called by the French "sanguines." (Int Studio 35: sup liv)

Ernest Knaufft says: "The mantle of Edwin A. Abbey has fallen upon the shoulders of Albert E. Sterner, who is almost the sole representative of sentiment in illustration. His technique is not so expert as that of Abbey .... but at his best he far transcends the average illustrator, and we find the genuine ring of art, the true poetic feeling dominating his productions."

"Like Blake and Poe in their poetry, Mr. Sterner sets aside the rules of convention and breaks loose from the leading strings of schools, his touch now poignant, now languid, is the touch of a musician turned draughtsman, and the result is most elusive."

STEVENS, HELEN B., (E.) b. Chicago, Ill., February 8, 1878. Pupil of the Art Institute, Chicago, and of Frank Brangwyn in England.

Teacher of etching at the Art Institute, Chicago.

STEWART, JULIUS L., (P.) b. Philadelphia, Pa., 1855. Was a pupil of Zamacöis, Gèrome, and R. de Madrazo.

Received honorable mention at Paris salon, 1885; third class medal salon of 1890; gold medal, Berlin, 1891; grand gold medal, Berlin, 1895; gold medal, Munich, 1897; Order of Leopold of Belgium, 1895; Legion of Honor, 1895, officer, 1901; grand gold medal, Munich, 1901. Associate Société Nationale des Beaux Arts, 1895; member, 1899.

"In result of Fortuny's influence Stewart has become a thorough man of the world, a painter of society, and one of captivating grace, whose 'Hunt ball' and 'Five o'clock tea' were amongst the most refined pictures of the Paris Exhibition of 1889." (Müther)

STILLWELL, SARAH S., (I.) is known as the delineator of fully clothed little girls, as for instance the pair investigating the lions' den in the back of a recent Harper.

She was a student in the Drexel Institute in Philadelphia and owes, as do all the younger artists of this group, much to the instruction of Mr. Howard Pyle. She is a close observer of child life; has illustrated a new edition of Mrs. Dodge's "Rhymes and jingles" which shows her characteristic style. She rarely uses other medium than oil in her work.

Her work is done in her Philadelphia studio.

STUART, GILBERT, (P.) b. Narragansett, R. I., December 3, 1755; d. Boston, Mass., July 27, 1828. Began painting at the age of ten and when thirteen years old was commissioned to paint portraits of Mr. and Mrs. John Bannister, which shows his early precocity. His first tutor was a Scotch painter of some note, Cosmo Alexander, who came to Newport when the boy was fifteen. Two years later Stuart traveled through the south with Alexander and later accompanied him to Scotland where he was established in the University of Glasgow and under the care of Sir George Chambers, but both peer and painter died within a short interval of each other, leaving Gilbert alone, friendless and penniless in a strange country; he worked his way back home, reaching his father's house in rags.

In 1775 he went to England where through Benjamin West, who recognized his talent, he obtained much favor and distinction in London. He painted three kings and many celebrated people. His representation of Kemble, the great actor, as "Richard the third," is considered one of the strongest examples of brushwork ever produced in England. Returning to the United States in 1792, he opened a studio in New York.

His famous portrait of Washington—the "Athenaeum portrait"—now in the Boston Museum of Fine Arts, is the only one to be universally accepted as a faithful likeness of the father of his country. The "Gibbs-Channing" Washington—the one showing the right side of the face—is in the Metropolitan Museum of Art, New York.

Gilbert Stuart still holds his place among our best painters, and even among his great contemporaries in England. Tuckerman says: "His best portraits are glimpses of character."

SULLY, THOMAS, (P.) b. Horncastle, Lincolnshire, England, June 8, 1783; d. Philadelphia, Pa., November 5, 1872. His parents were actors and in 1792 with their family of nine children came from England to Charleston, South Carolina. Lawrence Sully, his brother, was a miniature painter in Richmond, Va., and in 1799 Thomas joined him and painted with him until his (Lawrence) death in 1804.

In 1806 he removed to New York; then for a short time resided in Boston for instruction from Gilbert Stuart. He studied under Benjamin West in London in 1809, and settled permanently in Philadelphia in 1810 when he became the most fashionable painter of the day.

He visited England in 1837 and painted a full-length portrait of Queen Victoria. Between 1820-40 he exhibited ten portraits at the Royal Academy.

At an historical portrait exhibition at the Pennsylvania Academy of the Fine Arts, 1887-88, Thomas Sully was represented by 106 pictures, "showing great versatility and extraordinary powers of conception and execution."

"Sully is the.connecting link between the dawn and meridian of American art." (Tuckerman)

"Thomas Sully was called the 'Sir Thomas Lawrence of America.' .... His general style is similar to that of the famous painter of English women."

SYLVESTER, FREDERICK OAKES, (P.) b. Brockton, Mass., October 8, 1869. Mr. Sylvester was professor of drawing and painting at Newcomb College, New Orleans, 1881-2; instructor in drawing in St. Louis high school, 1892-1909. He has done mural work and is the author of "The great river" poems and pictures, but is better known as the "Painter of the Mississippi."

One of his best canvases is of the Eads bridge, St. Louis. The painting was awarded a medal at the St. Louis Exposition, 1904.

SYMONS, GEORGE GARDNER, (P.) b. Chicago, Ill., 1861. He studied art at the Art Institute, Chicago, in Paris, Munich, and London; is a member of the National Academy of Design, Royal Society of British Artists, Union Internationale des Beaux Arts et des Lettres, and Society of Washington Artists; has been warded the Carnegie prize, National Academy of Design; Evans prize, Salmagundi Club; prize and gold medal of National Arts Club and many others.

Several of Mr. Symons' best and most favorably received paintings have been snow scenes and he stands exceptionally high as a snow painter. In his western scenes he shows the gorgeousness of the Grand Canyon or the sombre green of the desert. He has painted the Berkshires in all seasons.

"Mr. Symons has painted many admirable snow scenes but his autumns have an immense charm and poetic quality and his springs a Chaucer-like freshness and undertone of potent life ...... In color Mr. Symons is vivid and powerful and in his distances particularly happy in the sense of far reaching depth and the gradation of values." (Outl 105:886)

"Winter sun" is owned by the Art Institute, Chicago; "Snow clouds," Corcoran Gallery of Art, Washington, D. C.; "Opalescent river," Metropolitan Museum, New York.

"Winter evening" was accorded a position of honor in the 1914 spring exhibition of the National Academy. It shows the late afterglow seen across snowfields and reflected in a brook in the foreground.

Other notable paintings are:

"Winter stood at the gate"
"Rock-ribbed hills in winter"
"Winding river"
"Winter glow"
"Youth"

"Under a blue sky"
"Snow clad fields in morning
light"
"Sorrow"
"The brook"

Mr. Symons is an out-door painter; he does his painting entirely out-of-doors.

"Gardner Symons records the cold, clear effect of New England winter. His line has the rhythmic flow of rivers and the curve of clear-cut mountains. He has a splendid sense of picture-making." (Scrib 72:766)

TAFT, LORADO, (S.) b. Elmwood, Ill., April 29, 1860. He was educated at the University of Illinois where his father, Don Carlos Taft, was a professor of geology. His artistic training was completed in Paris where he studied three years at the Ecole des Beaux Arts.

Mr. Taft has been instructor in the Art Institute of Chicago since 1886; lecturer of art, university extension department, University of Chicago, 1892-1902; professional lecturer on art since 1909. He was elected associate member of the National Academy of Design in 1909; full member, 1911. His "History of American Sculpture" is a standard work.

Mr. Taft's first great success was the commission for two groups which were at the entrance of the Horticultural Building of the World's Columbian Exposition—"The sleep of the flowers" and "The awakening of the flowers." The "Mountains" and the "Prairie" at the St. Louis Exposition were his next conspicuous work; "Solitude of the soul" won for him a gold medal, and is, by some critics, pronounced his finest work.

"The Spirit of the Lakes," the group on the summit of the Ferguson Fountain erected near the Art Institute on the lake front, Chicago, is the first large and purely ideal group erected in America. It represents the great lakes typified by five beautiful female figures grouped on a pyramid of rocks pouring water from shells—"Superior" poised on the summit bends to "Michigan" and "Huron," below are "Erie" and "Ontario."

"The blind," suggested by Maeterlink's "Les aveugles," is placed by scholarly critics among his most important works.

His colossal statue of Washington for the campus of the University of Washington at Seattle, is also an important work. The Columbus

Memorial Fountain which stands on the Plaza in front of the Union station at Washington, D. C., was dedicated in 1915 and is among his later works.

On Eagle's Nest Bluff at Rock River, Ill., a lofty promontory 150 feet high, stands his colossal statue of the Indian Chief Black Hawk. It is made of concrete, is 50 feet high and weighs 300 tons.

One of the greatest civic projects for beautification ever undertaken by a city is nearing completion in Chicago. The Midway Park of the World's Columbian Exposition, 1893, is to be transformed into a beautiful boulevard.

The plan, original with Mr. Taft, contemplates a canal spanned by three bridges of monumental design dedicated to Art, Science, and Religion. Along the roadways at a distance from the bridges will stand statues of the world's greatest idealists treated as architectural notes. At each end will be a large fountain: at the west, "Fountain of Time;" at the east, "Fountain of Creation," all to be the work of Mr. Taft. The "Fountain of Time" is completed and dedicated. It was suggested by a poetic couplet of Austin Dobson:

"Time goes, you say? Oh, no,
Alas, time stays; we go."

Ninety colossal figures seem to advance across an arched bridge which rises from sculptural waves at the north and descend into the surging sea at the south. East of this procession and in front of it is the nearly circular basin of the fountain in which stands the rugged, crag-like figure of "Time."

According to ancient custom, the sculptured portrait of the sculptor appears in one of the groups and thus identifies the work.

The other fountain, "Fountain of Creation," uses the old classic myth of Deucalion, the Noah of Greek religion.

One of Mr. Taft's latest works is a group of colossal figures called "Alma Mater, Learning, and Labor" to stand in the Auditorium building of the University of Illinois, at Urbana. "Alma Mater," a stately draped figure, with outstretched arms welcomes the youth of Illinois; at her left, "Learning" reaches her right hand towards "Labor" on the left.

"Lorado Taft represents a high type of citizenship as well as his professional service to art as sculptor, lecturer, and writer." He is original, impressive, artistic, and emotional.

During the summer of 1923 Mr. Taft lectured for three mornings at the British museum on the Elgin marbles.

TANNER, HENRY OSSAWA, (P.) b. Pittsburgh, Pa., June 21, 1859, the son of the late Bishop B. T. Tanner of the African Methodist church, is an Afro-American painter who became famous in Paris. He studied in the Pennsylvania Academy of the Fine Arts under Thomas Eakins; was a pupil of Jean Paul Laurens and Benjamin-Constant, Paris. Is a member of the Paris Society of American Painters, and Société Internationale Peinture et Sculpture, Paris; elected an associate member of the National Academy of Design, 1909.

Special interest attaches to the work of Henry O. Tanner because he is an American artist of African descent and in all the world the leading painter of his race, having an international reputation deservedly won through merit.

In the World's Work, 1909, Mr. Tanner gives an interesting account of his early experience. Animals and landscape were his first subjects, then he was drawn towards religious subjects, later taking up war subjects and scenes in Tangiers.

Since 1895 he has exhibited every year in the Paris salon.

His first official recognition came in 1896 when his "Daniel in the lion's den" won honorable mention at the salon.

It was his "Raising of Lazarus," purchased by the French government in 1897, that aroused the enthusiasm of artistic Paris and marked his recognition in the art world after twenty years of privation, struggles, and hardships. "Christ and the disciples at Emmaus" has also been placed in the Luxembourg.

In 1898 "The Annunciation" was exhibited and proved one of the successes of the year. "The picture has spirituality so far that it suggests the mystery of the conception." (Caffin in The Artist 24: sup xiv)

In 1900 he showed "Nicodemus coming to Christ." "In his 'Flight of Judas' his idea of dramatic power seems to be carried to the most forceful expression yet achieved; it has the accent of inspiration." (Outl 64:796)

His "Five wise and five foolish virgins" was given a place of honor in the salon of 1908.

Some of his famous Biblical subjects in the United States are:

"Christ at the home of Mary and Martha," Carnegie Institute, Pittsburgh

"Nicodemus," Pennsylvania Academy of the Fine Arts, Philadelphia
"Two disciples at the tomb," Art Institute, Chicago
"The three Marys," Art Institute, Chicago

"Christ walking on the water," Fine Arts Association, Des Moines, Iowa

"Holy family," Hackley Art Gallery, Muskegon, Mich.

Other prominent titles are:

"Jews waiting at the wall of Solomon"
"Stephen before the Council"
"Moses and the Burning Bush"
"The mothers of the Bible (Mary, Hagar, Sarah, Rachel, and the mother of Moses)

"Christ and His disciples on the road to Bethany" is one of the most remarkable of all the pictures for subdued coloring.

M. M. Benjamin-Constant, Gérome, and in fact all the leaders of French painting today have recognized in Mr. Tanner a true artist and man and have cóme to esteem him as much for his personal qualities as for those which he has shown in his work.

An eminent art critic says: "In religious feeling Mr. Tanner seems nearer to Fra Bartolommeo than to any other artist past or present." A marked and welcome quality in all his pictures is atmosphere.

One critic says there is a tendency to regard Mr. Tanner as a Negro artist and so as an object of wonder rather than as a very fine artist who happens to be a Negro.

Mr. Tanner has been called the poet-painter of the Holy Land, having made several trips to the Orient. Palestine is a setting for his Biblical subjects and the object of his sojourns in that land has been to gain an insight into the landscape and types of people.

His early reputation was gained from his Biblical subjects but his later subjects have been other than religious. Moonlight scenes appealed to him first but his "Old gateway, Tangiers," has the dazzling effect of white sunlight. One is reminded of Fortuny. "Neufchateau" is the most interesting of the war-time pictures—a rainy night in France. "The picture has the fine wet quality of a sticky drizzle and all the mystery of night and movement." In "Domremy, 1918" the artist seeks unusual light problems. The picture is of the house of Joan of Arc at dusk while an old woman holds a lantern at the doorway. "Head of a Bethlehem girl" is a souvenir of his last visit to Palestine.

A really great picture is his "Fetes des morts, Paris, July 13, 1919." A night picture represents the great catafalque erected under the Arc d'Triumphe made conspicuous by a strong artificial light against the dark bluish background. A procession of people paying homage to the dead are seen in the dim light.

Tanner's home at Etaples was in the war zone, so in 1917 he brought to the United States twelve of his before-the-war pictures which were exhibited in several art centers of this country.

Miss Clara MacChesney in writing of this gifted Negro artist says: "He is thoroughly romantic in tone and in spirit if not in technique. There is much to connect him with Holman Hunt, the Pre-Raphaelite painter."

Benjamin Brawley in his "Negro in literature and art" closes a chapter on Tanner as follows: "His whole career is an inspiration and a challenge to aspiring painters, and his work is a monument of sturdy endeavor and exalted achievement."

His color is especially distinguished and beautiful.

TARBELL, EDMUND C., (P.) b. Groton, Mass., April 26, 1862. Pupil of Grundmann at the Museum of Fine Arts, Boston; also studied under Boulanger and Lefebvre in Paris. He has been instructor in drawing and painting in the Boston Art Museum since 1889 and been awarded many prizes for his paintings, including Pennsylvania Academy of the Fine Arts medal of honor, 1908, and gold medal of the National Academy of Design, 1908.

Is a member of the Ten American Painters. Associate member National Academy of Design, 1894; full member, 1906.

Tarbell's interiors compare favorably with the paintings of the famous Dutch painters and none better than he has pictured our contemporary home life. Sunlight and atmosphere pervade the rooms which Tarbell pictures. "To Tarbell his art is primarily, almost exclusively, a medium of expression of abstract beauty."

Philip A. Hale, the well known artist critic, wrote in 1898: "Tarbell's 'Venetian blind' is the best picture that has been done in America" and the jury of the Carnegie Institute endorsed this opinion by awarding the picture the gold medal.

"One of the things that makes Tarbell's paintings different from that of other men is the way he treats shadows." (Arts & D 2:129)

Caffin said: "Girl reading" seems a lesson in the holiness of beauty. His art, in fact, has the quality of symbolism by which the modern mind is endeavoring to interpret "the substance of things hoped for, the evidence of things not seen." His vigorous, dashing brush work is always sure to attract attention. This was the principal merit of his prize picture—"The bath."

"Tarbell's characteristics are brilliant versatility, dexterity with the brush, and spontaneousness of effect; all regulated by innate good taste, for he has little or no reserve power." (Artist 27: sup xxvii)

Frederic W. Colburn, in an appreciative article on Tarbell, says: "Among various groups and factors of painters and by the public at large, he has come to be regarded as among the most able of living painters."

In writing of "Girl reading," Julia de Wolf Addison says: "Tarbell is past master in making intentional effects appear quite accidental, giving this picture a peculiarly natural and easy quality both in color and form."

"Tarbell . . . . . . regards the human brain merely as a medium for perceiving effects of light." (Müther)

Kenyon Cox has written: "In the work of Mr. Tarbell there is an elegance of arrangement, a thoroughness in the notation of gradation of light, a beauty and a charm that were learned of no modern."

And again: "The best example of Mr. Tarbell's draughtsmanship is perhaps the head of the 'Girl mending' . . . . . . The head of the girl in 'Preparing for the matinée' is not so fine in type, but its modeling in the delicate half-shadow cast by the hat and the upraised. arms, is nothing less than masterly."

"No one since Vermeer himself has made a flat wall so interesting—has so perfectly rendered its surface, its exact distance behind the figure, the play of light upon it for the amount of air in front of it." (Burlington M 14:259)

Mr. Tarbell was one of the eight American painters selected by the National Art Committee to paint the portraits of the leaders of the World War. He painted the portraits of President Wilson, General Leman of Belgium, Marshal Foch, and Herbert Hoover.

TAYLOR, WILLIAM LADD, (P., I.) b. Grafton, Mass., Dec. 10, 1854. Educated at Worcester, Mass., and in art schools of Boston and New York and studied 1884-85 under Boulanger and Lefebvre, Paris. Traveled extensively, making a particular study of mediaeval architecture, costumes, and customs. Settled in Boston, 1888, and has since that time been a well known painter and illustrator.

The work which has given Mr. Taylor most reputation, and rightly, is his illustration of Owen Meredith's poem entitled "The earl's return."

Illness and a year's sojourn in Colorado resulted in several paintings of the Rocky mountains. "The Caribou hunter" and "Shooting the Rapids" are excellent works of the period.

Recent works as an illustrator are selections from Longfellow's poem, the psalm series, a series of New England scenery, and a book of pictures of American life.

"The boy Christ"
"Evangeline"
"Minnehaha and Hiawatha"
"The village blacksmith"
"The hanging of the crane"
"Maidenhood"
"The old clock on the stairs"

"The building of the ship"
"The golden legend"
"Priscilla and John Alden"
"Rosita" (Illustrating Bret Harte's "The mystery of the hacienda")
"The children's hour"

Psalm series:

"When I consider the heavens." (Ps. viii)
"The Lord is my Shepherd." (Ps. xxiii)
"When I meditate on Thee in the night watches." (Ps. lxiii)
"He shall give his angels charge over thee." (Ps. xci)
"I will lift up mine eyes unto the hills." (Ps. cxxi)
"Children are an heritage of the Lord." (Ps. cxxvii)

THAYER, ABBOTT HENDERSON, (P., Mural P.) b. Boston, Mass., August 12, 1849; d. Monadnock, N. H., May 29, 1921. Began to draw and paint before he was ten years old. He was educated at Chauncy Hall School, Boston, and before he was eighteen received as high as fifty dollars for dog portraits.

He was first known in New York as an animal painter and it was not until he went to Paris (1875) and studied in the Ecole des Beaux Arts under Gérome and Lehmann that he began to make portrait painting a specialty and do some landscape work. Was a member of the Academia de San Luca, Rome, and of the National Academy of Design, New York.

"Sleep," an idealized likeness of his eldest daughter as a sleeping infant, was one of Mr. Thayer's earliest pictures to attract general attention. His three masterpieces are "The virgin," "The virgin enthroned" and "Caritas." (His children were the models.)

His chief work is the finely conceived mural decoration in Bowdoin College, Brunswick, Maine—a fresco representing "Florence" forms one of four lunettes.

A few landscapes are: "Sketch of Cornish headlands," "Capri," "Monadnock in winter." "In these his ability and sensitive feeling for the poetic beauty of nature are evident."

The keynote of his art is simplicity and the chief characteristic of the subjects he chooses is a deep spirited meaning.

"Abbott H. Thayer merited his inimitable position as a painter of the essential spirit of man since no one has fathomed deeper than he the mystery of infusing concrete human beauty with the most elusive of divine significance." (Critic 46:423)

Craftsman: "He paints symbolical figures and groups of great beauty in an austere but impressive style."

"It is however as an interpreter of virginity that this painter is especially distinguished .... His virgins, it has been well said, are obviously intended to be adored, but they are at the same time essentially human." (Int Studio 39:187)

The memorial exhibition at the Metropolitan Museum in 1922 was a large and interesting assembly of his paintings.

He was a great lover of the woods, and a scientific student of beasts and birds. A discovery set forth in his treatise "Concealing coloration of the animal kingdom" became known as "Thayer's law," the application of which brought the art of camouflage into the World War. In 1915 he went overseas to give advice on the concealment of arms and other objects in the field.

The Freer Gallery of Art, Washington, D. C., has fifteen paintings by Thayer in that collection, and the Corcoran Gallery of Art has recently purchased his self-portrait for $10,000, and his "Figure—half draped" has just been sold for $40,000.

Thayer believed that the high mission of the artist is: first to see beauty in nature to which other men may be blind, and then to report truthfully the great facts of nature that he sees. Upon such foundations his success rests.

THAYER, THEODORA W., (Min. P.) b. Milton, Mass., 1868; d. August 6, 1905. Studied with Joseph DeCamp, Boston, and was an active member of the American Society of Miniature Painters and of the Copley Society of Boston; taught for several years in the New York School of Art and was one of the instructors at the Art Students' League; was recognized as one of the best of teachers.

Her fine portrait of Bliss Carman is one of the memorable achievements in American miniature painting. At one of the society's exhibitions, she showed "a wee miniature of a wee speck of humanity, a baby's head painted in a cloud of sweet mist." (Brush & P 6:26)

The Metropolitan Museum of New York City has her portrait of Parke Godwin. "We see a person we should like to know—a charming portrait of an old gentleman, with a mass of white hair that dominates the picture." (Mentor 4:8)

Her work is wonderfully full of character and charm. She painted with grace and nobility of treatment.

TIFFANY, LOUIS COMFORT, (P., Stained-glass designer) b. New York, February 18, 1848. Pupil of George Inness and Samuel Colman in New York and Leon Bailly in Paris. Received gold medal for applied arts at the Paris Exposition, 1900; elected chevalier of the Legion of Honor of France, 1900; grand prize at Turin Exposition, 1904; associate member National Academy of Design, 1871; full member, 1880. Is art director of the Tiffany studios.

It is Mr. Tiffany's achievement in stained glass work that has brought him world fame. It is acknowledged by all experts that the great advance made in this country in both colored windows and wall mosaic work is largely due to the discoveries and inventions of Mr. Tiffany, particularly that of Favrile glass. He has received many personal honors, such as being made a member of the Société National des Beaux Arts, Paris; also of the Imperial Society of Fine Arts, Tokio, Japan.

In painting, Mr. Tiffany makes a specialty of oriental scenes. Well known subjects in oil are:

"Street scene in Tangiers"
"Feeding the flamingoes"
"Dock scene"
"The cobblers at Boufarick"

"Market day at Nuremberg"
"Study of Quimper, Brittany"
"Duane street, New York"

TILDEN, DOUGLAS, (S.) b. Chico, Cal., May 1, 1860. At the age of five he lost his hearing as a result of scarlet fever and was educated in the state institute for the deaf, Berkeley, Cal. He taught in the institute from 1879-87. It was not until 1887 that he took up the study of sculpture. Among his early work, the first to attract favorable comment, was the "Tired wrestler." This he produced while a teacher in the school at Berkeley. In 1887 he went to New York and became a student at the National Academy of Design. Later he went to Paris and became the private pupil of Paul Chopin, himself a deaf mute. After spending seven years in Paris, he returned to the United States and from 1894-1900 was instructor in modeling at the Mark Hopkins Institute of Art, San Francisco.

Mr. Tilden's "Baseball player," in Golden Gate Park, San Francisco, was exhibited in the Paris salon, 1889. "Tired boxer" won honorable mention in the salon of 1899. This work, unfortunately, was destroyed by fire. "Indian bear hunt" was exhibited in the salon, 1892, and has been placed in the grounds of the asylum for the deaf at Berkeley.

Of the last mentioned group, a sympathetic critic says: "Tilden has caught the unmeasured power of the Indian to endure torture unflinchingly; for he represents him as all unheedful of the bear's savage grip upon the bare arm, while he fights for the life of his companion." (Sunset M 30:818)

A recent work of Mr. Tilden's is a monument in honor of Abbe de l'Espee, the first teacher of the deaf. It was seen at the Panama-Pacific Exposition. A statue of Joaquin Miller placed in an Oakland park is his work, and he has also executed commissions for memorial monuments at Portland, Ore., Los Angeles, and San Francisco.

"Considering Mr. Tilden's work as a whole it impresses one principally by its simplicity, directness and strength; its absence of mere sentimental prettiness." (Overl 31:153)

TILLINGHAST, MARY ELIZABETH, (P., Stained-glass designer) b. New York; d. December 15, 1912. Pupil of John LaFarge in New York; Carolus-Duran and Henner in Paris; won several gold and bronze medals. Specialty: designs for stained-glass.

TRUMBULL, JOHN, (P.) b. Lebanon, Conn., June 6, 1756; d. New York, November, 1843. The son of the colonial governor of Connecticut, Jonathan Trumbull, he was the greatest historic painter of America. A graduate of Harvard University, his artistic taste was awakened by familiarity with the portraits of Copley and Smibert. He served with distinction in the armies of Washington and Gates. Early in 1777 he resigned from the army and devoted himself to art as a profession, going to London. In 1784 he conceived the idea of his historical pictures of the revolution and went to Paris where he painted his "Declaration of Independence" assisted by the information and advice of Thomas Jefferson.

In 1789 he returned to America. As an inaugurator of serious historical painting, Trumbull bore a very worthy part, and he carried portraiture to its highest limits by making portraits from life for all the chief figures introduced into his canvases. His portrait of General Washington (in the New Haven collection) must be regarded as a standard portrait of the father of his country. When Lafayette first beheld a copy of his picture on his visit to this country in 1824, he was delighted with its resemblance. Tuckerman says: "The most spirited portrait of Washington that exists—the only reflection of him as a soldier of freedom in his mature years, worthy of the name, drawn from life—is Trumbull's."

Trumbull was commissioned to paint four of the eight commemorative pictures in the capitol at Washington. He was eight years at the task and received $32,000 for the four paintings:

"Declaration of Independence"   "Surrender of General Burgoyne"
"Surrender of Lord Cornwallis"   "Resignation of Washington"

Other important historical paintings are: "Battle of Bunker Hill," "Death of General Montgomery," "Battle of Trenton," "Battle of Princeton."

"Trumbull's works still hold their rank not only for their historical interest but for their artistic merit." Critics rank his "Death of Montgomery" as the most spirited battle-piece ever painted. His portrait of Alexander Hamilton is one of the best portraits he ever did.

Trumbull was the first president of the Academy of Arts, New York.

TRYON, DWIGHT WILLIAM, (P.) b. Hartford, Conn., August 13, 1849. Pupil of C. Daubigny, Jacquesson de la Chevreuse, A. Guillemet, and H. Harpignies in Paris. Has received many prizes and medals. His "First leaves" was awarded the Webb prize in 1889, and his "Rising moon" won the first-class medal at the Munich International Exposition in 1892. He is professor of art in Smith College.

Mr. Tryon has added much to the world's store of poetic interpretation of nature. Equally refined as his "poems of early spring" are his moonlight scenes and his snowy landscapes. He has interpreted sunsets, storms, mountains, and rugged nature with as powerful a brush as has any painter.

"The objective world, its primitive and elemental grandeur, the naked truth of nature, as we see it in the works of other artists, concerns him not at all. His art is subjective and his interest is in the spiritual significance of the visible world as it is made intelligible in immaterial beauty . . . . . . His pictures are not so much remarkable as representations of the world in which we live as they are illuminating as expressions of something of the infinity of beauty that like a halo surrounds the earth.

"The 'Early morning—September, 1904' and the 'Twilight—November, 1912' show the development of his art and are representative examples of the later period. In them one discerns an individual type of landscape and the evidences of a rare technic which he has all but perfected." (Art in Am 7:38)

Examples of Mr. Tryon's work are permanently placed as follows:

"End of the day"—Corcoran Gallery, Washington, D. C.
"Moonrise at sunset"—Metropolitan Museum, New York City
"Spring morning"—Toledo, Ohio
"Autumn sunset"—Worcester, Mass.
"Evening"—Pennsylvania Academy of the Fine Arts, Philadelphia
"November morning"—Herron Art Institute, Indianapolis, Ind.
"Evening in May"—Albright Art Gallery, Buffalo, N. Y.
"Before sunrise—June"—Institute of Arts, Detroit, Mich.
"Rising moon"—Hackley Art Gallery, Muskegon, Mich.

"In his pictures may be seen, as in Daubigny's, a silvery grey atmosphere against which the tracery of young foliage stands out in relief, green shining meadows and softly rippling streams, cornfields, apple trees and fruit gardens." (Müther)

"In his earlier period Tryon's tones were dark. He loved black nights with troubled skies, a yellow morn casting fitful gleams over the hard and rough old earth ...... Tryon's art is the perfect expression of his personality. ...... The best landscapes of Dwight Tryon more or less unconsciously combine subtlety with precision ......

"Tryon might have been either a realist or a mystic if the two dominant qualities had not hung so persistently in the balance. It is just the perfect balance between the well-informed, plain spoken observer of facts and the scrupulous artist selecting lovingly and with delicate perception his chosen moment, which distinguishes the expression of Tryon from that of many other painters of similar subjects." (Am M of Art 9:391)

TUCKER, ALLEN, (P.) b. Brooklyn, N. Y., June 29, 1866. He has exhibited at the Paris salon and international exhibitions held in New York.

"The two painters who appear most obviously to have affected the work of Allen Tucker are Monet and Van Gogh ...... It is the landscapes by Allen Tucker that most successfully indicate his attainments ...... But it is Mr. Tucker's portraits that perhaps most clearly illustrate both his strongest and his weakest points."

"Ice storm," one of his characteristic landscapes, is "brilliant in key and delicate in color." (Int Studio 52: sup xix)

TURNER, CHARLES YARDLEY, (P., Mural P.) b. Baltimore, Md., November 25, 1850; d. New York City, January 1, 1919. In 1872 he went to New York and entered the National Academy of Design. After spending three years in the school and taking a bronze medal and a money prize, he went to Paris and studied under Laurens, Munkaczy, and Bonnat. In Holland he found the subject of his famous picture, "The grand canal at Dordrecht;" his best water-color is "Dordrecht milkmaid."

Mr. Turner was assistant director of decoration at Columbian Exposition, Chicago, 1893, and director of color at the Pan-American Exposition, Buffalo, 1901, and a member of the National Academy of Design.

His finest mural work is a series of wall paintings in the corridor of the Baltimore court house, the subject of which is the incident of the brig Peggy Stewart entering the harbor of Annapolis in 1774.

His puritan subjects are particularly fine, and great favorites. Most noted are:

"Courtship of Miles Standish"	"The bridal procession"
"John Alden's letter"	"Martha Hilton"

Mr. Turner painted four panels for the Capitol at Madison, Wis. The subject is "Transportation" and depicts the earliest mode of travel from the primitive canoe to the most modern automobile.

His mural work is also on the hotels Manhattan, Waldorf-Astoria, Martinique, and Bank of Commerce building, New York.

TURNER, HELEN M., (P., Min. P.) b. Louisville, Kentucky. Studied with Kenyon Cox. Elected associate member of National Academy of Design in 1913; full member in 1921.

Her miniature, "Girl with the green shawl," is in the Metropolitan Museum, New York City; and "Girl with lantern" in the Corcoran Gallery, Washington, D. C. "Flower girl" was awarded second Altman prize in 1921.

Miss Turner exhibited at a recent exhibition in New York City her latest canvas, "A lady reading," which was one of the outstanding pictures of the exhibition. Other canvases exhibited were: "The blonde," "The Italian," "Woman in blue," and "The Russian" which is a young Slavic girl of strange beauty.

Miss Turner is noted for the soft light of her interiors and the golden radiance of her sunshine.

TURNER, ROSS STERLING, (P., I.) b. Westport, N. Y., June 29, 1847; d. Nassau, Bahamas, February 12, 1915. Studied in Munich and in Italy. Was instructor Massachusetts Normal Art School and Massachusetts Institute of Technology.

A few of his best known works in oil and water colors are:

"A small court in Mexico"	"Flying Dutchman"
"El Jardin, Modesto"	"A Bermuda wedding"
"A painted ship"	

The inspiration for his "Golden galleon" is said to have been derived from Lockhart's Spanish ballad, "Count Arnaldo's gallery."

"Above and beyond any qualities he possesses, and they are many, Ross Turner is a colorist. His is the rare sense which discriminates between 'colors' and 'color.'"

TWACHTMAN, JOHN HENRY, (P.) b. Cincinnati, O., August 4, 1853; d. Gloucester, Mass., August 8, 1902. Pupil of the National Academy of Design, New York, and of Frank Duveneck in Munich and Italy; studied also at the Académie Julien and under Boulanger and Lefebvre, Paris.

He won the Webb prize, 1888; Temple gold medal, 1895; and was a member of the American Art Club, Munich. In 1898 he founded the organization known as the Ten American Painters.*

Caffin says: "In his 'Brook in winter' it is the soul, as it were, of the still cold dormant world that he has rendered. Never has been better expressed through the subtle resources of modern methods of painting the suggestion of the abstract."

His artistic qualities are also well represented in

"The hemlock pool"   "The end of winter"
"Drying sails"   "Round Hill road"
"The torrent"   "Landscape in spring"

"He recognized as few can, the poetic side of snowy pastures and snow-bound woodland rills and marshes. His painting of the damp winter weather surcharged with latent snowfall has never been surpassed." (Innes "School of Painting")

"In his handling of the elements of natural scenery, particularly in representing snow upon the branches of trees, he shows a high degree of skill." (Nat Cyc Am Biog)

Mr. Twachtman is supposed to have been the first American artist to employ blue shadows.

From "An appreciation" published in the North American Review shortly after the death of Mr. Twachtman, the following extract is made:

"In defining the quality of Twachtman's paintings, one would say that, first of all he was a master of 'values'—as much so as Whistler ...... One of his paintings instantly arrests the eye of the connoisseur by a certain espect, as original as Thoreau, and sometimes curiously like him." (T. W. Dewing)

"The great beauty of design which is conspicuous in Twachtman's paintings is what impressed me always ...... His use of line was rhythmic, and the movements were always graceful ...... His work as color had delicate refinement and truth." (Childe Hassam)

"He painted as all men have done who have made great art; he painted the atmosphere of his time." (Robert Reid)

"In the death of John H. Twachtman we lose one of our best landscape painters ...... The canvases which Twachtman has left us, like all

---

*Society of the Ten American Painters was organized January, 1898. No particular aim except that of exhibiting independently of juries once a year. Original members; Benson, DeCamp, Dewing, Hassam, Metcalf, Reid, Simmons, Tarbell, Twachtman, Weir.

work of signally original merit, may prove for a time too fine a food for the general palate." (Edward Simmons)

"To my mind, he was in advance of his age to the extent that like many others, he lived ahead of his epoch." (J. Alden Weir)

"No one has rendered the mysterious stillness of winter as he [Twachtman]; no one in American art has painted such beautiful whites, such elusive silvery greys, in which translucent halflights play endless variations. (J. Nilsen Laurvik)

None of our landscape painters surpass him in subtle delineation of atmospheric effects and values generally. To many art critics, Mr. Twachtman ranks as the greatest American landscape painter.

UFER, WALTER, (P.) b. Louisville, Kentucky, July 22, 1876. Studied in Chicago, Dresden, Munich, and Paris. Associate member National Academy of Design; also president of the Taos Society of Artists.

A one-man show of Mr. Ufer's paintings was held last year in Chicago. Several of the canvases indicated that Mr. Ufer is breaking into the field of modernists. The four outstanding were: "A June storm," "Fructuation" (symbolic), "The rider—Taos Canyon," and "My back yard."

" 'The rider—Taos Canyon' is the new Ufer because in it representation is freer in the sense that it is more abandoned to the rhythmic element; and because as a result of that abandon the movement plays more elaborately throughout every part." (The Arts 2:286)

"Hunger" and "Autumn" are recent interpretations of the life and the scene of his field of work in the southwest. In his "By the window" he brings together incongruous elements of civilization and savagery by giving a stolid Indian woman a background of a typically American room.

The American Magazine of Art, December, 1922, closes a long and interesting article on this "new-comer" in American art as follows: "Ufer is a many-sided painter, equally clever in handling the landscape and the figure. There is an incredible variety in the subject matter; his power of selection is a great factor in his being a big man. One feels that he is free, unbiased, a determined, untiring investigator, a man who has come a long way toward artistic excellence but whose effort will lead him to the highest point of achievement."

"Solemn pledge—Taos Indians" is in the Chicago Art Institute; "Don Pedro de Taos" in the Brooklyn Institute of Arts and Sciences; "Artist and model" in the Pennsylvania Academy of Fine Arts; and "Suzanna and her sister" in the Maryland Institute, Baltimore.

"His Indians are perhaps the least posed, the least self-conscious of all the Indians painted today."

ULRICH, CHARLES FREDERICK, (P.) b. N. Y., October 18, 1858; d. Berlin, Germany, May 15, 1908. Studied at the National Academy of Design in New York and with Loefftz and Lindenschmidt in Munich. In 1884 he was the first recipient of the Clark prize at the National Academy of Design and this picture, "The land of promise," now belongs to the National Gallery of Art, Washington, D. C.

His painting "The glass blowers of Murano" is now in the Metropolitan Museum of Art, N. Y., and marked the climax of his success.

An associate member National Academy of Design, 1883.

He resided in Venice for many years and was recognized in art circles in Germany, France, and England.

"Critics praised his pictures for their exquisite technique, their finish in detail, their purity of color and their strength of character."

VAIL, EUGENE, (P.) was born of American parents at Saint Servan, Brittany, September 29, 1856; studied in Art Students' League, N. Y., under Carrol Beckwith and William M. Chase and at Ecoles des Beaux Arts, Paris, under Cabanal; later under Dagnan-Bouveret and Raphael Collin. Medals, prizes, and distinguishing honors have come to Mr. Vail in recognition of his artistic ability.

Four scenes of seafaring life, very beautiful in color and among the very strongest and best pictures of the kind at the Paris Exposition, 1900, were "Ready about," "Port of Concarneau," "The widow," and "On the Thames."

Other admired works are:

"The hour of prayer"   "A rainy day"
"Evening in Brittany"   "Twilight"
"Autumn near Beauvais"   "Rio della Madonetta, Venice"
"Chemin de foi"

Vail's landscapes are marked by an exquisite sense of nature, at once delicate and full of force. The fisherfolk of Brittany are a favorite subject with him.

Müther says that Vail was influenced by Mesdag and DeNittis in his Dutch sea-pieces and pictures of the port of London, which are shrouded in a heavy, melancholy mist.

Caffin says: "Eugene Vail while seeing into the soul of his subjects, views it with a personal sympathy and interprets, so to speak, in terms of spirit rather than matter. That is to say, he does not compel your attention to the physical properties of the figures and the landscape; he envelopes the whole in atmosphere, enriching it with sombre but tenderly impressive harmony of color; so that the picture is as full of mystery as of suggestion. It puts us into spirit-communion with the place and its inhabitants; which as I understand it, involves a superior knowledge and at the same time an acknowledgment of how much there is unknowable. It represents the vision of a poet."

VAN ELTEN, HENDRICK DIRK KRUSEMAN, (P., E.) b. Alkmaar, Holland, 1829; d. Paris, France, July 12, 1904. When fifteen years of age was sent to Haarlem to study painting under C. Lieste, a landscape painter of repute. He won a gold medal at the International Exhibition at Amsterdam in 1860 and was made a chevalier of the Order of the Lion of the Netherlands. He was a member of the Amsterdam and Rotterdam academies; came to New York in 1865; was elected a member of the National Academy in 1883; also a member of the American Water Color Society, New York Etching Club, and the Royal Society of Painter-Etchers of London.

S. R. Koehler writes in the American Art Review, 1880; "Perhaps it would be permissible to class him as an 'international' artist, for at the Centennial Exhibition of 1876 he exhibited as an American in the American department and as a Hollander in that of the Netherlands ...... Mr. Van Elten's claim to be considered an American was long ago recognized by the National Academy of Design by his election in 1871 to the position of an associate in that body .... In his choice of subjects Mr. Van Elten seems to betray the Dutch blood that flows in his veins. He loves the flat expanse of the grain fields and the meadows, the quiet copse, the dilapidated hut or the river bank grown with reeds in which the fisherman may hide his boat, and he finds these subjects both here and in his native Holland."

A group of 200 of his paintings was sold at the American Art Galleries in New York, April 27 and 28, 1905, under the auspices of the Artists' Aid Society of New York, bringing $9,335.

VAN INGEN, WILLIAM BRANTLEY, (Mural P.) b. Philadelphia, Pa., August 30, 1858. Pupil of Eakins in Philadelphia; LaFarge in New York; Bonnat in Paris. Member Mural Painters; fellowship Pennsylvania Academy of the Fine Arts.

His best known mural work is a series of sixteen panels in the senate chamber of the state house, Trenton, N. J., entitled "The cause of independence and prosperity." "He has done much mural work in private residences in Philadelphia."

"His attack of the subject is bold and candid, his sketches carefully wrought, his brushwork adequate." (Arch Rec 13:323)

VEDDER, ELIHU, (P., S., I., Mural P.) b. New York, February 26, 1836; d. Rome, Italy, January 29, 1923. His parents' ancestry was in the Netherlands. It is related that as a child he chewed sticks into brushes and spent his money for cheap paints. Very early he received instructions in art and in 1856 he went to Europe, spending the winter in Paris studying in the atelier of Picot. In the following spring he went to Italy and had a few lessons in drawing from Buonajuti, in Florence. He received no further instructions but he spent four years there, returning to the United States in 1861. He was elected an associate member of the National Academy of Design in 1863; full member in 1865; and is said to be the youngest painter so honored.

It was during the Civil War, while in this country, that he imagined and created "The question of the Sphinx," "The fisherman and the genii," "The roc's egg," and "The lair of the sea serpent" and it has been said of these productions, "Few young painters have ever made a more solid and brilliant debut in imaginative design."

In 1866 Mr. Vedder returned to Rome and in that city and at his villa on the Island of Capri he resided until his death, rarely exhibiting in the United States.

Frank Jewett Mather, Jr., in writing of Vedder and his work divides it into three periods: Early imaginative pictures, 1863-1865; The Omar illustrations, 1883-1884; Murals, 1893-1897.

"A note of mystery, a recognition of the infinite and unknowable forms a characteristic of Vedder's work ...... It is calm, virile, intellectual, a mystery of which Darwin and Huxley might well approve." (Isham)

His illustrations of Edward Fitzgerald's translation of the "Rubaiyàt of Omar Khayyam," published in 1884, won him world-wide renown. Vedder called these illustrations "Accompaniments."

Mather says: "No painter of the century with the single exception of George Frederic Watts, has found such vivid and convincing symbols for those great reflective emotions which, if we will, are ours simply by our rights as human beings."

Elizabeth Luther Cary says: "His human forms are the abodes of foreign spirits, great unhuman powers personified ...... His mind is of an austere tendency and he holds us to the contemplation of these abstractions with an almost noble, but seldom fiery, line and without allurements of color or surface."

Vedder's "Head of Lazarus" is the best representative of his decorative art; "Sea serpent" shows his naturalistic painting, and in his "Sphinx" he becomes realistic in portrayal. Of his "Keeper of the threshold" an enthusiastic admirer says that if it is possible for a picture to hypnotize, he feels sure that this one has such power. "Its fascination for me is as

strong even yet, and I am still under its spell though an ocean lies
between us."

A few other characteristic paintings are:

"The African sentinel"   "Cumean sibyl"
"The monk upon the gloomy   "The lost mind"
  path"   "The crucifixion"
"The death of Abel"   "Greek actor's daughter"
"A scene on the Mediterranean"   "Young Marsyas"

In the Library of Congress Vedder's work consists of the mosaic of
Minerva and five lunettes representing Good and Bad Government and
their results. The lunette of "Anarchy" is considered one of the best
things in mural painting of the century. "The joy of ruthless destruction, of a power that has passed beyond human good and evil, could not
be better expressed."

His murals in the Walker Art Gallery at Bowdoin College has Nature
for the theme. In the style of the renaissance are personifications of
sculpture, architecture, poetry, harmony, love and painting.

He also accepted at that time a commission to decorate the New York
residence of C. P. Huntington. The subject chosen was the "Sun with
the four seasons."

"Elihu Vedder's contribution to the development of the time will
always be connected with that Italy of his first love and of the best
years of his life." (Nation 116:206)

"As it is, it may seem enough that he was the greatest intellectualist
painter of America in his day, and with few rivals among his contemporaries anywhere. With all his limitations—and painfully he knew
them—he had, in Mr. Brownell's words, emphatically expressed his own
'native inclination for whatever is large and noble in form' and as well
'a penetrating feeling for beauty in its full rather than in its fleeting
aspects.' " (Scrib M 74:128)

Vedder wrote his delightful autobiography in 1910, some poetry in
1914, and "Doubts and other things" in 1921. The last publication, a
thing of beauty, was placed in his hands the evening before he died.

His studio in Rome was a place of fascination for his friends and
acquaintances, and American tourists regarded it as a distinguishing
honor to be invited to attend one of his famous receptions.

VINTON, FREDERIC PORTER, (P.) Bangor, Maine, January 29, 1846;
d. Boston, Mass., May 19, 1911. Pupil of William Hunt and Dr. Rimmer
in Boston, Bonnat and Jean Paul Laurens in Paris, also at the Royal

Academy of Bavaria, where he studied under Mauger and Dietz. Honorable mention in Paris salon, 1890; member of the National Academy of Design, 1891.

"The early life of Mr. Vinton was passed in mercantile business in Boston, but the later years were devoted entirely to art. At a memorial exhibition of 124 of his paintings held at the Museum of Fine Arts, Boston, fifty were portraits.

"Vinton's sterling qualities as a portrait painter are well known. He was a strong, incisive, and thorough draughtsman, a serious and studious observer, with a deep respect for his art and for himself as an artist."

"His grasp of character in his men sitters—and he was almost exclusively a painter of men—is in the best of his portraits ...... and on a par with that of the great portrait painters. A large number of men who sat for him were statesmen, jurists, philanthropists, authors, soldiers, and successful professional men." (Art & P 3:474)

"His landscapes were made chiefly for recreation, for play, and in the intervals of more arduous undertakings. Based upon a silvery gray principle of coloring, they were delicate and sober, but free from dullness and heaviness."

VOLK, DOUGLAS, (P.) b. Pittsfield, Mass., February 23, 1856. When fourteen years of age accompanied his parents to Rome where he became interested in painting and studied in the Saint Luke Academy. In 1873 studied in Paris with Gérome. His "In Brittany" was exhibited in the salon of 1875.

He was instructor in Cooper Institute, New York, 1879-84; has been awarded many medals and prizes; was elected associate member of the National Academy of Design, New York, in 1898; full member in 1899.

He writes and lectures on the subject of art with a view to the introduction of more artistic methods and a higher standard of teaching as opposed to the usual mechanical system in art institutions.

"Mr. Volk is a figure painter who relies upon the subject of his work to suggest Americanism."

Generally he paints a bit of the pine forest, rude and solemn, and places in it a girl or boy with such differences of motive as are suggested by the titles:

"Song of the pines"	"Thoughts of youth"
"The woodland maid"	"Accused of witchcraft"
"A winter walk"	"Young pioneer"
"The boy with the arrow"	"A belle of the colonies"
"A colonial youth"	

"The spirit of the nation's past and of its best hopes for the future seems to be figured in these types." (Artist 29: sup xx)

Mr. Volk was one of the eight American painters selected by the National Art Committee to make portraits of the distinguished leaders of America and of the allied nations for a pictorial record of the World War. His work was the portraits of King Albert of Belgium, Premier Lloyd George, and General Pershing.

VONNOH, BESSIE POTTER, (Mrs. Robert W. Vonnoh), (S.) b. St. Louis, Mo., August 17, 1872. Pupil of Chicago Art Institute under Lorado Taft. Spent four months in Paris in 1895 and four months in Florence in 1897. Was married to Robert William Vonnoh, September 17, 1899. Is a member of the National Sculpture Society, and was elected an associate member of the National Academy of Design in 1906.

Mrs. Vonnoh's specialty is modeling diminutive portraits. Her work is suggestive of the figurines done in terra cotta by the sculptors of Tanagra, whose work was entirely unknown to her when she began her little figures. She presents modern life and modern costumes and conditions. Her work is impressionistic, suggesting character without expressing it. For representation of joy and buoyancy of childhood, for idealization of maternal love, for the art that speaks to us from within, Bessie Potter Vonnoh has not been surpassed by men or women.

"Mrs. Vonnoh's 'figurines' and little groups have the bigness of true plastic conceptions and at the same time that exquisite refinement possible only to works of small scale. Because of inherent merit the question of size does not signify. These bronzes have a charm and grace peculiarly their own. Her young mothers are essentially maternal, her young women delightfully feminine, yet womanly, her children are childish, lovable, sincere. Thus in her little groups, Mrs. Vonnoh touches upon those human relationships which are elemental, and stirs emotions both deep and profound. Her message is delivered with a lightness of touch and outward serenity, but it makes universal appeal." (Art & P 4:819)

Of her figurines seen at an exhibition last summer, a New York correspondent writes with discriminating appreciation: "One might say that she is the originator of an American genre in which small size does not for a moment imply either a trifling imagination or a petty rendering ...... It is the small things that most severely test discrimination."

"It has been her aim to sound the human note sweetly and reticently, without a sacrifice of a certain degree of gentle strength. She achieves the precious and delightful distinction of that kind of inconspicuousness which signifies proportion and restraint." (Int Studio 54: sup lii)

"The sketch" is noted for the realistic stare of the infant; "Enthroned" is unsurpassed portraiture of motherhood; "Fountain of youth" is a group of happy children.

Her bronzes have charm of subject and competence of craftsmanship. "Bust of baby" shows how vigorous Mrs. Vonnoh's art is, just as such figures as "The dance" and "Grecian draperies" reveal its grace, while "A young mother" and "His first journey" illustrate her warm human knowledge and sympathies.

"Perhaps the most remarkable power of Mrs. Vonnoh is seen in her treatment of the eyes of her statuettes. In a way quite inexplicable to the layman, she secures the most lifelike expression of eyes which on examination are seen not to possess any of the details of anatomy."

VONNOH, ROBERT WILLIAM, (P.) b. Hartford, Conn., September 17, 1858. Pupil of Massachusetts Normal Art School, Boston; also of Académie Julien, Paris, under Boulanger and Lefebvre. Instructor Massachusetts Normal Art School, Boston; Cowles Art School; Boston Museum of Fine Arts; Pennsylvania Academy of the Fine Arts. A member of the National Academy of Design, 1906.

Exhibited in the salons of 1888, 1889, 1890, 1891. Received honorable mention, 1888; medal at Paris Exposition, 1889. Exhibited several years at Munich expositions. Specialty; portraits.

After studying at Grez sur Loing, near the Forest of Fontainebleau he said: "I gradually came to realize the value of first impressions and the necessity of correct values, pure color and higher key, resulting in my soon becoming a devoted disciple of the new movement in painting." (Nat Cyc Am Biog)

Some highly decorative compositions are:

"Hydrangeas"   "In costume"
"Reverie"   "Phoebe"

"In his technique the artist is never ponderous, on the contrary there is a degree of elegance which shows the discrimination and elasticity of his mind." (Harper 116:254)

During the many years that he was instructor in portrait and figure painting in the Pennsylvania Academy of the Fine Arts, many of our well-known artists were pupils of his. In his portrait work Mr. Vonnoh has an enviable record, having painted by commission over five hundred portraits, many being of prominent and distinguished persons.

His portrait of his wife, the gifted sculptor, Bessie Potter Vonnoh, won the Proctor prize at the National Academy of Design in 1904 and has since been purchased by the Brooklyn Museum.

His "In Flanders fields," painted before the World War, is in the museum at Youngstown, Ohio. "Fantasy—blue and yellow," a girl in Chinese costume, is owned by the Los Angeles Museum.

"In his landscapes one sees a fine envelopment of atmosphere. They carry out the advice which he frequently gives to his pupils of not painting the sky down to the horizon line but down to the foreground." (Int Studio 77:232)

"Leah," a nude study, is a beautiful piece of modeling and painting of sunlight on flesh; "Sandman's a-comin'" is a delightful picture of a mother reading to a sleepy child; "Summer morn" is exquisite in mood and tone.

The Metropolitan Museum of Art, New York, has purchased Mr. Vonnoh's canvas "La mère Adèle." "It is one of the artist's first studies of old age, showing the old French cook in her black hooded cape, her keen eyes and tightly clenched hand giving evidence of undiminished nervous vitality."

WALDEN, LIONEL, (P.) b. Norwich, Conn., May 22, 1862. Studied with Carolus-Duran, Paris. Received honorable mention in the Paris salon; silver medal at Paris Exposition, 1900; third-class medal in salon of 1903.

Represented in the Luxembourg Gallery, Paris; Memorial Museum, Philadelphia; and Art Gallery, Cardiff, Wales.

Member of the Société Internationale de Peinture et Sculpture, Société de Peintre de Marine, Paris, and Society of Paris American Painters.

A noteworthy American in Paris, Mr. Walden is a painter of marine scenes and a proficient delineator of shipping and harbor life; has also painted some figure and landscape subjects, such as:

"The torrent"   "Out for a sail"
"The end of winter"   "Summer evening"

"Night on the Mount of Olives" is one of his pictures exhibited in the Paris salon.

WALKER, HENRY OLIVER, (P., Mural P.) b. Boston, Mass., May 14, 1843. After a common school education he took up mercantile pursuits, but soon gave up this line of work for the profession of art, going to Paris in 1879 to study under M. Bonnat. Returned to the United States three years later; settled in Boston but later removed to New York City.

Member of the Society of American Artists and of the National Academy of Design. In 1894 he received the Shaw fund prize for "The Singers," and the following year, the Clark prize for "A morning vision." "The boy and the muse" is another celebrated picture. Aside from his reputation as a figure painter, Mr. Walker is well known for his achievements in mural painting. His best wall decorations are to be seen in the Library of Congress, Washington, D. C.; appellate courts, New York; the Massachusetts and Minnesota state capitols.

WALKER, HORATIO, (P.) b. Listowel, Ont., 1858. Studied miniature painting under J. A. Fraser, Toronto, also in New York. Has been awarded medals at exhibitions in Paris and United States. Member of the Royal Institute of Painters in Water-Colors, England; also member of the National Academy of Design, New York, since 1891. Largely self-taught, his achievement constitutes one of the most notable conquests in the history of art.

He paints the rustic life of the peasant types on the Isle of Orleans in the St. Lawrence river. His subjects are the same as Millet's but he treats them in a more impersonal manner. "To Walker these peasants going to their daily tasks are a symbol of the eternal stability of life, of a quiet harmony with nature's laws."

"Horatio Walker handles his brush broadly. His color is always rich, pure and true, whether inclining to the sombre and deeper notes, or to brighter keys where it is joyous and vibrating, full of the intimate charm of sunshine." He combines realism and classicism to a decorative as well as a suggestive art, which satisfies the most modern taste."

Characteristic works are:

"Morning milking"	"A summer pastoral"
"Wood cutters"	"The harrower"
"Oxen drinking"	"Hauling the log"
"Shepherdess and sheep"	"Tree fellers"
"Sheepfold"	"A spring morning"
"The potato pickers"	"Man felling a tree"
"Girl feeding turkeys"	"Sheepyard—moonlight"
	"The thresher"

"Walker's art while immediately concerned with the local and individual character of that portion of the visible world he has chosen for his particular study, is concerned also with beauty in the abstract, and with the psychological relation of what is finite and temporary to that which we conceive to be universal and eternal." (Caffin)

"Harmony is the word which sums up the character of Walker's art; he interprets in harmonies of color."

Mr. Walker exhibited at the Royal Academy, London, in 1901 and of one of the collection, a leading art journal said: "Mr. Horatio Walker shows a Millet-like realism which is yet charged with poetry Charm, the outcome of power, and not of mere desire to achieve the pretty, is the characteristic of this water-color. England should give welcome to Horatio Walker."

"Always there is a sense of color in his canvases, even when the evening is grey or the morning misty."

It has been said that he has done for the farmers of Canada what Millet did for the peasants of Barbizon and of Normandy—caught the wonder and the greatness of their patient toil.

WALKER, NELLIE VERNE, (S.) b. Red Oak, Ia., December 8, 1874. Her father was a marble cutter and as a child and a young girl she played and experimented with the material and implements of the trade. At the age of sixteen she elected to become a sculptor and studied with Lorado Taft and at the Art Institute, Chicago.

Portrait busts and ideal groups for memorials are her specialty. One of her finest groups is "Her son"—"a mother gazing in awe and amazement at her son who stands erect, elated with the vision which he may not share with her .... He is the son of her body but his spirit transcends her in knowledge and in dreams."

The Stratton monument, Colorado Springs, Col.; memorials of the Diggins family, Cadillac, Mich.; and the Decker family, Battle Creek, Mich.; and a statue of Chief Keokuk at Keokuk, Ia., are well known.

Miss Walker is a member of the Chicago Society of Artists, Society of Western Artists, and the National Sculpture Society.

WALTER, MARTHA, (P.) b. Philadelphia, Pa. Studied art in the Philadelphia Art School and with William M. Chase; also a pupil of the Julien Academy and the Grande Chaumiére in Paris.

Miss Walter has won many prizes and has the distinction of winning the first award of the Cresson traveling scholarship in 1908 which made it possible for her to travel and study in Germany, Holland, Italy, and Spain. For a short time she had a studio in Paris and received criticism from Prinet and Simon Ménaud. She exhibited in the Paris salon and her pictures are now to be seen in exhibitions held in the cities of the United States. In 1909 she won the Mary Smith prize for the best work by a woman.

Miss Walter has been called the painter of joyous children. "She can never depict poignant misery without some note of cheer."

A few of her best known pictures are:

"Fresh air children"   "A parasol tea"
"Brittany family"   "The outing"
"The shore"   "Motherhood"

"She has a sense of form as well as of color, a feeling for composition which is rather rare and she has attained to a mastery of the tools of her profession which places her in a position to attain the highest in the artist's career .... Her brush work is broad and applied without hesitation, avoiding as far as possible the less important details." (Arts & D 1:303)

"Miss Walter shows all the range of tone white may have, from the sunlit white of a summer gown to the grey hues of a white dress in shadow ...... Her use of color is delightful, her treatment of draperies is broad and free." (Int Studio 52: sup xlii)

"Indeed color, air, light, and motion are Miss Walter's strong points and she is very clever with her little sketches of beaches with their tiny figures.

It all starts with Potthast and ends up with something very suggestive of Boldini." (American Art News)

WARD, JOHN Q. A., (S.) b. near Urbana, Champaign Co., Ohio, 1830; d. New York, May 1, 1910. Displayed a talent for plastic art at an early age. Studied under H. K. Brown in Brooklyn, N. Y., remaining his pupil for six years. In 1857 made his first sketch for "The Indian hunter" now in Central Park, New York, studying his subjects in the aboriginal state. In 1861 opened a studio in New York; was elected associate member of the National Academy of Design in 1862; full member in 1863 and president in 1874. Was first president of National Sculpture Society, 1896, and was reelected to the office for many years.

In 1866 he executed the group of "The good Samaritan" now in Boston, in honor of the discovery of anaesthetics, and in 1867 presented his design for the Shakespeare statue in Central Park, New York.

His "Freedman" was an early work, and of this bronze statuette, Jarves says: "We have seen nothing in our sculpture more soul-lifting or more comprehensively eloquent."

Tuckerman says: "Although Mr. Ward has never practiced modeling in any academy or foreign or famed studio, he has labored with rare assiduity to master the principles of his art. He understands porportion and anatomical conditions."

In the field of portrait statuary, Mr. Ward is one of the masters of the day. Perhaps his finest achievement in this field is the statue of Henry Ward Beecher in Borough Hall Park, Brooklyn; also statue of Commodore Perry at Newport, R. I., and statue of Israel Putman of Hartford, Conn.

Other triumphs are:

"Horace Greeley" in front of the Tribune building, "Washington" on the steps of the Sub-Treasury in Wall street, and "Roscoe Conkling" in Union Square, New York City.

"Lafayette," Burlington, Vt.

"William Gilmore Simms" (a southern author), Charleston, S. C.

Equestrian statues of General Thomas and General Sheridan, also colossal figure representing "Poetry" and the Michelangelo in the Library of Congress, Washington, D. C.

A statue of General Sheridan has recently been unveiled in Albany, N. Y. The model was Mr. Ward's last work and was completed before his death.

"Mr. Ward is essentially a sculptor ...... His technique may lack at times that charm of surface manipulation in which his younger colleagues excel, but it always shows a quiet simplicity, an expressiveness of mass, which is the first element in good monumental sculpture." (Taft's "History of American sculpture.")

WARNER, OLIN L., (S.) b. West Suffield, Conn., 1844; d. New York, August 14, 1896. The son of an itinerant Methodist minister, it was not until 1869 that he was able to sail for Europe. He went to Paris and studied sculpture in the Ecole des Beaux Arts under Jouffroy and afterwards in the studio of Carpeaux, making the acquaintance of Falguiére and Merciè. He returned to New York in 1872 and was one of the original members of the Society of American Artists. Associate member National Academy of Design, 1888; full member, 1889.

Among his most important works are statuettes entitled "May" and "Twilight," a colossal medallion of Edwin Forrest, a bust of J. Alden Weir (which excited profound admiration in the Paris salon), and the beautiful fountain in Portland, Oregon; also the fountain and spandrel figures for the entrance of the Library of Congress, Washington, D. C.

"His short career as an artist was sufficient to place him among the immortal masters of sculpture—those who have created a style of their own." (Nat Cyc Am Biog)

"His portrait of William Lloyd Garrison is among the best that our country has produced." (Taft)

WASHBURN, CADWALLADER, (E.) b. Minneapolis, Minn. A pupil of the Art League, N. Y.; he studied under Mowbray and Chase; Joaquin Sorolla in Spain. Received second prize of the American Art Association of Paris. An artist whose paintings were well known in leading art centers of Europe, it was in the year 1903 that Mr. Washburn first employed etching as a mode of expression. A series of Venetian plates revealed his harmony with the medium, and admitted him to the ranks of painter-etcher.

The direct influence of Sorolla is far-reaching, for not the least distinguishing quality of his plates, strikingly illustrated in the Mexican series, is his masterly interpretation of atmosphere and sun. His plates classify naturally:

Italian set—Venice, Padua and Verona
Japanese portfolio, etched in 1904
"The Nordlands," a series of landscapes
A group in Havana; Cathedral of Old Mexico

With the passing of the master, Seymour-Haden, recent attention has been called to the school of landscape etching. With the exception of a few scattered plates, Mr. Washburn is the only American in the list of the younger men to turn a sustained interest to landscape subjects.

It is of significance that he has revealed powers capable of worthily upholding his traditions in America.

WATKINS, SUSAN, (P.) b. California, 1875. A pupil Arts Students' League in New York; Collin in Paris; she received honorable mention in the Paris salon of 1899 and third gold medal in the salon of 1901. Her painting entitled "The fan" is well known and a critic refers to the "quaint yet alluring figure of the young woman."

WAUGH, FREDERICK JUDD, (P.) b. Bordontown, N. Y., September 13, 1861. A painter of American marines, comes from a family of artists; his father, S. B. Waugh, was a Philadelphia portrait painter; his mother, Eliza Waugh, was a miniature painter; and his sister, Ida Waugh, is also a portrait painter and an illustrator of children's books.

At eighteen he began the study of art in the Pennsylvania Academy of the Fine Arts under Thomas Eakins, after that he went to Paris and worked in Académie Julien under Bouguereau and Robert-Fleury.

Associate member National Academy of Design, 1909; full member, 1911.

The first beginnings of his marine work were laid while he lived on the Island of Sark, Channel Islands. He crossed the ocean frequently, thus familiarizing himself with every changing aspect of the water; and he also acknowledges the fact that the time spent at miniature portrait, decorative work, landscape, and figure painting, gives him strength and power in his marines.

"The surf off Cape Ann" is a powerful marine; this is permanently placed in the National Academy of Design, New York.

Other marines are:

"The great deep"   "A heavy sea"
"Outer surf"   "Little harbor, Bailey's Island,
"Roaring forties"   Maine"
"Incoming tide"   "Docks at Gloucester"
"Blue gulf stream"   "Southwesterly gale, St. Ives"

Mr. Waugh has a wonderfully trained "eye memory" and he produces his seascapes from memory: "He declares that if he never saw the sea again he could still go on painting it and constantly improving in his representations." (Arts & D 1: 111)

The real idealized is the art of Frederick Judd Waugh.

Recently Waugh exhibited fifteen new paintings, all of which were West Indian marines.

"The brilliancy and beauty of these West Indian subjects place Waugh in the very front rank of contemporary American painters."

His "Storm wave" has tremendous power and beauty.

"Where the sea is greenest" and "Sea at Bathsheba, Barbados" are described as "delicious."

WEBSTER, HERMAN A., (P., E.) b. New York City, 1878. Family home in Chicago; occupies a studio at No. 6, Rue Furstemberg, Paris. Graduated from Yale University in 1900 and in October of that year went abroad. After a winter in Paris among the studios and artists of the Latin Quarter, he joined Burton Holmes and Senator Albert J. Beveridge on a trip to the Orient. Returning to the United States he engaged in commercial work, also doing journalism in the office of the Chicago Record-Herald.

In February, 1904, he returned to Paris and entered the Académie Julien under Jean Paul Laurens. In 1905 four of his plates were accepted at the salon. In Grez on the edge of the Forest of Fontainebleau, Mr. Webster etched his first plates during the autumn of 1904; "Studio windows" of which there are two plates, "Rue del'Abbaye," "Loing at Grez," and "The Court, Bourron," the first of a series of Court-yard studies.

Spring, 1905, etchings were "St. Martin's bridge, Toledo," and "Mirada de las Reinas, Alhambra" seen from the Hall of the Ambassadors.

December, 1907, Mr. Webster's name was enrolled in the associate membership of the Royal Society of Painter-etchers in London, of which the late Sir Francis Seymour-Haden was president. He is the first etcher from Chicago, and one with less than a dozen other Americans who have been admitted to the Royal Society since its foundation in 1881.

"In some of his plates definite sureness of touch is linked with a certain severity; while in others there is a richness which in some original drawings becomes a lusciousness that makes one regret that he has not tried the lithographic crayon." (Weitenkampf)

WEEKS, EDWIN LORD, (P.) b. Boston, Mass., 1849; d. Paris, France, November 16, 1903. As a youth he studied art in Paris at the Ecole des Beaux Arts and afterwards under Lèon Bonnat and Gérome. At the age of twenty-nine he began to exhibit at the salon.

Received honorable mention in the Paris salon of 1885, and a medal in 1889; medals of the first-class at the Universal Exposition, Paris, 1889; gold medal from Philadelphia Art Club, 1891; a grand diploma of honor at Berlin, 1891; medal at London, 1896; Dresden, 1897; Munich, 1897; special medal and prize at the Empire of India Exposition, London, 1896; the same year was elected a chevalier of the Legion of Honor of France, and in 1898, an officer of the Order of St. Michael, Bavaria.

Mr. Weeks is particularly famous for his pictures of life in Cairo, Jerusalem, Damascus, Tangier, and India. He made frequent trips to Eastern cities, traveling extensively in India.

"The last voyage" shows his dramatic and scenic qualities and his careful observation of oriental air and color.

Other famous paintings are named:

"Jerusalem from the Bethany road"
"Scene in Tangier"
"Arab story-teller"
"A cup of coffee in the desert"
"Three beggars of Cordova"
"A rajah of Jodhpore"
"Hindoo marriage"

"Pilgrimage to the Jordan"
"Alhambra windows"
"A Moorish camel driver"
"Departure for the hunt, India"
"Packing the caravan"
"The porter of Bagdad"
"Steps in the mosque, Lahore"

His pictures are notable for their rendering of sunlight effects, fine color and artistic truth.

A well known art critic says: "Mr. Weeks is gifted with great facility; his skill and sureness of eye and of hand in dealing with vast scenes are remarkable. No one has treated with greater effect and with such unhesitating directness, the great architectural backgrounds of India with their pluri-color richness and splendor of detail."

"He is a skilful draughtsman and an excellent colorist." (John Rummell)

WEINMAN, ADOLPH ALEXANDER, (S.) b. Karlsruhe, Germany, December 11, 1870; came to America in 1880. Pupil of Art Students' League of New York under Augustus Saint-Gaudens and of Cooper Union. He also studied with the late Olin L. Warner and later was an assistant to Charles H. Niehaus and to Daniel Chester French. He won the Mitchell Vance prize for drawing at Cooper Union and the prize in the modeling class at the Art Students' League. Member National Sculpture Society, Society of American Artists; associate member National Academy of Design, 1906.

As a child he showed an aptitude for art and as a youth he was apprenticed to a carver of wood and ivory. At the age of sixteen he entered the evening classes in drawing and modeling at the Cooper Union.

Since taking up sculpture as his active work, he has been awarded many important commissions. His monument to Major-General Alexander Macomb, erected in Detroit, Michigan, in 1908, placed him in the front rank of the younger American sculptors; and his memorial of the late Mayor Maybury of Detroit is a magnificent heroic bronze. His portrait statue of the late president of the Pennsylvania Railroad system, Alexander J. Cassatt, is a conspicuous ornament of the new Terminal Station in New York City.

At the Panama-Pacific Exposition, San Francisco, 1915, he contributed the fountains of the "Rising Sun" and the "Setting Sun" for the Court of the Universe.

His pair of colossal sphinxes for the Scottish Rite Temple at Washington, D. C., won him much praise.

Mr. Weinman has also done some beautiful decorative work in connection with architecture. The Madison Square Presbyterian Church; the library of J. Pierpont Morgan; Pennsylvania Railroad Station, New York; and the capitol at Madison, Wisconsin, contain examples of his art in highly ornate work.

As a medalist he ranks second to none. His medallic work includes the medal of honor of the National Institute of Arts and Letters, the medal of honor of the National Institute of Architects, the medal of award of the St. Louis Exposition, and the United States medal for life-saving on railroads. Most recently he has designed a series of coins for the United States government.

Mr. Weinman has executed a number of remarkable statues of Lincoln; one is a standing figure for the rotunda of the state capitol at Frankfort, Kentucky.

The little service button which all enlisted men who served during the World War are entitled to wear, was designed and modeled by Mr. Weinman and was passed upon and approved by the National Commission of Fine Arts.

WEIR, JULIAN ALDEN, (P., E., Mural P.) b. West Point, N. Y., August 30, 1852; d. New York City, December 9, 1919. Studied art under his father, Robert Weir, who was instructor in drawing at West Point Military Academy, and with Gèrome at the Ecole des Beaux Arts, Paris. Received honorable mention in the Paris salon of 1881, also numerous medals and honors. Was elected associate member of the National Academy of Design, New York, in 1885; full member in 1886; president, 1915. In 1916 he was chosen by President Wilson for the National Commission of Fine Arts. Was one of the original members of the Ten American Painters.

Mr. Weir was an exquisite painter of flowers and a bold original etcher.

While studying in Paris he sent to the National Academy of Design, New York, in 1875, "A Brittany interior;" in 1877, "At the water-trough," "Brittany peasant girl," "Brittany washerwoman," and "Study of an old peasant." During these student days he was intimately associated with Bastien-Lepage.

He painted many kinds of pictures—still life, portraits, figure, land-scape. Examples are to be found in the Luxembourg Gallery, Paris, and in nearly every important museum in this country.

In the Metropolitan Museum, New York City, are his "Green bodice," "Idle hours," and "The red bridge." The first is regarded as one of his masterpieces. Of this ("The green bodice") Kenyon Cox wrote: "The paramount quality of his 'Green bodice' is perfection of tone and a delicate observation of the gradations of light which would make it hold its own in any company."

"Upland pasture" is a characteristic picture and his "Early morning" is strongly suggestive of Corot.

Other well known paintings are:

"A bough of green apples"	"Silver flagon and Delft plate"
"China bowl with flowers"	"The young student"
"The lane"	"The open book"
"A winter day"	"Lengthening shadows"
"Breton interior"	"The plowman"
"The good Samaritan"	"Young girl"
"Ideal head"	"The miniature"
"Return of the fishing party"	"Oriana"
"A gentlewoman"	"Dorothy and Cora"

"The longer one studies Mr. Weir's etchings the more one is impressed not only by the mastery of essentials, but by the power of the artist to create a composition in which the material gathered by his swift and certain observation is brought into unity with d controlling idea, and however trivial it may seem, made to belong to the essentials through its relation to the idea." (Scrib 68:512)

Duncan Phillips says: "At their best Weir's landscapes are the most important made in America since the death of George Inness."

"His landscapes are bits of nature presented with a degree of intimacy and poetic understanding quite uncommon in our day." (J. Nilsen Laurik)

"Always full of space and light his paintings are distinguished for a broad handling, truthful and luminous color, and harmony of tone.

"Whenever American artists meet they speak of Mr. Weir's work with respect and admiration. To him they have something more to give— their liking and love for a magnificent personality and a noble character." (Philip L. Hale)

WELCH, MABEL R., (Min. P.) b. New Haven, Conn. Pupil of Kenyon Cox, New York; Courtois, Paris. Member Art Students' League, N. Y., also American Society of Miniature Painters. A teacher.

Her miniature works possess much charm of color, much judicious placing of the subject within the frame, and no inconsiderable excellence of technical treatment.

Aside from color, the interesting quality of Miss Welch's miniatures is their breadth of treatment. "Breadth is easy of achievement, given the artist to do it, on a five-foot canvas; but breadth which has to compromise with refinement on less than a five-inch ivory is another matter."

(Int Studio 39: sup xcii.) "Miss Welch is one of the most promising of the newer miniature painters and her work has attracted much interest."

Her "Study of a child" is a delightful rendering of sweetness and innocence.

WENDT, JULIA M. BRACKEN (Mrs. William Wendt), (S., P.) b. Apple River, Ill., June 10, 1871. Pupil of Art Institute of Chicago under Lorado Taft.

The Craftsman (22:495) says: "Mrs. Wendt has already won distinction through the merit of her portrait-busts and bas-reliefs, her symbolic statues and the naive characterful studies of animals, but this imaginative work (a bronze group representing Art, Science, and History) places her among the foremost sculptors of America."

WENDT, WILLIAM, (P.) b. Germany, 1865. Settled in Chicago, 1880. Self-taught. First conspicuous successes were made as a result of a long sojourn in California. He has exhibited in the Paris salon, Royal Academy, London, and in leading American galleries.

Mr. Wendt is president of the California Art Club and elected associate member of the National Academy of Design in 1912.

"Wendt is a colorist and he is a success whenever he is reveling with warm tones and brilliant effects. He is original and his paintings have a distinct personal character and value."

"Scarlet robe" is a picture full of air, space, and movement and is professionally painted. "Old age" shows a village street empty of team and person. Its color scheme suggests the gray harmony of Cazin. "Wilderness" and "Canon Diablo" are notable California scenes. "Cornwall coast" is dramatic in treatment. "Autumn melody" was exhibited in the New Salon of 1899.

In his catalogue of some fifty works a considerable number were done in California and show at his best his love for strong color. (Brush & P 6:257)

At the 23d annual exhibition of American paintings at Chicago, a room was set apart for his paintings. An art critic writes: "The best trio of landscapes it is generally conceded is that by William Wendt. 'The silence of night,' which received honorable mention, is a landscape with slender birches in the foreground beyond which the darker reaches are illuminated by a subdued light. 'The land of the heart's desire' is as satisfying in a decorative sense and in mood more joyous, the golden sunlight gilding the open country. 'The Arcadian hills' is in the same manner a strong, independent painting." (Art & P 2:49)

"His work has the rare quality of standing true under a glaring light, and when in shadow it seems to radiate a light of its own. He has done much to raise the standard of art in the west, spending his energy lavishly in its service at all times."

Thirty landscapes painted by Mr. Wendt were recently exhibited in a one-man show in Los Angeles.

His affiliations have been for the past twenty-five years entirely of the west.

"No man paints the greens of spring better than he, and to him Southern California's tawny summer yields its richest gold."

A distinguished piece of painting is "Threatening weather," a fawn-colored hillside on a gray day, a mood of nature wonderfully well-rendered."

A fine seascape is "Freshening breezes."

Other notable canvases are:

"Lupin patch"   "Peace eternal"
"Patterned fields"   "Rocky ledges"
"Verdant hills"   "Another road"

"The originality and massiveness of Mr. Wendt's decorative mountain landscapes are charming."

WENTWORTH, CECILE DE, (P.) b. in New York City. Pupil of the Sacred Heart Convent and of Cabanel and Detaille in Paris.

Received gold medal at Tours, Lyons, and Turin; honorable mention, Paris salon, 1891; bronze medal, Paris Exposition, 1900; Chevalier of the Legion of Honor of France, 1901; officer of Public Instruction of France; Order of Holy Sepulchre from Pope Leo XIII.

Represented in the Luxembourg Gallery, Paris, and in the Metropolitan Museum of Art, New York.

WENZELL, ALBERT BECK, (I.) b. Detroit, Mich., 1864; d. Englewood, N. J., March 4, 1917. Pupil of Strahuber and Loefftz in Munich, and Boulanger and Lefebvre in Paris.

Received silver medal at Pan-American Exposition, Buffalo, 1901; silver medal at St. Louis Exposition, 1904.

His work as an illustrator is marked by great originality of treatment.

WHISTLER, JAMES MCNEILL, (P., E., Mural P.) b. Lowell, Mass., 1834; d. Chelsea, England, July 17, 1903. Was taken as a child to Russia; after his father's death he returned to America and entered the Military Academy at West Point. Being a poor student and failing in chemistry, he was recommended to be discharged in 1854; after a short employment in the United States Coast Survey at Washington he went to Paris and entered the studio of Charles Gabriel Gleyre, where Degas, Bracquemond, and Fantin-Latour were his favorite companions. Two or three years later he left Paris and took up permanent residence in London. In 1860 "At the piano" was exhibited at the Royal Academy, London. His success began with the "White girl" exhibited in 1863 in the Salon des Refusès, Paris.

In 1883 Mr. Whistler sent the portrait of his mother to the Paris salon and received a third-class medal; in 1889 he received the cross of the Legion of Honor.

He was a member of the Société Nationale des Artistes Francais, honorary member of the Royal Academy of St. Luke, Rome, commander of the Order of the Crown of Italy, honorary member of the Royal Academy, Bavaria, chevalier of the Order of St. Michael, and honorary member of the Royal Academy of Dresden, but most unjustly he was never elected to the Royal Academy of London.

Elizabeth Luther Cary, in her recent work on Whistler, gives a tentative list of Whistler's work. She catalogues 528 oils, water-colors, and pastels; 161 lithographs; and 426 etchings as his principal works.

He always called his pictures "harmonies," "symphonies," "nocturnes," and "arrangements." The portrait of his mother, the "Thomas Carlyle" and "Miss Alexander" are usually considered the height of his achievements.

C. H. Caffin most interestingly writes: "None but a man of peculiar sweetness of mind could have conceived that masterpiece in the Luxembourg, "The portrait of my mother."'

"It was with the night that Mr. Whistler set his seal and sign manual upon art," writes George Moore; "above all others he is surely the interpreter of the night."

C. H. Caffin also says: "His art was the product of most delicate selection; a hybrid derived from the intermingling of many strains— Velasquez, Rossetti, the impressionists and Japanese—with his own rarely gifted personality, itself a curious mingling of aristocratic hauteur and spiritual sensibility."

William C. Brownell, the art critic, has spoken of Whistler as, "perhaps the most typical painter and the most absolute artist of the time."

His fame is now an international one; his works and personality have been before the public for more than forty years.

Of Whistler's etchings, Bryant, in "Pictures and their painters," says: "But two men in the whole history of the world—Rembrandt and Whistler—have been able to use the etching needle with such skill that every object in the scene becomes as much a piece of portraiture as though it were a portrait. Both of them produced etchings that were without flaw."

WHITE, THOMAS GILBERT, (P.) b. Grand Rapids, Michigan. Pupil of Art Students' League in New York City under Twachtman; Julien Academy under Benjamin-Constant and Laurens; also Whistler and MacMonnies in Paris. Specialty: portraits.

WHITNEY, GERTRUDE VANDERBILT, (Mrs. Harry Payne Whitney), (S.) Has devoted much time to the study of modeling, principally with the well known American sculptor, James Earle Fraser.

Among her first work to attract attention was a male figure of heroic proportions called "Aspiration," placed before the New York building at the Pan-American Exposition, Buffalo, 1901.

"Well modeled and carefully executed this work expressed great originality in design, winning much praise from artists and laymen."

Mrs. Whitney won the $50,000 commission for the design of the Titanic Memorial to be erected by the women of the United States as a tribute to the men who lost their lives in the great ocean disaster of 1912.

"She has had a thorough education in craftsmanship and is a serious and sometimes imaginative sculptor ...... She has a sense of color, and a sense of color in terms of life is emotional power." (Arts & D 6:342)

Her "El Dorado" fountain was one of the most important fountains at the Panama-Pacific Exposition, 1915.

At a recent exhibition in New York Mrs. Whitney was represented by forty-nine works in sculpture, which were divided as follows: large memorial figures and groups, symbolical groups and figures, and portraits.

Mrs. Whitney's sculptural portraits are her finest works in realization of character, technical treatment of the whole design and of surfaces. "Flora," "Barbara," and "Sheilah" are charming little figure portraits.

At the exhibition popular interest centered in the study of the memorial to Buffalo Bill, a recent important commission Mrs. Whitney has received. "The pose of the horse and the figure of Buffalo Bill are extremely spirited."

Other works shown were:

"Titanic Memorial"   "Monument to a sculptor"
"Aztec fountain"   "The Law"
"Duryea Memorial"   "Doors of El Dorado"
"Pan"   Portrait medallion of
"Boy with pipes"   · Walter Damrosch.
"Bacchante"

The degree of Master of Arts was conferred on Mrs. Whitney by the New York University at the annual commencement exercises on June 7, 1922. The honor was bestowed on the artist as an "interpreter in sculpture of the American character as it found expression, regardless of rank, in the great war for the freedom of the world; and patron and friend of many who in the face of difficulty are making for excellence in artistic production."

In her sculptures of war, we find tenderness, sympathy and understanding. "All that Barbusse specializes in, Mrs. Whitney keeps away from her art, either consciously or unconsciously."

WHITTEMORE, WILLIAM JOHN, (Min. P.) b. New York City, March 26, 1860. Pupil in New York of William Hart, National Academy of Design, and Art Students' League under Beckwith; in Paris, Lefebvre and Benjamin-Constant.

Received silver medal for drawing at Paris Exposition, 1889. Member American Society of Miniature Painters; associate member of National Academy of Design, 1897.

His first success was a water-color landscape, and his most serious work has been in portraiture.

A critic calls attention most visibly to his sympathetic though never mawkish portrait studies of children.

"The burgomeister" has much strength and a wonderful color. "Pandora" is an interesting figure composition. (Critic 47:535)

WHITTREDGE, WORTHINGTON, (P.) b. Springfield, Ohio, May 22, 1820; d. Summit, N. J., February 25, 1910. When very young he studied landscape and portrait painting in Cincinnati. In 1849 he went abroad and continued his art studies in London, Paris, Antwerp, and in Düsseldorf under Andreas Achenbach. In 1859 he exhibited in the National Academy of Design his "Roman Campagna" and was at once elected an associate member, and in the following year was made a full member. He was president of the academy for the year 1875-6. "He possessed great faculty and originality as a landscape painter."

Among his most celebrated pictures are "A brook in the wood," "Plains at the base of the Rocky Mountains" and "Sunshine in the forest."

For many years Mr. Whittredge was active in art circles in New York City.

WIGGINS, CARLETON, (P.) b. Turners, N. Y., March 4, 1848. Educated in public schools of Brooklyn, N. Y. Studied art with H. Carmiencke of Brooklyn, drawing at the National Academy of Design, New York; and landscape painting with Inness. He was unsuccessful from both an artistic and commercial standpoint with his landscape work, and turned his attention to cattle painting. He met with immediate success and is now the most distinguished painter of cattle and sheep in the United States. (Innes' "School of painting") He was elected associate member of the National Academy of Design in 1890; full member in 1906.

The Paris salon accepted his "Shepherd and his flock."

Other paintings are:

"A Holstein bull"
"The wanderers"
"Plough horse"
"Down the lane at twilight"
"The pasture lot"
"Ploughing in France"
"Three oaks"

"Morning on the hills"
"Normandy bull"
"Evening—Forest of Fontaine-bleau"
"Near Great South Bay"
"After wind—rain"

"He chooses principally American motives and his pictures carry the evidence of their truth to nature. His technical skill is great, his color warm and vibrant and his construction shows he has a thorough knowledge of form." (Nat Cyc Am Biog)

"Mr. Wiggins is at his best when he paints landscape with animals rather than animals with landscape." (Artist 29: sup iv)

WILES, IRVING RAMSEY, (P., Mural P.) b. Utica, N. Y., April 8, 1861. Was educated at Sedgwick Institute, Great Barrington, Mass. His father, a gifted painter of landscapes, was his first instructor in art: he was also a pupil of William M. Chase and although he subsequently studied in Paris with Carolus-Duran and Jules Lefebvre, he returned to America to work, definitely to express himself as an American artist.

He has never been identified with any special school or any new movement. Has received third Hallgarten prize of the National Academy of
Design, New York; honorable mention in the Paris salon; and several
medals. Was elected member of the National Academy of Design,
New York, in 1897. He has been called the "Artist's painter" and
chiefly busies his brush with portrait and figure paintings. His illustrations are well known to art readers of Century, Harper, Scribner, etc.

"If low tones appeal to him with the greatest strength, however, the
bright luminous colors come often into his canvases with brilliant
effect." (Arts & D 1:403)

His work is characterized by a charming simplicity of idea and treatment, and "Memories," now owned by Mr. Carnegie, is an admirable
example of those qualities of his art." (Nat Cyc Am Biog)

Among his works are:

"On the beach"
"The student"
"Quiet corner"
"Sunshine and flowers"
"Sunshine in the studio"
"The southwest wind"
"A breezy day"
"The black shawl"
"An Autumn stroll" (Portrait of
    Gladys Wiles)
Portrait of Julia Marlowe
"Girl with peonies"

Portrait of "My father and
    mother"
"Girl and horse"
"Noon"
"The green gown"
"The window"
"With hat and veil"
"Among Canada thistles"
"Discouraged"
"Brown kimono"
"The Sonata" (prize picture)
"In summertime"

His portrait of Mrs. Gilbert is a masterpiece of portraiture.

"The wholesome realities of life are depicted in Mr. Wiles' canvases—
the gladness of childhood, the dignity of age—and the glory of good
work."

He represents no intricate symbolism in his work; no revelation of a
nature complicated beyond power to express its thoughts. He has found
the ideals of art in the realities of life. His daughter has been the
inspiration of some of her father's most distinguished works." (Arts
& D Aug. 1911)

Mr. Wiles was honored by the National Art Committee, being one of
the eight American painters selected to paint portraits for the pictorial
history of the World War. He was also commissioned and painted the
portrait of the Hon. William J. Bryan which hangs in the State Department at Washington, D. C.

WILLET, WILLIAM, (Stained glass designer) b. New York City, November 1, 1868; d. Philadelphia, Pa., March 29, 1921. Pupil of Whittaker, Chase, and LaFarge in New York; studied also in France and England. Author of "Stained glass in our churches;" lectured on applied arts at Carnegie Technical Schools.

The most important representative of the new school of stained glass workers. Beginning his art career as a portrait painter, he turned to decorative work. "It is this feeling for design joined with a subtle appreciation of color, that makes his work notable."

The design for "The spirit of the water lily," a memorial window in the home of Mr. George I. Whitney of Pittsburgh, shows exquisite draughtsmanship and mastery of symbolism.

In the "Marriage of Isaac and Rebecca" the artist has more scope for color. The finest work is undoubtedly the window recently executed in the Third Presbyterian Church at Pittsburgh, depicting the parable of "The wise and the foolish virgins." "It bears brilliant witness to the vitality and promise of American art."

WILLIAMS, FREDERICK BALLARD, (P.) b. Brooklyn, N. Y., October 21, 1872. When a little more than a lad he studied at night at the Cooper Union in New York City. Then for a while attended a school conducted by John Ward Stimson, an idealist. Later studied at the National Academy of Design and spent a short time traveling in England and France. Was elected member of the National Academy of Design, 1909.

"Mr. Williams' landscapes are not painted out-of-doors ...... He transcribes what he feels rather than what he sees .... The scenes are imaginative, gay, and fanciful. Their charm lies in their joyous spon-taneity, their rhythm of line and color."

"The women he paints are intensely feminine but are pictured impersonally, their object being, as it were, to decorate the earth."

"His pictures are atmospheric, without resort having been made to mists and vapors, and they are peculiarly spacious in suggestion."

"Form and color are paramount and light and shade take their places as in a purely decorative scheme."

A few paintings are:

"A glade by the sea"   "Chant d'amour"
"The confidantes"   "The inner harbor, Block Island"
"On the cliffs"   "Garrets Mountain, N. J."
(Int Studio 42: sup liii)

"A glade by the sea" and "Conway hills" are in the National Gallery, Washington; "Happy valley" and "L'Allegro" in the Metropolitan Museum, New York.

His Pacific Coast landscapes are "pictures painted with a full brush showing fine draftsmanship in construction, tonal quality, with spontaneity of execution and richness in effect ...... it is a California which pours her riches, as it were, at the feet of the least beggar and the mightiest prince, without price or the asking." (Am M of Art 13:463)

WINTER, EZRA AUGUSTUS, (Mural P.) b. near Traverse City, Michigan, March 10, 1886.

As a school boy his vacation days were spent on his grandfather's farm and while wandering in the woods he drew pictures on birch bark taken from the trees. His favorite subjects were "The cock fight" and "A landscape view." While a student in Traverse City he earned money drawing cartoons for newspapers, designing postcards, and working in a basket factory. Mr. Winter's artistic ability was recognized when a student in Olivet college and the annual, "The Oaks," put out by the class of 1907 contained some very clever cartoons by this now well-known artist. After graduating at the Chicago Academy of Fine Arts he took up the work of an illustrator. In 1911 he painted a picture, "The muse of the arts," which won the coveted prize and entitled him to three years study in the American Academy at Rome. At the time it was said that never before had a winner had so little art training in schools.

After returning from Europe he opened a studio in New York City and was selected to decorate the dome of the great hall in the Cunard building. Four great murals on pendatives are the most beautiful. First is Lief Ericson in his Viking ship; second, Columbus with Holy Crosses on his sails; third, Cabot with high decks and sails of many colors; fourth, Drake in an elaborately ornamented craft.

The entire color scheme of the interior of the two auditoriums of the Eastman school of music at Rochester, N. Y., was selected by Mr. Winter; and his murals on the wall of the large auditorium won for him in 1922 the gold medal awarded by the Architectural League of America. The paintings symbolize musical festivals, lyric, martial, and sylvan music.

The new high school in Traverse City, Michigan, (his boyhood home) is to be decorated by this now popular and artistic mural painter.

WOODBURY, CHARLES HERBERT, (P., E.) b. Lynn, Mass., July 14, 1864. A pupil of the Massachusetts Institute of Technology in Boston and of the Academie Julien in Paris under Bouguereau and Lefebvre. A member of the National Academy of Design, 1907.

"Few painters have painted the ocean with a more familiar knowledge of its aspects, a closer sympathy with its various moods or in a larger imaginative style." (Art & P 4:762)

His best marines are:

"The breaker"	"Ground swell"
"A quiet sea"	"The steamer"
"The open sea"	"Maine coast"
"Mid-ocean"	"On a lee shore"
"A heavy sea"	

Many who admire Mr. Woodbury's marines and landscapes will be surprised to learn that he has recently taken up etching. The Print division of the Library of Congress recently exhibited a group of his etchings.

"He pictures the stern, rock-bound coast of Maine with a few lines and gives an adequate impression of its bold grandeur; with a few more lines he brings before our vision the open sea and awakens the same sensibility that the limitless restless waves themselves may have stirred; he gives a picture of the mountain tops and the observer is bound to comprehend their lofty stateliness; or he presents a scene on the beach and instantly one is transported to the gayest center of an American summer resort." (Am M of Art 7:224)

At a recent exhibition Mr. Woodbury displayed two canvases of unusual interest: "The wreck," a marine with convincing technique, and "Coral reef." Of the latter the correspondent to the Boston Transcript says: "It is splendid in theme and in its rich coloration. One cannot help but read poetry into it. The gentle swirl of the emerald green sea and palm-covered island drenched in orange sunlight makes one recall with much delight the south seas of Somerset Maugham and Frederic O'Brien."

WOODWELL, JOSEPH R., (P.) b. Pittsburgh, Pa., 1843; d. Pittsburgh, Pa., May 30, 1911. Mr. Woodwell was chairman of the Fine Arts Committee of the Carnegie Institute and one of the best known of the Pittsburgh artists. He studied for four years at Barbizon and was the friend of both Millet and Jacques. In Paris he was associated with Monet, Sisley, Renoir, and Pissaro.

WRIGHT, M. LOUISE WOOD, (Min. P., I.) b. Philadelphia, Pa., 1875. Pupil Pennsylvania Academy of the Fine Arts, Whistler and Academie Julien, Paris; F. W. Jackson, England.

Received Toppan prize Pennsylvania Academy of the Fine Arts. A teacher.

WYANT, ALEXANDER HELWIG, (P.) b. Port Washington, O., January 11, 1836; d. New York, November 29, 1892. First occupation was that of a sign painter in his native village. At the age of twenty-two he consulted Inness on art matters; later went to Düsseldorf and studied under Hans Gude; subsequently in London he studied the works of Turner and Constable. Settled in New York after 1864. Losing the use of his right hand from paralysis, he learned to paint with the left with no diminution of skill.

The work done with the left hand is considered by some critics to be superior to that done previously. Long before his death he was ranked with Inness as a landscape painter. In a certain delicate refinement none of our artists have equalled him.

His first picture exhibited in New York, "A view of the valley of the Ohio river," was at the National Academy of Design in 1865. He was elected associate member of the academy in 1868 and full member in 1869.

"Many of his landscapes are truly idyllic in character and full of tender and poetic sentiment. Others are beautiful interpretations of the more dramatic moods of nature or representatives of the wild and rugged scenery of the Adirondacks." ("Aims and ideals of representative American artists")

"Of the exquisitely poetic feeling with which he loved to invest his scenes, 'Early morning' is a glorious example." (Caffin)

There is a combined realism and impressionism in Wyant's work. "Early spring" is a characteristic landscape.

"Wyant always looked for and grasped the specific essential truth of a scene ...... Some of his twilight scenes breathe only ineffable peace, others are astir with suggestions of the infinite mystery of the final sleep." (Eleanor Richardson Gage)

"He loved the gray sky and somber tints of November, the subtle mystery of twilight, the fading glory of the sunset." (Arts & D 2:349)

Many critics have rated "Passing clouds" as Wyant's most dramatic composition "which in its way he never surpassed."

Of his "Moonlight and frost" (painted at a single sitting) it is said: "It is bathed in the mystic sheen of the moonlight which has impressed itself on the soul of the painter and is instinct with the very spirit of frost, chilled to intensity in the picture, as it must have been in the artist."

A few of his pictures in oil are:

"Staten Island from the Jersey meadows"

"The bird's nest"

"Scene on the Upper Susquehanna"

"A view on Lake George"

"Broad silent valley"

"The wilds of the Adirondacks"

"The old road—Evening"

"Hoosatonic valley"

"Early twilight"

"A glimpse of the sea"

"View in County Kerry, Ireland"

"Spring"

"Gray days had more allurement than sunny ones and his works are found to have a lyric quality which in a measure Inness' lacks.

WYETH, N. C., (P., I.) b. Needham, Massachusetts, October 22, 1882. Pupil of Howard Pyle.

Some of his known murals are in the Missouri State Capitol; Hotel Traymore, Atlantic City; New York Public Library; and Hotel Utica, Utica, N. Y.

Mr. Wyeth's illustrations are noteworthy not only for their color and vigor, but for their fidelity to the author's text.

The revived public interest in classical historical romances is largely due to the attractive work of such illustrators as Mr. Wyeth.

YANDELL, ENID, (S.) b. Louisville, Ky., October 6, 1870. A pupil of the Cincinnati Art School; Philip Martiny in New York; MacMonnies and Rodin in Paris; is an officer de l'academie, French government; and has the distinction of being the first woman member of the National Sculpture Society.

At the Columbian Exposition in 1893, Miss Yandell was represented by the caryatids of the Women's building and a figure of Daniel Boone. At the Tennessee Centennial Exposition her Athena (in heroic size) stood before the Art Palace. This figure is said to be the largest figure ever designed by a woman. At the Pan-American Exposition in 1901 she exhibited two busts: Honorable John G. Carlisle of Kentucky and the Baroness de Braunecker; also the Carrie Brown Memorial Fountain, given to the City of Providence, R. I., by Paul Bagnotti of Turin, Italy. in memory of his wife. "The lines of the composition are large and dignified, especially noticeable in the modeling of the individual figures which is well studied and technically excellent." (Outl 70:82)

"Miss Yandell has made many small figures with admirable skill and abounds in happy inventions." (Taft)

YATES, CULLEN, (P.) b. Bryan, Ohio, January 24, 1866. Studied with Chase and Ochtman in New York, and at the Ecole des Beaux Arts, Colarossi and Julien academies in Paris. Elected an associate member of the National Academy of Design in 1908; full member, 1919.

As a child and youth he spent much time out of doors and early became familiar with animal, bird, and plant life. He manifested unusual artistic genius while a child and his parents took him to Paris for art instructions. After several years spent abroad he returned to the United States and became art instructor in a school at Cleveland, Ohio. Later he took up his residence in New York City where he became a successful landscape painter. Although better known as a painter of landscapes, Mr. Yates' marines, especially those of the Maine Coast, have technical qualities and impressive strength and poetry.

"A love of the sea grew upon him, and his marine subjects are quite as important as his landscapes, while all seasons of the year inspire his canvases in messages of gladness." (Country L 38:35-June)

YOHN, FREDERICK COFFAY, (I.) b. Indianapolis, Ind., February 8, 1875; made his debut when he was nineteen, in the pages of Harper periodicals. From his home in Indiana he went to New York to study at the Art Students' League where he was a pupil of Mr. Siddons Mowbray.

Was selected to supply the drawings that accompanied the frontier sketches of Theodore Roosevelt. This recognition was followed by a commission to illustrate Cabot Lodge's "Story of the American Revolution."

He makes the story-telling quality of a picture easily felt in his composition, and projects his motive with admirable appearance.

"Mr. Yohn's ultimate purpose is to paint battle-pieces, but in illustrating he prefers to do character work—it is the soldier type that has so far identified him."

"His military compositions have suggested him as a successor to De Neuville."

Invests his versatile compositions with stirring vigor and dramatic interest.

Noted for his spirited battle scenes. (Brush & P 2:161)

YOUNG, MAHONRI, (S., P., E.) b. Salt Lake City, Utah, 1877, and is a grandson of the famous Mormon leader, Brigham Young. Studied in the Julien Academy, Paris. Was elected associate member of the National Academy of Design, 1912. His bronze figure of an Alsatian boatman, Bovet Arthur, received honorable mention at Buenos Ayres and was awarded the Helen Foster Barnett prize at the National Academy exhibition of December, 1911.

"His best work is distinguished by nobility and breadth of conception, close and conscientious observation of nature, a predilection for virile form and plastic line of great beauty and power."

A noteworthy achievement of Mr. Young is the "Sea gull" monument erected in Salt Lake City, Utah. Other sculptured work exhibited at the Panama-Pacific Exposition, San Francisco, 1915, was awarded the silver medal.

Mr. Young is also known as an etcher. In this medium of expression he is represented in the Metropolitan Museum of Art and American Museum of National History, New York City.

That he is a painter as well as a sculptor and etcher is a surprise to many. Last year an exhibition of his work in oil proved that he can deal with color as well as line. He carries the strength of his sculpture into his painting. The subjects of his canvas work are mostly picturesque scenes from the Navajo country. The most conspicuous canvases at the exhibition referred to were:

"Under the Pino"
"The shepherdess"
"Navajo land"

A group of pastels was attractive, especially "Evening" with reds, exquisite blues, and greens. "The Arroyo" and "Noon rest" also appealed to the connoisseur and the artist. There were also groups of water colors and drawings.

BIBLIOGRAPHY

BIBLIOGRAPHY

GENERAL

Appleton's Cyclopaedia of American biography. New York: Appleton, 1888.

Bryan's Dictionary of painters and engravers. London: Bell, 1903.

Cyclopedia of painters and painting. Edited by Champlin and Perkins. New York: Scribner, 1892.

Dictionary of national biography. Edited by Stephen and Lee. New York: Macmillan, 1885-1901.

James, R. N. Painters and their works. London: Gill, 1897.

Lamb's Biographical dictionary of United States. Boston: Lamb, 1900.

Levy, Florence. American art annual. Vols. 1-20. Washington, D. C.: American Federation of Arts.

The national cyclopaedia of American biography. New York: White, 1898.

The new international encyclopaedia. New York: Dodd, 1914.

Slater, J. H. Engravings and their value. New York: Scribner, 1900.

Who's who in America. Vols. 1-12.

SPECIAL

Addison, Julia de Wolf. The Boston Museum of Fine Arts. Boston: Page, 1910.

Agar, John G. Address at testimonial to John W. Alexander. Fine Arts Federation of New York, 1916.

American art and artists by leading American writers. Boston: American Art Co., 1895.

Amory, Martha Babcock. Domestic and artistic life of John Singleton Copley. Boston: Houghton, 1882.

Bailey, Henry T. Twelve great paintings. (Whistler.) Chicago: Prang, 1913.

Bayley, Frank W. The life and works of John Singleton Copley. Boston: Taylor Press, 1915.

Benjamin, S. G. W. Our American artists. 1st and 2nd series. Boston: Lothrop, 1881.

Blakelock, his art and his family. Chicago: Young's Art Galleries, 1916.

Blashfield, Edwin H. Mural painting in America. New York: Scribner, 1913.

Bolton, Sarah K. Lives of poor boys who became famous. (Thomas Cole pp. 270-283) New York: Crowell, 1913.

Bowdoin, W. G. James McNeill Whistler, the man and his work. New York and London: Mansfield, 1901.

Brawley, Benjamin. The negro in literature and art. (H. O. Tanner and Meta Warrick Fuller) New York: Duffield, 1921.

Brinton, Christian. Modern artists. (Melchers, Sargent, Shannon, Whistler.) New York: Baker and Taylor, 1908.

Bryant, Lorinda M. Pictures and painters. New York: Lane, 1907.

Bryant, Lorinda M. What pictures to see in America. New York: Lane, 1915.

Bye, Arthur Edwin: Pots and pans. (American still-life painting, Chap. 8) Princeton: Princeton Univ. Press, 1921.

Caffin, C. H. American masters of painting. New York: Doubleday, 1902.

Caffin, C. H. American masters of sculpture. New York: Doubleday, 1903.

Caffin, C. H. How to study pictures. (Whistler and Sargent.) New York: Century, 1912.

Caffin, C. H. The story of American painting. New York: Stokes, 1907.

Calder, A. Stirling. The sculpture and mural decorations of Panama-Pacific Exposition. San Francisco: Elder, 1915.

Carr, Cornelia. Harriet Hosmer: letters and memories. New York: Moffat, 1912.

Carroll, Dana H. Fifty-eight paintings by Homer D. Martin. New York: Privately printed, 1913.

Cary, Elizabeth Luther. Artists past and present. New York: Moffat, 1909.

Child, Theodore. Art and criticism. New York: Harper, 1892.

Clement, Clara E. Women in the fine arts. Boston: Houghton, 1904.

Clement and Hutton. Artists of the nineteenth century. Boston: Houghton, 1899.

Cook, Clarence. Art and artists of our times. Vol. 3. (Weir.) New York: Hess, 1888.

Cortissoz, Royal. American artists. New York: Scribner, 1923.

Cortissoz, Royal. Art and common sense. (Sargent and Whistler.) New York: Scribner, 1913.

Cortissoz, Royal. John LaFarge. New York: Houghton, 1911.

Cox, Kenyon. Old masters and new. New York: Duffield, 1905.

Cox, Kenyon. Artist and public. (Sargent, Chap. V; American School, Chap. VI; Saint-Gaudens, Chap. VII.) New York: Scribner, 1914.

Daingerfield, Elliott. Ralph Albert Blakelock. New York: Privately printed, 1914.

Daingerfield, Elliott. George Inness. New York: Privately printed, 1911.

Downes, William Howe. Twelve great artists. Boston: Little, 1900.

Downes, William Howe. Life and works of Winslow Homer. Boston: Houghton, 1911.

Dunlap, William. History of the rise and progress of the arts of design in the United States. New York: 1834.

Eaton, D. Cady. A handbook of modern French painting. New York: Dodd, 1909.

Fairmount Park Art Association. Philadelphia: Published by the Association, 1922.

Famous etchers. Boston: Estes and Lauriat, 1889.

Fifty paintings by George Inness. New York: Privately printed, 1913.

Fowler, Harold North. A history of sculpture. (Chap. XXVI.) New York: Macmillan, 1916.

French, H. W. Art and artists of Connecticut. Boston: 1879.

Goodyear, W. H. Renaissance and modern painting. (Chap. XXXIII.) New York: Macmillan, 1900.

Hartmann, Sadakichi. A history of American art. Boston: Page, 1902.

Hawthorne, Nathaniel. The French and Italian note-books. (Harriet Hosmer, pp. 217,493.) New York: Houghton, 1883.

Heermann, Norbert. Frank Duveneck. New York: Houghton, 1918.

Henderson, Helen W. The Pennsylvania Academy of the Fine Arts. Boston: Page, 1911.

Hind, C. Lewis. Augustus Saint-Gaudens. New York: Lane, 1908.

Hoeber, Arthur. The treasures of the Metropolitan Museum of Art. New York: Russell, 1899.

Hubbard, Elbert. Little journeys to homes of prominent artists— Whistler. East Aurora, N. Y.: Roycrofters, 1902.

Huneker, James G. Bedouins. (George Luks, Chap. XI.) New York: Scribner, 1920.

Innes, Mary, and Dekay, Charles. Schools of painting. New York and London: Putnam, 1911.

Isham, Samuel. The history of American painting. New York: Macmillan, 1905.

Jackson, Henry E. Benjamin West, his life and work. Philadelphia: Winston, 1900.

James, Henry. William Wetmore Story and his friends. New York: Houghton, 1903.

Jarves, James Jackson. The art idea. Boston: 1864.

King, Pauline. American mural painting. Boston: Noyes, 1902.

Knowlton, Helen M. The art and life of William Morris Hunt. Boston: Little, 1900.

Koehler, S. R. Etching. New York, London, Paris, Melbourne: Cassell, 1885.

Koehler, S. R. and others. American etching. Boston: 1879.

Lanman, Charles. Letters from a landscape painter. (Cole's imaginative paintings, p. 64; Our New York painters, p. 233.) Boston: Monroe, 1845.

Laurvik, J. Nilsen. Catalogue de luxe of the Department of Fine Arts, Panama-Pacific International Exposition. (Vol. 1, Chaps. I-XII.) San Francisco: Elder, 1915.

Leonard, John W. Men of America. New York: Hamersly, 1908.

Lester, C. Edwards. Artists of America. (Allston, Inman, Stuart, Trumbull.) New York: Baker, 1846.

Lucas, E. V. Edwin Austin Abbey. New York: Scribner, 1921.

Mabie, Hamilton Wright. American ideals. (Chap. VII.) New York: Macmillan, 1913.

MacFall, Haldane. A history of painting. Vol. 8. Boston: Estes, 1912.

McSpadden, J. Walker. Famous painters of America. (Abbey, Alexander, Chase, Copley, Hassam, Homer, Inness, LaFarge, Sargent, Stuart, Vedder, Weir, West, Whistler.) New York: Dodd, 1916.

Marquand and Frothingham. A history of sculpture. (Chap. XXVII.) New York: Longmans, 1896.

Mason, George C. Life and works of Gilbert Stuart. New York: Scribner, 1879.

Masters in art. (Copley, Vol. 5; Hunt, William M., and Inness, Vol. 9; Whistler, Vol. 8.) Boston: Bates, 1900-1909.

Mather, Frank Jewett, Jr. Homer Martin. New York: Privately printed, 1912.

Mauclair, Camille. The French impressionists. (Mary Cassatt.) New York: Dutton, 1903.

Meynell, Wilfred. The modern school of art. (Vedder, Vol. 4.) London: Cassell.

Meynell, Mrs. Works of John Singer Sargent. New York: Scribner, 1903.

Modern paintings described by great writers. (Inness, Sargent, Abbey, Whistler.) New York: Dodd, 1911.

Moore, George. Modern painting. (Mark Fisher.) New York: Scribner, 1898.

Morris, Harrison S. Richards' masterpieces of the sea. Philadelphia: Lippincott, 1912.

Murray, Freeman H. M.   Emancipation and the freed in American sculpture. Washington, D. C.: Pub. by author, 1916.

Müther, Richard.   History of modern painting.   New York: Macmillan, 1896.

Neuhaus, Eugen.   The art of the exposition.   San Francisco: Elder, 1915.

Noble, Louis L.   Life and works of Thomas Cole.   New York: 1853.

One hundred early American paintings.   New York: Ehrich Galleries, 1918.

Parkes, Kineton.   Sculpture of today.   Vol. 1.   New York: Scribner, 1922.

Partridge, William Ordway.   Art for America.   Boston: Roberts, 1894.

Pennell, E. R. and J.   The life of James McNeill Whistler.   Philadelphia: Lippincott, 1911.

Pennell, E. R. and J.   The Whistler journal.   Philadelphia: Lippincott, 1921.

Pennell, Joseph.   Etchers and etchings.   New York: Macmillan, 1919.

Pennell, Joseph.   The graphic arts.   Chicago: University of Chicago Press, 1921.

Perkins, Augustus T.   John Singleton Copley.   Privately printed, 1873.

Post, Chandler R.   History of European and American sculpture.   Cambridge: Harvard University Press, 1921.

Pousette-Dart, Nathaniel.   Childe Hassam.   New York: Stokes, 1922.

Pousette-Dart, Nathaniel.   Robert Henri.   New York: Stokes, 1922.

Preyer, David C.   The art of the Metropolitan Museum of New York, Boston: Page, 1909.

Proceedings at the meeting in memory of Karl Bitter.   New York: Privately printed, Nation Press, 1915.

Radcliffe, A. G.   Schools and masters of sculpture.   New York: Appleton, 1900.

Rathbun, Richard.   The National Gallery of Art (Washington, D. C.) Washington: Government Printing Office, 1909.

Roof, Katherine Metcalf.   Life and art of William Merritt Chase.   New York: Scribner, 1917.

Rummell, John.   Aims and ideals of representative American painters. Buffalo: E. M. Berlin, 1901.

Saint-Gaudens, Homer.   The reminiscences of Augustus Saint-Gaudens. New York: Century, 1913.

Sheldon, George W.   American painters.   New York: Appleton, 1879.

Sherman, Frederic Fairchild.   American painters of yesterday and today.   New York: Privately printed, 1919.

Sherman, Frederic Fairchild. Landscape and figure painters of America. New York: Privately printed, 1917.

Simmons, Edward. From seven to seventy. New York: Harper, 1922.

Singleton, Esther. Modern paintings as seen and described by great writers. New York: Dodd, 1911.

Sparrow, Walter Shaw. Women painters of the world. (Cecilia Beaux, Mary Cassatt.) New York: Stokes, 1905.

Spencer, Edwina. Story of American painting. Chautauquan, Vols. 48, 49, 50.

Taft, Lorado. The history of American sculpture. New York: Macmillan, 1903.

Taft, Lorado. Modern tendencies in sculpture. Chicago: University of Chicago Press, 1917.

Tuckerman, Henry T. Book of the artists. New York: Putnam, 1870.

Tytler, Sarah. Modern painters. (Allston, Leutze, Church.) Boston: Roberts, 1874.

Van Dyke, John C. American painting and its tradition. New York: Scribner, 1919.

Van Dyke, John C. History of painting. (Chap. XX.) New York: Longmans, 1899.

Van Dyke, John C. The meaning of pictures. New York: Scribner, 1903.

Van Dyke, John C. Studies in pictures. New York: Scribner, 1907.

Vedder, Elihu. The digresssions of. New York: Houghton, 1910.

Viardot, Louis. Wonders of sculpture. New York: Scribner, 1896.

Way, T. R. and Dennis, G. R. The art of James McNeill Whistler. London: Bell, 1904.

Weir, John F. John Trumbull. New York: Scribner, 1901.

Weir, Julian Alden, an appreciation of his life and works. New York: Dutton, 1922.

Weitenkampf, F. American graphic art. New York: Holt, 1912.

Wharton, Anna Hollingsworth. Heirlooms in miniatures. (Edward Greene Malbone.) Philadelphia: 1898.

Wood, T. Martin. Whistler. New York: Stokes, 1913.

PERIODICAL REFERENCES.

Abbey, Edwin Austin
Art & P 2:347
Artist 29:169
Arts & D 1:444
Craftsm 21:11
Cur Lit 51:319
Harper 100:875; 105:525
Int Studio 15:sup lvi; 17:sup lxxix;
  44:sup lv
Mag of Art 19:224; 23:145, 193, 247
Nation 86:384
R of Rs 44:300
Scrib M 44:656; 51:1
W To-day 21:1218
W Work 16:10191

Adams, Herbert
Am M of Art 12:151

Aitken, Robert I.
Arts & D 19:184
Int Studio 50:sup iii; 54:sup xv
Overl 60:108; 61:218

Alexander, John White
Am M of Art 7:345
Art W 2:523
Arts & D 1:147
Cent o.s.70:642; 90:957
Craftsm 10:46
Critic 35:609; 46:239
Harper 99:694; 114:845
House B 15:67
Int Studio 34:sup lxxxv; 56:sup xxi
Lit Digest 50:1466
Mag of Art 18:226
Munsey 39:744
Outl 95:171
Scrib M 25:340; 45:45; 58:385
Studio 11:21
W Work 9:5682, 5993
W Work (London) 5:373

Anderson, Karl
Int Studio 76:132

Anschutz, Thomas Pollock
Brush & P 4:277

Barlow, Myron
Int Studio 46:284; 54:sup xxviii

Barnard, George Grey
Arts & D 5:129
Brush & P 3:50
Cent o.s.53:877
Cosmopol 49:667
Craftsm 15:270; 19:212
Critic 33:354
Harper W 60:299
Ind 89:355
Int Studio 36:sup xxxix; 71:sup lv
Munsey 20:456
Outl 109:198
R of Rs 19:49; 38:689
Touchst 8:201
W To-day 16:273
W Work 5:2837; 17:11256

Bartlett, Paul Wayland
Arch Rec 39:265
Art & Archaeol 1:163; 3:135
Art W 1:41
Craftsm 16:437
Mag of Art 25:133
New Eng M n.s.33:369
Scrib M 45:309; 48:125; 54:527
Studio 4:245

Beaux, Cecilia
Brush & P 6:81
Cent o.s.80:581
Critic 47:39
Delin 98:16
Harper 128:870
Harper B 45:119; 47:221
Int Studio 41:sup iii
Scrib M 22:477
Studio 8:215

Bouguereau, Elizabeth Gardner
 (Mme. W. A. Bouguereau)
 Cur Lit 39:391

Brenner, Victor
 Arts & D 2:24
 Cur Opin 60:50
 Survey 35:15

Breuer, Henry Joseph
 Int Studio 39:sup xlix

Bridgman, Frederic Arthur
 Artist 29:138
 Harper 63:694

Browne, George Elmer
 Brush & P 14:107
 Int Studio 36:286

Brush, George DeForest
 Art W 2:8
 Arts & D 6:187
 Brush & P 5:266; 6:205
 Delin 88:16
 Int Studio 34:sup xlvii; 39:187;
  76:187
 New Eng M n.s.14:149

Bryant, Nanna
 Int Studio 76:338

Cadwalader-Guild, Emma Marie
 Cur Lit 40:42
 Int Studio 27:sup xliv

Calder, A. Stirling
 Am M of Art 9:319
 Art W 1:402
 House & G 3:316
 Int Studio 67:sup xxxvii
 Touchst 1:22
 W Work 20:13377

Carlsen, Emil
 Arts & D 6:239
 Int Studio 27:sup xliii; 39:10;
  61:sup cv; 75:300
 Touchst 7:110

Cassatt, Mary
 Arts & D 3:265; 17:377
 Cent o.s.57:740
 Craftsm 19:540
 Cur Lit 46:167
 Delin 74:121
 Good H 50:141; 58:153
 Harper 123:596
 Harper B 45:490
 Int Studio 27:sup i; 35:sup xxxi;
  64:6,11
 Print Coll Q 16:397
 Scrib M 19:353; 46:734
 W To-day 21:1659

Chase, William Merritt
 Am M of Art 8:45; 8:432
 Art W 1:156
 Cent o.s.93:833
 Craftsm 18:33
 Critic 48:515
 Harper 78:549
 Int Studio 39:sup xxix; 60:sup cv;
  62:63
 New Repub 10:133
 Outl 115:344
 Scrib M 61:255
 Studio 21:151

Church, Frederick E.
 Bay View M 15:391
 Ecl M 65:688
 Galaxy 1:422
 Harper 59:488
 Liv Age 62:817; 63:318
 New Eng M 13:302

Clarke, Thomas Shields
 Brush & P 6:193

Cole, Thomas
 Am M 60:663
 Art W 1:13
 Bay View M 15:387
 Chaut 49:359
 Harper 59:251
 South Lit Mess 15:351

Conant, Lucy Scarborough
 Am M of Art 12:269,274

Cooper, Colin Campbell
Brush & P 18:72

Copley, John S.
Art in Am 5:200

Couse, Eanger Irving
Am M of Art 11:400
Artist 27:sup xvii
Craftsm 18:619

Cowles, Genevieve
McCl 54:62

Cox, Kenyon
Am M of Art 10:304
Art W 1:156
Arts & D 6:343
Cent n.s.19:333
Int Studio 32:sup iii

Dabo, Leon and T. Scott
Brush & P 17:3
Craftsm 13:261
Cur Lit 41:524
Int Studio 27:173; 39:sup lv
R of Rs 41:219
Sewanee Review 22:96
W To-day 12:76

Dallin, Cyrus Edwin
Arts & D 4:152
Brush & P 5:1
Catholic W 79:426
Int Studio 58:109
New Eng M n.s.21:196; 48:408; 53:32
Overl 54:435
Scrib M 57:779

Dannat, William T.
Craftsm 6:154

Davidson, Jo
Am M of Art 11:469
Art & Archaeol 9:289
Arts & D 3:170; 18:18
Bookm 45:637
Colliers 67:12 (Jan. 15)
Cur Lit 52:99
Int Studio 56:133; 70:114; 76:180

Lit Digest 58:26(Aug. 10); 62:28
(Aug. 9)
W Work 22:14746

Davies, Arthur B.
Art in Am 6:295
Int Studio 72:sup cxxvii; 75:213
Lit Digest 56:23 (Jan. 26)
Touchst 6:277

Davis, Charles Harold
Brush & P 4:40,122; 12:107
Cent n.s.26:319
Int Studio 75:177
New Eng M n.s.27:422

Dearth, Henry Golden
Am M of Art 10:196
Cent o.s.70:157
Int Studio 64:sup cxvi

DeCamp, Joseph R.
Am M of Art 14:182
Art & P 4:919
Arts & D 1:248
New Eng M n.s.39:239

Deming, Edward Willard
Arts & D 2:107
Craftsm 10:150; 21:456
Int Studio 27:sup xv

Dessar, Louis Paul
Artist 24:sup lix
Brush & P 5:97
Int Studio 27:sup lxvi

Dewing, Thomas W.
Art in Am 10:225
Scrib M 74:359

Dougherty, Paul
Craftsm 25:510
Int Studio 30:180; 36:sup iii;
38:sup xxxvii, xlvi

Dufner, Edward
Country L 38:41 (June)

Duveneck, Frank
Arts & D 1:382
Scrib M 58:643

Eakins, Thomas
Am M of Art 9:106
Art in Am 3:185
Art W 3:291

Eberle, Abastenia St. Leger
Art & Archaeol 6:87
Arts & D 2:105; 6:290
Craftsm 8:623; 18:475
Cur Opin 55:124
Good H 53:179
Illus W 24:328
Survey 30:196

Edstrom, David
Art & Archaeol 9:231; 14:50

Elliott, John
Arts & D 2:359
Everybody's 23:95
New Eng M n.s.50:26

Enneking, John
Am M of Art 8:320
Brush & P 10:335
Int Studio 76:3
W To-day 16:517

Evans, Rudulph
Cent o.s.90:208
Int Studio ,55:sup lxxxiv

Ezekiel, Moses Jacob
Am Artists 2:371
Art & Archaeol 5:307; 11:227
W Work 19:12255

Farnham, Sally James
Arts & D 16:26
Bul Pan Am U 52:433
Delin 98:16 (May)
Overl n.s.77:67
W Work 42:6

Fisher, Harrison
Bookm 11:53
Cosmopol 49:135
Harper B 50:13 (Aug.)
Ind 59:1357

Flagg, James Montgomery
Cent o.s.90:320
Harper B 50:13 (Aug. 15)
Int Studio 77:396

Foote, Will Howe
Arts 1:5

Fournier, Alexis Jean
Arts & D 1:18
Brush & P 4:243; 11:140

Fraser, James Earle
Am M of Art 8:276
Bul Pan Am U 46:648
Cent o.s.79:930
Craftsm 18:364
Cur Opin 70:531
Scrib M 68:427
Touchst 7:87

French, Daniel Chester
Am M of Art 13:3
Art W 1:44
Atlan 75:223
Brush & P 5:145; 8:43
Bul Pan Am U 44:66
Cent o.s.59:871
Cur Lit 30:727
Ind 83:288
Int Studio 41:sup lx; 46:211;
  53:sup lxi; 56:sup lv
Mag of Art 25:314

Frieseke, Frederick Carl
Art & P 3:747
Arts & D 3:13
Harper 118:291
Int Studio 43:273; 53:259; 54:sup
  xxiv
Scrib M 58:643

Frishmuth, Harriet
Arts 2:31

Fuller, George
Art in Am 7:84; 9:91
Brush & P 6:209
Harper 69:517
Int Studio 35:sup xcii; 75:265

Hitchcock, George
  Arts & D 3:401; 14:297
  Brush & P 2:258; 9:315
  Cent o.s.70:318
  Hearst M 22:131
  Int Studio 26:sup i
  Mag of Art 22:577

Homer, Winslow
  Am M of Art 7:68,74
  Art in Am 6:201
  Arts & D 6:278
  Brush & P 6:202; 10:40; 11:271
  Cent n.s.36:651
  Critic 43:548; 46:323
  Cur Lit 45:54
  Dial 58:333
  Forum 54:670
  Int Studio 34:sup cxxv
  Nation 100:206
  New Eng M n.s.14:131
  Outl 96:338
  R of Rs 38:102
  W Work 21:14009

Hornby, Lester G.
  Int Studio 27:123

Hosmer, Harriet
  Ecl M 77:245
  Liv Age 56:697
  Nation 86:203; 95:340
  New Eng M n.s.45:265
  Outl 102:545

Hunt, William Morris
  Am M 61:24
  Am M of Art 14:384
  Bookm 11:187
  Chaut 49:86
  Dial 28:20
  Int Studio 35:sup xciv
  Masters in Art 9:319
  New Eng M n.s.10:685
  No Am 217:643
  Scrib M 57:125

Hutt, Henry
  Bkbuyer 22:22
  Bookm 11:55
  Brush & P 2:15

Hyatt, Anna V.
  Am M of Art 7:313
  Art & P 4:773
  Arts & D 2:106
  Cent o.s.92:308
  Craftsm 8:623
  Harper B 51:32
  Int Studio 57:sup xlvii
  Lit Digest 51:1476
  Outl 111:885
  St N 43:402
  Touchst 5:286
  Woman's H C 43:40

Hyde, Helen
  Am M of Art 7:429
  Asia 17:639
  Brush & P 11:241
  Craftsm 15:186; 28:380; 29:337
  Harper B 40:12
  Int Studio 24:239; 45:51; 51:26

Inness, George
  Am M 61:35
  Art W 1:234,250,310
  Bookm 47:487
  Cent o.s.49:530
  Cosmopol 55:518
  Critic 26:17
  Forum 18:301
  Masters in Art 9:215, (bibliography)
  Mo Illus 3:258
  Outl 73:535
  Pub Opin 18:207

Johansen, John C.
  Am M of Art 10:290
  Arts & D 1:292
  Int Studio 26:264; 40:sup lxxviii;
    42:sup iii

Keith, William
  Craftsm 20:528
  Int Studio 33:36

Kemeys, Edward
  Cent o.s.28:213
  Int Studio 26:sup x
  McClure 5:120

Kendall, William Sergeant
Arts & D 1:15,40; 6:343
Cent o.s.50:478
Harper 117:568

Kent, Rockwell
Arts & D 11:70; 12:324
Cent o.s.106:323
Cur Opin 62:277; 67:52; 68:681
Int Studio 67:sup cv
Lit Digest 61:31 (May 31)
Scrib M 72:768

Knox, Susan Ricker
Arts & D 19:28

Lachman, Harry B.
Am M of Art 13:336

Ladd, Anna Coleman
Am M of Art 10:309
Art & P 2:251; 3:740
Craftsm 28:344
Harper B 50:39 (March)
Survey 39:707

LaFarge, John
Art in Am 8:85
Craftsm 8:312; 9:369, 19:330
Cur Lit 50:93
Int Studio 15:sup xxxvi; 38:sup
  lxxxiii, ciii
New Eng M n.s.14:136
Outl 84:479; 90:518
R of Rs 11:535
Scrib M 26:3; 37:604, 638
W Work 21:14085

Lamb, Charles Rollison
Lamb, Ella Condie
Lamb, Frederick Stymatz
Craftsm 13:420
Int Studio 40:sup xliv
Outl 70:571

Lawson, Ernest
Am M of Art 8:257
Art in Am 8:32
Arts & D 10:257

Lie, Jonas
Arts & D 12:91; 15:221
Bul Pan Am U 38:679
Craftsm 13:135; 21:455
Cur Lit 52:222
House B 35:126
Int Studio 51:sup cxcii; 53:sup lv;
  54:sup cxii

Linde, Ossip L.
Arts & D 4:437
Int Studio 61:sup xlvii; 64:sup xlix

Loeb, Louis
Artist 24:sup xiii
Bookm 10:548
Cent o.s.79:74
Harper 115:138
Harper W 53:33
Int Studio 27:sup lxxxvii
Outl 92:871

Longman, Evelyn Beatrice
Good H 53:178
Harper B 45:360
Int Studio 45:sup xcix
W To-day 14:526

Low, Will Hicok
Am M of Art 12:41
Bkbuyer 12:5
Forum 34:414
McCl 5:291
Scrib M 29:509

Lukeman, Henry Augustus
Am M of Art 13:476

Luks, George B.
Am M of Art 14:74
Arts 3:107
Arts & D 3:164; 4:335; 6:238
Craftsm 12:599
Int Studio 56:241; 71:sup xxi
Touchst 8:32

MacEwen, Walter
Brush & P 11:301; 19:21

McKenzie, R. Tait
Arts & D 13:258
Cent o.s.97:249
Cur Opin 69:378
Int Studio 41:sup xi; 72:133
Outing 65:586
Outl 127:246

MacLane, M. Jean
(Mrs. J. C. Johansen)
Arts & D 3:299
Harper 118:292

MacLaughlin, Donald Shaw
Print Coll Q 6:111

MacMonnies, Frederick W.
Arts & D 16:424
Brush & P 10:1
Cosmopol 53:207
Int Studio 29:319; 58:sup xl
Munsey 34:415
Scrib M 18:617
Studio 6:17
W Work 11:6965

McNeil, Hermon A.
Art W 3:366
Brush & P 5:68
Craftsm 16:709
W Work 14:9403

Macomber, Mary L.
Int Studio 54:sup lxvii

Manship, Paul
Arts & D 6:291; 15:384
Cur Opin 69:96 (July)
Harper Weekly 62:246
Int Studio 71:sup lxxv
Lit Digest 52:1278; 65:34 (June 19)
Nation 96:162
New Repub 6:207
Outl 106:335; 112:542
Scrib M 55:664

Marin, John
Art in Am 9:87
Arts 2:201
Arts & D 6:278
Forum 55:331

Martin, Homer Dodge
Art in Am 7:255
Bookm 31:236
Dial 53:488
Harper 59:678; 126:916
Int Studio 35:255
Nation 95:622

Melchers, J. Gari
Am M of Art 13:117
Arts & D 13:98
Brush & P 5:267
Cosmopol 55:4
Harper 114:430
House B 11:92
Int Studio 31:sup xi; 48:sup xxvii
Mag of Art 24:145
W Work 15:10092

Metcalf, Willard Leroy
Bk-Lovers M 6:511
Cent o.s.77:155
Country L 38:37 (June)
Int Studio 39:8
New Eng M n.s.39:374
Quart Illus 3:93

Millet, Francis Davis
Art & P 3:635; 4:1087
Artist 26:sup lxiv
Craftsm 15:426
Int Studio 32:sup cxi; 48:sup xxxiv
Nation 94:410
Scrib M 51:253
W Work 19:12378

Mora, Francis Luis
Arts & D 6:343
Craftsm 17:402
Harper 123:888

Moran, Edward
Brush & P 8:188

Moran, Mary Nimmo
Brush & P 8:3
Scrib M 46:731

Moran, Peter
Art Journal 31:26

Moran, Thomas
Brush & P 7:1
Harper 59:677

Mowbray, Henry Siddons
Harper 122:724

Murphy, John Francis
Art in Am 6:163
Arts & D 3:191
Brush & P 10:205
Int Studio 53:sup iii; 57:sup xi

Myers, Jerome
Am M of Art 8:481
Arts & D 10:257
Craftsm 29:25
Int Studio 57:sup cxxv
Touchst 5:396

Nourse, Elizabeth
Art & P 2:262
Cent o.s.59:481
Cosmopol 29:25
Cur Lit 48:90
Int Studio 27:247; 54:sup xxvi

Oakley, Violet
Am M of Art 13:157
Arch Rec 22:455
Arts & D 12:19
Bk News M 35:438
Cent o.s.70:265; 81:734; 85:239
Critic 36:521
Good H 54:470
Lit Digest 48:64
Scrib M 41:637; 62:125
W Work 23:606

Ochtman, Leonard
Artist 24:sup lix; 27:sup v,xi
Brush & P 4:125; 9:65

O'Connor, Andrew, Jr.
Arts & D 12:85
Cur Lit 42:281
Scrib M 45:637

Osthaus, Edmund Henry
Brush & P 18:81

Pape, Eric
Bookm 11:140
Brush & P 3:321
New Eng M n.s.39:455

Parker, Lawton S.
Int Studio 57:sup xxxvii

Parrish, Maxfield
Am M of Art 9:85
Bookm 11:55
Critic 46:512
Ind 59:1403
Int Studio 29:35
Outl 78:839

Paulus, Francis P.
Int Studio 46:141

Peale, Charles Willson
Scrib M 73:763

Peixotto, Ernest
Am M of Art 12:191

Pennell, Joseph
Art & P 4:766
Bookm 36:158
Brush & P 12:81
Canad M 38:333
Cent o.s.84:567; 89:340; 103:398
Craftsm 20:113; 29:132
Int Studio 30:312; 38:22; 40:200;
  48:132
Outl 81:172

Picknell, William L.
Cent o.s.62:710

Pratt, Bela L.
Arch Rec 35:508
Art & P 2:295; 4:1105
Cent o.s.78:722
Int Studio 38:sup iii; 57:sup cxxi
New Eng M n.s.39:632

Proctor, A. Phimister
Brush & P 2:241
Lit Digest 61:55 (April 26)
Scrib M 68:266

Thayer, Abbott Henderson
Am M of Art 12:329; 13:149
Arts 1:5
Brush & P 6:207
Critic 46:423
Int Studio 33:sup lxxxi; 39:187;
  74:sup vii
Lit Digest 69:29 (June 18)
Outl 130:535
Studio 6:247

Tiffany, Louis C.
Artist 24:sup iv
Arts & D 17:176
House B 34:179

Tyron, Dwight W.
Am M of Art 9:391
Art in Am 7:31

Twachtman, John Henry
Am M 61:599
Art in Am 7:129; 8:92
Art W & Arts & D 9:73
Arts 2:5
Arts & D 12:395
Bookm 27:355
Brush & P 12:243
Craftsm 14:597
Forum 52:245
Ind 58:147
Int Studio 35:sup xxiv; 38:sup
  xxxvii; 75:91
No Am 176:554

Ufer, Walter
Am M of Art 13:507
Arts 2:286
Int Studio 77:295

Van Ingen, William B.
Arch Rec 13:322

Vedder, Elihu
Artist 27:sup xv
Bookm 35:145
Cent o.s.86:917
Int Studio 35:sup xciv
Outl 96:693
Scrib M 74:123

Volk, Douglas
Cent o.s.68:654
Int Studio 54:sup cv; 55:sup lxxiii

Vonnoh, Bessie Potter
Brush & P 2:29
Good H 53:183
House B 35:125
Int Studio 54:sup xlviii
Mag of Art 24:522
Scrib M 19:126; 55:663

Vonnoh, Robert W.
Art & P 4:999
Artist 29:sup xii
Arts & D 2:381
Harper 116:254
Int Studio 27:sup lxxxvi; 54:sup
  xlviii; 77:231

Walker, Henry O.
Int Studio 27:sup lxxxvi

Walker, Horatio
Arts & D 1:63
Brush & P 6:82
Canad M 18:495
Craftsm 14:138
Harper 117:947
Int Studio 77:359
Touchst 5:482

Ward, John Q. A.
Artist 26:224
Harper 57:62
Int Studio 40:sup lxxxi; 58:sup
  xxxvii
R of Rs 41:694
Scrib M 32:385

Warner, Olin L.
Arch Rec 16:488
Cent o.s.46:436
Scrib M 20:429

Waugh, Frederick J.
Am M of Art 13:15
Arts & D 1:111
Int Studio 51:273; 74:sup cxxv

Webster, Herman A.
Int Studio 40:sup vi; 45:208

Weinman, Adolph Alexander
Arch Rec 33:519
Bul Pan Am U 45:775
Cent o.s.81:705
Int Studio 39:sup xliv

Weir, John Alden
Am M of Art 8:213
Art in Am 8:232,243
Arts & D 2:55
Burlington M 15:131
Cent o.s.57:956
Cosmopol 32:596
Harper 114:286; 131:246
Int Studio 75:127
Outl 110:120,136
Scrib M 59:129; 68:507

Wendt, William
Am M of Art 7:232
Brush & P 6:257

Wenzell, Albert Beck
Brush & P 2:65
Good H 61:860
Harper B 50:15 (Aug.)

Whistler, James McNeill
Am M of Art 10:168
Art W 3:12
Brush & P 12:305,319,334; 6:143
Cent o.s.80:219; 86:694; 90:710
Int Studio 21:3,208; 25:224; 72:sup
  xxxvii
Masters in Art 8:503 (bibliography)
W Work 6:3923

Whitney, Gertrude Vanderbilt
Arts & D 6:342
Good H 53:176

Int Studio 76:351
Lit Digest 70:28 (July 2)
Touchst 6:188

Wiles, Irving Ramsey
Arts & D 1:402
Bkbuyer 11:387
Cent o.s.54:799
Craftsm 14:602; 18:347
Harper 109:802; 114:608
Int Studio 77:256
R of Rs 34:40

Willet, William
Am M of Art 12:314

Winter, Ezra A.
Am Architect & Arch Review 23:181

Woodbury, Charles H.
Art & P 4:761
Brush & P 6:1
Int Studio 42:sup lxxi

Wyant, Alexander Helwig
Arts & D 10:197
Brush & P 11:184
Harper 59:678; 110:802

Yandell, Enid
Good H 53:182

Yates, Cullen
Country L 38:35 (June)

Yohn, F. C.
Brush & P 2:161

Young, Mahonri
Am M of Art 13:109
Art & Archaeol 6:83
Cur Opin 57:200
Int Studio 47:sup lv; 64:sup liii
Touchst 4:8